IN GOOD COMPANY

DEDICATION
*To my wife, Christine,
whose gift of a word processor
encouraged me to attempt this book.
With you I am indeed in good company!*

In Good Company

A Year's Readings
from Scripture and Church History
Chosen and Edited
by

Stuart H. Cook

Marshall Pickering
An Imprint of HarperCollinsPublishers

Marshall Pickering is an Imprint of
HarperCollins*Religious*
Part of HarperCollins*Publishers*
77–85 Fulham Palace Road
Hammersmith, London W6 8JB

First published in Great Britain
in 1993 by Marshall Pickering

1 3 5 7 9 10 8 6 4 2

Copyright in this compilation © 1993 Stuart H. Cook

Stuart H. Cook asserts the moral right to
be identified as the compiler of this work

A catalogue record for this book is
available from the British Library

ISBN 0 551 02245-0

Printed and bound in Great Britain by
HarperCollinsManufacturing, Glasgow

CONDITIONS OF SALE

This book is sold subject to the condition that it
shall not, by way of trade or otherwise, be lent, re-sold,
hired out or otherwise circulated without the publisher's
prior consent in any form of binding or cover other
than that in which it is published and without a
similar condition including this condition being
imposed on the subsequent purchaser.

All rights reserved. No part of this publication may be
reproduced, stored in a retrieval system, or transmitted,
in any form or by any means, electronic, mechanical,
photocopying, recording or otherwise, without the prior
permission of the publishers.

Contents

Foreword	9
Acknowledgements	11
The Company	13
One Year's Readings	25
Index	435
Sources of Readings	439

Foreword

In Good Company has a threefold aim. First of all, I hope that you will be stimulated by the writings of some people who have gone before us in the history of the Church. Church history has some complex issues, many of which are still with us today and they cannot easily be introduced in such a work as this. I would like therefore to suggest some books which will help put the people I have chosen into a wider perspective. My recommendations are two Lion books, *The History of Christianity*, and *The Book of Christian Thought*. Two very helpful American books are: *Church History in Plain Language*, Bruce L. Shelly, Word Books, and *From Jerusalem to Irian Jaya, a Biographical History of Christian Missions*, Ruth A. Tucker, Zondervan.

I trust, secondly, that you will be encouraged to want to know more about the people in this book and the history of Christianity generally. To help in this, as well as the books listed above, I have also, where possible, suggested further reading along with the biographical notes. Where each person appears can be found in the index. This also includes subjects so that hopefully then the book may be of further use, especially for preachers like myself who need stimulation and illustration!

The third part of my aim is the most important and that is to provide a devotional aid for one year. That has governed my choice of material. The use of people from different periods of history enables a varied approach and the different types of material such as letters, sermon extracts, verse, etc., assist in this also. (The presence of [ ] indicates where I have inserted extra information.) My hope and prayer is that this book will really help you in your walk with God. May you experience His blessing, as you set out in good company!

I would like to express my appreciation to Christine Smith, Marshall Pickering's Publishing Manager, for her encouragement.

Acknowledgements

Scripture quotations for each daily reading, apart from 1st January and 7th February, are taken from the HOLY BIBLE, NEW INTERNATIONAL VERSION. Copyright © 1973, 1978, 1984 by International Bible Society. Used by permission.

I have generally sought to use material not requiring copyright permission but I am grateful to the following Publishers for permission to use extracts from the books stated:

Epworth Press
The Heidelberg Catechism for Today, Karl Barth, 1964.
Westminster Sermons, Volume 1, W. E. Sangster, 1960.
Let me commend, W. E. Sangster, Wyvern, 1961.

Herald Press, Scottdale, PA 15683, USA
Anabaptism in Outline, Walter A. Klassen, Editor, 1981.

Overseas Missionary Fellowship, Hudson Taylor's "Retrospect".

SCM Press Ltd
Call for God, Karl Barth, 1967.
Lord Shaftesbury, Florence Higham, 1948.
The Reformed Pastor, Richard Baxter, Hugh Martin, Editor, 1956.

SPCK
Fragments That Remain, Amy Carmichael, Bee Trehane, Editor, 1987.

WEC International
Fool and Fanatic? Jean Walker, now out of print.

The Company

With the biographical notes I have provided where possible suggestions for currently available further reading, by and/or about the writer. An * indicates someone whose writings have also been used in the book.

AMBROSE (c. 339–97) Bishop of Milan. Ambrose was a noted preacher and defender of Jesus Christ as both human and divine. In the Roman Empire where Christianity had become patronised by Emperors he fought to maintain the independence of the Church and the accountability of Christian rulers. He encouraged hymn singing and wrote some hymns himself. He was an important influence in the conversion of Augustine*. *The Early Church*, Henry Chadwick, Pelican Books.

ANSELM OF CANTERBURY (c. 1033–1109) Much of his time as Archbishop of Canterbury was spent in exile because of controversies about the independence of the English Church from the Crown and about the authority of the Pope in England. Anselm is best remembered as a theologian, in particular for his arguments on why it was necessary for Christ to come into the world and to be crucified. *The Prayers and Meditations of Anselm*, Penguin Classics. *Christian England*, David Edwards, Fount.

ATHANASIUS (c. 296–373) Bishop of Alexandria. His place in history is established through his courageous defence and advocacy of the divinity of Christ against Arian opposition. He was exiled five times, and sometimes felt that he was "Athanasius against the World", but his later years were more peaceful. He introduced ideas of monasticism into the West. *St Athanasius on the Incarnation*, A. R. Mowbray. *A Cloud of Witnesses*, Alister E. McGrath, IVP.

AUGUSTINE OF HIPPO (354–430) North African theologian. As one of the major theologians of all time Augustine's influence has been considerable on both Catholics and Protestants. Converted from a dissolute life, his *Confessions* remain a spiritual classic. Augustine lived in a period of frightening change and his work *The City of God* coincided with the sacking of Rome by the Visigoths. *The Confessions of St Augustine*, Hodder Christian Classics. *A Cloud of Witnesses*, Alister E. McGrath, IVP.

KARL BARTH (1886–1968) Barth is probably the major theologian of the twentieth century. During the First World War he found the theological liberalism of his day inadequate and turned to Scripture and the Reformers such as Luther and Calvin. His massive output of books caused controversy amongst both liberals and conservatives in theology. Barth was expelled from his professorship in Bonn because of his opposition to Hitler and returned to his native Switzerland. *Deliverance to the Captives*, Karl Barth, SCM Press. *A Cloud of Witnesses*, Alister McGrath, IVP.

RICHARD BAXTER (1615–91) Baxter's life and ministry mirrored something of the dramatic events in seventeenth-century England in that he was both part of and then expelled from the Church of England, and both a supporter of Parliament and then of the return of the Monarchy. A noted pastor, Baxter was concerned that Christians should not be divided over non-essentials. *The Reformed Pastor*, Richard Baxter, Banner of Truth. *Saints Everlasting Rest*, Richard Baxter, Evangelical Press.

THE VENERABLE BEDE (c. 673–735) Bede has been called the "Father of English History" because of the way in which he told the story of the English Church with the use of sources and in the setting of the nation. A monk at Wearmouth and then Jarrow, his work became known throughout Europe, though he himself never left his native Northeast. *History of the English Church and People*, Bede, Penguin Classics. *Christian England*, David Edwards, Fount.

BERNARD OF CLAIRVAUX (1090–1153) Bernard was the great influence in the growth of the Cistercian order of monks which was founded in 1098. He was a controversial figure in his day. His writings emphasise the mystical and contemplative life. Best known of them are his 86 sermons on the Song of Solomon. *The Song of Songs*, Hodder Christian Classics. *On Loving God, Twelve Steps of Humility and Pride*, Hodder Christian Classics.

CATHERINE BOOTH (1829–90) The "Mother of the Salvation Army". She and her husband William formed a remarkable movement which despite early opposition was to spread out from the East End of London and become worldwide. Catherine travelled much as a preacher and also began the women's work which has been an important aspect of the Salvation Army. *God Used a Woman: Catherine Booth*, Joan Metcalfe, Salvationist.

PHILLIPS BROOKS (1835–93) An American Episcopal Minister. Brooks served as rector of Trinity Church, Boston, for 22 years and was then made Bishop of Boston in 1891. His Yale Lectures on Preaching which defined preaching as truth through personality are often quoted in books on the subject. He wrote the hymn "O Little Town of Bethlehem". *The Joy of Preaching*, Phillips Brooks, Kregel Publications.

JOHN BUNYAN (1628–88) Writer and preacher. Bunyan's *Pilgrim's Progress* has become a classic of English literature. He produced a number of his writings while suffering persecution and imprisonment. *Pilgrim's Progress*, Bunyan, Hodder Christian Classics. *Riches of Bunyan*, Evangelical Press.

WILLIAM CAREY (1761–1834) English Baptist minister and missionary. Carey's influence was crucial for the great outpouring of Protestant missionary activity in the nineteenth century. He himself was challenged by the example of the Moravian Brethren. Carey showed how the Great Commission of Matthew 28 was still binding on the Church. His example in going to India, never to return home, inspired people like Charles Simeon.* *William Carey. By Trade a Cobbler*, Kellsye Finnie, OM Publishing, Baptist Missionary Society. *Faithful Witness*, Timothy George, IVP.

AMY CARMICHAEL (1867–1951) English missionary and writer. She first worked as a missionary in China and then went to India. She established the Donavur Fellowship to rescue children from the evils of service at pagan temples. She was crippled after a fall in 1931. Her writings have become popular devotional aids. *Learning of God, Readings from Amy Carmichael*, Triangle, SPCK. *Amy Carmichael*, Elizabeth Eliot, Kingsway.

JOHN CHRYSOSTOM (c. 344/345–407) John was Bishop of Constantinople from 398 and was one of the most gifted preachers of the Early Church, hence his name Chrysostom ("golden mouthed"). He came into conflict with the Empress Eudoxia and with some other church leaders. He died in exile after being banished for a second time. *The Early Church*, Henry Chadwick, Pelican.

CLEMENT OF ROME (fl. c. 90–100) Clement was a Christian leader in Rome. From his letter to the church in Corinth we can see something of the character of that church after the apostles. It is clear that the problems of division in Corinth about which the apostle Paul had written were still there! *The Early Church*, Henry Chadwick, Pelican.

CYPRIAN (c. 201/210–258) Bishop of Carthage. Cyprian was a controversial figure. After the persecution of Christians by the Roman Emperor Decius, Cyprian was involved in conflict over whether Christians who had denied the Faith under duress ("the lapsed") should be readmitted to the Church. He was also in controversy over theology with the church in Rome. *New Eusebius*, edited by J. Stevenson, SPCK. *The Early Church*, Henry Chadwick, Pelican.

ROBERT WILLIAM DALE (1829–95) An English Congregational minister. Dale exercised a powerful ministry at Carr's Lane Chapel in Birmingham which became England's second largest city. He was involved in the political, social and educational life of the city. He published a number of books, most notably *The Atonement*. *Evangelical Spirituality*, James M. Gordon. SPCK.

JAMES DENNEY (1856–1917) A Scottish theologian. Denney served as a minister of East Church, Broughty Ferry, during which he began his work as an author. He became a lecturer at the Free Church College, Glasgow, where he himself had trained for ministry. Eventually he became college Principal. Like Forsyth* he wrote passionately on the death of Christ.

THE DIDACHE (1st–3rd century) This anonymous writing on morals and church life has been assigned by scholars to various dates from the first century onwards. *The Early Church*, Henry Chadwick, Pelican.

THE EPISTLE TO DIOGNETUS (c. 2nd century) This anonymous letter sets out to prove how Christianity is unique and therefore superior to both Judaism and Paganism. *The Early Church*, Henry Chadwick, Pelican.

JONATHAN EDWARDS (1703–58) American minister and theologian. Edwards, one of America's greatest theologians, wrote on a number of subjects. He defended the Revival in New England (*The Great Awakening*). The influence of his writings extended beyond the New World. William Carey* was challenged by his call for united prayer. *On Revival*, Jonathan Edwards, Banner of Truth. *A Cloud of Witnesses*, Alister E. McGrath, IVP.

EUSEBIUS (c. 260–c. 340) Bishop of Caesarea and an historian. The writings of Eusebius are the main source of early church history from the apostolic era. He took part in the controversies which were raging over the Person of Christ. *Eusebius: Ecclesiastical History*, Penguin Classics.

CHARLES GRANDISON FINNEY (1792–1875) An American evangelist. Finney trained as a lawyer but became an ordained Presbyterian minister. He became noted for the revivals which he conducted in the eastern states. Leaving the Presbyterian church he became professor of theology at a new college, Oberlin, but still took time to conduct revivals. He was passionately opposed to slavery and taught that the Church must take a stand against it. His Lectures on Revival reflect the travelling evangelist's impatience with the Church's status quo!

PETER TAYLOR FORSYTH (1848–1921) Scottish Congregational theologian. Forsyth was Principal of New College, London, for twenty years. His writings emphasise the importance of the cross of Christ. *Evangelical Spirituality*, James M. Gordon, SPCK.

ELIZABETH FRY (1780–1845) An English Quaker prison reformer. Elizabeth Fry ministered at Newgate and other prisons, at a time when capital punishment was the penalty for crimes like petty thieving and forgery. She campaigned for better prison conditions such as the separation of male and female prisoners, and having women warders for women prisoners. She also became concerned for the care of discharged prisoners.

FRANCES RIDLEY HAVERGAL (1836–79) An English poet and hymn-writer. Frances Ridley Havergal was a gifted linguist and after her conversion she devoted herself to Christian work. A number of books of her poems and hymns were published. Several of her hymns are still sung today, including "Take my life and let it be". *Evangelical Spirituality*, James M. Gordon, SPCK.

The Company

BALTHASAR HUBMAIER (c. 1480–1528) Anabaptist leader in Southern Germany. Hubmaier was influenced by the Zurich Reformer Zwingli and introduced the Reformation at Waldshut. He later became an Anabaptist ("Rebaptizer"). He was burnt at the stake in Vienna. *The Anabaptist Story*, William R. Estep, Eerdmans.

JAN HUS (1373–1415) Bohemian reformer. Hus was led to criticisms of the Catholic Church by his view of the authority of the Bible. This together with the turbulent nationalist events of the time led to his execution. His ideas were known to Martin Luther and in some ways Hus anticipated him. *The Great Reformation*, R. Tudor Jones, IVP.

THOMAS A KEMPIS (1380–1471) German mystic. His book *The Imitation of Christ* has been valued by Catholics and Protestants alike. His emphasis on a direct personal relationship with Christ was a preparation for the Reformation. Thomas's writings were instrumental in the conversion of the slave trader John Newton.* *The Imitation of Christ*, Hodder Christian Classics.

WILLIAM LAW (1686–1761) An English devotional writer. Law's *A Serious Call to a Devout and Holy Life* influenced some of the early Evangelicals such as Wesley* and Whitefield*. His fierce spirituality should be seen against the background of church attendance accompanied by moral laxity. *A Serious Call*, William Law, Hodder and Stoughton. *Spiritual Awakening*, edited by Sherwood Eliot Wirt, Lion Publishing.

LEO THE GREAT (c. 400–461) Pope Leo I from 440. Leo extended the jurisdiction and claims of the Roman Church. He was an able administrator and preacher. In a time when the Roman Empire was disintegrating, he persuaded Attila the Hun not to attack Rome and when the city was captured by the Vandals, he managed to secure minimum destruction. *The Early Church*, Henry Chadwick, Pelican.

ALEXANDER MACLAREN (1826–1910) Scottish Baptist minister. Like R. W. Dale* in Birmingham, Maclaren ministered in a fast-growing industrial city. He was a noted expository preacher and was minister of Union Chapel, Manchester, from 1858–1903. His books *Expositions of Holy Scripture* were greatly valued by preachers. He became the first president of the Baptist World Alliance in 1905.

FREDERICK BROTHERTON MEYER (1847–1929) English Baptist minister and devotional writer. While a minister in York he played a crucial part in the encouragement of D. L. Moody* who was beginning evangelism in Britain. Meyer had an important social and evangelistic ministry through his founding of Melbourne Hall in Leicester. He was a speaker at the Keswick Convention and his biblical character studies are still popular.

DWIGHT LYMAN MOODY (1837–99) American evangelist. Moody worked as an evangelist in America after being in business. He came to international prominence following his tour of Great Britain (1873–5) with singer Ira Sankey. Moody was always keen to see different denominations working together in evangelism. He founded the Bible Institute in America which now bears his name. *Evangelical Spirituality*, James M. Gordon, SPCK.

JOHN NEWTON (1725–1807) English Anglican minister and hymn-writer. John Newton was converted while captain of a slave ship. Although he continued in the slave trade for a time, in later life he encouraged William Wilberforce in the battle for its abolition. *Spiritual Awakening*, edited by Sherwood Eliot Wirt, Lion Publishing. *The Collected Letters of John Newton*, Hodder Christian Classics.

POLYCARP OF SMYRNA (c. 70–155/160) Polycarp was a noted Christian leader in the Roman province of Asia. His martyrdom was therefore recorded and commemorated. Of his letters, the only one which has survived was written to the Christians in Philippi. *The Early Church*, Henry Chadwick, Pelican.

PETER RIEDEMAN (1506–56) Riedeman was an important leader of the Hutterites, an Anabaptist group which required the communal ownership of possessions. He wrote their Confession of Faith. Unlike so many of the early Anabaptists he died a natural death. *The Anabaptist Story*, W. R. Estep, Eerdmans. *The Great Reformation*, R. Tudor Jones, IVP.

WILLIAM EDWYN SANGSTER (1900–1960) A noted Methodist leader and preacher who made a study of holiness (an important emphasis in the teaching of John Wesley*). He ministered in Westminster Central Hall for sixteen years after which he became Methodist Home Mission Secretary. Sangster's collections of sermons and books about preaching are still greatly valued. *The Craft of Sermon Illustration*, Sangster, Marshall Pickering. *The Craft of Sermon Construction*, Sangster, Marshall Pickering.

HANS SCHLAFFER (d. 1528) An Anabaptist leader. Schlaffer who had been a priest became an Anabaptist and during his imprisonment wrote nine tracts. He was executed by the sword in Schwatz, Tyrol. *The Anabaptist Story*, W. R. Estep, Eerdmans.

LORD SHAFTESBURY (1801–85) The famous status of Eros at the end of London's Shaftesbury Avenue is a memorial to this Evangelical social reformer. Shaftesbury championed many worthy causes. He fought to improve working conditions in factories and mines, and the treatment of the mentally ill and retarded. He was the president of many societies, including the British and Foreign Bible Society. *Shaftesbury*, John Pollock, Lion Publishing. *Genius and Grace*, Gaius Davies, Hodder and Stoughton.

CHARLES SIMEON (1759–1836) An English Anglican minister. Simeon faced much opposition to his Evangelical views when he was appointed Vicar of Holy Trinity, Cambridge. In time, however, he became an important Christian influence on Cambridge students. He helped to found the Church Missionary Society and the London Jews Society (now The Church's Ministry Among Jews). *Evangelical Spirituality*, James M. Gordon, SPCK. *Charles Simeon: Preacher Extraordinary*, Hugh Evan Hopkins, Grove Booklets.

MENNO SIMONS (c. 1496–1561) Anabaptist leader. Simons was a monk and priest before becoming an Anabaptist. He travelled considerably as a preacher and church planter. His followers, the Mennonites, still exist today with the largest number of them living in the USA. They continue Simons's witness to non-violence. *The Theology of the Reformers*, Timothy George, Apollos. *The Great Reformation*, R. Tudor Jones, IVP.

CHARLES HADDON SPURGEON (1834–92) An English Baptist minister. Spurgeon exercised a remarkable preaching ministry in London which was then carried worldwide through print. He encouraged the planting of churches, created a college for training ministers (now Spurgeon's College) and set up an orphanage (now Spurgeon's Child Care). His sermons and writings are still greatly valued. *C. H. Spurgeon: Morning and Evening*, Marshall Pickering. *Spurgeon: A New Biography*, Arnold Dallimore, Banner of Truth.

CHARLES THOMAS STUDD (1862–1931) Pioneer missionary. Studd was one of the "Cambridge Seven", students who offered themselves for missionary work. He served successively in China, India and Africa. The mission which he founded in Africa continues today as Worldwide Evangelization Crusade and still has his founding principle of not appealing directly for financial support. *No Sacrifice Too Great*, Eileen Vincent, OMF. *C. T. Studd*, Norman Grubb, Lutterworth.

JAMES HUDSON TAYLOR (1832–1905) An English pioneer missionary. Hudson Taylor's name will always be linked with China where he first went in 1864. He was a man of great vision who sought to identify himself as much as possible with the Chinese people. The China Inland Mission which Hudson Taylor founded continues today as the Overseas Missionary Fellowship. *Man In Christ*, Roger Steer, Overseas Missionary Fellowship. *On Fire for God*, John Pollock, Marshall Pickering.

JOHN WESLEY (1703–91) The founder of Methodism. Wesley's experience of his heart being "strangely warmed" was to give him an evangelistic fervour which led him to give his life to preaching. He believed that God had raised up Methodism to witness to holiness and he organised his converts into small groups to encourage this. Within his lifetime Methodism was contained within the Church of England, of which Wesley was a minister. *Spiritual Awakening*, edited by Sherwood Eliot Wirt, Lion Publishing. *John Wesley*, John Pollock, Lion Publishing.

GEORGE WHITEFIELD (1714–70) An English preacher. Whitefield was influenced by John Wesley* but he in turn was to influence Wesley by persuading him to preach as he did himself in the open air. Whitefield is reckoned to have been the most gifted preacher of the Methodist Revival. He and Wesley differed over the question of human free will. Whitefield travelled seven times to America. *George Whitefield and the Great Awakening*, John Pollock, Lion Publishing. *Spiritual Awakening*, edited by Sherwood Eliot Wirt, Lion Publishing.

ALEXANDER WHYTE (1836–1921) A Scottish minister and author. Whyte served for nearly 40 years at Free St George's Church, Edinburgh, and was a noted preacher. Among his books were biblical character studies and studies of the characters in the writings of John Bunyan*. Whyte keenly supported the meetings of D. L. Moody* in Edinburgh. He became Principal of New College, Edinburgh, in 1909. *Evangelical Spirituality*, James M. Gordon, SPCK.

NIKOLAUS LUDWIG, COUNT VON ZINZENDORF (1700–1760) Leader of the Moravian Brethren which was an important influence on John Wesley*. Zinzendorf was himself influenced by the Pietist movement, a renewal movement within Lutheranism. He gave sanctuary to religious refugees from Bohemia whose origins went back to a movement led by Jan Hus*. A Christian community called Herrnhut was so formed. This became a powerful force for missions, by sending out its own missionaries and by its continuous prayer watch. Zinzendorf travelled widely and his desire was to see all Christians united in evangelism. *Spiritual Awakening*, edited by Sherwood Eliot Wirt, Lion Publishing. *The Church and the Age of Reason*, C. R. Cragg, Pelican.

One Year's Readings

January

1st January

My time is secure in your hands.
(Psalm 31:15, from the German)

My time does not belong to me; it is only lent to me, and can at any time be recalled and taken from me. And then I shall be asked: Who were you in your time? What have you done with the time you were given? What shall our answer be then? Excuses, pretexts and apologies will be of no use to us then. For he – the one in whose hands our time is secure – will then answer. And everything will depend for us on how he answers. And if there is anything left for us to mention, then it can only be this one thing:

> *Jesus' blood and righteousness,*
> *My only ornament and dress,*
> *In heaven shall keep me from all fear,*
> *Before my God when I appear.*

That and that alone . . .

There is a point where the figurative and symbolic ceases, where the question of God's hands becomes quite literally serious – that is where all the deeds, works, and words of God have their beginning, middle and end: Your hands – these are the hands of our Saviour Jesus Christ. They are the hands which he held out stretched when he called: "Come unto me, all you that labour and are heavy laden, and I will give you rest." They are the hands with which he blessed the children. They are the hands with which he touched the sick and healed them. They are the hands with which he broke the bread and shared it out to the five thousand in the desert place and then again to his disciples before his death. Finally and above all, they are his hands nailed to the cross, so that we might be reconciled to God. These my brothers and sisters, these are the hands of God: the strong hands of a father, the good, soft, gentle hands of a mother, the faithful, helping hands of a friend, the gracious hands of God, in which our time is secure, in which we ourselves are secure.

Karl Barth (1886–1968)

2nd January

As for man, his days are like grass, he flourishes like a flower of the field; the wind blows over it and it is gone, and its place remembers it no more. But from everlasting to everlasting the Lord's love is with those who fear him, and his righteousness with their children's children – with those who keep his covenant and remember to obey his precepts.

(Psalm 103:15–18)

While with ceaseless course the sun
Hasted through the former year,
Many souls their race have run,
Never more to meet us here:

They have done with all below;
We a little longer wait,
But how little none can know.

As the winged arrow flies,
Speedily the mark to find;
As the lightning from the skies
Darts, and leaves no trace behind:
Swiftly thus our fleeting days

Bear us down life's rapid stream;
Upwards, Lord, our spirits rise,
All below is but a dream.

Thanks for mercies past receive,
Pardon for our sins renew;
Teach us henceforth how to live,
With eternity in view:
Bless thy word to young and old,
Fill us with a Saviour's love;
And when life's short tale is told,
May we dwell with thee above.

John Newton (1725–1807)

3rd January

When you come, bring the cloak that I left with Carpus at Troas, and my scrolls, especially the parchments.

(2 Timothy 4:13)

We are taught in this passage how precisely similar one child of God is to another. I know we look upon Abraham, and Isaac, and Jacob as being very great and blessed beings – we think that they lived in a higher region than we do. We cannot think that if they lived in these times, they would have been Abraham, Isaac, and Jacob. We suppose that these are very bad days, and that any great height of grace, or self denial, is not very attainable. Brethren, my own conviction is, that if Abraham, Isaac, and Jacob had lived now, instead of being less, they would have been greater saints – for they only lived in the dawn, and we live in the noon. We hear the apostles often called "Saint" Peter and "Saint" Paul; and thus they are set up on an elevated niche. If we had seen Peter and Paul, we should have thought them ordinary sort of people – wonderfully like ourselves; and if we had gone into their daily life and trials, we should have said, "Well you are wonderfully superior to what I am in grace; but somehow or other, you are men of like passions with me. I have a quick temper, so have you, Peter. I have a thorn in the flesh, so have you, Paul. I have a sick house, Peter's wife's mother lies sick of a fever. I complain of rheumatism, and the apostle Paul, when aged, feels the cold, and wants his cloak."

Ah! we must not consider the Bible as a book intended for transcendental super-elevated souls – it is an everyday book; and these good people were everyday people, only they had more grace, but we can get more grace as well as they could; the fountain at which they drew is quite as full and free to us as to them. We only have to believe after their fashion, and to trust Jesus after their way, and although our trials are the same as theirs, we shall overcome through the blood of the Lamb. I do like to see religion brought out in everyday life. Do not tell me about the godliness of the Tabernacle, tell me about the godliness of your shop, your counter, and your kitchen. Let me see how grace enables you to be patient in the cold, or joyful in hunger, or industrious in labour. Though grace is no common thing, yet it shines best in common things. To preach a sermon, or sing a hymn, is but a paltry thing compared with the power to suffer cold, and hunger, and nakedness, for Christ's sake.

Courage then, courage then, my fellow pilgrims, the road was not smoothed for Paul any more than it is for us. There was no royal road to heaven in those days other than there is even now. They had to go through sloughs, and bogs, and mire, as we do still.

> *They wrestled hard as we do now*
> *With sins, and doubts, and fears;*

but they have gained the victory at last, and even so shall we.

C. H. Spurgeon (1834–92)

4th January

And tomorrow will be like today, or even far better.

(Isaiah 56:12)

These words, as they stand, are the call of boon companions to new revelry. They are part of the prophet's picture of a corrupt age when men of influence and position had thrown away their sense of duty, and had given themselves over, as aristocrats and plutocrats are ever tempted to do, to mere luxury and good living. They are summoning one another to their coarse orgies. The roistering speaker says, "Do not be afraid to drink: the cellar will hold out. Today's carouse will not empty it; there will be enough for tomorrow." He forgets tomorrow's headaches; he forgets that on some tomorrow the wine will be finished; he forgets that fingers of a hand may write the doom of the rioters on the very walls of the banqueting chamber.

What have such words, the very motto of insolent presumption and short-sighted animalism, to do with New Year's thoughts? Only this, that base and foolish as they are on such lips, it is possible to lift them from the mud, and take them as the utterance of a lofty calm hope which will not be disappointed, and of a firm and lowly resolve which may ennoble life. Like a great many other sayings, they may fit the mouth either of a sot or of a saint. All depends on what the things are which we are thinking about when we use them. There are things about which it is absurd and worse than absurd to say this, and there are things about which it is the soberest truth to say it. So looking forward into the merciful darkness of another year, we may regard these words as either the expressions of hopes which it is folly to cherish, or of hopes that it is reasonable to entertain ...

Let us humbly take the confidence which these words may be used to express, and as we stand on the threshold of a new year and wait for the curtain to be drawn, let us print deep on our hearts the uncertainty of our hold on all things here, nor seek to build nor anchor on these, but lift our thoughts to Him, who will bless the future as He has blessed the past, and will even enlarge the gifts of His love and the help of His right hand.

Let us hope for ourselves not the continuance or increase of outward good, but the growth of our souls in all things lovely and of good report, the daily advance in the love and likeness of our Lord.

Alexander Maclaren (1826–1910)

5th January

Consecrate the fiftieth year and proclaim liberty throughout the land to all its inhabitants. It shall be a jubilee for you; each one of you is to return to his family property and each to his own clan.
(Leviticus 25:10)

The singular institution of the Jubilee year had more than one purpose. As a social and economic arrangement it tended to prevent the extremes of wealth and poverty. Each fiftieth year the land was to revert to its original owners, the lineal descendants of those who had "come in with the conqueror", Joshua. Debts were to be remitted, slaves emancipated, and so the mountains of wealth and the valleys of poverty were to be somewhat levelled, and the nation carried back to its original framework of a simple agricultural community of small owners, each "sitting under his own vine and fig-tree" and like Naboth (1 Kings 21), sturdily holding the paternal acres.

As a ceremonial institution it was the completion of the law of the Sabbath. The seventh day proclaimed the need for weekly rest from labour, and as was the Sabbath in the week, so was the seventh year among the years – a time of quiet, when the land lay fallow and much of the ordinary labour was suspended. Nor were these all; when seven weeks of years had passed, came the great Jubilee year, charged with the same blessed message of Rest, and doubtless showing dimly to many wearied and tearful eyes some gleams of a better repose beyond.

Besides these purposes, it was appointed to enforce and to make the whole fabric of the national wealth consciously rest upon this thought ("the land is Mine"). The reason why the land was not to pass out of the hands of the representatives of those to whom God had originally given it, was that He had not really given it to them at all. It was not theirs to sell – they held it, it was still His, and neither they, nor any one to whom they might sell use of it for a time, were anything more than tenants at will. The land was His, and they were only like a band of wanderers, squatting for a while by permission of the owner, on his estate. Their campfires were here today, but tomorrow they would be gone. They were "strangers and sojourners". That might sound sad, but all the sadness goes when we read on "with Me". They are God's guests, so though they do not own a foot of soil, they need not fear want.

All this is true for us. We can have no better New Year's thoughts than those which were taught by the blast of the silver trumpets that proclaimed liberty to the slaves, and restored to the landless pauper his alienated heritage.

Alexander Maclaren (1826–1910)

6th January

Remember those in prison as if you were their fellow-prisoners, and those who are ill-treated as if you yourselves were suffering.
(Hebrews 13:3)

I desire to remember a few of the principal events, and some of the mercies and deliverances of the last year [1830] – an important one in the political world – the French revolution, and its consequences in other countries, and in our own in measure. I think, I unusually see the hand of providence in some of these things. I never remember my prayers to have been more raised by any public event, than on behalf of the French, during their revolution. Their conduct in it has given me great comfort, because it shows a wonderful advancement, at least in Christian practice, since the last revolution. I am still deeply interested about the French, and have a hope that a great and good work is going on amongst them. I have a hope also that the general stirring amongst the European nations is for good, and I have the same hope respecting our own country. I see that it is in rather an unsettled state, yet, as I also see that many things want a remedy, and as the process of fermentation must be passed through before a liquid can be purified, so at times with nations – such a process, though painful whilst it lasts, ends in the good of the people. May it prove so with us, and with other nations, and may all these turnings and overturnings advance the coming of that blessed day, when the "earth shall be full of the knowledge of the Lord as the waters cover the sea".

My interest in the cause of prisons remains strong, and my zeal unabated; though it is curious to observe how much less is felt about it by the public generally. How little it would answer in these important duties, to be much affected by the good or bad opinion of man. Through all we should endeavour to go steadily forward, looking neither to the right hand or to the left; with the eye fixed on that Power which can alone bless our labours, and enable us to carry on these works of charity to the good of others, our own peace and His praise.

Elizabeth Fry (1780–1845)

7th January

Let us fix our eyes on Jesus, the author and perfecter of our faith.
(Hebrews 12:2)

Someone has said: "There are three ways to look. If you want to be wretched, look within; if you wished to be distracted, look around; but if you would have peace, look up." Peter looked away from Christ, and he immediately began to seek. The Master said to him, "O thou of little faith! Wherefore didst thou doubt?" (Matthew 14:31). He had God's eternal word, which was sure footing, and better than either marble, granite, or iron; but the moment he took his eyes off Christ down he went. Those who look around cannot see how unstable and dishonouring is their walk. We want to look straight at the "Author and Finisher of our faith."

When I was a boy I could only make a straight track in the snow, by keeping my eyes fixed upon a tree or some object before me. The moment I took my eye off the mark set in front of me I walked crooked. It is only when we look fixedly on Christ that we find perfect peace. After He rose from the dead He showed His disciples His hands and His feet (Luke 24:40). That was the ground of their peace. If you want to scatter your doubts, look at the blood; and if you want to increase your doubts, look at yourself. You will get doubts enough for years by being occupied with yourself for a few days.

Then again: look at what He is, and at what He has done; not at what you are, and what you have done. That is the way to get peace and rest.

Abraham Lincoln issued a proclamation declaring the emancipation of three millions of slaves. On a certain day their chains were to fall off, and they were to be free. That proclamation was put up on the trees and fences wherever the Northern Army marched. A good many slaves could not read; but others read the proclamation, and most of them believed; and on a certain day a glad shout went up, "We are free!" Some did not believe it, and stayed with their old masters; but it did not alter the fact that they were free. Christ, the captain of our salvation, has proclaimed freedom to all who have faith in Him. Let us take Him at His word. Their feeling would not have made the slaves free. The power must come from outside. Looking at ourselves will not make us free, but it is looking to Christ with the eye of faith.

D. L. Moody (1837–99)

8th January

Trust in the Lord with all your heart and lean not on your own understanding; in all your ways acknowledge him, and he will make your paths straight.

(Proverbs 3:5–6)

[Lord Shaftesbury's funeral, 4 March 1885.]

It was raining. The procession made its way through crowded streets towards the Abbey. In Parliament Street, delegates from innumerable societies waited behind their banners to join it as it passed. But despite bands and banners it was a sad occasion, for those who watched were thinking of a friend whom they would not see again. They stood side by side on the pavement, at one for a brief moment in their love for a man who had loved them all; and then they went their different ways, peers of the realm and Piccadilly flower-girls; black-coated clerks and waifs from the London streets; seamstresses and chimney-sweeps and statesmen and clergymen; the costermongers who played in the band and the boys from H.M.S. *Arethusa*. Thus London paid its tribute to the seventh Earl of Shaftesbury ...

Anthony Ashley Cooper, whom the world knew as Lord Ashley until his fiftieth year and who then succeeded his father as seventh Earl of Shaftesbury, dallied as a youth with the idea of studying science, but knew in his heart that his name and his inheritance marked him down for politics. In this sphere he had great and legitimate ambitions. He did not lack ability or influence or opportunity. He needed only to be somewhat more adaptable, rather more conventional in his regard for party ties, a little less truly himself, to have been a leader of the Tory party. But one by one he put these ambitions behind him. On his twenty-seventh birthday he wrote of his future career: "The first principle God's honour, the second man's happiness, the means prayer and unremitting diligence." To this recipe for a good life he remained faithful for fifty-odd years, deliberately devoting himself to helping others, by giving freely of himself to all who asked his aid and by inquiring ruthlessly into every injustice with which he came into contact.

Lord Shaftesbury (1801–85)

9th January

For here we do not have an enduring city, but we are looking for the city that is to come.

(Hebrews 13:14)

> Jesus, still lead on,
> Till our rest be won;
> And although the way be cheerless,
> We will follow, calm and fearless:
> Guide us by Thy hand
> To our fatherland.
>
> If the way be drear,
> If the foe be near,
> Let no faithless fear o'ertake us,

> Let not faith and hope forsake us;
>   For, through many a foe,
>   To our home we go.
>
> When we seek relief
> From a long-felt grief.
> When oppressed by new temptations,
> Lord, increase and perfect patience;
>   Show us that bright shore
>   Where we weep no more.
>
> Jesus, still lead on
> Till our rest be won;
> Heavenly leader, still direct us.
> Still support, console, protect us,
>   Till we safely stand
>   In our fatherland.

Nikolaus Ludwig, Count von Zinzendorf (1700–1760)

10th January

For the grace of God that brings salvation has appeared to all men. It teaches us to say "No" to ungodliness and wordly passions, and to live self-controlled, upright and godly lives in this present age, while we wait for the blessed hope – the glorious appearing of our great God and Saviour, Jesus Christ, who gave himself for us to redeem us from all wickedness and to purify for himself a people that are his very own, eager to do what is good.

(Titus 2:11–14)

Though there is a height, a breadth, a length, and a depth, in this mystery of redeeming love, exceeding the comprehension of finite minds; yet the great and leading principles which are necessary for the support and comfort of our souls, may be summed up in very few words. Such a summary we are favoured with in Titus 2:11–14, where the whole of salvation, all that is needful to be known, experienced and practised, and hoped for, is comprised within the compass of four verses. If many books, much study, and great discernment, were necessary in order to be happy, what must the poor and the simple do? Yet for them especially is the gospel designed; and few but such as these attain the knowledge and comfort of it . . .

The doubts and fears you speak of, are, in a greater or less degree, the common experience of all the Lord's people, at least for a time. Whilst any unbelief remains in the heart, and Satan is permitted to tempt, we shall feel these things. In themselves they are groundless and evil; yet the Lord permits and overrules them for good. They tend to make us know more of the plagues of our own hearts, and feel more sensibly the need of a Saviour, and make his rest (when we attain it) doubly sweet and sure. And they likewise qualify us for pitying and comforting others.

Fear not; only believe, wait, and pray. Expect not all at once. A Christian is not of hasty growth, like a mushroom, but rather like the oak, the progress of which is hardly perceptible, but which in time becomes a great deep-rooted tree.

John Newton (1725–1807)

11th January

To the only wise God be glory for ever through Jesus Christ! Amen.
(Romans 16:27)

Prayer should rise more out of God's word and concern for His Kingdom than even out of our personal needs, trials or desires. That is implied in prayer in Christ's name or for Christ's sake, prayer from His place in the midst of the Kingdom. *Our* Prayerbook, the Bible, does not prescribe prayer, but it does more – it inspires it. And prayer in Christ's name is prayer inspired by His first interest – the gospel. Do not use Christ simply to countersign your egoist petition by a closing formula, but to create, inspire, and glorify it. Prayer in Christ's name is prayer for Christ's object – for His Kingdom, and His promise of the Holy Ghost.

If we really pray for that and yet do not feel we receive it, probably enough we have it; and we are looking for some special form of it not ours, or not ours yet. We may be mistaking the fruits of the Spirit for His presence. Fruits come late. They are different from signs. Buds are signs and so are other things hard to see. It is the Spirit that keeps us praying for the Spirit, as it is grace that keeps us in grace. Remember the patience of the missionaries who waited in the Spirit fifteen years for their first convert. If God gave His son *unasked*, how much more will he give His Holy Spirit to them that *ask* it! But let us not prescribe the form in which He comes.

The true close of prayer is when the utterance expires in its own spiritual fullness. That is the true Amen. Such times there are. We feel we are at last laid open to God. We feel as though we (in the words of Handel in writing *Messiah*) "did see heaven opened, and the holy angels and the great God Himself." The prayer ends itself; *we* do not end it. It mounts to heaven and renders its spirit up to God, saying "It is finished." It has its perfect consumation and bliss, its spiritually natural close and fruition, whether it has answer or not.

P. T. Forsyth (1848–1921)

12th January

How can I repay the Lord for all his goodness to me?
(Psalm 116:12)

The spirit of thankfulness and praise tends to holy practice. Sincere thankfulness to God leads us to render again according to the benefits received. This we look upon as a sure evidence of true gratitude or thankfulness towards our fellow-men. If anyone does his neighbour any remarkable kindness, and he is really thankful for it, he will be ready, when an occasion offers, to do him good in return. And though we cannot requite God's kindness to us by doing anything that shall be profitable to him, yet a spirit of thankfulness will dispose us to do what we can, which is well-pleasing or acceptable to him or which may tend to his declarative glory.

If one man should take pity on another who was in some great distress, or in danger of some terrible death, and, moved by pity, should lay himself out for his defence and deliverance, and should undergo great hardships and sufferings in order to do it, and by these means should actually deliver him; and if the latter should express great thankfulness towards his deliverer, and yet in his actions and course of conduct should oppose and dishonour and cast contempt upon him, and do him great injury, no one would give much heed to all his professions of thankfulness. If he is truly thankful, he will never act thus wickedly toward his benefactor.

And so no man can be truly thankful to God for the dying love of Christ, and for the infinite mercy and love of God toward himself, and yet lead a wicked life. His gratitude, if sincere, will lead him to be holy.

Jonathan Edwards (1703–58)

13th January

What shall we say, then? Shall we go on sinning, so that grace may increase? By no means! We died to sin; how can we live in it any longer? Or don't you know that all of us who were baptised into Jesus Christ were baptised into his death? . . . Therefore do not let sin reign in your mortal body so that you obey its evil desires.

(Romans 6:1–3, 12)

We must consider that our old self was crucified with Christ and that in the Cross we have passed into the glorious liberty of His resurrection. The death that Jesus died was a death to sin once and for all; and the life He lives, He lives to God. So we must regard ourselves as dead to sin and self, but as living to God through union with our Saviour. *The self-life may not be dead but we are dead to it!*

One summer afternoon when I reached the great Auditorium at Northfield, I found Mr [D.L.] Moody and his brother on the platform, and between them a young apple tree dug up and brought from the neighbouring orchard. There were about eight hundred or a thousand people in the audience. When I reached the platform the following dialogue took place:

Mr Moody to his brother: "What have you here?"

"An apple tree."

"Was it always an apple tree?"

"Oh no, it was a forest-sapling, but we have inserted apple-graft."

Mr Moody to me: "What does that make you think of?"

"You and I were forest-saplings, with no hope of bearing fruit, but the Jesus-nature has been grafted into us by the Holy Spirit."

To his brother: "Does the forest-sapling give you trouble?"

"Why, yes, it is always sending out shoots under the graft, and they drain off the sap."

"What do you do with them?"

"We pinch them with finger and thumb, but they are always coming up, lower down the tree."

Then he turned to me, and asked if there was anything like it in the life of the *Spirit*; to which he replied: "It is a parable of our experience. The old self-life is always sending out its shoots, but we must be merciless to them. In our earlier stages we deal with the more superficial appeals of the self-life to our vanity and the like. But as we grow older we become aware of their presence always lower down."

F. B. Meyer (1847–1929)

14th January

Do not offer the parts of your body to sin, as instruments of wickedness, but rather offer yourselves to God, as those who have been brought from death to life; and offer the parts of your body to him as instruments of righteousness. For sin shall not be your master, because you are not under law, but under grace.

(Romans 6:13–14)

[Continued from yesterday.]

A further illustration may be given from the experience of Dr Tauler of Strasburg, who did much to prepare the way for Luther and the Reformation. He was a fine preacher, and the whole city hung upon his lips. He was greatly startled, therefore, when a humble Switzer, one of the Society of "the Friends of God," named Nicholas of Basle, crossed the mountains, entered his church, and said, "You must die, Dr Tauler! Before you can do greatest work for God, the world and this city, you must die to yourself, your gifts, your popularity, and even your own goodness, and when you have learned the full meaning of the Cross you will have new power with God and man."

At first he greatly resented this intrusion, but ultimately left his pulpit for a time, and retired for meditation, prayer, and heart-searching. As the inner vision grew clearer, he came to realise how much of his ministry had been inspired by the inveterate wish to make an impression, not simply for Christ's sake, but with the view of maintaining and increasing his own prestige. Finally he left "life's glory dead" at the foot of the Cross, and resolved to have one objective, and one only, Jesus Christ and Him crucified. From that moment his preaching began to help people as never before, and prepared the way for Luther and the new Age.

That story might be indefinitely repeated. Some of us can never forget the hymn composed by the late Pastor Theodore Monod of Paris in his first radiant vision of a life hidden in Christ with God:

> *All of Self and none of Thee!*
> *Some of Self and some of Thee!*
> *Less of Self and more of Thee!*
> *None of Self and all of Thee!*

F. B. Meyer (1847–1929)

15th January

You were taught, with regard to your former way of life, to put off your old self, which is being corrupted by its deceitful desires; to be made new in the attitude of your minds; and to put on the new self, created to be like God in true righteousness and holiness.

(Ephesians 4:22–4)

The Ephesian Christians when they acknowledged the authority of

God and trusted in His love and power for eternal redemption, did not at once escape from the spirit and habits of their old life; nor did we. Their old life was more gross and foul than ours, and their life in the church was therefore stained with grosser and fouler sins; but we too have brought the ethics of the world into the kingdom of God. Sometimes indeed, when the supreme revelation comes to a man, many of his vicious habits fall away from him at the touch of Christ, as the chains of Peter fell at the touch of the angel. And sometimes after a Christian man has been trying for years to rid himself of a disposition, a temper, a habit alien from the spirit of Christ, the gracious lightning of heaven falls on it suddenly and blasts it to the very roots. But, normally, Christian righteousness is achieved slowly. A Divine life is given to us, but the life has to grow. "Love, joy, peace, long-suffering, kindness, goodness, faithfulness, meekness, temperance" are "the fruit of the Spirit"; and the fruit is not ripened in an hour or a day.

There will however be real ethical progress wherever there is genuine loyalty to Christ. There will be a persistent effort to do the will of God as far as the will of God is known. With this fidelity there will be a steady increase of ethical knowledge. The ethical ideal will gradually become loftier. By influences which we cannot trace, the prevailing temper of a Christian man will become more like the temper of Christ. He will be drawn beyond the reach of many temptations by the new and noble interests of the Divine kingdom; other temptations he will have the strength to master. The Divine life will perish if it is so obstructed by evil tempers and evil habits that it cannot grow. Its growth will gradually bring about a complete moral transformation.

R. W. Dale (1829–95)

16th January

To him be glory in the church and in Christ Jesus throughout all generations, for ever and ever! Amen.

(Ephesians 3:21)

The one true Church ... is where the Gospel heartily is, where it is taken seriously as man's chief end; where that Gospel is lived for and worked for; where it is the source of our supreme action, namely, worship, common worship; where it takes its native form in the existence of a Church speaking by Word and Sacrament; where it is the inspiration of all energy and kindness that flow out toward men when we have really been dealing with God; and where it makes the Church the prophet of righteousness to the nations and their States, bearding kings, sobering soldiers, and moralising finance. The true Church is where the Gospel creates its own institutions, prescribed by the situation, and flexible to it for God's purpose; and where the existence of a professional ministry witnesses that a Gospel for life must issue in a life for the Gospel. This true Church is in all the Churches. It is unseen, yet most manifest, like God Himself. It is unknown yet well known. In its purity it is everywhere to faith, nowhere to sight.

I will offer an illustration. When strangers come to Cambridge, and when they have seen the colleges, it would be natural to say, "Now take me to the University." It is a puzzling request. The Senate-House – it is not there. The Library – it is not there. The Schools – it is not there. If you say it is the aggregate of the colleges – it is not that either. It has a personality of its own; it is not a mere group, or sum, or amalgam. It has a history, a tradition, a life, a power, a spell, which is not simply the added-up history or influence of the colleges. To the curious stranger you cannot show the University – which yet is Cambridge. Who can deny the University? It is a great reality, a great spiritual reality in which its colleges inhere. It gives the colleges their true value. It is that which they serve. It is the one spiritual corporation in which the palpable sodalities of the colleges hold together. It dignifies them all. It is the mother of them all from above.

So it is with the Church. The universal Church is, so to say, the University of the Churches. They are all, as it were, collegiate Churches in the great Church they express and serve. They are true Churches in proportion as they lay hold of this spiritual reality which is their life.

P. T. Forsyth (1848–1921)

17th January

He is "the stone which the builders rejected, which has become the capstone." Salvation is found in no-one else, for there is no other name under heaven given to men by which we must be saved.

(Acts 4:11–12)

[Continued from yesterday.]

All the Churches draw their right from the Church which Christ created in His Blood and equipped with His Gospel. A famous statesman once said of a great seaport which arose in the terrible commerce of the eighteenth century that its stones were cemented with the blood of slaves. What was meant bitterly of that city is gloriously true of the City of God. It was founded in a crime, and is built together in the outcast blood of the Son of God. But history has power by Grace to undo the past and erase the taint of origin. The spirit of commerce has outgrown the age of slavery. It is bad business as it is bad morals. And in the Church the blood of Christ is now the stream which flows fast by the living oracles of God, and makes one, and makes glad, the City of our King. That is the unity of the reconcilement which God makes and not man. And that is the life and secret of the One Holy Catholic and Apostolic Church.

The Church's one foundation is not simply Jesus Christ, but Him as crucified and atoning. The message and power of that at once creates the Church and moralises it. Without that it dies into a moralist sterility and sentimental futility. A positive Gospel is the only base of an effective catholic, holy, and united Church, as it was its creator.

P. T. Forsyth (1848–1921)

18th January

So he said he would destroy them – had not Moses, his chosen one, stood in the breach before him to keep his wrath from destroying them.

(Psalm 106:23)

What shall I say of Moses? With what rich perfume had he too filled his heart! That rebellious house, in the midst of which he was for a time occupied, was never able, with all its murmurs, or its angry passions, to make him lose that unction of spirit with which he had once been imbued, or to hinder his gentleness of temper among their constant strifes and daily quarrels. Well deserved, therefore, was the witness which the Holy Spirit bore to him, that "he was the meekest of all men who were on the face of the earth" (Numbers 12:3). Even with those who hated peace, he was peacefully disposed, insomuch that he not only did not indulge anger against an ungrateful and rebellious people, but even interceded for them, so that Divine anger was softened at his mediation . . . He said, "Forgive, if Thou wilt, their sin: but if not, block me out of the book Thou hast written" (Exodus 32:32). A man truly filled with the unction of mercy!

He obviously speaks with the feeling of a father, whom no happiness can delight apart from his children. It is as if a rich man should say to some poor woman who is a mother, "Enter and dine with me, but leave outside the infant you carry in your arms, for fear that it should cry, and be a trouble to us." What would that mother answer, do you suppose? Would she not rather choose to remain without food, than to dine with the rich man alone, after having abandoned her dear pledge of affection? So also Moses did not choose to be admitted alone, even into the joy of his Lord, while his people remained outside. Although they were restless and ungrateful, he retained for them the affection, as he held the place, of a mother.

Bernard of Clairvaux (1090–1153)

19th January

Jesus has been found worthy of greater honour than Moses, just as the builder of a house has greater honour than the house itself.
(Hebrews 3:3)

Moses was a patriot, and punished the enemies of his race with tremendous chastisement; he was a legislator, and his laws had retained their authority for more than sixteen hundred years; he founded a national literature, and his writings had been the daily reading of the kings and priests and commonality of the Jewish people throughout their subsequent history, and no doubt was ever urged, no appeal was ever made against a solitary sentence that had come from his pen; he established religious institutions, and through generation after generation inspired men had been commissioned to defend their sanctity; and the fortunes of the nation had proved that no commandment of Moses could be forgotten or violated without provoking the vengeance of heaven. No other name in the history of the world has ever had the power to stir the heart of a nation like his. More than Luther is to Germany, more than Napoleon is to France, more than Alfred, or Elizabeth, or Cromwell, or William III is to England, Moses was to the Jewish people – prophet, patriot, warrior, lawgiver, all in one.

How strange a contrast between this romantic, brilliant, and splendid history, and the life of Jesus Christ! He was called a Nazarene; He was despised and calumniated by the rulers of His nation; His religious claims were branded by the priesthood as blasphemous, and He was crucified by the civil power as a turbulent political criminal. And yet Moses was only God's servant – Christ was God's Son. "Consider the Apostle and High Priest of our profession," "for He has been held more worthy of honour than Moses."

R. W. Dale (1829–95)

20th January

The Queen of the South will rise at the judgment with this generation and condemn it; for she came from the ends of the earth to listen to Solomon's wisdom, and now one greater than Solomon is here.
(Matthew 12:42)

There is nothing in heaven or earth, in God or in man, so interesting to us as the working of our Lord's mind: especially when he is working on Himself. Well, as it appears to me, we have here an example of how our Lord read, and thought, and saw, and felt about Himself, till He had fully discovered Himself, and had fully and for ever taken possession of Himself. The apostle says that it is not wise in us too much to measure ourselves by ourselves, or to compare ourselves with ourselves, But He who is the Wisdom of God itself here measures and compares Himself with Solomon, and that, to us, in a most interesting and instructive way.

As the Holy Child read the story of Solomon, as that so beautiful and tragical story is told in the First Book of Kings – as he read and saw how Solomon was born of David and Bathsheba; how he was named first the Divine Darling, and then the Son of Peace: how the young king chose wisdom and understanding as his royal portion; how wise he already was, and how wise he became, above all the wise men of the East; what a great kingdom he had, and what untold wealth, and what far and near renown he had; what a service he did in building and finishing the House of the Lord; how the Queen of Sheba came to Jerusalem to hear his wisdom; and then, after all that, Solomon's songs and sermons and proverbs – as the Child Jesus read all that, and asked questions about all that; and then when He became a man, and saw Himself as in a glass in all that, – ere ever He was aware, the Holy Ghost had witnessed it and had sealed it on His mind and His heart, that in all that He, the Son of Mary, was made of God a far greater than Solomon.

The same thing must have come to Him as He read, and prayed, and pondered about David, and Moses, and Abraham, and Adam, till our Lord stood alone among all men, and above all men, and till of the people there none with Him. And this went on, and increased in all clearness and in all assurance, till He was enabled and constrained to say, I and My Father are One. In some such way as that, as I believe, our Lord was led up of the Spirit from strength to strength, till He stood before God and Man the Messiah of Israel, the Son of God, and the Saviour of all them that believe.

Alexander Whyte (1836–1921)

21st January

Going a little farther, he fell with his face to the ground and prayed, "My Father, if it is possible, may this cup be taken from me. Yet not as I will, but as you will."

(Matthew 26:39)

> Behold your King! Though the moonlight steals
> Through the silvery sprays of the olive tree,
> No star-gemmed sceptre or crown it reveals,
> In the solemn shade of Gethsemane.
>   Only a form of prostrate grief,
>   Fallen, crushed, like a broken leaf!
> Oh, think of His sorrow! that we may know
> The depth of love in the depth of woe.
>
> Behold your King! Is it nothing to you,
> That the crimson tokens of agony
> From the kingly brow must fall like dew,
> Through the shuddering shades of Gethsemane?
>   Jesus Himself, the Prince of Life,
>   Bows in mysterious mortal strife;
> Oh, think of His sorrow! that we may know
> The unknown love in the unknown woe.
>
> Behold your King, with His sorrow crowned,
> Alone, alone in the valley is He!
> The shadows of death are gathering round,
> And the Cross must follow Gethsemane.

> Darker and darker the gloom must fall,
> Filled is the Cup, He must drink it all!
> Oh, think of His sorrow! that we may know
> His wondrous love in His wondrous woe.

Frances Ridley Havergal (1836–79)

22nd January

There they offered Jesus wine to drink, mixed with gall; but after tasting it, he refused to drink it. When they had crucified him, they divided up his clothes by casting lots.

(Matthew 27:34–5)

What a gap there is between verses 34 and 35! The unconcerned soldiers went on to the next step in their ordinary routine on such an occasion, – the fixing of the cross and fastening of the Victim to it. To them it was only what they had often done before; to Matthew it was too sacred to be narrated. He cannot bring his pen to write it. As it were, he bids us turn away our eyes for a moment; and when we next look the deed is done, and there stands the cross, and the Lord hanging, dumb and unresisting on it.

We see not Him, but the soldiers busy at their next task. So little were they touched by compassion or awe, that they pay no heed to Him, and suspend their work to make sure of their perquisites – the poor robes which they stripped from His body. Thus gently Matthew hints at the ignominy of exposure attendant on crucifixion, and gives measure of the hard stolidity of the guards. Gain had been their first thought, comfort was their second. They were a little tired by the march and their work, and they had to stand on guard for an indefinite time, with nothing to do but two more prisoners to crucify; so they take a rest, and idly watch over Him till He shall die.

How possible it is to look at Christ's sufferings, and see nothing! These rude legionaires gazed for hours on what has touched the world ever since, and what angels desired to look into, and saw nothing but a dying Jew. They thought about the worth of the clothes, or about how long they would have to stop there, and in the presence of the most stupendous event in the world's history were all unmoved. We too may gaze on the cross and see nothing. We may look at it without emotion, because without faith, or any consciousness of what it may mean for us. Only they who see there the sacrifice for their sins and the world's, see what is there. Others are as blind as, and less excusable than, these soldiers who watched all day by the cross, seeing nothing, and tramped back at night to their barrack, utterly ignorant of what they had been doing.

Alexander Maclaren (1826–1910)

23rd January

And sitting down, they kept watch over him there. Above his head they placed the written charge against him: THIS IS JESUS, THE KING OF THE JEWS.

(Matthew 27:36–7)

[Continued from yesterday.]

But their work was not quite done. There was still a grim piece of mockery to be performed, which they would much enjoy. The "cause" as Matthew calls it, had to be nailed to the upper part of the cross. It was tri-lingual, as John tells us, – in Hebrew, the language of revelation; in Greek, the tongue of philosophy and art; in Latin, the speech of law and power. The three chief forces of the human spirit gave unconscious witness to the King; the three chief languages of the western World proclaimed His universal monarchy, even while they seemed to limit it to one nation.

It was meant as a gibe at Him and at the nation, and as Pilate's statement of the reason for his sentence; but it meant more than Pilate meant by it, and it was fitting that His royal title should hang above His head, for the cross is His throne, and He is the King of men, because He has died for them all.

One more piece of work the soldiers had still to do. The crucifixion of the two robbers (perhaps of Barabbas's gang, though less fortunate than he) by Christ's side was intended to associate Him in the public mind, with them and their crimes, and was the last stroke of malice, as if saying, "Here is your King, and here are two of His subjects and ministers." Matthew says nothing of the triumph of Christ's love, which won the poor robber for a disciple even at that hour of ignominy. His one purpose seems to be to accumulate tokens of suffering and shame, and so to emphasise the silent endurance of the meek Lamb of God.

Alexander Maclaren (1826–1910)

24th January

"Men of Galilee," they said, "why do you stand here looking into the sky? This same Jesus, who has been taken from you into heaven, will come back in the same way you have seen him go into heaven."

(Acts 1:11)

I could not help admiring while I was reading it, that when Christ ascended to heaven, one angel, one particular angel, it must have been a blessed one, left those who were attending Christ in glory, stopped in the way, for what? why, to preach to the apostles: Why stand ye gazing into heaven? I am ashamed of you, says he; here is an angel, one of the convoy, waiting upon them: he does not say, let me go to heaven with thee, and let me come down again and preach, no; he stays down to preach for a few poor fishermen. Lord search us, Lord try us, Lord God Almighty help us to examine ourselves that we may know whether we are beloved of the Lord or not.

Some may say, I think I can apply all the marks, though I don't depend on marks, I have a number of bills tonight; one says, if I am beloved of the Lord, why am I so poor? another says, if I am beloved of the Lord, why am I so afflicted? says another, if I am beloved of the Lord, why am I left to starve? can I think God loves me, when I see thousands squandering away every day, and yet my poor babes groaning . . . If I am so beloved of the Lord, how is that I have so many domestic trials . . . If I am beloved of the Lord, how is it that I am harassed with blasphemous thoughts?

Our dear Jesus was never more beloved of his father than when he cried out, My God! my God! why hast thou forsaken me? never more beloved of his father than when he was sweating great drops of blood, when he cried, Father if it be possible let this cup pass from me.

I remember a dear minister of Christ, now in Suffolk, told me, when he was in Scotland, going to receive the sacrament, he was dry and dark, and benumbed and tempted, that he thought that he would go away. As he was going away this word came to his mind, when was Jesus Christ most acceptable of his Father? when did he give the greatest trial of his love? when he cried out, My God! my God! why hast thou forsaken me? Why then, says he, upon this I will venture; if I perish, I perish at Christ's feet; and he came away filled with comfort from his blessed God and Father in Christ.

George Whitefield (1714–70)

25th January

For whenever you eat this bread and drink this cup, you proclaim the Lord's death until he comes.

(1 Corinthians 11:26)

We believe and confess concerning the Lord's holy Supper that it is a holy sacramental sign, instituted of the Lord himself in bread and wine, and left to his disciples in remembrance of him. Matthew 26; Mark 14; Luke 22; 1 Corinthians 11. It was also taught and administered as such by the apostles among the brethren, according to the commandment of the Lord, in which in the first place the Lord's death is proclaimed. 1 Corinthians 11. And it also serves as a remembrance how he offered his holy flesh and shed his precious blood for the remission of our sins. Matthew 26:27; Mark 14:24; Luke 22:19.

Second, it is an emblem of Christian love, of unity, and of peace in the church of Christ. Paul says, "For we, being many, are one bread and one body; for we are all partakers of the one loaf" 1 Corinthians 10:17. For as a loaf being composed of many grains is but one bread; so we also being composed of many members are but one body in Christ. And as the members of a natural body are not disharmonious, but altogether united and at one among themselves; so it is with all those who are in the Spirit and faith true members of the body of Christ. For this very reason this same supper was called by Tertullian a brotherly meal or love feast.

Third it is a communion of the flesh and blood of Christ. As Paul says, "The cup of blessing which we bless, is it not the communion of the body of Christ?" 1 Corinthians 10:16. This communion consists in the fact that Christ has accepted us in his great love, and we are become partakers of him. As Paul says, "We are made partakers of Christ, if we hold the beginning of our confidence steadfast unto the end." Hebrews 3:14.

Since it is a sign of such force which is left of Christ, that it is to represent and admonish us of his death, the love, peace, and unity of the brethren, and also the communion of his flesh and blood as was said, therefore none can rightly partake of this Supper except he be a disciple of Christ, flesh of his flesh, and bone of his bone, who seeks the forgiveness of sins in no other means than in the merits, sacrifice, death, and blood of Christ alone; who walks in unity, love, and peace with his brethren, and who leads a pious, unblamable life in Christ Jesus, according to the Scriptures.

Menno Simons (c. 1496–1561)

26th January

As it is, there are many parts, but one body. The eye cannot say to the hand, "I don't need you!" And the head cannot say to the feet, "I don't need you!"

(1 Corinthians 12:20–21)

For wherefore, tell me, enviest thou? Because thy brother hath received spiritual grace? And from whom did he receive it? answer me. Was it not from God? Clearly then He is the object of the emnity to which thou art committing thyself, He the bestower of the gift. See thou which way the evil is tending, and with what sort of a point it is crowning the heap of thy sins; and how deep the pit of vengeance which it is digging for thee?

Let us flee it, then, beloved, and neither envy others, nor fail to pray for our enviers, and do all we can to extinguish their passion: neither let us feel as the unthinking do, who being minded to exact punishment of them, do all in their power to light up their flame. But let us not do so; rather let us weep for them and lament. For they are the injured persons, having a continual worm gnawing through their heart, and collecting a fountain of poison more bitter than any gall.

Come now, let us beseech the merciful God, both to change their state of feeling, and that we may never fall into that disease: since heaven is indeed more inaccessible to him that hath this wasting sore, and before heaven too, even this present life is not worth living in. For not so thoroughly are timber and wool wont to be eaten through by moth and worm abiding therein, as doth the fever of envy devour the very bones of the envious, and destroy all self-command in their soul.

In order then that we may deliver both ourselves and others from these innumerable woes, let us expel from within us this evil fever, this that is more grievous than any gangrene: that having regained spiritual strength, we may both finish the course, and obtain the future crowns; unto which we may all attain, by the grace and mercy of our Lord Jesus Christ, with whom to the Father, with the Holy Ghost, be glory, power, honour, now and for ever, and world without end. Amen.

John Chrysostom (c. 344/345–407)

27th January

And let us consider how we may spur one another on towards love and good deeds.

(Hebrews 10:24)

"Consider one another to provoke to love and good works." The minister cannot do it, he has not time; it is impossible he should study and prepare sermons, and at the same time visit all the members of the Church as often as is necessary to keep them advancing. The members are bound to watch over one another's spiritual welfare. But how is this done? Many do not know each other. They meet and pass as strangers, and never ask about one another's spiritual condition. But if they hear anything bad of one, they go and tell it to the others. Instead of watching over them for good, they watch for their halting. How can they watch for good when they are not even acquainted with each other?

The Church should watch for the effect of preaching. If the members are *praying* for the success of the preached Word, they will watch for it of course. They should keep a look-out, and when any in the congregation give evidence that the Word of God has taken hold of them, they should follow it up. Wherever there are any exhibitions of feeling, those persons should be attended to, instantly, and not left until their impressions wear off. They should be spoken to, or visited, or got into the anxious meeting, or into the Bible class, or brought to the minister. If members do not attend to this, they neglect their duty. If they attend to it, they may do incalculable good.

There was a pious young woman, who lived alone in a very cold and wicked place. She alone had the spirit of prayer, and she had been praying for a blessing upon the Word. At length she saw an individual in the congregation who seemed to be affected by the preaching, and as soon as the minister came from the pulpit, she came forward, agitated and trembling, and begged him to go and converse with the person immediately. He did so, the individual was converted, and soon a revival followed.

Charles G. Finney (1792–1875)

28th January

My brothers, if one of you should wander from the truth and someone should bring him back, remember this: Whoever turns a sinner from the error of his way will save him from death and cover over a multitude of sins.

(James 5:19–20)

We must restore the penitent to the fellowship of the church. As we must not teach an offender to make light of discipline by too much facility, so neither must we discourage him by too much severity. If he appears to be truly sensible of the criminality of his conduct, and penitent on account of it, we must see that he confess his guilt, and that he promise to fly from such sins for the time to come. He must promise to watch more narrowly, and to walk more warily, to avoid temptation, to distrust his own strength, and to rely on the grace which is in Christ Jesus.

We must assure him of the riches of God's love, and the sufficiency of Christ's blood to pardon his sins, if he believe and repent. We must see that he beg the communion of the church, and their prayers to God for his pardon and salvation.

We must charge the church that they imitate Christ, in forgiving and in retaining the penitent person; or, if he were cast out, in receiving him into their communion. They must never reproach him with his sins, nor cast them in his teeth, but forgive them, even as Christ hath forgiven them.

Finally, we must give God thanks for his recovery, and pray for his confirmation and future preservation.

Richard Baxter (1615–91)

29th January

Repentance and forgiveness of sins will be preached in his name to all nations, beginning in Jerusalem.

(Luke 24:47)

Sometimes an awakened sinner is comforted by being told that "religion does not consist in feeling bad." I once heard of a Doctor of Divinity giving an anxious sinner such counsel, when he was actually writhing under the arrows of the Almighty. Said he: "Religion is cheerful, religion is not gloomy; do not be distressed, but dismiss your fears; be comforted, you should not feel so bad," and such like miserable comforts, when, in fact, the man had infinite reason to be distressed, for he was resisting the Holy Ghost, and was in danger of grieving Him away for ever.

It is true, religion does not consist in "feeling bad"; but the sinner has reason to be distressed because he has no religion. If he had religion, he would not feel so. Were he a Christian, he would rejoice. But to tell an impenitent sinner to be cheerful!

Why, you might as well preach this doctrine in hell, and tell them there: "Cheer up here, cheer up: do not feel bad!"

The sinner is on the very verge of hell, he is in rebellion against God, and his danger is infinitely greater than he imagines. Oh, what a doctrine of devils it is to tell a rebel against Heaven not to be distressed! What is all his distress, but rebellion itself? He is not comforted, because he refuses to be comforted. God is ready to comfort him. You need not think to be more compassionate than God. He will fill the sinner with comfort, in an instant, on submission. There stands the sinner, struggling against God, and against the Holy Ghost, and against conscience, until he is distressed almost to death, but still he will not yield; and now someone comes in, saying: "Oh, I hate to see you feel so bad, do not be distressed: cheer up, cheer up; religion does not consist in being gloomy; be comforted." Horrid!

Charles G. Finney (1792–1875)

30th January

For it is by grace you have been saved, through faith – and this not from yourselves, it is the gift of God – not by works, so that no-one can boast.

(Ephesians 2:8–9)

I sometimes think that I might have been in darkness and despair until now had it not been for the goodness of God in sending a snowstorm, one Sunday morning when I was going to a certain place of worship. When I could get no further, I turned down a side street, and came to a little Primitive Methodist Chapel. In that chapel there may have been a dozen or fifteen people. I had heard of the Primitive Methodists, how they sang so loudly that they made people's heads ache; but that did not matter to me. I wanted to know how I might be saved, and if they could tell me that, I did not care how much they made my head ache. The minister did not come that morning; he was snowed up I suppose. At last a very thin-looking man, a shoemaker, or tailor, or something of that sort, went up into the pulpit to preach. Now it is well that preachers be instructed, but this man was really stupid. He was obliged to stick to his text, for the simple reason that he had little else to say. The text was —

"LOOK UNTO ME, AND BE YE SAVED, ALL THE ENDS OF THE EARTH." He did not even pronounce the words rightly, but that did not matter. There was I thought, a glimpse of hope for me in that text. The preacher began thus: "My dear friends, this is a very simple text indeed. It says, 'Look.' Now lookin' don't take a deal of pain. It ain't liftin' your foot or finger; it is just, 'Look.' Well a man needn't go to College to learn to look. You may be the biggest fool, and yet you can look. A man needn't be worth a thousand a year to be able to look. Anyone can look; even a child can look. But then the text says, 'Look unto *ME*' Ay!" said he, in broad Essex, "many on ye are lookin' to yourselves, but it's no use lookin' there. You'll never find any comfort in yourselves. Some look to God the Father. No, look to him by-and-by. Jesus Christ says, 'Look unto *ME*.' Some on ye say, 'We must wait for the Spirit's workin'.' You have no business with that just now. Look to *CHRIST*. The text says, 'Look unto ME.'"

C. H. Spurgeon (1834–92)

31st January

Then I heard the voice of the Lord saying, "Whom shall I send? And who will go for us?"

(Isaiah 6:8)

"Whom shall I send? And who will go for us?" Why does the Lord ask that question with such anxiety when He has all these shining seraphs standing at his side, and each of them with six wings? Why was Isaiah, the son of Amoz, a man of such unclean lips, and a man so woeful and undone, so accepted and so sent? Seraphs, not sinners, should surely be preachers of such holiness as that of the God of Israel, and the heralds of such a Saviour – that is what we would have expected.

But God's thoughts in these things are not as our thoughts. It was not the seraph burning with heavenly love that was sent to preach to Jerusalem in Uzziah's day, but a man who but a moment before had been full of leprosy to his lips, and laden to the earth with his own and his people's sin. It was Isaiah, the son of Amoz, who took boldness to say, Here am I, send me. And it was to that same Isaiah that the Lord said, Go and tell this people. And this has always been God's way in choosing and in ordaining and in sending both prophets, and psalmists, and priests, and preachers for His Church on earth. Only once did God choose a completely sinless preacher. Always, but that once, God has chosen sinful men; and not seldom, the most sinful of men He could get to speak to their fellow-men about sin and salvation.

Gabriel might come with his six wings to announce to Mary that the fulness of time had come and that the Word was to be made flesh, but it was John, who was less than the least in the kingdom of heaven (Matthew 11:11), who was sent to preach repentance to the vipers of his day, and to urge them to flee from the wrath to come . . .

Isaiah . . . of all men on the face of the earth at that moment, and of all angels of heaven, was the man chosen to preach repentance to Jerusalem, and to prophesy to her, as never before, the coming of her Messiah. And he preached on all these matters as no angel in heaven could have preached. He preached as only a leper could preach to his elder brother lepers, and as only a man undone could preach to other undone men.

Alexander Whyte (1836–1921)

February

1st February

Jesus said to them, "It is not the healthy who need a doctor, but the sick. I have not come to call the righteous, but sinners".

(Mark 2:17)

The Samaritan must come – that is Christ – who brings medicine with him, wine and oil, and pours it upon the wounds of the sinner. Wine represents man's repentance for his sins, and the oil annoints his sores and mollifies them. Christ says believe in the gospel which clearly states that I am the physician that has come into the world to make the sinner righteous and godly. The gospel teaches also that I am the only gracious, reconciling, interceding mediator and peacemaker with God our Father. He who believes on me shall not be damned but has eternal life. Through such comforting words the sinner is quickened, comes to himself, becomes joyful, and entrusts himself to his physician. He commits and entrusts his sickness to the physician, surrenders as much as a wounded man can, and calls to him for healing. The physician helps, advises, and promotes whatever the wounded man cannot do in his own strength so that he can follow his word and commandment.

Now all the teachings which diagnose diseases and point to the physician are only "the letter that kills" before they are believed. But in faith God makes them to live, wax green, and bear fruit.

Thus by faith water becomes wine at the wedding. One must put on the rough coat of John the Baptist before one can receive the soft, mild and meek lamb, Jesus Christ. Then a man surrenders himself sincerely from the heart and purposes to lead a new life, according to the rules and teaching of Christ, the physician, who had made him whole, and from whom he derives his life. So Paul acknowledges openly that it is not he that lives, but Christ that lives in him. Christ is the life in him. Outside of Christ, he confesses that he and his works are vain, of no account, and an accursed sinner.

Balthasar Hubmaier (c. 1480–1528)

2nd February

Is any one of you in trouble? He should pray. Is anyone happy? Let him sing songs of praise. Is any one of you sick? He should call the elders of the church to pray over him and anoint him with oil in the name of the Lord. And the prayer offered in faith will make the sick person well; the Lord will raise him up. If he has sinned, he will be forgiven. Therefore confess your sins to each other and pray for each other so that you may be healed. The prayer of a righteous man is powerful and effective.

(James 5:13–16)

(When I had to leave home on business) some thought the healings would cease. I was glad to have the chance to prove to all who the Healer was. When I left, Arulai led at Prayers, backed up by the whole family.

There was only one who dropped out. Some people from the Dohnavur village had a child with hip disease and I had asked them to come to Prayers that they might understand things better. When they saw Arulai in my place they were not pleased and did not come again.

"So it was not *God* they were looking at," was the children's true comment.

A new baby was sent to us, a lovely little Brahman boy of ten days or so. He developed water on the knee and a swollen foot, and of course a high temperature. He was far too ill to be taken to

Neyoor hospital. He could not have borne the shaking (in the bullock cart).

After prayer, the prayer of the whole Family, his temperature fell and he slept. Yesterday for the first time he moved his little leg almost straight out. He is not perfectly healed yet. One waits, not knowing with any easy assurance what the will of the Lord is, but longing for the very touch that was of old, the touch that perfectly restored at once. Why is it not so now?

Is this sentence, which is often in my mind, the answer to that question? "We must remember in contrite humility that the way of healing is like a broken, long disused road – it is overgrown with the thorns and briers of our long neglect; it is blocked with the boulders of thoughts and ways of the world that are not the thoughts and ways of God." The bridges of faith have been half broken, the gates of prayer have been too often closed – should we dare to ask or expect our Lord to come in healing and to do His mighty works among us, as though the way were made straight for His feet?

Sometimes I wonder if even we of Dohnavur may be allowed to roll just one small boulder out of the way, that the path may be by just so much the straighter for His feet.

Amy Carmichael (1867–1951)

3rd February

For though we live in the world, we do not wage war as the world does. The weapons we fight with are not the weapons of the world. On the contrary, they have divine power to demolish strongholds.
(2 Corinthians 10:3–4)

And when they were come to By-path Meadow, to the stile over which Christian went with his fellow, Hopeful, when they were taken by Giant Despair and put into Doubting Castle, they sat down and consulted what was best to be done, to wit; now they were so strong, and had got such a man as Mr Great-heart for their conductor, whether they had not best to make an attempt upon the giant, demolish his castle, and, if there were any pilgrims in it, to set them at liberty before they went any further. So one said one thing, and another said the contrary. One questioned if it was lawful to go upon unconsecrated ground; another said they might, provided their end was good. But Mr Great-heart said, "Though this assertion offered last cannot be universally true, yet I have a commandment to resist sin, to overcome evil, to fight the good fight of faith (1 Timothy 6:12). And I pray, with whom should I fight this good fight if not with Giant Despair? I will therefore attempt the taking away of his life and the demolishing of Doubting Castle." Then said he, "Who will go with me?" Then said old Honest, "I will." "And so will we too," said Christian's four sons, Matthew, Samuel, James, and Joseph, for they were young men and strong.

So they left the women in the road, and with them Mr Feeble-mind, and Mr Ready-to-halt, with his crutches, to be their guard until they came back. For in that place, though Giant Despair dwelt so near, they keeping in the road, a little child might lead them.

So Mr Great-heart, old Honest, and the four young men went to go up to Doubting Castle to look for Giant Despair. When they came at the castle gate, they knocked for entrance with an unusual noise. At that, the old giant comes to the gate, and Diffidence, his wife, follows. Then said he, "Who, and what is he that is so hardy as after this manner to molest the Giant Despair?" Mr Great-heart replied, "It is I, Great-heart, one of the King of the Celestial Country's conductors of pilgrims to their place. And I demand of thee that thou open thy gates for my entrance. Prepare thyself to fight, for I am come to take away thy head and to demolish Doubting Castle."

John Bunyan (1628–88)

4th February

We demolish arguments and every pretension that sets itself up against the knowledge of God, and we take captive every thought to make it obedient to Christ.

(2 Corinthians 10:5)

[Continued from yesterday.]

Now Giant Despair because he was a giant, thought no man could overcome him. And again, thought he, "Since heretofore I have made a conquest of angels, shall Great-heart make me afraid?" So he harnessed himself and went out. He had a cap of steel upon his head, a breastplate of fire girded to him, and he came out in iron shoes, with a great club in his hand. Then these six men made up to him and beset him behind and before. Also when Diffidence, the giantess, came up to help him, old Mr Honest cut her down at one blow. Then they fought for their lives. And Giant Despair was brought down to the ground but was very loath to die. He struggled hard, and had as they say, so many lives as a cat. But Great-heart was his death, for he left him not till he had severed his head from his shoulders.

Then they fell to demolishing Doubting Castle, and that you know might with ease be done since Giant Despair was dead. They were seven days in destroying of that, and in it of pilgrims they found one Mr Despondency, almost starved to death, and one Much-afraid, his daughter. These two they saved alive. But it would a made you a wondered to have seen the dead bodies that lay here and there in the castle yard, and how full of dead men's bones the dungeon was.

When Mr Great-heart and his companions had performed this exploit, they took Mr Despondency and his daughter, Much-afraid, into their protection, for they were honest people though they were prisoner, in Doubting Castle, to that tyrant, Giant Despair. They, therefore, I say, took with them the head of the giant (for his body they had buried under a heap of stones), and down to the road and to their companions they came and showed them what they had done. Now when Feeble-mind and Ready-to-halt saw that it was the head of Giant Despair, indeed, they were very jocund and merry. Now Christiana if need was, could play upon the viol, and her daughter, Mercy, upon the lute. So, since they were so merry disposed, she played them a lesson, and Ready-to-halt would dance. So he took Despondency's daughter, named Much-afraid, by the hand, and to dancing they went in the road. True, he could not dance without one crutch in his hand, but, I promise you, he footed it well: also the girl was to be commended, for she answered the music handsomely.

As for Mr Despondency, the music was not much to him; he was for feeding rather than dancing, for that he was almost starved. So Christiana gave him some of her bottle of spirits for present relief and then prepared him something to eat. And in little time the old gentleman came to himself and began to be finely revived.

John Bunyan (1628–88)

5th February

For no matter how many promises God has made, they are "Yes" in Christ. And so through him the "Amen" is spoken by us to the glory of God.

(2 Corinthians 1:20)

Jesus Thy blood and righteousness
My beauty are, my glorious dress;
Midst flaming worlds, in these arrayed.
With joy I lift up my head.

Bold shall I stand in Thy great day:
For who aught to my charge shall lay?
Fully through Thee absolved I am.
From sin and fear, from guilt and shame.

When from the dust of death I rise
To claim my mansion in the skies,
Even then this shall be all my plea –
Jesus hath lived and died for me!

Jesus, be endless praise to Thee,
Whose boundless mercy hath for me,
For me and all Thy hands have made,
An everlasting ransom paid.

Lord, I believe, were sinners more
Than sands upon the ocean shore,
Thou hast for all a ransom paid,
For all a full atonement made.

Lord, I believe Thy precious blood,
Which at the mercy-seat of God
For ever doth for sinners plead,
For me, even for my soul, was shed.

Thou God of power, Thou God of love,
Let the whole world Thy mercy prove!
Now let Thy world o'er all prevail;
Now take the spoils of death and hell.

O let the dead now hear Thy voice,
Now bid Thy banished ones rejoice,
Their beauty this, their glorious dress.
Jesus, the Lord our righteousness!

Nikolaus Ludwig, Count von Zinzendorf (1700–1760)

6th February

To keep me from becoming conceited because of these surpassingly great revelations, there was given me a thorn in my flesh, a messenger of Satan, to torment me

(2 Corinthians 12:7)

In our own day interpretation [of Paul's thorn in the flesh] has taken a line of its own in this matter. Lightfoot holds that it was epilepsy. And while Dean Farrar admits that there is something to be said for epilepsy, he decides on the whole for ophthalmia. And then Professor Ramsay, Paul's latest, and in his own field one of Paul's best commentators, has no doubt at all but that it was one of the burning up fevers so frequent to this day in Asia Minor. Whatever his thorn really was, we are left in no doubt as to what Paul did with it. And we are left in just as little doubt as to what his Master's mind and will were about it. And then all that leads up to this magnificent resolve of the Apostle – "Most gladly, therefore, will I rather glory in my infirmities, that the power of Christ may rest upon me." A splendid parenthesis, in a splendid argument. An autobiographic chapter of the foremost instructiveness and impressiveness, and of all kinds of profit and delight, to read and remember.

Now while it will be the most fruitless of all our studies to seek to find out what Paul's secret thorn was; on the other hand it will be one of the most rewarding of all our best studies, both of ourselves and of Holy Scripture also, if we can find out what our own thorn is, and can then go on to make the right use of our own thorn. To be told even by himself just what Paul's thorn actually was would not bring to us one atom of real benefit. But if I have a thorn in my own flesh, and if I know what it is, and why it is there, and what I am to do with it – that will be one of the divinest discoveries in the world to me; that will be the salvation of my own soul to me.

Never mind the commentators on Paul's thorn; no not the very best of them, lest they draw your attention away from your own. Be your own commentator on all such subjects. Be your own thorn-student especially. What is it then that so tortures you, and rankles in you, till your life is absolutely intolerable to you? What is it that gnaws and saps and undermines all your joy in this life? What is it that makes you beseech the Lord thrice, and without ceasing, that it may depart from you? Tell me that, and then I will tell you Paul's thorn.

Alexander Whyte (1836–1921)

7th February

My grace is enough.

(2 Corinthians 12:9 from the German)

My dear friends, that is a very short text – only four words – I think it is the shortest on which I have ever preached. The advantage of this is that you can remember it all the better. It is, by the way my most important concern, each time that I am permitted to be here [Basel Prison], that the word from the Bible should stick in your minds and stay with you afterwards rather than my sermon. So today the text is: My grace is enough. The point of this text lies in its brevity – it illustrates, as it were, what it describes. These four words are enough. Some of you have perhaps heard it said that in the last forty years I have written a great many books and some of them are very fat ones. Let me, however, frankly and even gladly confess that the four words: "My grace is enough" say much more and say it better than the whole pile of paper with which I have surrounded myself. They are enough – something that I am very far from being able to say about my books. Whatever might be good about my books could at best consist only in pointing out from the distance what these four words say. And when my books have long since been superseded and forgotten, and the books of the whole world with them, then these words will still shine on in all their eternal richness: My grace is enough.

And now a second preliminary remark. If you want to look up this text afterwards in your Bibles, you will find in the German translation of Luther, which is still the one most widely used, the text has a rather different wording from that given by me: the version there is "Let yourselves be satisfied with my grace." It is very true that you may and must let yourself by satisfied with what is enough for you. But the original word is better still. Whether you let yourself be satisfied with it, whether you are satisfied with it or not, my grace is *enough* for you. It stands like a solidly based tower or like the Matterhorn or like the Pole Star around which our whole universe seems to revolve. My grace is *enough*. Because it is enough for you in all cases, *therefore* you can, may and must *let* yourself be satisfied with it, today as yesterday and tomorrow as today.

Karl Barth (1886–1968)

8th February

As I was with Moses so I will be with you; I will never leave you nor forsake you. Be strong and courageous, because you will lead these people to inherit the land I swore to their forefathers to give them.

(Joshua 1:5b–6)

Did Joshua remember how, nearly forty years since, he had fronted the mob of cowards with the very same assurance, and how the answer had been a shower of stones? The cowards are all dead – will their sons believe the assurance now? If we do believe that God is with us, we shall be ready to cross Jordan in flood, and to meet the enemies that are waiting on the other bank. If we do not, we shall not dare greatly, nor succeed in what we attempt. The small successes of material wealth and gratified ambition may be ours, but for all the higher duties and nobler conflicts that become a man, the condition of achievement and victory is steadfast faith in God's presence and help.

That assurance – which we may all have if we cling to Jesus, in whom God comes to be with every believing soul – is the only basis on which the command to Joshua, thrice repeated, can wisely or securely be rested. It is a mockery to say to a man conscious of weakness, and knowing that there are evils which must surely come, and evils that may possibly come, against which he is powerless, "Don't be afraid" unless you can show him a reason why he need not be.

And there is only one reason which can still reasonable dread in a human heart that has to front "all the ills that flesh is heir to," and sees behind them all the grim form of death. He ought to be afraid, unless – unless what? Unless he has heard and taken into his inmost soul the Voice that said to Joshua, "I will not fail thee, nor forsake thee: be strong and of good courage," or, still more sweet and peace-bringing, the Voice that said to the frightened crew of the fishing boat in the storm and the darkness, "It is I, be not afraid." If we know that Christ is with us, it is wise to be strong and courageous; if we are meeting the tempest alone, the best thing we can do is to fear, for the fear may drive us to seek for His help, and He ever stretches His hand out to him who is afraid, as he ought to be, when he feels the cold water rising above his knees, and by his very fear is driven to faith, and cries, "Lord, save; I perish!"

Alexander Maclaren (1826–1910)

9th February

Therefore encourage one another and build each other up, just as in fact you are doing.

(1 Thessalonians 5:11)

When we come together, we do so with the desire to encourage and awaken our hearts in the grace of God, to walk in the Lord's sight with greater diligence and attention. Therefore, the people are first encouraged to mark diligently and to consider why we have met and come together, that they may prepare their hearts for prayer, so that they may come worthily before the Lord and pray for what concerns the church and all her members.

After this we give thanks to God for all the good that he has given us through Christ, and for accepting us into his grace and revealing to us his truth. This is followed by an earnest prayer that he keep us faithful and devout therein to the end, and supply all our desires and needs, and open our hearts that we may use his word with profit, hear, accept and keep it. When this is done, one proceeds to proclaim the Lord's word faithfully, according to the grace given by God, encouraging the heart to fear the Lord and to remain in his fear. When all this is completed the minister commends the church to God the Lord and lets them depart one from another, each to his place. When, however, we come together to keep the Lord's memory or Supper the people are encouraged and taught for one, two or three days and told vividly what the Lord's Supper is, what happens there and what one does thereby, and how one should prepare himself worthily to receive the same. Every day, however, has also its thanksgiving and prayer. When all this has taken place, and the Lord's Supper has been kept, a hymn of praise is sung to Lord. Then the people are admonished to walk in accordance with what they have shown to be in their hearts, and then they are commended to the Lord and allowed to separate.

Peter Riedeman (1506–56)

10th February

I long to see you so that I may impart to you some spiritual gift to make you strong – that is, that you and I may be mutually encouraged by each other's faith.

(Romans 1:11–12)

The interest of Elizabeth Fry was not confined to the prisons of her native country. She opened a correspondence with St Petersburg, through the medium of Walter Venning, who devoted himself to visiting and instructing prisoners in that city.

"Respected friend, Though personally unknown to thee, I am confident, from the interest we both feel in one cause, that thou wilt excuse the liberty in writing to thee, to express my heartfelt satisfaction at the interesting and important accounts thou hast given my brother Hoare, of the proceedings of the Gentlemen and Ladies' Prison Associations in Petersburg. Most warmly do I desire their encouragement in this work of charity and utility; for the more I am acquainted with the subject, and the more extensive my observation of the effects of prison discipline is, the more confident I feel of its importance; and, that although the work will be gradual, yet through the Divine blessing, its results will be sure.

"Not only that many will be stopped in their career of vice, but some truly turned from their evil ways, and the security and comfort of the community at large increased, by our prisons, that have been generally the nurseries of vice, and the scenes of idleness, filth and debauchery, being so arranged and so attended to, that they became schools where the most reprobate may be instructed in their duty towards their Creator and their fellow-mortals; and where the very habits of their lives may be changed.

"It will be found in this, as in every good work, that some trials and discouragements will attend it; but the great end in view must induce those engaged in it to persevere, and use increased diligence to overcome them. Doing what we do to the Lord, and not unto man, and then we shall do it well."

Elizabeth Fry (1780–1845)

11th February

But when the kindness and love of God our Saviour appeared, he saved us, not because of righteous things we had done, but because of his mercy.

(Titus 3:4–5)

[Continued from yesterday.]

We continue to have much satisfaction in the results of our efforts in Newgate: good order appears to be increasingly established, there is much cleanliness among our poor women, and some very encouraging proofs of reformation in habit, and what is more, in heart. This, in a prison so ill arranged, with no classification, except tried from untried, no good inspection, and many other great disadvantages, is more than the zealous advocates of prison discipline could look for. We find the same favourable result follows the labours of several other Ladies' Associations in this kingdom; as I have the pleasure to state that in England, Scotland and Ireland, many are now established . . .

It is more than three years since we first began our operations in Newgate, and how encouraging it is, that the experience of every year should increase our hopes and diminish our fears as to the beneficial results of these exertions. Indeed it is wonderful to observe the effects of kindness and care upon some of these poor forlorn creatures – how it tenders their hearts and makes them susceptible of impression. I am of the opinion, from what I have observed, that there are hardly any amongst them so hard, but that they may be subdued by kindness, gentleness and love; so as very materially to alter their general conduct.

Some of the worst prisoners have, after liberation, done great credit to the care taken of them. In two particular instances, young women who had sunk into almost every depravity and vice, upon being liberated, conducted themselves with much propriety, as far as we know, and after long illnesses died peaceful deaths. They were striking instances; through a blessing upon the care taken of them, they in remarkable manner were turned from Satan unto God, and we humbly trust, through the mercy of Redeeming love, they are received into Glory. Some are settled in service, others we hope are doing well in different situations. We wish it were in our power to attend to more of the prisoners upon leaving the prisons, as we think this an important part of the duty of such associations; but in London the numbers are so very great that it is almost out of our power to do it, as we desire; though we endeavour to extend a little care over them.

Elizabeth Fry (1780–1845)

12th February

The disciples were called Christians first at Antioch.
(Acts 11:26)

It is interesting to remember how all which has happened to Christianity happened first to Christ. All the welcome and rejection, all the eager love, the passionate hatred, and the perplexed questionings which have greeted the religion of the Saviour greeted the Saviour first, and have left their record on the pages of the Gospels, in which the story of His earthly life is told. If men have always wondered whether the final salvation of this world has been attained in Jesus, has there not been in their questioning the echo of John the Baptist's message, "Art thou He that should come, or do we look for another?" If men have taunted Christianity because with all its vast claims to mastery it still has been despised and trodden under foot of men, we can hear through their mockery the words which greeted Jesus in His agony, "If thou be the Son of

God, come down from the cross." If men's pride in their own self-sufficiency and in the competence of their earthly associations and traditions has been wounded, they have cried out to the Redeemer, who offered His redemption with such importunate insistence, "Art thou greater than our father Abraham? Art thou greater than our father Jacob, which gave us this well?" If the spiritual region from which Christianity issued has seemed too obscure, too remote from the great accredited interests of mankind, the voice which declared that such a religion could not save the world has only taken up again the old objections, "Can any good thing come out of Nazareth?" "Search and look, for out of Galilee ariseth no prophet." It is a sign of the vitality and reality of Jesus, it is a sign of how Christianity is but the extension and perpetuation of Christ in the world, that all which is said of Christianity today was said years and years ago of Christ.

Phillips Brooks (1835–93)

13th February

Then Simeon blessed them and said to Mary, his mother: "This child is destined to cause the falling and rising of many in Israel, and to be a sign that will be spoken against, so that the thoughts of many hearts will be revealed. And a sword will pierce your own soul too."

(Luke 2:34–5)

"And for a sign that shall be spoken against." We wonder to hear that. We are shocked to hear that. We say in amazement at that: What did He ever say or do that He should be spoken against by any man? He did the very opposite. He went about speaking and doing only good. But that made no difference to those men in that day who spake so spitefully against Him. Some spake against Him out of sheer ignorance of Him. They had never even seen Him. But they spake against Him in their distant villages as if He had come and done them and theirs some great injury. And many who saw Him every day spake against Him every day, just because they did not understand Him, and would not take the pains and pay the price to understand Him and to love Him. Some, again, were poisoned against Him by what other people and people of power, said against Him; some through envy, and some just because they had once begun to speak against Him, and could never give over what they had begun to do. And they went on so speaking till they were swept on to cry, Crucify Him! not knowing what they were saying, or why.

Take good care how you begin to speak against any man, good or bad. The chances are that, once you begin it, you will never be able to give it over. When once you have begun the devil's work of evil-speaking, he will hold his hook in your jaws, and will drag you on, and will give you a stake and an interest in lies and slander, till it will enrage and exasperate you to hear a single word of good spoken about your innocent victim. "Judge not," said our Lord, feeling bitterly how He was misjudged Himself.

Alexander Whyte (1836–1921)

14th February

John's clothes were made of camel's hair, and he had a leather belt round his waist. His food was locusts and wild honey. People went out to him from Jerusalem and all Judea and the whole region of the Jordan. Confessing their sins, they were baptised by him in the Jordan River.

(Matthew 3:4–6)

People tell us that they do not believe in revivals. There never was a country moved so suddenly and awakened so quickly as was Judea under the preaching of John and Jesus Christ. Talk about sensational preaching! If by that term you mean preaching designed merely to impress the outward senses, then their preaching was not sensational; but if you mean preaching calculated to produce a striking effect, then it was indeed sensational. The greatest sensation that any nation ever witnessed was brought about by these mighty preachers. Some great patriarchs, prophets and kings – some wonderful men had arisen; but now the Jewish world was about to gaze on its greatest . . .

It was not long before you could hear the tramp of thousands flocking from the towns into the desert to hear a man who had no commission from his fellow-men; who had gone through no seminary or college; who had not been brought up in the temple among the sons of Levi; who belonged to no sect or party; who had no D.D., LL.D., or any handle to his name, but simply JOHN; a heaven-sent man, with a heaven-sent name. He had no *prestige* in Jerusalem, nor any influential committee meetings. He was simply John the Baptist, preaching in the wilderness! And away went the crowds to hear him, and many believed him! Why? Because he was sent from God.

In New York, Edinburgh, or London, almost any man of note can gather a large audience; but let him go away into the desert and see if he can draw the inhabitants from the large cities to hear him, as John did. Like Elijah, he was intrepid and uncompromising. He did not preach to please people, for he denounced their sins . . .

That is the beginning; but he did not leave them there. You may bring the law, and cry "Reform! Reform!" "Repent! Repent!" but that leaves a man outside the Kingdom of God; that does not bring him to Christ; and it will not be long before he goes back to his sins. In every one of his sermons John alluded to the coming Messiah.

D. L. Moody (1837–99)

15th February

There the angel of the Lord appeared to him in flames of fire from within a bush. Moses saw that though the bush was on fire it did not burn up.

(Exodus 3:2)

Very much what the burning bush was to Moses – that His baptism at the Jordan must have been to our Lord. He that dwelt in the bush called Moses to the work of his life on that eventful day on Horeb; and, so far as we can gather, our Lord received and accepted His full and final call also at the Jordan. So far as we can see, our Lord had the great seal of His Messiahship set upon His heart that day. And with that there came that unparalleled outpouring and indwelling of the Holy Ghost which made Him without measure equal to all His high call.

Never did mortal man set out to such a task as that which was set to Moses at the bush. But a far greater call was that which came to the Lord at Bethabara for your salvation! Look into your own heart and you will see there what Jesus Christ was called, and baptised, and anointed, and sworn in that day to do. You will never wonder and stand amazed and aghast at His awful task by studying it in any book – not even in the New Testament. But you will so stand, and so fall down, every day and all your days, if you only begin to study all the call and all the offices of Christ in yourself. As He studied His call; as He saw more and more what was in the heart of man, and what came out of the heart of man, He sometimes seemed inclined to repent of and to resign His awful call, and to despair of His terrible office. And you will not wonder at that; you will expect that, when you look into yourself as He looks into you.

But He went through with His call. He did not throw it up. He finished it. And he is finishing it still . . . in you and in me.

Alexander Whyte (1836–1921)

16th February

Grow in the grace and knowledge of our Lord and Saviour Jesus Christ. To him be glory both now and for ever! Amen
(2 Peter 3:18)

Although, dearly-beloved, as the Easter festival approaches, the very recurrence of the season points out to us the Lenten fast, yet our word also must add their exhortations which, the Lord helping us, may not be useless to the active, nor irksome to the devout. For since the idea of these days demands the increase of all our religious performances, there is no one, I am sure, that does not feel glad at being incited to good works. For though our nature which, so long as we are mortal, will be changeable, is advancing to the highest pursuits of virtue, yet always has the possibility of falling back, so has it always the possibility of advancing.

And this is the true justness of the perfect, that they should never assume themselves to be perfect, lest flagging in the purpose of their unfinished journey, they should fall into the danger of failure, through giving up the desire for progress.

And, therefore, because none of us, dearly-beloved, is so perfect and holy as not to be able to be more perfect and more holy, let us all together, without difference of rank, without distinction of desert, with pious eagerness pursue our race from what we have attained to what we need to aspire to, and make some needful additions to our regular devotions. For he that is not more attentive than usual to religion in these days, is shown at other times to be not attentive enough.

Leo the Great (c. 400–461)

17th February

The wisdom that comes from heaven is first of all pure; then peace-loving, considerate, submissive, full of mercy and good fruit, impartial and sincere. Peacemakers who sow in peace raise a harvest of righteousness.

(James 3:17–18)

Religion is a serious and personal concern. It rises from a right knowledge of God and ourselves; a sense of the great things that he has done for fallen man; a persuasion, or at least a well-grounded hope, of our own interest in his favour; and a principle of love to him who first loved us. It consists in an entire surrender of ourselves, and our all to God; in setting him before us, as the object of our desires. It means that he is the inspector of our actions and our only refuge and hope in every trouble. Finally it calls us to make God's goodness to us the motive and model of our behaviour to our fellow-creatures. Thus, we love, pity, relieve, instruct, forebear and forgive them as occasions offer. We ourselves too need to experience these things at the hand of our heavenly Father.

The two great points to which it tends, and to which it urges the soul, where it has taken place, incessantly to press after, are, communion with God and conformity to him. Since neither of these can be fully attained in this life, it teaches us to pant for something better; to withdraw our thoughts and affections from temporal things, and fix them on that eternal state, where we trust our desires will be abundantly satisfied. The work begun by grace shall be crowned by glory!

John Newton (1725–1807)

18th February

On the third day a wedding took place at Cana in Galilee. Jesus' mother was there, and Jesus and his disciples had also been invited to the wedding. When the wine was gone, Jesus' mother said to him, "They have no more wine." "Dear woman, why do you involve me?" Jesus replied, "My time has not yet come."
(John 2:1–4)

Mary was probably about fifty years of age, and her head was becoming streaked with grey hairs. But probably there was a new light in her eyes and a fresh spring in her step. The tidings which had reached her from the Jordan valley had probably altered the whole outlook of her life. She had been told by some of the celestial light that had gathered about the dear figure of Jesus as He had emerged from the river in which John had baptised Him. Others had heard rumours of a voice.

For thirty years she had been waiting for something to happen which would vindicate her honour and reward her husband for his noble action in screening her. Nothing of the kind had, however, happened and Joseph had died. Now, at last, it seemed as though she was likely to witness great unfoldings, and when the servants – probably friends and companions of the bridegroom – told her that, in consequence of the group of men whom Jesus had brought, the wine was nearly exhausted, a new hope sprang up in her breast, and the conviction of miraculous intervention on the part of Jesus seems to have broken upon her heart. So she whispered to Him across the table that the wine was running short.

He was already aware of it, and addressing her by the same noble title that emperors would address their queens, the Lord replied that he was carefully watching the dial, and waiting for the exact moment to present itself for His interposition. "Woman! Mine hour has not yet come!" Herein is a deep lesson for us all. We, apt to be too hasty and precipitate in our actions, need this reminder! We must watch and pray! Our eyes must be fixed on the hands of our Saviour, like those on the swift movement of the hands of master or mistress in the old Hebrew households. In the case of Lazarus, the Master remained two days longer in the place where He was. Let us not forget that to everything "there is a season and a time for every purpose under heaven." "It is good that a man should hope and quietly wait for the salvation of the Lord."

F. B. Meyer (1847–1929)

19th February

May I never boast except in the cross of our Lord Jesus Christ, through which the world has been crucified to me, and I to the world.

(Galatians 6:14)

When we consider, worthy brethren, our very weak and sinful nature, how that we are prone to evil from our youth, how that in our flesh no good thing dwelleth, and how that we drink unrighteousness and sin like water, even as Eliphaz the Temanite said to Job, and when we consider how that we have a tendency at all times (although we do seek and fear God) to mind earthly and perishable things, then we see that the gracious God and Father, who through his eternal love cares for all his children, had left behind in his house an excellent remedy against all this, namely, the pressing cross of Christ. Thus we who now through Jesus Christ are taken up to eternal grace to the glory of the Father, who with a pure heart believe on Christ Jesus whom we love in our weakness, may through the aforesaid cross, that is through much oppression, tribulation, anxiety, apprehension, bonds, seizure, and so forth, let go of all the transitory things of earth, and that which delights the eyes. And so we die unto the world and unto the flesh, love God alone, and seek the things that are above where Christ sitteth at the right hand of God . . .

We know very well dear brethren, how that this cross seems to be to the flesh grievous, harsh, and severe, and in the present is not considered a matter of joy, but rather of sorrow, even as Paul says. But since it contains within itself so much of profit and delight, in that it constantly adds to the piety of the pious, turns them away from the world and the flesh, makes them revere God and his Word, as was said above, and since it is also the Father's holy will that by it saints be approved, and the pretender exposed in his hypocrisy, therefore all the true children of God are prepared to love, to do the will of God rejoicing in it . . .

If you allow yourselves as meek lambs for the testimony of Christ to be led with perfect constancy to the slaughter, then in you the name of God will be praised and made holy and glorious, the name of the saints be revealed, the kingdom of heaven extended, the Word of God made known, and your poor weak brethren in the Lord be strengthened and taught by your courage.

Menno Simons (c. 1496–1561)

20th February

And pray in the Spirit on all occasions with all kinds of prayers and requests. With this in mind, be alert and always keep praying for all the saints.

(Ephesians 6:18)

The most admirable Polycarp, when he first heard that he was called for, was not at all concerned at it, but resolved to remain in the city. Nevertheless, he was at the last persuaded, at the desire of many, to go out of it. He departed therefore, into a little village, not too far distant from the city, and there tarried with a few about him. He was doing nothing, night or day, but praying for all men, and for the churches which were in all the world. This was Polycarp's usual custom. And as he was praying, he saw a vision three days before he was taken in which the pillow under his head seemed to be on fire. Whereupon, turning to those that were with him, he said prophetically, that he should be burnt alive.

Now, when those who were to take him drew near, he departed

to another village . . . they seized upon two young men that were there; one of which, being tormented, confessed . . . The sergeants, therefore, and horsemen, taking the young lad with them, departed about supper-time (being Friday) armed, as it were, against a thief or a robber. They came to the place where he was about the close of evening, where they found him lying down in a little upper room. He could easily have escaped from there into another place, but he would not, saying, "The will of the Lord be done."

When he heard that they had come into the house, he went down and spoke to them. They were wondered at his age and constancy, some of them began to say, "Was there need of all this care to take such an old man?" Then presently he ordered that food be got ready, so that they might eat and drink their fill.

Polycarp asked them that they would give him one hour's liberty to pray without disturbance. And when they had permitted him, he stood praying, and being full of the grace of God, he did not cease for two whole hours, to the admiration of all that heard him. Many of the soldiers began to repent that they were to come out against so godly an old man.

Polycarp (c. 70–155/160)

21st February

If you suffer as a Christian, do not be ashamed, but praise God that you bear that name.

(1 Peter 4:16)

[Continued from yesterday.]

As soon as he had done his prayer – in which he remembered all men, whether little or great, honourable or obscure, that had at any time been acquainted with him; and with them, the whole catholic church, over all the world – the time came for him to be taken away. The guards set him upon a donkey and so brought him into the city. It was the day of the great Sabbath. Herod, the chief officer, with his father Nicetes, met him in a chariot. Having taken him up to them and set him in the chariot, they began to persuade him saying, "What harm is there in it, to say, Lord Caesar, and sacrifice, (with the rest that is usual on such occasions) and so be safe?"

Polycarp at first did not answer but when they continued to urge him, he said, "I shall not do what you persuade me to." So being out of all hope of prevailing with him, they began to rail at him. Then, with much violence, Polycarp was thrown out of the chariot so that he hurt his thigh in the fall. But he did not turn back, and went on readily with all diligence, as if he had not received any harm at all. Thus he was brought to the lists, where there was so great a tumult, that nobody could be heard.

As he was going into the lists, there came a voice from heaven to him – "Be strong, Polycarp, and quit thyself like a man." No one saw who it was that spake to him; but for the voice, many of the brethren, who were present, heard it. And when he was brought in, there was great disturbance when they heard how that Polycarp was taken. The proconsul asked him whether he was Polycarp and when he confessed that he was, persuaded him to deny the faith. "Reverence, thy old age;" said the proconsul with many other similar things that are said on these occasions. He concluded thus, "Swear by Caesar's fortune. Repent, and say, take away the wicked."

Then, Polycarp looked with a stern countenance upon the whole multitude of wicked Gentiles that was gathered together in the lists, and shook his hand at them. He looked up to heaven, and groaning said, "Take away the wicked." But the proconsul insisted saying, "Swear, and I will set thee at liberty; reproach Christ."

Polycarp replied, "Eighty and six years have I served Christ, and He has never done me wrong; how then can I blaspheme my King, and Saviour?"

Polycarp (c. 70–155/160)

22nd February

Then the angel carried me away in the Spirit into a desert. There I saw a woman sitting on a scarlet beast that was covered with blasphemous names and had seven heads and ten horns ... I saw that the woman was drunk with the blood of the saints, the blood of those who bore testimony to Jesus.

(Revelation 17:3, 6)

[Continued from yesterday.]

When the proconsul nevertheless still insisted, saying, "Swear by the genius of Caesar," Polycarp answered, "Seeing, thou art so vainly urgent with me that I should swear, as thou callest, it, by the genius of Caesar, it seems as if thou didst not know what I am. Hear me professing it to thee, that I am a Christian. But if thou further desirest an account what Christianity is, appoint a day and thou shalt hear it." The proconsul replied, "Persuade the people." Polycarp answered. "To thee have I offered to give a reason of my faith: for so are we taught to pay all honour (such only excepted as would be harmful to ourselves), to the powers and authorities which are ordained of God. But for the people, I esteem them not worthy that I should give any account of my faith to them."

The proconsul continued, and said unto him, "I have wild beasts ready: to those I will cast thee, except thou repent." He answered, "Call for them, then; for we Christians are fixed in our minds not to change from good to evil. But for me it will be good to be changed from evil to good." The proconsul answered, "Seeing thou despised the wild beasts, I will cause thee to be devoured by fire, unless thou shalt repent." Polycarp answered, "Thou threatenest me with fire which burns for an hour and so is extinguished; but knowest not of the fire of future judgement, and of that eternal punishment which is reserved for the ungodly. But why tarriest thou? Bring forth what thou wilt."

Having said this, and many similar things, he was filled with confidence and joy. Polycarp's countenance was full of grace so that not only did he not let it fall with any confusion at what was spoken to him, but on the contrary, the proconsul was struck with astonishment.

He sent his crier into the middle of the lists, to proclaim three times – "Polycarp has confessed himself to be a Christian." When this had been done by the crier, the whole multitude, both of the Gentiles and of the Jews which dwelt at Smyrna, were full of fury. They cried out with a loud voice, "This is the doctor of Asia, the father of the Christians, and the overthrower of our gods; he that has taught so many not to sacrifice, nor pay any worship to the gods." . . . Then it pleased them to cry out with one consent that Polycarp should be burnt alive.

Polycarp (c. 70–155/160)

23rd February

As obedient children, do not conform to the evil desires you had when you lived in ignorance. But just as he who called you is holy, so be holy in all you do; for it written: "Be holy, because I am holy."

(1 Peter 1:14–16)

The man of strength and power is to forgive and pray for his enemies, and the innocent sufferer, that is chained in prison, must, with Paul and Silas, at midnight sing praises to God. For God is to be glorified, holiness is to be practised, and the spirit of religion is to be the common spirit of every Christian, in every state and condition of life.

For the Son of God did not come from above to add an external form of worship to the several ways of life that are in the world, and so to leave people to live as they did before, in such tempers and enjoyments as the fashion and spirit of the world approves; but as He came down from Heaven altogether divine and heavenly in His own nature, so it was to call mankind to a Divine and heavenly life; to the highest change of their own nature and temper; to be born again of the Holy Spirit; to walk in the wisdom and light and love of God, to be like Him to the utmost of their power; to renounce all the most plausible ways of the world, whether of greatness, business, or pleasure; to a mortification of all their most agreeable passions; and to live in such wisdom, and purity, and holiness, as might fit them to be glorious in the enjoyment of God to all eternity.

Whatever, therefore, is foolish, ridiculous, vain, earthly, or sensual, in the life of a Christian, is something that ought not to be there; it is a spot and a defilement that must be washed away with tears of repentance. But if any thing of this kind runs through the course of our whole life, if we allow ourselves in things that are either vain, foolish, or sensual, we renounce our profession.

For as sure as Jesus Christ was wisdom and holiness, as sure as He came to make us like Himself, and to be baptised into His Spirit, so sure it is, that none can be said to keep their Christian profession, but they who, to the utmost of their power, live a wise and holy and heavenly life. This and this alone, is Christianity; a universal holiness in every part of life, a heavenly wisdom in all our actions, not conforming to the spirit and temper of the world, but turning all worldly enjoyments into means of piety and devotion to God.

William Law (1686–1761)

24th February

His mother said to the servants, "Do whatever he tells you."
(John 2:5)

There is something to be done in order that Jesus may show out completely what He is trying to make manifest. And here, I think, is where a human action mounts to its highest dignity, and puts on its fullest meaning. There are two views of human actions. One looks on them as they are in themselves, seeing only the force and friction which is involved in the specific thing that is done, and in the will of the immediate doer; the other regards them as setting free for expression and effect some higher force and purpose of God which are waiting behind. One is the purely human, the other is the divine view of human action. It is as when you turn a screw in some great engine. A child who sees it turned thinks only of the hand which he sees turning it, and sees only the twisting of that bit of brass; but to the man who knows the engine the turning of that screw is the setting free of the imprisoned steam to do its work. And so with human actions. Take any one. You engage tomorrow, it may be, in a new business, take a new partner, and begin to sell new goods in a new store. To one man that may mean the setting forth by your own will in search of fortune, – nothing more than that; to another man it may mean what we can reverently call the opening up to God of chances to show Himself, and work effects which have been seemingly impossible before. New combinations, new contacts, will result out of that act of yours, new needs of divine illumination, of divine guidance are sure to come; and if man's need is indeed God's opportunity, then this new enterprise of yours will surely open some new chink through which the everlasting light can shine, or build some wall against which the everlasting and all-loving voice can echo. And so it is with everything you do. You make a friend, you read a book, you take a journey, you buy a house, you write a letter, and so full is the great world of God, so is He waiting everywhere to make Himself known and to give Himself away, that through this act of yours, to men who are looking and listening, there comes some revelation of His nature and some working of His power. Acts become little or great only according to the degree in which God manifests Himself and works through them.

Phillips Brooks (1835–93)

25 February

Jesus said to the servants, "Fill the jars with water"; so they filled them to the brim.

(John 2:7)

Be careful in the service of Christ, always to give brimful measure. It may be a very small thing! To take a class of poor children; to pay a visit to a dying man or woman; to write a letter; to give a tract or a pocket Testament. To fill a jar of opportunity may be a very simple, common act; but it is more likely, that, if done at the command of Jesus and in His fellowship, it may lead to a marvellous unfolding of God's purposes. Only do your bit with all your soul, and mind and strength! Let there be no lacking on your side! It is amazing that the Lord should help and honour us as fellow workers; let us prove ourselves worthy of His confidence!

Those jars were not filled apart from strenuous labour on the part of the servants. It is not a light matter for them to draw water from a neighbouring well, and fill those big vessels. But they were proud to co-operate with One whose name and fame were beginning to be recognised. So, also, the measure of our sacrifice will always be the measure of our success. Is not this the lesson which the Lord intended to teach? . . . Let us see to it that we do our best in all service that we render. Never give a message without previous thought and prayer! Never take a class or engage in service to the school, the church, or the community, without putting your best into it! . . . Give your best, your finest, your most loving answer to any appeal made to you in the name of Jesus!

Then a wonderful thing will happen. It has happened in the experience of many of us! We may have spent a week in thinking out and preparing our address. We have filled the waterpot to the brim, but as time approaches for its delivery we are compelled to feel that it is a very poor attempt, comparable to water. But as we begin to speak, and see faces suffused with tears or eyes filled with new hope, we realise that the Master has been collaborating with us, and has turned the water into wine. "The servants that drew the water knew!" Only the Master and they were in the secret! But how beautiful it is, when there is a secret understanding between Jesus and the servant who is endeavouring to serve Him . . .

We will fill the jars to the brim. Then let us reckon on Him to do His share. Let people forget the servant (and put him in a bracket) whilst all glory is given to Jesus.

F. B. Meyer (1847–1929)

26th February

His master replied, "Well done, good and faithful servant! You have been faithful with a few things; I will put you in charge of many things. Come and share your master's happiness!"

(Matthew 25:23)

MY DEAR BETSY,

I was a little surprised at a letter from sister D-, in which she seems to approve of all that Mrs C. has done; and speaks as if it were just and right, and done in obedience to the order of Providence! I could not help saying, "There is but one advice which I can give upon the present occasion: 'Remember from whence thou are fallen. Repent and do thy first works.'"

Some years ago, I committed a little company of lovely children to the care of one of our sisters at Haverford. I was concerned yesterday to find she was weary of well doing, and had totally given up her charge. I hope, my dear Betsy, this will never be your case! You will never leave off your labour of love; though you should not always (immediately at least) see the fruit of your labours. You may not immediately see Mrs H- so established in grace as you desire and hope. But in this, as well as many other instances, in due time "you shall reap, if you faint not."

I have been often musing upon this, – why the generality of Christians, even those that really are such, are less zealous and less active for God, when they are middle aged, than they were when they were young. May we not draw an answer to this question from the declaration of our Lord (no less than eight times repeated by the Evangelists), "To him that hath," uses what he hath, "shall be given; but from him that hath not, shall be taken away that he hath?" A measure of zeal and activity is given to everyone, when he finds peace with God. If he earnestly and diligently uses this talent, it will surely be increased. But if he ceases (yea, or intermits) to do good, he insensibly loses both the will and the power. So there is no possible way to retain these talents, but to use them to the uttermost. Let this never be the case of my dear friend! Never abate anything of your diligence of doing good. Sometimes, indeed, the feeble body sinks under you; but when you do all you can, you do enough.

Remember in all your prayers,
Yours most affectionately,
JOHN WESLEY

John Wesley (1703–91)

27th February

Who is greater, the one who is at the table or the one who serves? Is it not the one who is at the table? But I am among you as one who serves.

(Luke 22:27)

Sometimes the Lord honours faithful servants by giving them more to do. If they have been faithful in that which is least, he tries them in that which is great. If they have looked after a few little children, and fed the lambs, he says, "Come hither and feed my sheep." If they have trimmed a vine, or a fig tree in a corner, he calls them out and sets them among the chief vines of the vineyard, and says to them, "See after these clusters." Many a man would have been called to wider fields of labour if he had not been discontented or slothful in his narrow sphere. The Lord watches how we do little things, and if great care be taken in them he will give us greater things to do. Elisha poured water upon the hands of Elijah, and then the Lord says, "Elijah's mantle shall fall upon his faithful servant, and he shall do even greater miracles."

God also honours the faithful in the eyes of their fellow servants. When I take down from my library-shelf the biography of a holy man I honour him in my soul; I do not mind whether he was a bishop or a Primitive Methodist preacher, a blacksmith or a peer. I do him honour in my heart. If he served his Master, he will be sure to be elevated into a position of honour in the memory of succeeding ages.

There are some men whose doctrines you and I could not endorse, who yet were faithful to the light they had, and therefore we number them among the honoured dead, and we are glad to recollect how bold they were against the foe, how meek they were with the little ones, how faithful they were in believing in their God, and how courageous in rebuking sin. If you would get honour from your fellow servants, you will never get it by seeking honour from them; you must go to your Master and honour him by waiting upon him, and then there will come to you honour in the eyes of your fellow men.

But, beloved, the chief honour of a faithful servant comes from the blessed Trinity. "If anyone will serve me, him will my Father honour." Does it not appear too good to be true that a poor man should be honoured of God the Father, the Creator, the great I Am! I will not speak about it, but leave you to think it over.

C. H. Spurgeon (1834–92)

28th February

Finally they said, "Who are you? Give us an answer to take back to those who sent us. What do you say about yourself?" John replied in the words of Isaiah the prophet, "I am the voice of one calling in the desert, 'Make straight the way for the Lord.'"

(John 1:22–3)

I want to call your attention to the life and character of John the Baptist. The contemplation of no Bible character quickens me more than his. I never touch that life but I get a blessing. I used to think that I should like to have lived in his day, and in the times of the prophets; but I have given up that idea years ago: for when a prophet appears, it is when the priests have been unfaithful, religion is at a low ebb, and everything is in disorder and confusion. When John appeared, it was as black as midnight. The Old Testament had been sealed up by Malachi's proclamation of the Lord's coming, and of the forerunner who should introduce Him.

With Malachi prophecy ceased for four hundred years; then John came, preaching repentance and preparing the way for the dispensation of the grace of God. The word "John" means the grace and mercy of God. He looked upon the past, and looked forward to the future . . .

Notwithstanding the wonders attending John's birth, for thirty years he dropped out of sight. Many events had taken place during that period. The Roman Emperor had died; Herod, who had sought the lives of the young children when he heard that Jesus was born King of the Jews, was dead; the shepherds were gone; Simeon and Anna, the prophet and prophetess, were gone; the father of John the Baptist was gone, and all the rumours that were afloat at the time of John's birth had died out and were forgotten, when all at once he burst upon the scene like the flashing of a meteor.

There was a voice heard in the wilderness, and the cry came, "Repent: for the kingdom of heaven is at hand!" There had been a long line of prophets. He was the last prophet of the Law; he was to close up that dispensation; he stood on the threshold of the new age, with one foot upon the old and the other foot upon the new dispensation. He told them what had taken place in the past and what would take place in the future.

D. L. Moody (1837–99)

29th February

I tell you, among those born of women there is no-one greater than John; yet the one who is least in the kingdom of God is greater than he.

(Luke 7:28)

It does not matter whether the greatness of John [the Baptist] is conceived of as that of official dignity or that of personal character; he had both. He had an incomparably high vocation as the immediate messenger of the Kingdom, and his personality was equal to it. What does matter is that there is a still higher greatness than John's, which belongs even to the least in the Kingdom. It is impossible to suppose that Jesus here thinks of the Kingdom as purely transcendent, and means that whoever finds an inheritance in it when it comes – all its future citizens – will stand on a higher plane than John. The "least" of whom he speaks in the passage, are only the most typical example of the "little ones", to whom he refers so often.

Taking them as a body, the citizens of the Kingdom as Jesus knows them are insignificant people – "these little ones", or "these little ones who believe"; but the cause with which they are identified makes them partakers in its incomparable greatness. He asserts this in all kinds of indirect ways. The smallest service done to them is registered and repaid: Whoever shall give to drink to *one of these little ones* a cup of water only, in the name of a disciple, verily I say unto you, He shall in no wise lose his reward (Matthew 10:42). The most terrible indignation flames out against those who lead them astray: Whoever shall offend *one of these little ones* which believe (on Me), it were better for him that a great millstone were hanged round his neck, and that he were drowned in the depth of the sea (Matthew 18:6) ...

The greatness of the little ones is a familiar thought with Jesus, illustrated in these and other ways, and it is only put with startling boldness when He declares that the most insignificant of them all is greater than John. But the only difference was that for the little ones Jesus and the Kingdom were realities which interpenetrated; all their hopes were realised through Him; whereas John when this word was spoken, stood looking towards Jesus indeed, but with a look critical and perplexed. No one who takes this attitude to Jesus knows or can know the supreme good which God bestows upon man; whatever his eminence in other respects – in ability, in public service, in native capacity for spiritual life – the most insignificant disciple of Jesus stands on a higher plane.

James Denney (1856–1917)

March

1st March

If you are insulted because of the name of Christ, you are blessed, for the Spirit of glory and of God rests on you.

(1 Peter 4:14)

[Charles Simeon faces opposition and ridicule in Cambridge because of his evangelical beliefs.]

On one occasion in that early time a party of these men determined to assault Simeon personally as he left the church after service. They assembled at the chief entrance, the north door in Market Street, in such numbers that it would have been difficult to disperse them before some cruel violence had been inflicted; and Simeon had always left the church by the north door on his way back to King's. But that Sunday, without thinking about it, and certainly without the least suspicion of a plot, he went out by the south door and returned to college by the street called Petty Cury.

Quite as hard to bear as open insults and attempts at outrage were the coldness and half-expressed contempt of men of his own standing. Indeed, this must have been to him the heavier burden of the two. The disorderly student challenged and called out his personal courage as well as his patience; the slow trials of social estrangement, surely one of the severest tests of principle to a man of refinement and sensibility, could not be met by action. "I remember the time that I was quite surprised that a Fellow of my own College ventured to walk with me for a quarter of an hour on the grass-plot before Clare Hall; and for many years after I began my ministry I was 'as a man wondered at,' by reason of the smallness of number of those who showed any regard for true religion."

He records one incident of the inner history of those trying years: "When I was an object of much contempt and derision in the University, I strolled forth one day, buffeted and afflicted, with my little Testament in my hand. I prayed earnestly to my God that He would comfort me with some cordial from His word, and that, on opening the book, I might find some text which should sustain me. It was not for direction I was looking, for I am no friend of such superstitions ... but only for support. The first text that caught my eye was this: *'They found a man of Cyrene, Simon by name; and they compelled him to bear His cross.'* You know Simon is the same name as Simeon. What a word of instruction was here – what a blessed hint for my encouragement! To have a cross laid upon me, that I might bear it for Jesus – what a privilege! It was enough. Now I could leap and sing for joy as one whom Jesus was honouring with a participation of His sufferings."

Charles Simeon (1759–1836)

2nd March

Let us, then, go to him outside the camp, bearing the disgrace he bore.

(Hebrews 13:13)

Why is it that this reproach centres so often in the name of Jesus?

A fine Christian woman I know, who bears witness for our Lord in an unsavoury factory, brought that very problem to me some time ago. She said, "I can talk to the girls I work with about religion now and then, about moral standards, even about God, and they take it in silence, if not in acquiescence. But if I talk about Jesus, they will *not* take it; they seem to find his name offensive."

I knew what she meant.
Do you?

> *Jesus is the Name we treasure,*
>   *Name beyond what words can tell;*
> *Name of gladness, Name of pleasure,*
>   *Ear and heart delighting well;*
> *Name of sweetness passing measure,*
>   *Saving us from sin and hell.*

But it is a name others find offensive. They turn it into a swear word, a blasphemous oath. It is one of the bitterest experiences a Christian must endure to hear that holy name profanely used.

When that tide of reproach is rolling over you, when for Christ's sake, you are made an object of reviling, "rejoice and be exceeding glad, for great is your reward in heaven; for so persecuted they the prophets which were before you."

W. E. Sangster (1900–1960)

3rd March

The apostles left the Sanhedrin, rejoicing because they had been counted worthy of suffering disgrace for the Name.

(Acts 5:41)

[Continued from yesterday.]

In the late seventies of the last century there was a girl named Priscilla Livingstone Stewart. She was lovely to look upon: blue eyes, bright coloured golden hair, Irish gaiety. All the boys in the neighbourhood thought she was grand. Her admirers lined up for a smile!

Then she met Christ. Having been heartily opposed to religion before, she became as ardent a disciple, and soon after, the Salvation Army came to those parts. It was altogether characteristic of her that she could throw in her lot for a while with that despised people, and she chose to walk in their procession in days when they were pelted with old boots, stones, bad oranges, and worse eggs.

Now notice this! I give you the exact words of her reminiscences. She said, "None of my friends recognised me in the street, and all the young men who were fond of me walked on the other side."

I have no doubt that, being a normal girl, there was something of pain for her in that, but she found infinitely more than she had lost, and, truth to tell, God had other things in store for her. She went as a missionary to China and became the wife of that extraordinary missionary, C. T. Studd.

"None of my friends recognised me now" – "without the camp" – "bearing his reproach". What do you do when, without eccentricity and censoriousness and with no willing severance of old friendships on your part, they put you out?

You exalt in it!

Don't miss the willing eagerness of the first phrase in my text: "Let us therefore go forth unto him . . ." I am not going to be dragged. I am going willingly. Indeed, I am running. It is an honour of which I am all unworthy. I am going to thrust my shoulder underneath his cross and bear whatever I can of his reproach.

> *I'm not ashamed to own my Lord,*
> *Or to defend His cause,*
> *Maintain the glory of His Cross,*
> *And honour all His laws.*

W. E. Sangster (1900–1960)

4th March

Charm is deceptive, and beauty is fleeting; but a woman who fears the Lord is to be praised.

(Proverbs 31:30)

[C. T. Studd writes on the death of his wife to Stanley Smith, one of the Cambridge Seven who went with him to China.]

Very, very many thanks to you and Gracie for your love and sympathy. I was only writing to a lady the other day and telling her of Scilla's and my contract when we married: that we would not keep each other back from any work that the Lord gave us to do, even though it might mean separation for a time. I was saying to her (for it is nice to be able to bear a testimony to God's unspeakable grace) that God kept us together all the early years in China, England and India. Only when we were pretty well worn out did He claim our promise from us, but He commenced to claim by simply giving us an extra fifteen years' life.

I have done nothing particular, but Scilla did an amazement. In her case it was specially plain because God took away her life before giving her the new one. The doctors absolutely gave her up. Lord Radstock went to Carlisle and prayed for her and she rose again. Then the doctors pronounced that she would be an invalid for life, and it looked as though they were right. Their verdict was quite justified, but you know that the Almighty now and again does things out of the ordinary that men cannot do, and this was one. She had never spoken at any meetings for years; she had never come to any of the meetings, they were too great a strain upon her heart (that was my wild talking, I suppose). But when I came out here and God touched the spring, her life became a cyclone, and whatever I might say about what she did would not be an exaggeration. She was a wonder to many, but most of all to myself. She had such energy, vision and faith and she could capture anybody.

Of course, you probably knew it was she who ran the home work . . . I think you have heard her talk? I have too, you bet, and I never heard a woman, and very few men, talk like her. She got the knack, a Scriptural one, did not speak from memory, not from the library, but from vision. What she saw she said, made others see it too, and there is no speaking like that . . .

Well, she is a great loss, but I think she is doing better work for God and for the evangelisation of the world where she is than if she were down here, for she is with the Saviour, and I am quite sure He does not do much sleeping and so she won't either. Meanwhile we on the earth are forced into closer communion with the Lord.

C. T. Studd (1862–1931)

5th March

Then Jesus came from Galilee to the Jordan to be baptised by John. But John tried to deter him, saying, "I need to be baptised by you, and do you come to me?" Jesus replied: "Let it be so now; it is proper for us to do this to fulfil all righteousness." Then John consented.

(Matthew 3:13–15)

The very act in which Jesus comes upon the stage of human history – His baptism by John – is . . . of profound significance. No doubt the baptism has many aspects which can be independently emphasised: it was the annointing of Jesus as the Messianic King; it was the hour in which He was signally conscious of His relation to the Father and of His Messianic calling, it was in some sense a great act of self-dedication or self-consecration to a work which only time and Providence would define: but no such conceptions of it enable us to answer the question which evidently exercised the mind of the Church from the beginning, – Why did the sinless one come to be baptised with what was explicitly declared to be a baptism of repentance looking to remission of sins?

There is no answer to this question, equal to its importance, but that which allows us to see Jesus, at the very outset of his career, identifying Himself, as far as love enabled Him to do, with sinful men. We might have expected that where the work of God was being done, as through the prophetic ministry of John, Jesus would be present; but we should have looked for Him at John's side, confronting the people, assisting the prophet to proclaim the word of God.

Yet nothing is more true to the character of Jesus and to the spirit in which He carries through His mission than that He appears not at John's side, but among the people who came to be baptised; His entrance on His work, like the whole work from beginning to end, was an act of loving communion with us in our misery. He numbered Himself with the transgressors, and made the burden of our sins His own.

James Denney (1856–1917)

6th March

John came neither eating nor drinking, and they say, "He has a demon." The Son of Man came eating and drinking, and they say, "Here is a glutton and a drunkard, a friend of tax collectors and 'sinners'." But wisdom is proved right by her actions.
(Matthew 11:18–19)

[Continued from yesterday.]

A similar relation to sin is implied in all Jesus' dealings with sinners for their forgiveness and restoration to God. Nothing is more certain than His power to win sinners from their sin and to bring them to the Father, and nothing is more certain than that such power depends absolutely on the bearing of sin in the sense at present in view – on entering lovingly, sympathetically, and profoundly into the sinner's experience, and realising through love and sympathy the crushing weight which sin is for him.

This is the vital difference between Jesus and the Pharisees, between goodness which bears the sinner's burden and says, "Come unto Me, and I will give you rest," and goodness which has no sympathy with the sinner, which bears no burden for him, which says, "Stand by thyself; come not near me, for I am holier than thou." Pharisaic goodness has no redemptive power in it just because it has no love in it and bears no burden; the sinner is not moved by it except to curse it, and in doing so he shows at least some sense for what goodness is.

But the goodness of Jesus has the redeeming virtue which unquestionably belongs to it just because love is the soul of it, love which in its very nature makes the burden of others its own, whatever these burdens be. If sin is the most fatal and crushing of all, then sin will weigh heaviest upon Him. When Jesus received sinners in the gospel they were conscious of this. He did not talk about sin-bearing love; He exhibited it. They knew in His presence what forgiveness cost. They saw it in His face, and heard it in the tones of His voice. They were aware that He had carried on His own spirit the weight that was lifted from theirs, and that their debt to Him was immeasurable. That is why they poured their precious ointment on His head, and wet His feet with their tears.

If there was not an articulate word in the New Testament on the subject of Christ bearing sin, we should argue quite confidently from the redemptive power of goodness as displayed in Him, that He unquestionably did bear it. He bore it in a love which entered victoriously into sinful hearts and reconciled them to God.

James Denney (1856–1917)

7th March

Jesus went up on a mountainside and called to him those he wanted, and they came to him. He appointed twelve – designating them apostles – that they might be with him and that he might send them out to preach and to have authority to drive out demons.
(Mark 3:13–15)

Christ's compassion stands out in its *spiritual fellowship*. The King of kings makes eternal friends of the fishermen. "He did not visit the poor," "He did not elevate their sad lot," and walk on in His own high path, having His fellowship, His joys, His sorrows apart from them; but He shared His life with them in a holy comradeship. He did not live in the style and companionship of the worldly Pharisee, and occasionally visit Peter, James, and John, and hold meetings for the working classes; no, He lived with them and became education, elevation, salvation, and all to them by His blessed fellowship. "Ye are my friend," said He, and "all things that I have heard of My Father, I have made known to you." His heart had no reserves from these men. John's head could lean on His breast, and Mary could sit at His feet, with the consciousness that they were taken into His confidence, and were indeed as brethren.

That they could not always understand Him was their fault, not His; but their slowness and dullness never wearied His compassion, nor caused Him to seek friends elsewhere. He called His three fishermen to Him when He was about to put forth any wonderful exercise of power. He wanted Peter, James, and John, when He was raising the dead, and took them to share His joy on the mount of transfiguration. He craved for their presence in His last agony, and desired no better provision for His mother, when He hung upon the cross, than the home that one of them could afford.

Catherine Booth (1829–90)

8th March

He then began to teach them that the Son of Man must suffer many things and be rejected by the elders, chief priests and teachers of the law, and that he must be killed and after three days rise again.
(Mark 8:31)

In the person and sufferings of Christ, there is at once a discovery of the misery of fallen man, and the means of his complete recovery . . . Christ frequently spoke of the necessity and certainty of his sufferings and he spoke of them as the great design of his incarnation. It was by this means that he should draw all unto himself . . .

Isaiah had foretold that the Lord would lay upon him the iniquities of us all; that he was wounded for our transgressions, and by his stripes we should be healed. Here then we see the manifold wisdom of God; his inexpressible love to us commended. Here his mercy is exalted in the salvation of sinners; his truth and justice are vindicated in the true satisfaction for sin extracted from the Surety. Here we see his glorious holiness and opposition to all evil, and his invariable faithfulness to his threatenings and promises.

Considered in this light, our Saviour's passion is the most momentous, instructive, and comfortable theme that can affect the heart of man. But if his substitution and proper atonement are denied, the whole is unintelligible. We can assign no sufficient reason why a person of his excellence was abandoned to such miseries and indignities; nor can we account for that agony and distress which seized him at the prospect of what was coming upon him. It would be highly injurious to his character to suppose he was thus terrified by the apprehension of death or bodily pain, when so many frail and sinful men have encountered death, armed with the severest tortures, with far less emotion.

John Newton (1725–1807)

9th March

Then he called the crowd to him along with his disciples and said: "If anyone would come after me, he must deny himself and take up his cross and follow me."

(Mark 8:34)

Young converts should be taught that the duty of self-denial is one of the leading features of the Gospel. They should understand that they are not pious at all, any further than they are willing to take up their cross daily, and deny themselves for Christ. There is but little self-denial in the Church, and the reason is that the duty is so much lost sight of, in giving instructions to young converts. How seldom are we told that self-denial is the leading feature of Christianity! In pleading for benevolent objects, how often will you find that ministers and agents do not even ask Christians to deny themselves for the sake of promoting the object! They only ask them to give what they can spare as well as not; in other words, to offer unto the Lord that which costs them nothing. What an abomination! They only ask for the surplus, for what is not wanted, for what can just as well be given as not.

There is no religion in this kind of giving. A man might give a very large sum to a benevolent object, and there would be no religion in his doing so, if he could give the money as well as not; nor would there be any self-denial in it. Jesus Christ exercised self-denial to save sinners. So had God the Father exercised self-denial in giving His Son to die for us, and in sparing us, and in bearing with us in our perverseness. The Holy Ghost exercises self-denial, in condescending to strive with such unholy beings to bring them to God. The angels exercise self-denial in watching over this world. The apostles planted the Christian religion among the nations by the exercise of self-denial.

And are we to think of ourselves Christians, the followers of

Christ, the "temples of the Holy Ghost" (1 Corinthians 6:19), and to claim fellowship with the apostles, when we have never deprived ourselves of anything that would promote our personal enjoyment for the sake of promoting Christ's kingdom? Young converts should be made to see that unless they are willing to lay themselves out for God, and ready to sacrifice life and everything else for Christ, they "have not the Spirit of Christ, and are none of His" (Romans 8:9).

Charles G. Finney (1792–1875)

10th March

When he saw the crowds, he had compassion on them, because they were harassed and helpless, like sheep without a shepherd.
(Matthew 9:36)

It is a curious race of beings that these philanthropists have taken in hand [through running "Ragged Schools"]. Every one who walks the streets of the Metropolis must daily observe several members of the tribe – bold, and pert, and dirty as London sparrows, but pale, feeble, and sadly inferior to them, in plumpness of outline. Their business or pretended business, seems to vary with the locality. At the West End they deal in lucifer matches, audaciously beg, or tell a touching tale of woe. Pass on to the central parts of the town, to Holborn or the Strand, and the regions adjacent to them, and you will find the numbers greatly increased; a few are pursuing the avocations above mentioned of their more Corinthian fellows; many are spanning the gutters with their legs, and dabbling with earnestness in the latest accumulation of nastiness; while others, in squalid and half-naked groups, squat at the entrances of the narrow, fetid courts and alleys that lie concealed behind the deceptive frontages of our larger thoroughfares.

Whitechapel and Spitalfields teem with them like ants' nests; but it is in Lambeth and in Westminster that we find the most flagrant traces of their swarming activity. There the foul and dismal passages are thronged with children of both sexes, and of every age from three to thirteen. Though wan and haggard, they are singularly vivacious, and engaged in every sort of occupation but that which would be beneficial to themselves and creditable to their neighbourhood. Their appearance is wild; the matted hair, the disgusting filth that renders necessary a closer inspection before the flesh can be discerned between the rags which hang about it; and the barbarian freedom from all superintendence and restraint, fill the mind of a novice in these things with perplexity and dismay.

Visit these regions in the summer, and you are overwhelmed by the exhalations; visit them in the winter, and you are shocked by the spectacle of hundreds shivering in apparel that would be scanty in the tropics; many are all but naked; those that are clothed are grotesque; the trousers, where they have them, seldom pass the knee; the tail-coats very frequently trail below the heels. In this guise they run about the streets, and line the banks of the river at low tide, seeking coals, sticks, corks, for nothing comes amiss as treasure-trove; screams of delight burst occasionally from the crowds, and leave the passer-by, if he be in contemplative mood, to wonder and to rejoice that moral and physical degradation have not yet broken every spring of their youthful energies.

Lord Shaftesbury (1801–85)

11th March

For the Son of Man came to seek and to save what was lost.
(Luke 19:10)

To me this is one of the sweetest verses in the whole Bible. In one little short sentence we are told what Christ came into this world for. He came with a purpose; He came to do a work, and in this little verse the whole story is told. He came not to condemn the world, but that the world through Him, might be saved.

A few years ago, the Prince of Wales went to America, and there was great excitement about your Crown Prince coming to our country. The papers took it up, and began to discuss it, and a great many were wondering what he came for. Was it to look into Republican government? Was it for his health? Was it to see our institutions? or for this, or for that? He came and went, but he never told us what he came for. But when the Prince of Heaven came down into this world, He told us what He came for. God sent Him, and He came to do the will of His Father. What was that? "To seek and to save that which was lost."

And you cannot find any place in Scripture where a man was ever sent by God to do a work in which he failed. God sent Moses to Egypt to bring three millions of bond-men up out of the house of bondage into the promised land. Did he fail? It looked, at first, as if he were going to. If we had been in the Court when Pharaoh said to Moses, "Who is God, that I should obey Him?" and ordered him out of his presence, we might have thought it meant failure. But did it? God sent Elijah to stand before Ahab, and it was a bold thing when he told him there should be neither dew nor rain; but did he not lock up the heavens for three years and six months?

Now here is God sending his own beloved Son from his bosom, from the throne down into this world. Do you think He is going to fail? Thanks be to God, He can save to the uttermost, and there is not a man in this city who may not find it so, if he is willing to be saved.

D. L. Moody (1837–99)

12th March

He withdrew about a stone's throw beyond them, knelt down and prayed, "Father, if you are willing, take this cup from me; yet not my will, but yours be done." An angel from heaven appeared to him and strengthened him.

(Luke 22:41–3)

Every true prayer has its background and its foreground. The foreground of prayer is the intense, immediate desire for a certain blessing which seems to be absolutely necessary for the soul to have; the background of prayer is the quiet, earnest desire that the will of God, whatever it may be, should be done. What a picture is the perfect prayer of Jesus on Gethsemane! In front, burns the strong desire to escape death and live; but behind, there stands, calm and strong, the craving of the whole life for the doing of the will of God. In front, the man's eagerness for life; behind, "He that formeth the mountains and createth the winds and declareth unto man His thought, that maketh the morning darkness, and treadeth upon the high places of the earth" (Amos 4:13). In front, the teeming plain; behind the solemn hills. I can see the picture of prayer with absolute clearness. Leave out the foreground – let there be no expression of the wish of Him who prays – and there is left a pure submission which is almost fatalism. Leave out the background – let there be no acceptance of the will of God – and the prayer is only an expression of self-will, a petulant claiming of the uncorrected choice of Him who prays. Only when the two, foreground and background, are there together, – the special desire resting on the universal submission, the universal submission opening into special desire, – only then is the picture perfect and the prayer complete!

What Christ's prayer was all prayers may be, all true prayers must be. What is it that you ask for when you kneel and pray? Directly, no doubt, it is some special mercy. It is the coming in of your ship; it is the recovery of your friend; it is the opportunity of usefulness which you desire for yourself. But do you want any of those things if God does not see that it is best that you should have them? Would they not fade out of your desire if you should know that they were not of His will? Do you not wish them because it seems to you that they must be best, and therefore must be His will? Is it not then, His will which is your real, your fundamental, essential prayer? You must keep that essential prayer very clear or the special prayer becomes wilful and trivial. You must pray with the great prayer in sight. You must feel the mountains above you, while you work upon your little garden. Little by little your special wishes and the eternal will of God will grow into harmony with one another, – the background will draw the foreground to itself. Foreground and background at last will blend in perfect harmony. All conflict will die away and the great spiritual landscape from horizon to horizon be but one. That is the prayer of eternity – the prayer of heaven – to which we may come, no one can say how near, on earth.

Phillips Brooks (1835–93)

13th March

After six days Jesus took with him Peter, James and John the brother of James, and led them up a high mountain by themselves. There he was transfigured before them. His face shone like the sun, and his clothes became as white as the light. Just then there appeared before them Moses and Elijah, talking with Jesus.
(Matthew 17:1–3)

In this Transfiguration the foremost object was to remove the offence of the cross from the disciples' heart, and to prevent their faith being disturbed by the humiliation of His voluntary Passion for it revealed to them the excellence of His hidden dignity. But with no less foresight, the foundation was laid of the Holy Church's hope, that the whole body of Christ might realise the character of the change which it would have to receive, and that the members might promise themselves a share in that honour which had already shone forth in their Head.

The Lord Himself said, when he spoke of the majesty of His coming, "Then shall the righteous shine as the sun in their Father's Kingdom." The blessed Apostle Paul bears witness to the self-same thing and says: "for I reckon that the sufferings of this time are not worthy to be compared with the future glory which shall be revealed in us:" and again, "for ye are dead, and your life is hid with Christ in God. For when Christ our life shall appear, then shall ye also appear with Him in glory." But to confirm the Apostles and assist them to all knowledge, still further instructions was conveyed by that miracle.

For Moses and Elijah, that is the Law and the Prophets, appeared talking with the Lord so that in the presence of those five men might most truly be fulfilled what was said: "In two or three witnesses stands every word." What is more stable, what is more steadfast than this word, in the proclamation of which the trumpet of the Old and of the New Testament joins, and the documentary evidence of the ancient witnesses combine with the teachings of the Gospel? For the pages of both covenants corroborated each other, and He Whom under the veil of mysteries the types that went before had promised, is displayed clearly and conspicuously by the splendour of the present glory.

This is because, as the blessed John says, "the law was given through Moses: but grace and truth came through Jesus Christ." In Him is fulfilled both the promise of prophetic figures and the purpose of the legal ordinances: for He both teaches the truth of prophecy by His presence, and renders the commands possible through grace.

Leo the Great (c. 400–461)

14th March

While he was still speaking, a bright cloud enveloped them, and a voice from the cloud said, "This is my Son, whom I love; with him I am well pleased. Listen to him!"

(Matthew 17:5)

These things dearly beloved, were said not for their profit only, who heard them with their own ears, but in these three Apostles the whole Church has learnt all that their eyes saw and their ears heard. Let all men's faith then be established, according to the preaching of the most holy Gospel, and let no one be ashamed of Christ's cross, through which the world was redeemed.

And let not any one fear to suffer for righteousness' sake, or doubt of the fulfilment of the promises, for this reason, that through toil we pass to rest and through death to life. Since all the weakness of our humility was assumed by Him, if we abide in the acknowledgement and love of Him, we conquer as He conquered, and receive what he promised. Whether to the performance of His commands or to the endurance of adversities, the Father's fore-announcing voice should always be sounding in our ears, saying, "This is My beloved Son, in whom I am well pleased; hear ye Him!" Who liveth and reigneth with the Father and the Holy Ghost, for ever and ever. Amen.

Leo the Great (c. 400–461)

15th March

So the Lord gave Israel all the land he had sworn to give their forefathers, and they took possession of it and settled there.
(Joshua 21:43)

The Church has always been prone to hero-worship, and to the idolatry of its organisation, its methods, or its theology. Augustine did so and so; Luther smote the "whited wall" (the Pope) a blow that made him reel; the Pilgrim Fathers carried a slip of the plant of religious liberty in a tiny pot across the Atlantic, and watered it with great tears till it has grown a great tree; the Wesleys revived a formal Church – let us sing hallelujahs to these great names! By all means; but do not let us forget whence they drew their power; and let us listen to Paul's question, "Who then is Paul, and who is Apollos, but servants through whom ye believed, even as the Lord gave to every man?"

And let us carve, deep-cut and indelible, in solitary conspicuousness, on the trophy that we rear on each well-fought field, the name of no man save "Jesus only". We read that on a pyramid in Egypt the name and sounding titles of the king in whose reign it was erected were blazoned on the plaster facing, but beneath that transitory inscription the name of the architect was hewn, imperishable, in the granite, and stood out when the plaster dropped away. So, when all the short-lived records which ascribe the events of the Church's progress to her great men have perished, the one name of the true builder will shine out, and "at the name of Jesus every knee shall bow."

Let us not rely on our own skill, courage, talents, orthodoxy, or methods, nor try to "build tabernacles" for the witnessing servants besides the central one near the supreme Lord, but ever seek to deepen our conviction that Christ, and Christ only, gives all their powers to all, and that to Him, and Him only, is all victory to be ascribed. That is an elementary truth; but if we really lived in its power we should go into battle with more confidence, and come out of it with less self-gratulation.

Alexander Maclaren (1826–1910)

16th March

This is love: not that we loved God, but that he loved us and sent his Son as an atoning sacrifice for our sins.

(1 John 4:10)

In the sinless bearing of sin – the one thing that needed to be done for man's redemption – Christ has a solitary greatness. We understand the motive of it, as we understand the motive of the incarnation; it was because He loved us that He took our doom upon Himself.

Every action then, and every suffering, which pure love prompts, is in the line of Christ's work; but that work, though its motive is thus brought within our reach, is not assimilated to anything we can do for each other. The scale of it is different – love made a sacrifice there to which earth has no parallel; and the inmost nature of it is different – there only God made to be sin for the world Him who knew no sin.

The love of a father for his erring son, the love of a patriot for his country, the love of a martyr for his faith, and all the sufferings and sacrifices these various kinds of love make, are included in the love of Christ; they are included in it, but it transcends them all. *Herein is love* not that we loved God, not that the world has had the passion of parents, of patriots, of martyrs, but that God loved us and sent His Son as a propitiation for our sins.

The other loves do not explain this; it is here and here only – in the Cross, where the sinless Son of God died for the sins of men – that we see what love itself is, and find a scale for the measurement of all these lesser loves. This solitariness of Christ, this uniqueness of His work, is to be maintained over all analogies; and modes of speaking which outrage it, such as that Christians should themselves be Christs, miniature Christs, little Christs, are to be decidedly rejected. It is little to say they are in bad taste; they are as false as they are offensive, for salvation is of the Lord.

James Denney (1856–1917)

17th March

There he was transfigured before them. His face shone like the sun, and his clothes became as white as the light. Just then there appeared before them Moses and Elijah, talking with Jesus.

(Matthew 17:2–3)

Their appearance set forth Christ's death, which was their theme, as the climax of revelation. The law with its requirements and its sacrifices, prophecy with its forward-looking face, stand there in their representatives, and bear witness that their converging lines meet in Jesus. The finger that wrote the law, and the finger that smote and parted Jordan, are each lifted to point to Him. The stern voices that spoke the commandments, and that hurled threatenings at the unworthy occupants of David's throne, both proclaim "Behold the Lamb of God, the perfect fulfiller of law, the true king of Israel!"

Their presence and their speech was the acknowledgement that this was He whom they had seen from afar; their disappearance proclaim that their work is done when they have pointed to Him. Their presence also teaches us that Jesus is the life of all the living dead. Of course, care must be exercised in drawing dogmatic conclusions from a manifestly abnormal incident, but some plain truths do result from it.

Of these two, one had died, though mystery hung round his death and burial; the other had passed into the heavens by another gate than that of death; and here they both stand with lives undiminished by their mysterious changes, in fullness of power and consciousness, bathed in glory which was congruous with them now. They are witnesses of an immortal life, and proofs that His yet unpierced hands held the keys of life and death ... They speak, too, of the eager onward gaze with which the Old Testament believers turned to the coming Deliverer.

Alexander Maclaren (1826–1910)

18th March

Therefore, since we are surrounded by such a great cloud of witnesses, let us throw off everything that hinders and the sin that so easily entangles, and let us run with perseverance the race marked out for us.

(Hebrews 12:1)

We know the power of any appeal to the great names of our secular history. There is no scholar, however humble or obscure, whose exhausted energy is not renewed when he is reminded of famous students of former times. The honours which cluster and thicken, as the ages roll by, round the names of great poets, artists, philosophers, statesmen, stimulate the enthusiasm and sustain the energy of those who, in distant times and countries, strive for the same glory. When nations are struggling for freedom, it is not living patriotism alone which gives strength to their arms and daring to their hopes — the memory of the patriots of other lands and of other centuries kindles enthusiasm and inspires heroic endurance. Defeated, while living, in their conflicts with tyranny, they triumph gloriously after death.

It is no doubt the prerogative of men who have been endowed with great powers, or held great positions, thus to act permanently on the imaginations and passions of mankind; but, without learning, without genius, without official rank, without social distinction, it is yet possible for every Christian man to illustrate to the hearts of some, the beauty of holiness, and to vindicate by his personal holiness, the authority of God.

Every holy life is a visible republication of the Divine law, a solemn appeal to the consciences of men, an unanswerable proof that in this world of temptation and sin, it is possible to recover the image of God and to live so as to please Him. Your life may not be famous. Orators, in coming ages, may not recall your names amidst the plaudits of crowded assemblies. But the craving for an immortal reputation, natural, I suppose, to the heart of man, may yet be satisfied; for if the soul of the humblest, poorest, most ignorant among your friends and acquaintances, is prompted or encouraged to live a holy life by your example, the memory of your deed will endure as long as the blessedness of the glorified.

R. W. Dale (1829–95)

19th March

But our citizenship is in heaven. And we eagerly await a Saviour from there, the Lord Jesus Christ.

(Philippians 3:20)

Christians are not distinguished from the rest of mankind by country or by speech or by customs. For they do not dwell in cities of their own, or use a different language or practise a peculiar life. This knowledge of theirs has not been discovered by the thought and effort of inquisitive men; they are not champions of a human doctrine, as some men are. But while they dwell in Greek or barbarian cities according as each man's lot was cast, and follow the customs of the land in clothing and food, and other matters of daily life, yet the condition of citizenship which they exhibit is wonderful, and admittedly beyond all expectation.

They live in countries of their own, but simply as sojourners; they share the life of citizens, they endure the lot of foreigners; every foreign land is to them a fatherland, and every fatherland a foreign land. They marry like the rest of the world, they beget children, but they do not cast their offspring adrift. They have a common table, but not a common bed. They exist in the flesh, but they live not after the flesh. They spend their existence upon earth, but their citizenship is in heaven.

They obey the established laws, but in their own lives they surpass the law. They love all men, and are persecuted by all. They are unknown, and yet they are condemned; they are put to death, and yet they give proof of new life. They are poor, and yet make many rich; they lack everything, and yet in everything they abound. They are dishonoured, and their dishonour becomes their glory; they are reviled, and yet are vindicated. They are abused, and they bless; they are insulted, and repay insult with honour. They do good, and are punished as evildoers; and in their punishment they rejoice finding new life therein. The Jews war against them as aliens; Greeks persecute them; and yet they that hate them can state no ground for their enmity.

In a word what the soul is in the body the Christians are in the world.

The Epistle of Diognetus (c. 2nd century)

20th March

If you harbour bitter envy and selfish ambition in your hearts, do not boast about it or deny the truth. Such "wisdom" does not come down from heaven but is earthly, unspiritual, of the devil.

(James 3:14–15)

Contention tends so much to the ruin of religion. The Scriptures tell us that it has this tendency – "Where envying and strife is, there is confusion and every evil work" (James 3:16). And so we find it by experience. When contention comes into a place, it seems to prevent all good. And if religion had been flourishing before, it presently seems to chill and deaden it; and everything that is bad begins to flourish. And in the light of our doctrine, we may plainly see the reason for all this; for contention is directly against that which is the very sum of all that is essential and distinguishing in true Christianity, even a spirit of love and peace. No wonder, therefore, that Christianity cannot flourish in a time of strife and contention among its professors. No wonder that religion and contention cannot live together.

Hence, then, what a watch and guard should Christians keep against envy and malice, and every kind of bitterness towards their neighbours! For these things are the very reverse of the real essence of Christianity. And it behoves Christians, as they would not, by their practice, directly contradict their profession, to take heed to themselves in this matter.

They should suppress the first beginnings of ill-will and bitterness and envy; watch strictly against all occasions of such a spirit; strive and fight to the utmost against such a temper as tends that way; and avoid, as much as possible, all temptations that may lead to it. A Christian should at all times keep a strong guard against everything that tends to overthrow or corrupt or undermine a spirit of love. That which hinders love to men, will hinder exercise of love to God . . .

If love is the sum of Christianity, surely those things which overthrow love are exceedingly unbecoming Christians. An envious Christian, a malicious Christian, a cold and hard-hearted Christian, is the greatest absurdity and contradiction. It is as if one should speak of dark brightness, or a false truth!

Jonathan Edwards (1703–58)

21st March

May our Lord Jesus Christ himself and God our Father, who loved us and by his grace gave us eternal encouragement and good hope, encourage your hearts and strengthen you in every good deed and word.

(2 Thessalonians 2:16–17)

Teach them [young converts] that religion does not consist in raptures, ecstasies, or high flights of feeling. There may be a great deal of those where there is religion. But it ought to be understood that they are all involuntary emotions, and may exist in full power where is no religion. They may be the mere workings of the imagination, without any truly religious affection at all. Persons may have them to such a degree as actually to swoon away with ecstasy, even on the subject of religion, without having any religion. I have known a person almost carried away with rapture, by a mere view of the natural attributes of God, His power and wisdom, as displayed in the starry heavens, and yet the person had no religion. Religion is obedience to God, the voluntary submission of the soul to His will.

Neither does religion consist in going to services, or of reading the Bible, or praying, or any other of what are commonly called religious duties. The very phrase "religious duties", ought to be struck out of the vocabulary of young converts. They should be made to know that these acts are not religion. Many become strict in performing certain things, which they call "religious duties", and suppose that is being religious; while they are careless about the ordinary duties of life, which, in fact, constitute A LIFE OF PIETY. Prayer may be an expression and an act of piety, or it may not be. Going to church or to a prayer-meeting, may be considered either as a means, an act, or an expression of pious sentiment; but the performance of these does not consitute a man a Christian; and there may be great strictness and zeal in these, without a particle of religion. If young converts are not taught to discriminate, they may be led to think there is something peculiar in what are called religious duties, and to imagine they have a great deal of religion because they abound in certain actions that are commonly called "religious duties", although they may at the same time be very deficient in honesty, or faithfulness, or punctuality, or temperance, or any of what they choose to call their common duties. They may be very punctilious in some things, may "pay tithe of mint and anise and cummin" (Matthew 23:23), and yet neglect "the weightier matters of the law"; justice and the love of God.

Charles G. Finney (1792–1875)

22nd March

Whoever has my commands and obeys them, he is the one who loves me.

(John 14:21)

Suppose I say to my boy, "Willie, I want you to go out and bring me a glass of water."

He says he doesn't want to go.

"I didn't ask you whether you wanted to go or not, Willie – I told you to go."

"But I don't want to go," he says.

"I tell you, you must go and get me a glass of water."

He does not like to go. But he knows I am very fond of grapes, and he is very fond of them himself; so he goes out, and some one gives him a beautiful cluster of grapes. He comes in and says –

"Here, papa; here is a beautiful cluster of grapes for you."

"But what about the water?"

"Won't the grapes be acceptable, papa?"

"No, my boy, the grapes are not acceptable; I won't take them; I want you to get me a glass of water."

The little fellow doesn't want to get the water; but he goes out and someone gives him an orange. He brings it in, and places it before me.

"Is that acceptable?" he asks.

"No, no, no!" I say; "I want nothing but water; you cannot do anything to please me until you get the water."

And so, my friends, to please God you must first obey Him.

D. L. Moody (1837–99)

23rd March

For as the soil makes the young plant come up and a garden causes seeds to grow, so the Sovereign Lord will make righteousness and praise spring up before all nations.

(Isaiah 61:11)

During the past week the air has been balmy with the breath of spring, and all nature has felt the influence of the "ethereal mildness". The earth – of which, through the long winter, we might have said, "she is not dead but sleepeth" – has now awakened, and she beginneth already to put on her garments of glory and beauty. Wild flowers are springing up in the hedgerows, buds upon the trees are hastening to burst, the time of the singing of birds is come, and if the voice of the turtle be not heard in our land, yet we trust the winter is past – the rain is over and gone. Now, nature is not at work to amuse and please us merely – its mission is instruction. Spring, Summer, Autumn, and Winter are God's four Evangelists, bringing each one a different version of the self-same gospel of divine love. Spring has its own particular evangel, and it is for us to read it, and interpret it, by the light of God's Spirit. A close analogy is often hinted at in the Old and New Testaments between the spring-time and the work of God in the hearts of men. As God has promised in the outward world, that there will be seed time, and then a harvest – winter and a following summer, so he declares over and over again, that his word which, when it goeth forth, is like unto the sowing, shall not return until him void, but shall prosper in the thing whereto he hath sent it. As surely as in due season the earth bringeth forth her buds, and the garden causeth the things that are sown in it to spring forth, so shall God's great purpose be accomplished, and righteousness and praise shall spring forth before all the nations.

The teaching of this morning is, that there is a spiritual springtime appointed of God, and it will surely come; as certainly as spring comes to the earth physically, so surely it will come to the church spiritually: as certainly as God keeps his covenant with the elements, so will he keep his covenant with his church, and with his Son . . . Be not impatient with regard to the result of what you are doing. A little child puts his seed into the ground, and he goes in an hour or two and stirs the ground, to see whether the seed is growing. This is because he is a little child; if he were a man he would know better . . . grace insures the harvest. If you want your seed to come up more quickly, water it again with your tears and your prayer, but never despair, success will come to it. Work on! work on! and never be unhappy about it.

C. H. Spurgeon (1834–92)

24th March

For you were like sheep going astray, but now you have returned to the Shepherd and Overseer of your souls.

(1 Peter 2:25)

You all know, that sheep of all creatures in the world are most apt to stray and be lost; Christ's people may justly, in that respect be compared to sheep. Therefore in the introduction to our morning service, we say, We have erred and strayed from thy ways like lost sheep. Turn out a horse or a dog, and they will find their way home, but a sheep wanders about, he bleats here and there, as much as to say, dear strangers, shew me my way home again. Thus Christ's sheep are too apt to wander from the fold; having got their eyes off the great shepherd, they go into this field, and that field, over this hedge and that, and often return home with the loss of their wool.

But at the same time sheep are the most useful creatures in the world; they manure the land, and thereby prepare it for the feed; they clothe our bodies with wool, and there is not the least part of a sheep but is useful to man. O my brethren, God grant that you and I may, in this respect, answer the character of sheep. The world says, because we preach faith we deny good works; this is the usual objection against the doctrine of imputed righteousness [Romans 4:23–5], but it is a slander, an impudent slander ...

Christ's sheep study to be useful, and to clothe all they can; we should labour with our hands, that we may have to give to all those that need.

George Whitefield (1714–70)

25th March

My prayer is not for them alone. I pray also for those who will believe in me through their message, that all of them may be one, Father, just as you are in me and I am in you.
(John 17:20–21)

In this union they can have no share who deny that in the Son of God, Himself true God, man's nature abides, assailing the health-giving mystery and shutting themselves out from the Easter festival. For, as they dissent from the Gospel and gainsay the creed, they cannot keep it with us, because although they dare to take to themselves the Christian name, yet they are repelled by every creature who has Christ for his Head.

You rightly exult and devoutly rejoice in this sacred season as those who, admitting no falsehood into the Truth, have no doubts about Christ's Birth according to the flesh, His Passion and Death, and the Resurrection of His body. Without any separation of the Godhead you acknowledge a Christ, Who was truly born of a Virgin's womb, truly hung on the wood of the cross, truly laid in an earthly tomb, truly raised in glory, truly set on the right hand of the Father's majesty. From which as the Apostle says "we look for a

Saviour our Lord Jesus Christ Who will refashion the body of our humility to be conformed to the body of His glory."

Leo the Great (c. 400–461)

26th March

The next day as they were leaving Bethany, Jesus was hungry. Seeing in the distance a fig-tree in leaf, he went to find out if it had any fruit. When he reached it, he found nothing but leaves, because it was not the season for figs. Then he said to the tree, "May no-one ever eat fruit from you again." And his disciples heard him say it.
(Mark 11:12–14)

He did not merely do miracles for the miracles' sake; but in order that the things which He did should inspire wonder in those who saw them, and convey truth to them who understand. As he who sees letters in an excellently written manuscript, and knows not how to read, praises indeed the transcriber's hand, and admires the beauty of the characters; but what those characters mean or signify he does not know; and by the sight of his eyes he is a praiser of the work, but in his mind has no comprehension of it; whereas another man both praises the work, and is capable of understanding it; such a one, I mean who is not only able to see what is common to all, but who can read also; which he who has never learned cannot. So they who saw Christ's miracles, and understood not what they meant, and what they in a manner conveyed to those who had understanding, wondered only at the miracles themselves; whereas others both wondered at the miracles and attained to the meaning of them.

Such ought we to be in the school of Christ. For he who says that Christ only worked miracles for the miracles' sake, may say too that He was ignorant that it was not the time for fruit, when He sought figs upon the fig-tree. For it was not the time for that fruit, as the Evangelist testifies; and yet being hungry He sought for fruit upon the tree. Did Christ not know what any peasant knew? What the dresser of the tree knew, did not the tree's Creator know? So then when being hungry He sought fruit on the tree, He signified that He was hungry, and seeking after something else than this; and He found that tree without fruit, but full of leaves, and He cursed it, and it withered away. What had the tree done in not bearing fruit? What fault of the tree was its fruitlessness? No; but there are those who through their own will are not able to yield fruit. And barrenness is their fault, whose fruitfulness is their will. The Jews then who had the words of the Law, and had not the deeds, were full of leaves, and bare no fruit. This have I said to persuade you, that our Lord Jesus Christ performed miracles with this view, that by those miracles He might signify something further, that besides that they were wonderful and great, divine in themselves, we might learn also something from them.

Augustine of Hippo (354–430)

27th March

They all ate and were satisfied, and the disciples picked up twelve basketfuls of broken pieces of bread and fish. The number of the men who had eaten was five thousand.

(Mark 6:42–4)

The front rows of the Five Thousand are getting the loaves and the fishes over and over again – till it seems as though they have to be bribed and sought to accept them – while the back rows are almost forgotten. Is it that we are so busy with the front rows which we can see, that we have no time for the back rows out of sight? But is it fair? Is it what Jesus our Master intends? Can this unequal distribution of the Bread of Life really be called fair?

Could you say to a heathen woman, "I am very sorry for you. I know this will not show you the way from the dark where you are to the light where I am. To show you the way I must go to you, or send someone whom I want for myself, or go without something which I wish to have. And this of course is impossible. It might be done if I loved God enough. But I love myself more than God or you".

You would not say such a thing. But – "Whoever has this world's goods, and sees his brother in need, and shuts up his heart from him, how does the love of God abide in him?" (1 John 3.17 NKJ).

The evangelisation of the world is a great word, but boil it down to its essence and you come to the conversion of individual people. To evangelise must mean giving each man, woman, and child an opportunity to hear and understand the gospel. Then, if there be response, surely there should be obedience to Matthew 28:19–20 "... make disciples of all the nations, baptising them into the name of the Father and of the Son and of the Holy Ghost: teaching them to observe all things whatsoever I commanded you."

All this takes time. It means personal work like the work of our Lord Jesus by the side of the well (John 4). In India at least, souls are not saved in bunches, but one by one.

Work in the villages is not spectacular. It is a hot, sometimes dull plod, with many a discouragement. But our Commander said "Go", and there is joy in obedience.

Amy Carmichael (1867–1951)

28th March

Jesus had compassion on them and touched their eyes. Immediately they received their sight and followed him.

(Mattthew 20:34)

Christ's compassion is distinguished from all other compassions by its *plain, cuttting, personal dealing.* "He would eat with sinners," talk familiarly and tenderly with the worst on earth, and lay His hands upon the most loathsome, but He was incapable of dealing lightly with their sin.

Imagine Christ giving an entertainment, and spending the evening in frivolous talk, in order that He might humour sinners and attract them to Himself! Imagine Him allowing His little band of disciples to sing current songs and read "amusing selections" for a couple of hours at a time to keep people out of worse company! No, He was too tenderly compassionate for souls, who He knew might end their time on earth at any moment, thus to fool away His chance. He never lost the opportunity of talking straight to them about their sins, the interests of their souls, and the claim of His Father's law. The young ruler comes to Him and he is so lovable, so moral, so good, might he not have been allowed to join the little band of disciples, and to have gained light gradually? "Yet lackest thou one thing" was pronounced all the more clearly because "He loved him." "Sell that thou hast and follow Me" rang out all the more distinctly because He could offer treasure for the *soul*.

The compassion of Jesus was not of the maudlin kind which leaves men their "little indulgences", and shrinks from being "too hard" on them, where hardness is the indispensible condition of salvation. "If thy right hand offend thee, cut it off; if thy right eye offend thee, pluck it out," He mercilessly prescribes; better, He decides, be maimed and suffering here, than be cast into "eternal fire".

As for the religious ideas of His day, He walked straight across them with a cutting "Woe unto you!" Woe! woe! was the one cry with which He met the teachers and professors of His time, provoking their deepest hate and animosity. "Making clean the outside platter, while within are dead men's bones," was His short description of them and their doings. He upset the nice little fashions which had sprung up around the temple worship with a whip of cords. "Publicans and harlots shall enter the kingdom before you," He told the grand professors who listened to Him. He inflicted the wounds of a friend, in order that He might awaken them to their danger and lead them to seek the only remedy.

Catherine Booth (1829–90)

29th March

"Do you want me to release to you the king of the Jews?" asked Pilate, knowing it was out of envy that the chief priests had handed Jesus over to him.

(Mark 15:9–10)

Our Lord's life and teaching and wonderful works, and the multitudes that were attracted to Him by all that; – it would have been New Jerusalem above, and Caiaphas would have been a sanctified saint in heaven, not to have had his heart burned up with envy within him at our Lord's popularity with the people. It is at this moment in the Passion Play at Ober-Ammergau that the chorus comes forward with warning to us:

> *'Tis envy – which no mercy knows,*
> *In which hell's flame most fiercely glows –*
> *Lights this devouring fire.*
> *All's sacrificed unto its lust –*
> *Nothing too sacred, good or just*
> *To fall to its desire.*
> *Oh! woe to those this passion sweeps*
> *Helpless and bound into the deeps!*

Pilate had never heard of the Jerusalem that is above, but no man knew better than he did the Jerusalem that was yelling like all the furies around him. Caiaphas had put on his holiest of masks that holiest of mornings, and he had demanded swift execution to be done on this traitor against Caesar and this blasphemer against God.

But Pilate was not a child. Heathen as Pilate was, and hardened as stone in his heart as he was, he both saw into and despised and detested every high priest, and scribe, and elder of them all. It was a noble hyperbole that was put upon Plato's tombstone: "Here lies a man too good and too great for envy." But that literally true epitaph, and no hyperbole, could not have been written even on Joseph's new tomb as long as Caiaphas remained alive in Jerusalem. Our Lord Himself was neither too good or great for Caiaphas's envy and ill-will, nor for Pilate's selfish cowardice and open sale of truth and justice. For, all this time, with all his power, and with all his pride, and with all his astuteness, and with all his resources, the chain of his terrible fate was fast closing around Pontius Pilate.

Alexander Whyte (1836–1921)

30th March

Now that I, your Lord and Teacher, have washed your feet, you also should wash one another's feet. I have set you an example that you should do as I have done for you.

(John 13:14–15)

To me one of the saddest things in all the life of Jesus Christ was the fact that just before his crucifixion, his disciples should be striving to see who should be the greatest of all, that night He instituted the Supper, and they ate the Passover together. It was his last night on earth, and they never saw Him so sorrowful before . . . He took a towel and girded Himself like a slave, and He took a basin of water and stooped and washed their feet . . .

When the Holy Ghost came, and these men were filled, from that time on mark the difference: Matthew takes up his pen to write, and he keeps Matthew out of sight. He tells what Peter and Andrew did; but he calls himself Matthew "the publican". Jerome says that Mark's gospel is to be regarded as memoirs of Peter's discourses, and to have been published by his authority. Yet we are constantly finding that damaging things are mentioned about Peter, and things to his credit are not referred to. Mark's gospel omits all allusion to Peter's faith in venturing on the sea, but goes into detail about the story of his fall and denial of our Lord. Peter put himself down, and lifted others up.

If the Gospel of Luke had been written today, it would have been signed by the great Dr Luke, and you would find his photograph as a frontispiece. But you cannot find Luke's name; he keeps it out of sight. He wrote two books, and his name is not to be found in either. John covers himself always under the expression – "the disciple whom Jesus loved". None of these four men whom history and tradition assert to be the authors of the gospels, lay claim to the authorship in their writings. Dear men of God, I would that I had the same spirit, that I could just get out of sight – hide myself.

D. L. Moody (1837–99)

31st March

Because the Lord kept vigil that night to bring them out of Egypt, on this night all the Israelites are to keep vigil to honour the Lord for generations to come.

(Exodus 12:42)

The Passover was a type of our Lord's passion. He is the Lamb of God's Passover. It is by his blood that we are preserved; it is by virtue of his sacrifice that God passes over us who through faith have received the sprinkling of that blood. Never let us forget that night which is to be much remembered – that night when the Lord was taken from prison and from judgement, – when there was none to declare his generation – when for the transgression of his people, he was smitten. It was a dark night when he arose from the table where he had supped for the last time with his disciples, and went to Gethsemane, there he began to suffer, in the very beginning to be sorrowful, even unto death; then to be taken off to Pilate, and to Herod, and to Caiaphas, to be condemned to die; to be lifted high upon the cross, to bleed, to suffer physical pain, and mental anguish and spiritual grief, unknown sufferings never to be estimated by us. It was a night to be remembered in all our generations.

Let it never be forgotten. Whatever else we do not know, my brethren, let us know the cross; whatever subject may have second place in our estimation, always let the ransom-price paid on Calvary be first and foremost. I would have you study much the four records of the evangelists. Dwell upon them. Christians ought to be familiar with every little incident of their Saviour's death: there is teaching in every nail; the sponge, the vinegar, and the hyssop all have a meaning in them, and the spear that pierced his side is full of instruction.

We ought to study them – study them again, and again, and again. Here is the very essence of our confidence; this is the pillar on which our souls lean. If there be any hope for sinners; if there be any consolation for sufferers; if there be any cleansing for the guilty; if there by any life for the dead, it is here. In thy words Emmanuel – it is here and only here. O, dwell at the cross then.

Whatever your minds may forget to consider, let them never lose the savour of this, or leave the meditation of Christ crucified. Keep to this. Remember that to help our frail memories, God has given us an ordinance. Even as he gave the Jews the Passover, he has given us the Lord's Supper. "This do ye, as oft as ye drink it, in remembrance of me."

C. H. Spurgeon (1834–92)

April

1st April

He who did not spare his own Son, but gave him up for us all – how will he not also, along with him, graciously give us all things?
(Romans 8:32)

The justice and the severity of God is no less conspicuous than his goodness in these words: as he spared not to give his Son for our sakes. When Christ appeared in our nature, he undertook our cause, and was charged with our sins. Even though he was the Father's well-beloved Son, he was not spared. He drank the bitter cup of the wrath of God to the very dregs: he bore all the shame, sorrow, and pain, all the distress of body and mind, that must otherwise have fallen on our heads.

His whole life, from the manger to the cross, was one series of humiliations and suffering. Observe him in the world, despised, vilified, persecuted even to death, by unreasonable and wicked men; ridiculed, buffeted, spat upon, and at length nailed to the accursed tree! Consider him in the wilderness, given up to the power and assaulted by the temptations of the devil! Behold him in the garden (Luke 22), and say, "Was there ever sorrow like unto his sorrow, wherewith the Lord afflicted him in the day of his fierce anger?" How inconceivable that agony must have been, which caused the blood to forsake its wonted channels, and start from every pore of his body!

Behold him, lastly, upon the cross, suffering the most painful and ignominious death: suspended between two thieves, surrounded by cruel enemies, who make sport of his pangs; derided by all that pass by! Attend to his dolorous cry, expressive of inward distress beyond all we have yet spoken of, "My God, my God, why hast thou forsaken me?"

John Newton (1725–1807)

2nd April

When I came to you, brothers, I did not come with eloquence or superior wisdom as I proclaimed to you the testimony about God. For I resolved to know nothing while I was with you except Jesus Christ and him crucified.

(1 Corinthians 2:1–2)

To lay the stress of Christ's revelation elsewhere than on the atoning Cross is to make Him no more than a martyr, whose testimony was not given by His death, but only sealed by it. His message must then be sought in His words; and His death only then certifies the strength of conviction behind them. Or it may be sought in the spell of His character to which His death but gives an impressive close.

But His message was of Himself, even through His word and deeds. "Come unto Me," "Confess Me if in the judgement you would have Me confess you." The cup of cold water was blessed like the cup of the supper – for His sake. I need not add to these passages. If, then, He was a martyr, He was a martyr to Himself. But a man who is a martyr to Himself on this scale is either a megalomaniac egotist, or He is a redeeming God. But Christ's long majestic influence with man forbids the former alternative, unless the whole race is moral lunatic, and His death was God in action. He was God, therefore, and His death was God in action.

He was not simply the witness of God's grace, He was its fact, its incarnation. His death was not merely a seal to His work; it was His consummate work. It gathered up His whole person. It was more than a confirmatory pledge, it was the effective sacrament of the gracious God, with His real presence at its core. Something was done there once and for all, and the subject doer of it was God. The real acting person in the Cross was God. Christ's death was not the sealing of a preacher's testimony; it altered from God's part the whole relation between God and man for ever. It did not declare something, or prove something, it achieved something decisive for history, nay for eternity.

P. T. Forsyth (1848–1921)

3rd April

And if Christ has not been raised, your faith is futile; you are still in your sins.

(1 Corinthians 15:17)

How he [R. W. Dale] hated "flashy" preaching! Once I told him of a striking and brilliant sermon I had heard from a popular preacher; he listened as I described it, and then said with considerable warmth: "Yes, I used to preach like that when I was a young man; but now, thank God, I have more sense."

The Living Christ and the Four Gospels next to *The Atonement* was he believed, one of the most helpful things he had ever written. Dr Amory Bradford of New Jersey told me that Dr Dale has done through that book more for the people of America in making them realise that Christ was really alive than any other preacher or book he knew.

How he came to write *The Living Christ* – so he said – was in this way. He was writing an Easter sermon, and when half-way through, the thought of the risen Lord broke in upon him as it had never done before. "Christ is alive," I said to myself; "alive! and then I paused; – alive! and then I paused again; alive! Can that really be true? living as really as I myself am? I got up and walked about repeating 'Christ is living!' 'Christ is living!' At first it seemed strange and hardly true, but at last it came upon me as a burst of sudden glory; yes, Christ is living. It was to me a new discovery, I thought that all along I had believed it; but not until that moment did I feel sure about it. I then said, 'My people shall know it; I shall preach about it again and again until they believe it as I do now.'"

For months afterwards, and in every sermon, the Living Christ was his one great theme; and there and then began the custom of singing in Carr's Lane on every Sunday morning an Easter hymn. When I first attended a service there I was surprised to hear on a November morning the hymn given out "Christ is risen: Hallelujah!" I mentioned it to Dr Dale afterwards and he said: "I want my people to get hold of the glorious fact that Christ is alive, and to rejoice over it; and Sunday, you know, is the day on which Christ left the dead."

R. W. Dale (1829–95)

4th April

For he has rescued us from the dominion of darkness and brought us into the kingdom of the Son he loves, in whom we have redemption, the forgiveness of sins.

(Colossians 1:13–14)

Through Christ he [the Christian] has passed into the eternal and Divine order. He belongs to two worlds. He is just as certain that he is environed by things unseen and eternal as that he is environed by things seen and temporal. In the power of the life given to him in the new birth he has entered into the kingdom of God. He is conscious that that Diviner region is now the native land of his soul. It is there that he finds perfect rest and perfect freedom. It is a relief to escape to its eternal peace and glory from the agitations and vicissitudes, the sorrows and successes of this transitory world. It is not always that he is vividly conscious of belonging to that eternal order; this supreme blessedness is reserved for the great hours of his life; but he knows that it lies about him always, and that at any moment the great apocalypse may come. And even when it is hidden, its "powers" continue to act upon him, as the light and the heat of the sun pass through the clouds by which the burning splendour is softened and concealed.

R. W. Dale (1829–95)

5th April

Jews demand miraculous signs and Greeks look for wisdom, but we preach Christ crucified: a stumbling-block to Jews and foolishness to Gentiles, but to those whom God has called, both Jews and Greeks, Christ the power of God and the wisdom of God.
                                                       (1 Corinthians 1:22–4)

Vast is the import of the things here spoken! For he means to say how by contraries God hath overcome, and how the Gospel is not of man. What he saith is something of this sort. When, saith he, we say unto the Jews, Believe; they answer, Raise the dead, Heal the demoniacs, Shew us signs. But instead thereof what say we? That he was crucified, and died, who is preached. And that is enough, not only to fail in drawing over the unwilling, but utterly to drive away those even who are willing. Nevertheless, it drives not away, but attracts, and holds fast, and overcomes.

Again; the Greeks demand of us a rhetorical style, and the acuteness of sophistry. But we to these also preach the Cross: and that which in the case of the Jews is deemed to be weakness, this in the case of the Greeks is foolishness. Wherefore, when we not only fail in producing what they demand, but also produce the very opposites of their demand; (for the Cross has not merely no appearance of being a sign sought out by reasoning, but even the very annihilation of a sign; – is nor merely deemed no proof of power, but a conviction of weakness; – not merely no display of wisdom, but a ground for surmising weakness;) – when therefore they who seek for signs and wisdom not only receive not the things for which they ask, but even hear the contrary to what they desire and then by means of contraries are persuaded; – how is not the power of Him that is preached unspeakable? As if to some one tempest-tost and longing for a haven, you were to shew not a haven, but another wilder portion of the sea, and so could make him follow with thankfulness! Or as if a physician could attract to himself the man that was wounded and in need of remedies, by promising to cure him not with drugs, but with burning of him again! For this is the result of great power indeed.

So also the Apostles prevailed, not simply by a sign, but even by a thing which seemed contrary to all known signs. Which thing also Christ did in the case of a blind man. For when He would heal him, He restored him by a thing which increased blindness: that is, He put on clay [John 9:6]. As then by means of clay He healed the blind man, so also by means of the Cross hath He brought the world to Himself. That certainly was adding an offence, not taking an offence away.

John Chrysostom (c. 344/345–407)

6th April

So when the crowd had gathered, Pilate asked them, "Which one do you want me to release to you: Barabbas or Jesus who is called Christ?" For he knew it was out of envy that they had handed Jesus over to him.

(Matthew 27:17–18)

It was through jealousy that Esau was enemy of his brother Jacob. For because the one had received the blessing of his Father, the other became inflamed by the firebrands of envy. Moreover when Joseph's brethren sold him, the cause of their selling him was derived from enviousness. When he with simplicity set forth to them, as a brother to brethren, that prosperous thing which had been shewn to him in visions, their unkindly spirit broke forth into envy.

What else moreover than the spur of jealousy provoked King Saul to hate David, and seek with persecutions oftentimes repeated, to kill that innocent and merciful man, full of meek and gentle patience? When Goliath was killed, and that great enemy destroyed through the help and goodness of God, the admiring people broke forth in acclamation, praising David. Saul then conceived through envious feeling, the mad spirit of hatred and persecution. And not to lengthen on in numbering all, let us mark the fate of a nation that entirely perished. Did not the Jews for this cause perish, because they would rather envy Christ, than believe in Him? Carping at those great works which He performed, they were deceived by jealousy that blinded them, and could not open the eyes of their heart to the acknowledgement of divine things.

Thinking now on these things, dearest brethren, let us watchfully and boldly arm our heaven-surrendered breasts, against this great instrument of destruction. Let others' death avail for our saving; let the sufferings of unwatchful men contribute health to those who take thought.

Cyprian (c. 201/210–258)

7th April

The God of Abraham, Isaac and Jacob, the God of our fathers, has glorified his servant Jesus. You handed him over to be killed, and you disowned him before Pilate, though he had decided to let him go.

(Acts 3:13)

We may turn our eyes inward and ask ourselves what we would have done that passover morning had we been in Pilate's place; had we stood between the deadly anger of Caesar at us on the one hand, and with only a just man to be scourged and crucified on the other hand! We would have done just what Pilate did. To protect ourselves; to stand well with our masters, to preserve our paying post; we would have washed our hands, and would have scourged Jesus, righteousness man and all. Who here, in this hour of truth, will dare to cast a stone at Pontius Pilate? What self-seeking, what self-sheltering, what truth-selling, what soul-selling man?

> *O break, O break, hard heart of mine!*
> *Thy weak self-love and guilty pride*
> *His Pilate and Judas were:*
> *Jesus, our Lord, is crucified!*

I know all the old legends, sacred and profane, about Pontius Pilate, and about his miserable end. But I shall not believe any of them. I shall continue to hope against hope for poor Pontius Pilate. If my sale of my Saviour, and of my own soul, has so often chased me up to the Cross of Christ, so I think that Pilate's remorse must have chased him.

And as he washed his hands in water that passover morning, so shall I hope he washed his hands and his heart ten thousand times in after days in that Fountain for sin which he had such an awful hand in opening. The world would not contain the books if all the names of all the chief priests, and scribes, and inhabitants of Jerusalem; and all the governors, and centurions, and soldiers of Rome, who came to believe in Christ were written in them.

Who can tell? With that glorious Gospel preached far and wide, with the Redeemer's prayer offered with His own blood to back it on the Cross, Father, forgive them; who can tell? I, for one, shall continue to hope for Pontius Pilate, as for myself. For –

> *O love of God! O sin of man!*
> *In this dread act your strength is tried,*
> *And victory remains with love:*
> *Jesus, our Lord, is crucified!*

Alexander Whyte (1836–1921)

8th April

He himself bore our sins in his body on the tree, so that we might die to sins and live for righteousness; by his wounds you have been healed.

(1 Peter 2:24)

Now, I saw in my dream that the highway up which Christian was to go was fenced on either side with a wall that was called Salvation. Up this way, therefore did burdened Christian run, but not without great difficulty, because of the load on his back.

He ran thus till he came to a place somewhat ascending and upon that place stood a cross, and a little below, in the bottom, a sepulchre. So I saw in my dream that just as Christian came up with the cross, his burden loosed from off his shoulders, and fell from his back, and began to tumble, and so continued to do till it came to the mouth of the sepulchre, where it fell in, and I saw it no more.

Then was Christian glad and lightsome, and said with a merry heart, "He hath given me rest by his sorrow, and life by his death." Then he stood awhile to look and wonder; for it was very surprising to him that the sight of the cross should thus ease him of his burden. He looked, therefore, and looked again, even till the springs that were in his head sent the water down his cheeks.

Now, as he was looking and weeping, three Shining Ones came to him and saluted him with, "Peace!"

So the first said to him, "Your sins be forgiven you." The second stripped him of his rags and clothed him with a change of raiment. The third also set a mark on his forehead, and gave him a roll with a seal upon it, which he told him to look at as he ran; and that he should turn it in at the celestial gate. So they went their way.

Then Christian gave three leaps for joy and went on, singing:

> *Thus far did I come laden with my sin;*
> *Nor could aught ease the grief that I was in,*
> *Till I came hither: what a place is this!*
> *Must here be the beginning of my bliss?*
> *Must here the burden fall from off my back?*
> *Must here the strings that bound it to me crack?*
> *Blest cross! blest selpulchre! blest rather be*
> *That Man that was there put to shame for me!*

John Bunyan (1628–88)

9th April

The Lord will rescue me from every evil attack and will bring me safely to his heavenly kingdom. To him be glory for ever and ever. Amen.

(2 Timothy 4:18)

Then said he, "I am going to my Father's: and though with great difficulty I am got thither, yet now I do not repent me of all the trouble I have been at to arrive where I am. My sword I give to him that shall succeed me in my pilgrimage, and my courage and skill to him that can get it. My marks and scars I carry with me to be a witness to me, that I have fought his battles who now shall be my rewarder."

When the day that he must go hence was come, many accompanied him to the river side, into which as he went he said, "Death where is thy sting?" And as he went down deeper, he said, "Grave, where is thy victory?" And so he passed over and all the trumpets sounded for him on the other side.

John Bunyan (1628–88)

10th April

The two of them, sent on their way by the Holy Spirit, went down to Seleucia and sailed from there to Cyprus. When they arrived at Salamis, they proclaimed the word of God in the Jewish synagogues. John was with them as their helper.

(Acts 13:4–5)

The missionaries must be men of great piety, prudence, courage and forbearance; of undoubted orthodoxy in their sentiments, and must enter with all their hearts into the spirit of their mission; they must be willing to leave all the comforts of life behind them, and to encounter the hardships of a torrid or frigid climate, an uncomfortable manner of living, and every other inconvenience that can attend this undertaking . . .

When they arrive at their destination, their first business must be to gain some acquaintance with the language of the natives, (for which purpose two [people] would be better than one). They must endeavour to convince them that it was their good alone, which induced them to forsake their friends, and all the comforts of their native country. They must be careful not to resent injuries which may be offered to them, or to think highly of themselves, so as to despise the heathens, and by those means lay a foundation for their resentment, or rejection of the gospel.

They must take every opportunity of doing them good, and labouring, and travelling night and day, they must instruct, exhort, and rebuke, with all long suffering, and anxious desire for them, and, above all, must be instant in prayer for the outpouring of the

Holy Spirit upon the people in their charge. Let but missionaries of the above description engage in the work, and we shall see that it is not impractical [to preach the gospel in all the world].

It might likewise be of importance, if God should bless their labours, for them to encourage any appearance of gifts amongst the people of their charge; if such be raised up many advantages would be derived from their knowledge of the language and customs of their countrymen; and their change of conduct would give great weight to their ministrations.

William Carey (1761–1834)

11th April

I tell you the truth, if you have faith as small as a mustard seed, you can say to this mountain, "Move from here to there" and it will move. Nothing will be impossible for you.

(Mattthew 17:20–21)

But how came the little church of the [Moravian] brethren to put its hand to missions to the heathen, and so to open a new chapter in the history of missions? In a manner which may be clearly recognised, it was the work of God. "He tied the threads, prepared the paths, chose and fitted the men, and then spake His Almighty word, 'Let it be.'"

First, as to the human instruments whom God prepared to carry on His work among the heathen, these were Nikolaus Ludwig, Count von Zinzendorf, and the Moravian Brethren, for whom he made ready a home in Herrnhut. Manifestly it was by the special leading of Divine Providence that Count Zinzendorf, who was to become so eminent an instrument for the work of converting the heathen, came as a boy into [August] Francke's institutions in Halle. He says himself later of that time: "The daily opportunity in Professor Francke's house of hearing edifying tidings of the kingdom of Christ, of speaking with witnesses from all lands, of making acquaintance with missionaries (especially Bartholomew Ziegenbalg), of seeing men who had been banished and imprisoned, as also the institutions then in their bloom, and the cheerfulness of the pious man himself in the work of the Lord . . . mightily strengthened within me zeal for the things of the Lord." Under these influences the pious boy, when only fifteen years of age, formed with some like-minded comrades an "Order" [of the Grain of Mustard Seed], whose chief rule ran thus: "Our unwearied labour shall go through the whole world, in order that we may win hearts for Him Who gave His life for our souls." With his friend Frederic von Wattewille in particular he made a compact "for the conversion of the heathen, and of such as no one else would go to, by instruments to whom God would direct them."

Already in early youth Zinzendorf was filled with burning love to the Person of the crucified Saviour, so that he could declare, "I have but one passion, and it is He, He only." And this man aflame with glowing love for the Saviour, had a peculiar instinct for fellowship. His was not a nature quietly in-turned upon himself, but the craving of his heart was to form societies which were bound to the Lord Jesus. "I admit no Christianity without fellowship," he declared. Besides Zinzendorf possessed quite a pre-eminent talent for organisation, which made him a blessed "Ordinarius" (ruling bishop), who knew how to give to every society and to every work fitting order, form and fashion.

Nikolaus Ludwig, Count von Zinzendorf (1700–1760)

12th April

He told them another parable: "The kingdom of heaven is like a mustard seed, which a man took and planted in his field. Though it is the smallest of all your seeds, yet when it grows, it is the largest of garden plants and becomes a tree, so that the birds of the air come and perch in its branches."

(Matthew 13:31–2)

[Continued from yesterday.]

But what could the best organiser with the most ardent love of the Saviour begin without instruments? With men of commonplace cast even a Zinzendorf could effect nothing. In order to establish an expansive missionary work among the heathen in that age, there was need of men of extraordinary faith and courage. "The storming column of the missionary host must be a chosen troop of daring energy and persistent endurance." God furnished to the Count that chosen troop. It consisted of a number of Moravian Brethren, who for the sake of their faith had been forced to leave their fatherland, and whom Count Zinzendorf . . . had hospitably sheltered on his estate of Bethelsdorf. On the 17th of July 1722 the first tree at Hutberg, near Bethelsdorf, was felled, on which occasion Christian David the carpenter exclaimed prophetically, "Here hath the swallow found her house and the bird its nest, Thine altars, O Lord of Hosts." That was the beginning of the church of the Brethren, which gradually attracted to itself at Herrnhut many especially of the ever increasing numbers of settlers from Moravia, and which hid within itself the human material out of which the Spirit of God makes His witnesses: men of inflexible resolve, stern towards themselves, ready for every labour and privation, perfectly calm amid great dangers, and burning with zeal to save souls.

As to their character, only some examples. When the first missionaries, David Nitzschmann, a carpenter, and Leonard Dober, a potter, went to the West Indies in 1732, their purpose, to convert the negro slaves, was declared in Copenhagen to be a foolish freak, and the directors of the Danish West India Company refused them a passage on their ships. That, however could not turn aside men with the courage of faith, who were certain of their divine call. When the chief chamberlain, Von Pless, who was well disposed towards them, asked, "But how will you manage at St Thomas?" Nitzschmann made answer, "We will work as slaves with the negroes." And when he rejoined, "You cannot do that; it will never be permitted," Nitzschmann averred, "Then I am willing to work as a carpenter at my trade." "Good, but what will the potter do?" – "I shall just pull him through along with me." "Verily then," said the chamberlain, "in that fashion you can go with one another through the whole world."

Of a great company of brethren and sisters who in 1734 were also sent to the West Indies, principally to St Croix, ten died in the course of the year. When the startling news of this sore loss reached the Herrnhut, there was indeed, in the first moment, deep depression because of the severe and unexpected blow. But it did not last for long: with the full joy of faith the congregation sang the verse which Zinzendorf composed on receipt of the tidings, and which has become so celebrated –

> *Ten were sown right faraway,*
> *as were they lost indeed, –*
> *But o'er their beds stands, "These are they*
> *Of Afric's race the seed."*

Nikolaus Ludwig, Count von Zinzendorf (1700–1760)

13th April

Now to him who is able to do immeasurably more than all we ask or imagine, according to his power that is at work within us, to him be glory in the church and in Christ Jesus throughout all generations, for ever and ever! Amen.

(Ephesians 3:20–21)

By Loch Tay, Eighth Month 9th, First-day [1834] – not having a Meeting to go to, and not believing it right to attend any other place of worship; I desire to spend a time in solemn searching of heart before the Lord, and may I be enabled to hold communion with Him in spirit.

On the morning of the 1st, the day appointed for the liberation of all slaves in the British dominions, and on which my dear niece, Priscilla B-- was to be married, I poured out my soul in deep supplication before my heavenly Father, on behalf of the poor slaves; that a quiet spirit may be granted to them – that their spiritual bonds might also be broken – that the liberty prepared for the children of God might be their portion. I also prayed for my beloved niece and her companion in life, that the Lord would be with them, keep them, and bless them.

My son Gurney, accompanied me from Newcastle, and we arrived at Dunkeld on the 5th, where we met my husband and daughters. I ought thankfully to remember how my way has been made, where I could hardly see an opening to join them; how difficulties have vanished, and how a kind Providence has been with me, and provided for me, and brought me to these dear ones; may I be edified and refreshed by beholding the wonderful and beautiful works of God; may I rightly attend to such little services as may open towards others.

Lord be with me, and help me by Thy Spirit, to perform all my duties to Thy praise. I pray Thee be very near to us all; protect us by Thy providential care over us, and above all, further visit us by Thy love, power, and Spirit. Oh Lord! turn us, and we shall be turned; help us, and we shall be helped; keep us, and we shall be kept. Amen.

Elizabetth Fry (1780–1845)

14th April

Righteousness exalts a nation, but sin is a disgrace to any people.
(Proverbs 14:34)

Lord Ashley [Shaftesbury] then proceeded to give a vivid description of the general effects upon its victims of indulgence in opium as a luxury – their physical, mental, and moral debility, their hideous disfigurement and premature decay – resulting in misery almost beyond belief, destroying myriads of individuals annually, and casting its victims into a bondage with which no slavery on earth could compare, and from which there was scarcely a known instance of escape.

There was immorality involved even in the cultivation of the plant, for such pressure was put upon the [Indian people] that in many cases, they were compelled to accept the Government grant and supply the needed quantity of poppy. In fact at every step the system was associated with evil, and only evil. Splendid regions were laid waste to supply the commodity (for poppies require a special soil); the trade was in the hands of desperate fellows who carried it on by fraud, violence, and oppression. It was an intolerable outrage to the feelings of the civilised and Christian nations of the world, that this iniquitous trade should be part of the fiscal arrangements of the Government – an important part of the Imperial policy of India. The opium was grown by advances from the Imperial Government; carried down to Calcutta, and put up for sale under Government authority; shipped in opium clippers lying in the river, and the clippers supplied with arms from the arsenals of the Government.

Lord Ashley frankly admitted that, for the sake of the revenue, Parliament in 1832 sanctioned the opium monopoly. "I was in Parliament myself at the time," he said, "and I share in the responsibility; but I had not, at that time, the most remote idea of the enormities which the details of the system have since brought to light." Having now [1834] studied the whole question, the revelation of the facts of the case had filled him with horror. He saw that it stood in the way of the progress of society, the civilisation of man, and the advancement of the Gospel. It could never be that Opium and the Bible could enter China together; he was constrained to endorse the testimony of missionary agents, who asserted that "the proud escutcheon of the nation which declares against the slave trade, is made to bear a blot broader and darker than any other in the Christian world."

Lord Shaftesbury (1801–85)

15th April

The Lord detests the way of the wicked but he loves those who pursue righteousness.

(Proverbs 15:9)

[Continued from yesterday.]

I am fully convinced that, for the country to encourage this nefarious [opium] traffic, is bad, perhaps worse than encouraging the slave trade. That terrible system of slavery does not necessarily destroy the physical and moral qualities of its victims. It tortures and degrades the man, but it leaves him susceptible of regeneration. But the opium trade destroys the man, both body and soul; and carries a hideous ruin over millions, which can never be repaired. You may abolish the evil this night, but you cannot restore the millions who have been tempted, by the precedings of the Government of India, to indulge in the use of the pernicious drug.

Now, a fact has just occurred, than which nothing, I am certain, can relect greater disgrace on all our conduct: it occurred on Wednesday last. The Baptist Missionary Society – a Society which has done a great deal in effecting the spread of the Gospel among heathen nations, and which has produced some most eminent and pious men – at a meeting last Wednesday took into consideration the propriety of sending out missionaries to China; and it was decided to work through the agency of the American missions, because the public feeling in China was so strong against the English, that if missionaries hoped to work at all, it must be through America, which has kept aloof from the disgraceful traffic. And what was the result? Why the Baptist Missionary Society of England voted £500 to be put at the disposal of the American Missionaries, for the propagation of the Gospel in China!

So, Sir, it has come to this, that England, which professes to be at the head of Christian nations, is precluded by her own immoral conduct from sending her own missionaries to that part of the world which she herself has opened for the advancement of civilisation and the enlightenment of Christianity.

Lord Shaftesbury (1801–85)

16th April

A student is not above his teacher, nor a servant above his master. It is enough for the student to be like his teacher, and the servant like his master.

(Matthew 10:24–25b)

The gospel leads us to love Christ as a humble person. Christ is the God-man, including both the divine and human natures; and so has not only condescension, which is a divine perfection, but also humility, which is a creature excellency. Now the gospel holds forth Christ to us as one that is meek and lowly of heart; as the most perfect and excellent instance of humility that ever existed; as one in whom the greatest performances and expressions of humility were manifest in his abasement of himself. Though he was "in the form of God", he "made himself of no reputation, and took the form of a servant", and "humbled himself, and became obedient unto death, even death of the cross" (Philippians 2:6–8)

Now the gospel leads us to love Christ as such an humble person; and, therefore, to love him with such a love as is proper to be exercised towards such a one, is to exercise an humble love. And this is more true, because the gospel leads us to love Christ not only as an humble person, but as an humble Saviour and Lord, and Head. If our Lord and Master is humble, and we love him as such, certainly it becomes us who are his disciples and servants to be so too; for surely it does not become the servant to be prouder or less abased than his master.

Jonathan Edwards (1703–58)

17th April

Grow in the grace and knowledge of our Lord and Saviour Jesus Christ. To him be glory both now and for ever! Amen.
(2 Peter 3:18)

Young converts should be faithfully warned against adopting a false standard in religion. They should not be left to fall in behind old professors [of the Faith], or keep such before their minds as a standard of holy living. They should always look to Christ as their model. Not aim at being as good Christians as the old Church members, and not think that they are doing pretty well because they are as much awake as the old members of the Church; but they should aim at being holy. The Church has been greatly injured for the want of attention to this matter. Young converts have come forward, and their hearts were warm, and their zeal ardent enough to aim at a high standard, but they were not directed properly, and so they soon settled down into the notion that what was good enough for others was good enough for them, and therefore they ceased to aim higher than those who were before them. And in this way the Church instead of rising higher with every revival, higher and higher in holiness, is kept nearly stationary.

Young converts should be taught to do all their duty. They should never make a compromise with duty, nor think of saying: "I will do *this* as an offset for neglecting *that*." They should never rest satisfied till they have done their duties of every kind, in relation to their families, the Church, Sabbath Schools, the impenitent around them, the disposal of their property, and the conversion of the world. Let them do their duty, as they feel it when their hearts are warm; and never attempt to pick and choose among the commandments of God.

They should be made to feel they have no separate interest. It is time Christians were made actually to feel that they have no interest whatever apart from the interests of Jesus Christ, and His Kingdom. They should understand that they are incorporated into the family of Jesus Christ, as members in full, so that their whole interest is identified with His. They are embarked with Him, they have gone on board, and taken all; and henceforth they have nothing to do, or anything to say, except as it is connected with this interest, and bearing on the cause and Kingdom of Christ.

Charles G. Finney (1792–1875)

18th April

Brothers, I could not address you as spiritual but as worldly – mere infants in Christ. I gave you milk, not solid food, for you were not yet ready for it.

(1 Corinthians 3:1–2)

There are many of our flock that are young and weak, who, though they are of long standing, are yet of small proficiency or strength. This, indeed is the most common condition of the godly. Most of them content themselves with low degrees of grace; and it is no easy matter to get them higher. To bring them to higher and stricter opinions, is comparatively easy, that is to bring them from the truth into error, on the right hand as well as on the left; but to increase their knowledge and gifts is not easy, and to increase their graces is the hardest of all. It is a very sad thing for Christians to be weak: it exposeth us to danger, it abateth our consolations, and taketh off the sweetness of wisdom's ways; it maketh us less serviceable to God and man – to bring less honour to our Master, and to do less good to all about us.

Now, seeing the case of weakness in the converted is so sad, how diligent we should be to cherish and increase their grace! The strength of strong Christians is the honour of the church. They are inflamed with the love of God, and live by a lively working faith. They set light by the profits and honours of the world, and love one another with a pure heart fervently. They can bear and heartily forgive a wrong, and suffer joyfully for the cause of Christ. They study to do good and walk inoffensively and harmlessly in the world. They are ready to be servants to all men for their good, becoming all things to all men in order to win them to Christ. Yet they abstain from the appearance of evil, and season all their actions with a sweet mixture of prudence, humility, zeal, and heavenly-mindedness.

O what an honour are such to their professions! What an ornament to the church! and how serviceable to God and man! Many would sooner believe that the gospel is from heaven, if they saw more such effects of it upon the hearts and lives of those who profess it.

Richard Baxter (1615–91)

19th April

I tell you the truth, unless a grain of wheat falls to the ground and dies, it remains only a single seed. But if it does, it produces many seeds.

(John 12:24)

Our all merciful and beneficent Father has . . . compassion towards them that fear Him, and kindly and lovingly bestows His graces upon all such as come to Him with a simple mind. Wherefore let us not waver, neither let us have any doubts in our hearts of His excellent and glorious gifts. Let that be far from us which is written,

"Miserable are the double-minded, and those who are doubtful in their hearts, who say, 'These things have we heard, and our fathers have told us these things. But behold, we are grown old, and none of them has happened unto us.' O ye fools! consider the trees, take the vine for an example: first it sheds its leaves, and then it buds; after that it spreads leaves, then it flowers; and then come the sour grapes, and after them follows the ripe fruit." Ye see how in a little time the fruit of the trees comes to maturity. Of a truth, yet a little while, and His will shall suddenly be accomplished. The Holy Scripture itself bearing witness, "that He shall quickly come and not tarry, and that the Lord shall suddenly come to His temple, even the Holy One whom ye look for."

Let us consider, beloved, how the Lord does continually show us, that there shall be a future resurrection, of which He has made our Lord Jesus Christ the first fruits, raising Him from the dead. Let us contemplate, beloved, the resurrection, that is continually made before our eyes. Day and night manifest a resurrection to us. The night lies down and the day arises; again the day departs, and the night comes on. Let us behold the fruits of the earth: everyone sees how the seed is sown: the sower goes forth, and casts it upon the earth, and the seed which, when it was sown fell upon the earth dry and naked, in time dissolves; and, from the dissolution the great power of the providence of the Lord raises it again and of one seed many arise, and bring forth fruit.

Having therefore this hope, let us hold fast to Him who is faithful in all His promises, and righteous in all His judgements, who has commanded us not to lie: how much more will He not Himself lie? For nothing is impossible with God but to lie. Let His faith then be stirred up again in us; and let us consider that all things are nigh unto Him.

Clement of Rome (fl. c. 90–100)

20th April

What you heard from me, keep as the pattern of sound teaching, with faith and love in Christ Jesus. Guard the good deposit that was entrusted to you – guard it with the help of the Holy Spirit who lives in us.

(2 Timothy 1:13–14)

The real preparation of the preacher's personality for its transmissive work comes by the opening of his life on both sides, towards the truth of God and towards the needs of man. To apprehend in all their intensity the wants and woes of men, to see the problems and dangers of this life, then to know all through us that nothing but Christ and His Redemption can satisfy these wants, that is what makes a man a preacher.

Alas for him who is only open on the man-ward side, who only knows how miserable and wicked man is, but has no power of God to bring to him! He lays a kind but helpless hand upon the wound. He tries to relieve it with his sympathy and his philosophy. He is the source of all he says. There is no God behind him. He is no preacher. The preacher's instinct is that which feels instantly how Christ and human need belong together, neither thinks Christ too far off for the need, nor the need too insignificant for Christ.

Never be afraid to bring the transcendent mysteries of our faith, Christ's life and death and resurrection, to the help of the humblest and commonest of human wants. There is a sort of preaching which keeps them for the great emergencies, and soothes the common sorrow and rebukes the common sins with lower considerations of economy. Such preaching fails. It neither appeals to the lower nor to the higher perceptions of mankind. Never fear as you preach, to bring the sublimest motive to the smallest duty, and the most infinite comfort to the smallest trouble. They will prove that they belong there if only the duty and trouble are real and you have read them thoroughly aright.

Phillips Brooks (1835–93)

21st April

So when the Midianite merchants came by, his brothers pulled Joseph up out of the cistern and sold him for twenty shekels of silver to the Ishmaelites, who took him to Egypt.

(Genesis 37:28)

The good work that the pit in Dothan began in Joseph, these still more terrible days and nights on the way to Egypt carried on. Lashed to the loaded side of a huge cane-wagon, and himself loaded with the baggage of Gilead for the Egyptian market, Joseph toiled under the mid-day sun, thankful to be left alone of his churlish masters in the red-hot air. Put yourself in Joseph's place. The fondling of his father; a child on whom no wind was ever to blow, and no sun was ever let strike; with servants to wait on his every wish, and to dress and anoint him for every meal; with loving looks and fond words falling continually upon him from the day he was born; and now, lashed to the side of a slave caravan, and with the whistling whip of his Ishmaelite owner laid on his shoulder till he sank into the sand.

But you must add this to the picture, else you will not have the picture complete: "The Lord was with Joseph, and Joseph found grace in the sight of the Lord." Yes, the Lord was more with Joseph, more and better far, than ever He had been as long as Joseph was the spoiled child of his father, and the continual snare of his brothers.

And there are young men in this city suffering hardships and persecutions in workshops and in offices as sore to bear as was Joseph's load of labour and ill-usage of the Ishmaelites. And the Lord is with them also as He never was so long as they were spoilt sons at home, getting all things their own way. And as they silently and prayerfully take up their cross daily, and wait out the will of God, they are thereby putting off a past that would have been their own sure destruction – and had almost been – and are preparing themselves for a future as sure, and as full of the providence of God, as ever was Joseph's future.

Alexander Whyte (1836–1921)

22nd April

Though I am free and belong to no man, I make myself a slave to everyone, to win as many as possible. To the Jews I become like a Jew, to win the Jews. To those under the law I become like one under the law (though I myself am not under the law), so as to win those under the law. To those not having the law I become like one not having the law (though I am not free from God's law but am under Christ's law), so as to win those not having the law. To the weak I become weak, to win the weak. I have become all things to all men so that by all possible means I might save some.

(1 Corinthians 9:19–22)

A few months previously the Rev. William Burns, of the English Presbyterian Mission, arrived in that port [Shanghai] on his journey home ... he made his headquarters in Shanghai for a season, devoting himself to the evangelism of the surrounding populous regions. Thus in the autumn of the year I was providentially led into association with this beloved and honoured servant of God.

We journeyed together, evangelising cities and towns in Southern Kiangsu and North Chekiang, living in our boats, and following the course of the canals and the rivers which here spread like a network over the whole of the rich and fertile country. Mr Burns was at that time wearing English dress; but saw that while I was young and in every way less experienced, I had the quiet hearers, while he was followed by the rude boys, and by the curious but careless; that I was invited to the homes of the people, while he received an apology that the crowd would follow precluded his being invited. After some weeks observation he also adopted the native dress, and enjoyed the increased facilities which it gave.

Those happy months were an unspeakable joy and privilege to me. His love for the Word was delightful, and his holy, reverential life and constant communings with God made fellowship with him satisfying to the deep cravings of my heart. His accounts of revival work and of persecutions in Canada, and Dublin, and in South China were most instructive, as well as interesting; for with true spiritual insight he often pointed out God's purpose in trial in a way that made all life assume quite a new aspect and value. His views, especially that about evangelism as the great work of the Church, and the order of lay evangelists as a lost order that Scripture required to be restored, were seed-thoughts which were to prove fruitful in the subsequent organisation of the China Inland Mission.

James Hudson Taylor (1832–1905)

23rd April

Until I come, devote yourself to the public reading of Scripture, to preaching and to teaching.

(1 Timothy 4:13)

A man is not invited into a pulpit just to say how things strike him at his angle, any more than he is expected to lay bear to the public the private recesses of his soul. Nor is it the preacher's first duty to be up-to-date, to be in the van of tentative thought. He can do his work well without the newest machinery. The professor should know the last thing written, but the preacher need not. If he is young, and has not been well trained in his subject perhaps not.

He is there to declare the eternal, which is always in the van, equally present, equally real for every soul, everlasting, final, insuperable for every age. He is not in the pulpit primarily, as the place where he can get most scope for his own individuality, and most freedom for his own idiosyncrasy. He is there, as the servant both of the Word and the Church, to do a certain work, to declare a certain message, to discharge a certain trust. He is not in the pulpit as the roomiest place he has found to enable him to be himself, and develop his genius. Some young preachers are more concerned about their own freedom than their people's service. They are prone to think they must get freedom to develop their individuality before they have any positive idea what they are to do. You cannot develop your individuality except obliviously, in the doing of some definite objective thing. Without that you are taking yourself too seriously . . .

You must grow in the doing of some definite thing; to learn which thing and the handling of it your individuality ought to go to a very severe school. Your duty is not to be yourself. "To thyself be true" is not a Christian precept. It is automatic for the Christian man, whose one concern is to be true to Christ.

P. T. Forsyth (1848–1921)

24th April

I know your deeds, that you are neither cold nor hot. I wish you were either one or the other

(Revelation 3:15)

To be hot ensures opposition – 1st, From Pharisees. They look with contempt on hot people, call them fanatics, extreme people, troublers of Israel, disturbers of the peace of the Church, occasions of reproach to the respectable and reasonable part of the Church.

The Pharisees were the bitterest enemies of Him who said, "The zeal of thine house hath eaten Me up." And they are still the bitterest enemies of those who are filled with His Spirit. It matters not that they have now a Christian creed instead of Jewish; the spirit is the same, and will not tolerate "God manifest in the flesh". A formal, ceremonious, respectable religion they do not object to; but a living, burning, enthusiastic Christianity is still Beelzebub! to them.

2nd, To be hot ensures opposition from the world. The world hates hot saints, because they look with contempt on its pleasures, set at naught its maxims and customs, trample on its ambition and applause, ignore its rewards, abjure its spirit, and live altogether above its level. "Because ye are not of the world, therefore the world hateth you." It can tolerate warm religionists – rational, decent people, who appreciate this world as well as the next, and can see how to make the best of it; but these "hot", "pestilent", "mad", "fools", who intrude their religion everywhere, who are always at everybody about their souls, who are always talking about God, death, judgement, heaven, and hell – "Away with them! they are not fit to live."

3rd. To be hot ensures opposition from the devil. Oh, how he hates these hot saints! What trouble he takes to trip them. He knows they are worth it. Many a council is held in hell over these. They set fire to his standing corn. They rout his best trained legions. They shake the foundations of his throne. They take the prey out of his jaws; they pull it out of his fires. He *must* do something! He sets his principalities and powers to work on *them* . . . Hallelujah! our arch enemy is a conquered foe.

Let me remind you, in conclusion, that to be hot ensures God's special favour, protection and fellowship and our final victory. "Be thou *faithful* unto death, and I will give thee a crown of life." Whereas to be lukewarm is to be spued out of His mouth, which indicates special dislikes, disgrace and final abandonment.

WHICH WILL YOU BE, HOT OR LUKEWARM?

Catherine Booth (1829–90)

25th April

So then, just as you received Christ Jesus as Lord, continue to live in him, rooted and built up in him, strengthened in the faith as you were taught, and overflowing with thankfulness

(Colossians 2:6–7)

I was thinking this morning, amidst all my business, my many engagements, my numerous cares, and little time I have for reflection and quiet; what I should do if my dependence was not placed upon the Eternal word of life which is with me in every place. I could not but feel this an invaluable gift; the Scriptures that testify of it are truly valuable, but though proceeding from it, they are not it. I think it a blessing to feel the operative power of this word of life, and through abundant mercy, it leads me at seasons, sometimes at very low seasons, to feel it my meat and drink to do the will of my Heavenly Father . . .

Entering my public life again is very serious to me, more particularly my readings at Newgate [Prison]. They are to my feelings too much like making a show of a good thing, yet we have been so often favoured in them to the tendering of many hearts, that I believe I must not be hasty in putting an end to them or hindering people coming to them; and it is the desire and prayer of my heart, that way might rightly open about them; and that when engaged in them, I might do heartily unto the Lord and not unto man; and look not either to the good or evil opinions of men.

The prudent fears that the good have for me, try me more than most things, and I find that it calls for Christian forbearance, not to be put out by them. I am confident that we often see a Martha-like spirit about spiritual things. I know by myself what it is to be overbusy. O Lord! enable us to keep our ranks in righteousness, and pardon the iniquity of even holy things, of our omissions and commissions; and be pleased to enable Thy unworthy child and servant, to cleave very close to Thee in spirit; and if it should please Thee, that she should again be brought forth even as a spectacle among the people, Oh! be pleased to keep her from ever hurting or bringing discredit upon Thy ever blessed cause; but enable her to do justly, love mercy and walk humbly before Thee; and so to abide in the light and life of Christ her Saviour and Redeemer, that many may be led to glorify Thee, her Father who art in heaven. Amen, and Amen.

Elizabeth Fry (1780–1845)

26th April

Jesus answered, "It is written: 'Man does not live on bread alone, but on every word that comes from the mouth of God.'"
(Matthew 4:4)

People take up God's book, read a few pages, and condemn the whole of it. Of all the sceptics and infidels I have ever met speaking against the Bible, I have never met one who read it through. There may be such men, but I have never met them. It is simply an excuse. There is no man living who will stand up before God and say that kept him out of the kingdom. It is the devil's work trying to make us believe it is not true, and that it is dark and mysterious. The only way to overcome the great enemy of souls is by the written Word of God. He knows that, and so tries to make men disbelieve it. As soon as a man is a true believer in the Word of God, he is a conqueror over Satan.

Young man! the Bible is true. What have these infidels to give you in its place? What has made England but the open Bible? Every nation that exalteth the Word of God is exalted, and every nation that casteth it down is cast down. Oh, let us cling close to the Bible.

Of course, we shall not understand it all at once. But men are not to condemn it on that account. Suppose I should send my little boy, five years old, to school tomorrow morning, and when he came home in the afternoon I say to him, "Willie, can you read? can you write? can you spell? Do you understand all about algebra, geometry, Hebrew, Latin and Greek?" "Why, papa," the little fellow would say, "how funny you talk; I have been all day trying to learn the A B C!" Well, suppose I should reply, "If you have not finished your education, you need not go any more." What would you say? Why, you would say, I had gone mad.

There would be just about as much reason in that, as in the way that people talk about the Bible. My friends, the men who have studied the Bible for fifty years – the wise men and the scholars, the great theologians – have never got down to the depths of it yet. There are truths there that the Church of God has been searching out for the last eighteen hundred years, but no man has fathomed the depths of that ever-living stream.

D. L. Moody (1837–99)

27th April

The Scripture cannot be broken

(John 10:35b)

> Upon the Word I rest,
> Each pilgrim day;
> This golden staff is best
> For all the way.
> What Jesus Christ hath spoken,
> Can*not* be broken!
>
> Upon the Word I rest,
> So strong, so sure,

So full of comfort blest,
So sweet, so pure!
The charter of salvation,
Faith's broad foundation.

Upon the Word I stand!
That cannot die!
Christ seals it in my hand,
He cannot lie!
The word that faileth never
Abiding ever!

Chorus.
The Master hath said it! Rejoicing in this,
We ask not for sign or for token;
His word is enough for our confident bliss, –
"The Scripture *cannot* be broken!"

Frances Ridley Havergal (1836–79)

28th April

Some trust in chariots and some in horses, but we trust in the name of the Lord our God.

(Psalm 20:7)

The Bible, God's holy Word, will do its own work, and therefore it is that I urge the Bible Society to put forth its best energies; to relax no effort in carrying on the work they have undertaken. Ay, the Bible will do its work in another way. It will counsel those who take a dark political view of the present times to look to God for protection against the evils which will be coming upon us. The Word of God will prove itself to be the chief defence of nations, the chief assurer of internal peace, the great bulwark against dangers from abroad.

Who can be blind to the fact that there are many who desire the Empire we possess? Who can doubt that there are many who look with hatred upon the civil and religious liberty which we enjoy, and who would band themselves together with infinite satisfaction to curb, suppress, and extinguish the last spark of liberty to be found in this great country? And do you think we are able to cope, single-handed, with all these powers? No, we are not able to do so.

Where, then, shall we look for alliances? Shall we look for merely earthly alliances? I tell you that merely earthly alliances have always been uncertain. They are not only uncertain, but they are feeble and treacherous. If you look for alliances, if you look for strength I tell you not to look there. Our strength lies in that old, effete Book – the Book so full of "old wives' fables" – that Book which they say is so unsuited to the present generation – that Book which they say is not equal to the present intelligence of man.

Ay, that old Book, THAT shall be the source of our safety, and of our greatness. Amid all the conflicts of the nations that are coming upon the earth, that Book shall be our life, our light, our security, our joy, our pillar of cloud by day, our pillar of fire by night, our guide through all our perils; and it will be found in that great day that none but those who are engaged in this work, none but those who have the Bible in their hands and in their hearts, will be able to meet the great conflict, and stand in their lot at the end of days.

Lord Shaftesbury (1801–85)

29th April

In this world you will have trouble. But take heart! I have overcome the world.

(John 16:33b)

I preached in the morning at Newport, on, "What must I do to be saved?" to the most insensible, ill-behaved people I have ever seen in Wales. One ancient man, during a great part of the sermon, cursed and swore almost incessantly; and, towards the conclusion, took up a great stone, which he many times attempted to throw. But that he could not do – Such the champions, such the arms against field-preaching!

At four I preached at the Shire-Hall of Cardiff again, where many gentry, I found, were present. Such freedom of speech I seldom had, as was given me in explaining those words, "The kingdom of God is not meat and drink; but righteousness, and peace, and joy in the Holy Ghost." At six almost the whole town (I was informed) came together, to whom I explained the last six Beatitudes; but my heart was so enlarged, I knew not how to give over, so that we continued three hours. O may the seed they have received, have its fruit unto holiness, and in the end, everlasting life!

Sat. 20th [October 1739] I returned to Bristol. I have seen no part of England so pleasant for sixty of seventy miles together, as those parts of Wales I had been in. And most of the inhabitants are indeed ripe for the Gospel. I mean (if the expression seem strange) they are earnestly desirous of being instructed in it; and as utterly ignorant of it, as any Creek or Cherikee Indians. I do not mean they are ignorant of the name of Christ. Many of them can say both the Lord's Prayer and the Belief. Nay, and some of them the Catechism: But take them out of the road of what they have learned by rote, and they know no more (nine in ten of those with whom I conversed) either of Gospel salvation, or of that faith whereby we alone can be saved, than Chicali or Tomo Chachi . . .

Finding a slackness creeping in among them who had begun to run well, on Sunday, 21st, both in the morning and afternoon, I enforced the words, "As ye have received Christ Jesus the Lord, so walk ye in him." In the evening I endeavoured to quicken them further, by describing pure and undefiled religion: And next day, to encourage them in pursuing it, by enforcing those words of our blessed Master, "In the world, ye shall have tribulation: But be of good cheer; I have overcome the world."

John Wesley (1703–91)

30th April

When Silas and Timothy came from Macedonia, Paul devoted himself exclusively to preaching, testifying to the Jews that Jesus was the Christ.

(Acts 18:5)

If there never had been a single commandment to that effect, I know not how the Christian Church or the Christian individual could have abstained from declaring the great and sweet Name to which it and he owe so much. I do not care to present this matter as a commandment, nor to speak of obligation or responsibility. The *impulse* is what I would fix your attention upon. It is inseparable from the Christian life. It may vary in force, as we see in the incident [of Acts 18] before us. It will vary in grip, according as other circumstances and duties insist upon being attended to. The form in which it is yielded to will vary indefinitely in individuals. But if they are Christian people it is always there.

Well, then, what about the masses of so-called Christians that know nothing of any such constraining force? And what about the many that know enough of it to make them feel they are wrong in not yielding to it, but not enough to make their conduct be influenced by it? Brethren, I venture to believe that the measure in which this impulse to speak the word, and use direct effects for somebody's conversion, is felt by Christians, is a very fair test of the depth of their own religion. If a vessel is half empty it will not run over. If it is full to the brim, the sparkling treasure will fall on all sides. A weak plant may never push its green leaves above the ground, but a strong one will come into the light. A spark may be smothered in a heap of brushwood, but a steady flame will burn its way out. If this word has not a grip of you, impelling you to its utterance, I would have you not to be sure that you have a grip on it.

Alexander Maclaren (1826–1910)

May

1st May

And we pray this in order that you may live a life worthy of the Lord and may please him in every way: bearing fruit in every good work, growing in the knowledge of God, being strengthened with all power according to his glorious might so that you may have great endurance and patience.

(Colossians 1:10–11)

The spirit of Christian long-suffering and of meekness in bearing injuries, is a mark of true greatness of soul. It shews a true and noble nature, and real greatness of spirit, thus to maintain the calmness of mind in the midst of injuries and evils. It is an evidence of excellence of temper, and of inward fortitude and strength. "He that is slow to anger", says Solomon (Proverbs 16:32), "is better than the mighty: and he that ruleth his spirit than he that taketh a city"; that is he shews a more noble and excellent nature, and more true greatness of spirit, than the greatest conquerors of the earth. It is from littleness of mind that the soul is easily disturbed and put out by the reproaches and ill-treatment of men; just as little streams of water are much disturbed by the small unevennesses and obstacles they meet with in their course, and make a great deal of noise as they pass over them, whereas great and mighty streams pass over the same obstacles calmly and quietly, without a ripple on the surface to shew that they are disturbed.

He that possesses his soul after such a manner that, when others harm and injure him, he can, notwithstanding, remain in calmness and hearty good-will towards them, pitying them and forgiving them from the heart, manifests therein a godlike greatness of spirit.

Jonathan Edwards (1703–58)

2nd May

Blessed are the peacemakers, for they will be called sons of God.
(Matthew 5:9)

This blessedness, beloved, belongs not to any and every kind of agreement and harmony, but to that of which the Apostle speaks: "have peace towards God"; and of which the Prophet David speaks: "Much peace have they that love Thy law, and they have no cause of offence." This peace even the closest ties of friendship and the exact likeness of mind do not really gain, if they do not agree with God's will. Similarity of bad desires, leagues in crimes, associations of vice, cannot merit this peace. The love of the world does not consort with the love of God, nor doth he enter the alliance of the sons of God who will not separate himself from the children of this generation.

Whereas they who are in mind always with God, "giving diligence to keep the unity of the Spirit in the bond of peace", never dissent from the eternal law, uttering that prayer of faith, "Thy will be done as in heaven, so on earth." These are "the peacemakers", these are thoroughly of one mind, and fully harmonious, and are called sons of "of God and joint-heirs with Christ", because this shall be the record of the love of God and the love of our neighbour, that we shall suffer no calamities, be in fear of no offence, but all the strife of trial ended, rest in God's most perfect peace, through our Lord, Who with the Father and the Holy Spirit, liveth and reigneth for ever and ever. Amen.

Leo the Great (c. 400–461)

3rd May

Be self-controlled and alert. Your enemy the devil prowls around like a roaring lion looking for someone to devour.

(1 Peter 5:8)

To feel jealousy of what you regard as good, and to envy those who are better than yourself, to some, dearest brethren, seems a light and minute offence. When it is thought light and minute, it is unfeared; and when unfeared it is held in contempt. When held in contempt, it is with difficulty escaped from. It then becomes a dark and covert destruction, which, from not being perceived and thereby provision made against it, works latent affliction upon incautious minds. Further, the Lord has commanded us to exercise prudence, and has instructed us to watch with thoughtful anxiety, against an Adversary, who is ever watchful, and ever on the alert to ensnare. After having stolen entrance into the breast, out of sparks he kindles flame, from little things building up the greatest. While flattering the inert and incautious with gentler air and softer breeze, he lifts storms and whirlwinds up. All this is to compass the downfall of faith and shipwreck of our life.

For this cause, dearest brethren, we must be keeping sentry, and toil with all our might, that against a raging enemy, who is directing his darts against all parts of our body wherein we can be stricken and wounded, we may with anxious and abundant vigilance carry on the fight ... He goeth about each of us; and, as an enemy that makes seige upon men who are shut within, he spies the walls, and tries whether there maybe some part of our members less steadfast and less sure, by access of which he may gain entrance to the inner places.

To your eyes, he offers luring images and easy pleasures, that by sight he may destroy chastity. He tries the ears with melodious music, that by listening to sweetest sounds, he may relax and enervate our Christian vigour. The tongue he provokes by revilings, the hand by provocation of injuries he stirs up to the wantonness of murder. To make a man dishonest, he sets unjust sins before him; that money may make the soul its captive, he loads up the heap of pernicious gatherings. He promises earthly honours, that he may take away the heaven and holds out the show of false things, that may steal the real.

Cyprian (c. 201/210–258)

4th May

Brothers, if someone is caught in a sin, you who are spiritual should restore him gently. But watch yourself, or you also may be tempted.
(Galatians 6:1)

Another class who demand our special help, are declining Christians, that are either fallen into some scandalous sin, or else they abate their zeal and diligence, and show that they have lost their former love! As the case of backsliders is very sad, so our diligence must be very great for their recovery. It is sad to them to lose so much of their life, and peace, and serviceableness to God; and to become so serviceable to Satan and his cause!

It is sad to us to see that all our labour is come to this, and that, when we have taken such pains with them, and have had so much hopes of them, all should be so far frustrated! It is saddest of all, that God should be so dishonoured by those whom he hath so loved, and for whom he hath done so much, and that Christ should be so wounded in the house of his friends. Besides, partial backsliding hath a natural tendency to total apostasy, and would effect it, if special grace did not prevent it.

Now the more melancholy the case of such Christians is, the more must we exert ourselves for their recovery. We must "restore those that are overtaken in a fault, in the spirit of meekness," and yet see that the sore be thoroughly searched and healed, and the joint be well set again, whatever pain it may cost. We must look especially to the honour of the gospel, and see that they give . . . evidence of repentance.

Richard Baxter (1615–91)

5th May

What I mean is this: One of you says, "I follow Paul"; another, "I follow Apollos"; another, "I follow Cephas"; still another, "I follow Christ."

(1 Corinthians 1:12)

Take the epistle of the blessed Paul the apostle into your hands. What was it that he wrote to you [in Corinth] at first preaching of the gospel among you? Verily he did by the Spirit admonish you concerning himself, and Cephas, and Apollos, because that even then ye had begun to fall into partitions and factions among yourselves. Nevertheless your partiality then led you into much less sin, forasmuch as ye placed your affections upon apostles, men of eminent reputation in the church; and upon another who was greatly tried and approved of by them. But consider, we pray you, who were they that have now led you astray, and lessened the reputation of that brotherly love that was so eminent among you? It is a shame, my beloved, yea a very great shame, and unworthy of your Christian profession, to hear that the most firm and ancient church of the Corinthians should, by one or two persons, be led into a sedition against its priests. And this report is come not only to us, but to those also that differ from us; insomuch that the name of the Lord is blasphemed through your folly, and even ye yourselves are brought into danger by it.

Let us therefore with all haste, put an end to this sedition; and let us fall down before the Lord, and beseech Him with tears that He would be favourably reconciled to us, and restore us again to a seemly and holy course of brotherly love. For this is the gate of righteousness, opening unto life: as it is written, "Open unto me the gates of righteousness; I will go in into them, and will praise the Lord. This is the gate of the Lord; the righteous shall enter into it." Although therefore many gates are opened yet this gate of righteousness is that gate in Christ at which blessed are all they that enter in, and direct their way in holiness and righteousness, doing all things without disorder. Let a man be faithful; let him be powerful in the utterance of knowledge; let him be wise in making an exact judgement of words; let him be pure in all his actions; but still by how much the more he seems to be above others by reason of these things, by so much the more will it behove him to be humble-minded, and to seek what is profitable to all men and not his own advantage.

Clement of Rome (fl. c. 90–100)

6th May

Meanwhile a Jew named Apollos, a native of Alexandria, came to Ephesus. He was a learned man, with a thorough knowledge of the Scriptures . . . He began to speak boldly in the synagogue. When Priscilla and Aquila heard him, they invited him to their home and explained to him the way of God more adequately.

(Acts 18:24, 26)

I admire all three so much, that I really do not know which to admire the most; Aquila and Priscilla in their quite extraordinary wisdom and tact and courage, and especially love; or Apollos in his still more extraordinary humility, modesty, and mind of Christ. A shining student of Alexandria, a popular and successful preacher, not standing-room when he preached in the synagogue, followed about by admiring crowds, and with many seals to his ministry among them; such a famous man to take to task about his pulpit work by two old workers in sail-cloth and carpets, and to be instructed by them how to preach, and how not to preach – "the whole thing is laughable, if it were not for its impudence." So would I have said had I been in Apollos's place. But like the true Alexandrian he was, and the true preacher, and the true coming colleague and successor of Paul, Apollos instantly saw who and what he had in Aquila and Priscilla. In a moment he felt they were by far his superiors in the things of the pulpit at any rate, and he at once made it both easy and successful for them to say to him all that was in their minds and hearts. I would far rather have Apollos's humble mind and quiet heart at that supreme moment of his life than all his gold medals, first-class certificates, and all his crowds to boot; the noble young

Christian gentleman that Apollos at that moment proved himself to be.

Alexander Whyte (1836–1921)

7th May

Greet Priscilla and Aquila, my fellow-workers in Christ Jesus.
(Romans 16:3)

[Continued from yesterday.]

It was their own experience of the way of God that enabled and authorised Aquila and Priscilla to take Apollos and teach him that way more perfectly. It was not Paul's preaching that did it. Their own experience, in their case, went before Paul's preaching, accompanied it, and came after it . . . Every true preacher comes on the same thing continually among his own people. And every wide reader of such literature knows where to find illustrations of the same thing. Brother Lawrence, the humble cook, instructing the theologians of his day about the practice of the presence of God . . . But the classical passage is in [John Bunyan's] Grace Abounding . . . "Upon a day the good providence of God did cast me to Bedford to work on my calling. And in one of the streets of that town I came where there were two or three poor women sitting in the sun, and talking about the things of God . . . they were to me as if they had found a new world . . . I found two things within me at which I did sometime marvel; the one was a very great softness and tenderness of heart; and the other was a great bending of my mind to a continual meditating on them, and on all the other good things which at any time I had read and heard of." All that might have been found in the best Alexandrian Greek among Apollos's papers after his death. Better Greek he could not have written, nor a better description of his experiences as he came and went to Aquila's and Priscilla's house in Ephesus. "By these things", adds Bunyan, "my mind was now so turned that it lay like a horse-leech at the vein, still crying out, give, give."

They complain that there threatens to be a dearth of candidates for the Christian ministry. But that can never be. For where can the flower of our youth find a field for their scholarship and their eloquence like the evangelical pulpit? What other calling open to a talented young man can compete with spiritual preaching? What other occupation can possess a pure mind and noble heart, and that more and more, to the end of life? Where will our intellectual youth find a literature for one moment to compare with the literature of Jerusalem and Alexandria? And a sphere of work like a congregation full of such people as Aquila and Priscilla? How long halt the flower of Scottish youth between two opinions? If the Lord be God, follow Him.

Alexander Whyte (1836–1921)

8th May

Carry each other's burdens, and in this way you will fulfil the law of Christ.

(Galatians 6:2)

They [young converts] should be watched over by the Church, and warned of their dangers, just as a mother watches over her young children. Young converts do not know at all the dangers by which they are surrounded. The devices of the devil, the temptations of the world, the power of their own passions and habits, and the thousand forms of danger, they do not know; and if not properly watched and warned, they will run right into such dangers. The Church should watch over and care for her young children – just as mothers watch their little children in this great city, lest carts run over them, or they stray away; or as they watch over them while they are growing up, for fear they may be drawn into the whirlpools of iniquity. The Church should watch over all the interests of her young members, know where they are, and what are their habits, temptations, dangers, privileges – the state of religion in their hearts, and their spirit of prayer.

Look at that anxious mother when she sees paleness gather round the brow of her little child. "What is the matter with you, my child? Have you eaten something improper? Have you taken cold?

What ails you?" Oh, how different it is with the children of the Church, the lambs that the Saviour has committed to the care of His Church! Alas! instead of restraining her children, and taking care of them, the Church lets them go anywhere and look out for themselves. What should we say of a mother who should knowingly let her children totter along the edge of a precipice? Should we not say she was horribly guilty for doing so, and if that child should fall and be killed, its blood would rest on the mother's head?

What, then, is the guilt of the Church, in knowingly neglecting her young converts? I have known Churches where young converts were totally neglected, and regarded with suspicion and jealousy; nobody went near them to strengthen or encourage them or counsel them; nothing was done to lead them to usefulness, or to teach them what to do or how to do it, to open to them a field of labour. And then – what then? Why, when they find that young converts cannot stand everything, when they find them growing cold and backward at such treatment, they just turn round and abuse them, for not holding out!

Charles G. Finney (1792–1875)

9th May

On one occasion, while he was eating with them, he gave them this command: "Do not leave Jerusalem, but wait for the gift my Father promised, which you have heard me speak about. For John baptised with water, but in a few days you will be baptised with the Holy Spirit."

(Acts 1:4–5)

Just as when soldiers are to charge a multitude, no one thinks of letting them issue forth until they have armed themselves, or as horses are not suffered to start from the barriers until they have got their charioteer; so Christ did not suffer these to appear in the fields before the descent of the Spirit, that they might not be in a condition to be easily defeated and taken captive by the many. Nor was this the only reason, but also there were many in Jerusalem who should believe. And then again that it might not be said, that leaving their own acquaintance, they had gone to make a parade among strangers, therefore among those very men who had put Christ to death do they exhibit the proofs of His Resurrection, among those who had crucified and buried him, in the very town in which the iniquitous deed had been perpetrated; there by stopping the mouths of all foreign objectors.

For when those even who had crucified Him appear as believers, clearly this proved both the fact of the crucifixion and the iniquity of the deed, and afforded a mighty evidence of the Resurrection. Furthermore, lest the Apostles should say, How shall it be possible for us to live among wicked and bloody men, they so many in number, we so few and contemptible, observe how he does away their fear and distress, by these words, "But wait for the promise of the Father, which ye have heard of Me."

You will say, When had they heard this? When He said, "It is expedient for you that I go away; for if I go not away, the Comforter will not come unto you." And again, "I will pray the Father and He shall send you another Comforter, that He may abide with you."

John Chrysostom (c. 344/345–407)

10th May

"But you will receive power when the Holy Spirit comes on you; and you will be my witnesses in Jerusalem, and in all Judea and Samaria, and to the ends of the earth." After he said this, he was taken up before their very eyes, and a cloud hid him from their sight.

(Acts 1:8–9)

But why had the Holy Ghost not yet come? It was fit that they should first be taught to have a longing desire for that event, and so receive the grace. For this reason Christ himself departed, and then the Spirit descended. For had He Himself been there, they would not have expected the Spirit so earnestly as they did. On this account neither did He come immediately after Christ's Ascension, but after eight or nine days. It is the same with us also: for our desires towards God are then mose raised, when we stand in need. Accordingly, John chose that time to send his disciples to Christ when they were likely to feel their need of Jesus, during his own imprisonment. Besides, it was fit that our nature should be seen in heaven, and that the reconciliation should be perfected, and then the Spirit should come, and the joy should be unalloyed. For, if the Spirit being already come, Christ had then departed, and the Spirit remained; the consolation would not have been so great as it was. For in fact they clung to Him, and could not bear to part with Him; wherefore also to comfort them He said, "It is expedient for you that I go away." On this account He also waits during those intermediate days, so they might first despond for a while, and be made, as I said, to feel their need of Him, and then reap a full and unalloyed delight.

John Chrysostom (c. 344/345–407)

11th May

When they came back from the tomb, they told all these things to the Eleven and to all the others. It was Mary Magdalene, Joanna, Mary the mother of James, and the others with them who told this to the apostles. But they did not believe the women, because their words seemed to them like nonsense.

(Luke 24:9–11)

Since the blessed and glorious Resurrection of our Lord Jesus Christ, whereby the Divine power in three days raised the true Temple of God, which the wickedness of the Jews had overthrown, the sacred forty days, dearly beloved, are today ended. By most holy appointment they were devoted to our most profitable instruction, so that, during the period that the Lord was still bodily present, our faith in the Resurrection might be fortified by needful proofs.

Christ's death had much disturbed the disciples' hearts, and a kind of torpor of distrust had crept over their grief-laden minds at His torture on the cross, at his giving up the ghost, at His lifeless body's burial. When the holy women, as the Gospel story has revealed, brought word of the stone rolled away from the tomb, the sepulchre emptied of the body, and the angels bearing witness to the living Lord, their words seemed like ravings to the Apostles and other disciples.

That doubtfulness, the result of human weakness, the Spirit of Truth would most assuredly not have permitted to exist in His own preachers' breasts, had not their trembling anxiety and careful hesitation laid the foundations of our faith. It was our perplexities and our dangers that were provided for in the Apostles! It was ourselves who in these men were taught how to meet the mockings of the ungodly and the arguments of earthly wisdom. *We* are instructed by their lookings, *we* are taught by their hearings, *we* are convinced by their handlings.

Let us give thanks to the Divine management and the holy Fathers' necessary slowness of belief. Others doubted, that we might not doubt.

Leo the Great (c. 400–461)

12th May

While he was blessing them, he left them and was taken up into heaven. Then they worshipped him and returned to Jerusalem with great joy.

(Luke 24:51–52)

Dearly-beloved, throughout this time which elapsed between the Lord's Resurrection and Ascension, God's Providence had this in view, to teach and impress upon both the eyes and hearts of His own people that the Lord Jesus Christ might be acknowledged to have as truly risen, as He was truly born, suffered and died. And hence the most blessed Apostles and all the disciples, who had been bewildered at His death on the cross and backward in believing His Resurrection, were so strengthened by the clearness of the truth that when the Lord entered the heights of heaven, not only were they affected with no sadness, but were even filled with joy.

And truly great and unspeakable was their cause for joy, when in the sight of the holy multitude, above the dignity of all heavenly creatures, the Nature of mankind went up, to pass beyond the angels' ranks and to rise beyond the archangels' heights ... received to sit with the Eternal Father, to Whose Nature it was united in the Son.

Since then Christ's ascension is our uplifting, and the hope of the Body is raised, whither the glory of the Head has gone before, let us exult, dearly-beloved, with worthy joy and delight in the loyal paying of thanks. For today [Ascension Day] not only are we confirmed as possessors of paradise, but have also in Christ penetrated the heights of heaven, and have gained still greater things than we lost through the devil's malice. For us, whom our virulent enemy had driven out from our blest abode, the Son of God has made members of Himself and placed at the right hand of the Father, with Whom He lives and reigns in the unity of the Holy Spirit, God for ever and ever. Amen.

Leo the Great (c. 400–461)

13th May

... he raised him from the dead and seated him at his right hand in the heavenly realms.

(Ephesians 1:20)

Our time is the time of his present and his future, his lordship. It stands under the sign of the *change* which has happened in his death and resurrection, in expectancy of his perfect future revelation. It is the *end time*, the time hurrying from this hither to this thither ...

The expression "sitting at the right hand of God", properly understood, clearly sets forth two fundamental principles of the Christian ethic:

1. Whoever understands this phrase correctly must understand this: what is Christian takes unqualified *precedence* over everything else. Man is of course never only a Christian. He has also his body, his ears, his nose. He is a whole little cosmos. But everything else that he is, is subordinated to this one thing, that he is first of all a

Christian. This sequence is not reversible. So, for instance, one can never be a politician and also in the second place a Christian. Christianity cannot be co-ordinated. It takes absolute precedence – because Christ sits at the right hand of the Father.

2. But from a correct understanding of this "sitting at the right hand of God" there also follows the absolute necessity of *the relatedness of the Christian to the world*, the relatedness of the Christian to everything human. It is not so that as a Christian one may or may not be interested in what is human, perhaps have open eyes for what is beautiful and great and pleasant in the world and perhaps not. Relatedness of the Christian to the world is not optional. He cannot set himself against the world with the somewhat shabby mistrust in which as a Christian he thinks he knows everything better, or perhaps even with hostility. This is impossible because through his church and as its Head, Christ rules over *all*. We would be guilty of breaking up the lordship of Christ if we did not live in the world with open eyes and open hearts and did not live in all seriousness to be Greeks to the Greeks [1 Corinthians 9:21]. After all, Christians are also creatures, and therefore they cannot evade the problems of the realm of creation. This realm is subject to Christ, and we also are at home in it.

Karl Barth (1886–1968)

14th May

Therefore, since we have a great high priest who has gone through the heavens, Jesus the Son of God, let us hold firmly to the faith we profess. For we do not have a high priest who is unable to sympathise with our weaknesses, but we have one who has been tempted in every way, just as we are – yet without sin.

(Hebrews 4:14–15)

The High Priest bore the names of the twelve tribes upon his heart, each name being engraved as a seal in the costly and imperishable stone chosen by God, each seal or stone being set in the purest gold; he likewise bore the same names upon his shoulders, indicating that both the love and the strength of the High Priest were pledged on behalf of the tribes of Israel. The bride [the Church] would thus be upborne by Him who is alike her Prophet, Priest, and King, for love is strong as death; and jealousy, or ardent love, retentive as the grave. Not that she doubts the constancy of her Beloved, but that she has learned, alas! the inconstancy of her own heart; and she would be bound to the heart and arm of her Beloved as with chains and settings of gold, ever the emblem of divinity. Thus the Psalmist prayed, "Bind the sacrifice with cords, *even* unto the horns of the altar."

It is comparatively easy to lay the sacrifice on the altar that sanctifies the gift, but it requires divine compulsion – the cords of love – to retain it there. So here the bride would be set and fixed on the heart and on the arm of Him who is henceforth to be her all in all, that she may evermore trust only in that love, be sustained only by that power.

Do we not all need to learn a lesson from this? and to pray to be kept from turning to Egypt for help, from trusting in horses and chariots, from putting confidence in princes, or in the son of man rather than in the living God? How the Kings of Israel, who had won great triumphs by faith, sometimes turned aside to heathen nations in their later years! The Lord keep His people from this snare.

James Hudson Taylor (1832–1905)

15th May

Command those who are rich in this present world not to be arrogant nor to put their hope in wealth, which is so uncertain, but to put their hope in God, who richly provides us with everything for our enjoyment. Command them to do good, to be rich in good deeds, and to be generous and willing to share.

(1 Timothy 6:17–18)

Ladies and gentlemen who walk in purple and fine linen, and fare sumptuously every day, can form no adequate idea of the pain and toil, which the founders and conductors of these schools have joyfully sustained in their simple and fervent piety. Surrendering nearly the whole of the Sabbath, their only day of rest, and often, after many hours of toil, giving besides, an evening in the week, they have plunged into the foulest localities, fetid apartments, and harassing duties. We have heard of school-rooms so closely packed that three lads have sat in the fireplace, one on each hob, and the third in the grate with his head up the chimney; and frequent are the occasions on which the female teachers have returned to their homes, covered with the vermin of their tattered pupils. All this they have done, and still do, in the genuine spirit of Christian charity, without the hope of recompense, of money, or of fame – it staggers at first our belief, but nevertheless it is true; and many a Sunday-school teacher, thus poor and zealous, will rise up in judgement with lazy ecclesiastics, boisterous sectarians, and self-seeking statesmen . . .

Here is the subject-matter enough for the sentimental, for spare tears, and wandering sympathies! Those who, amidst the enjoyment of existence, seek the luxury of woe in a poem or a romance may learn the realities of life are more touching than fiction; and the practical alleviation of sorrow, quite as delightful as the happy conclusion of a novel.

Lord Shaftesbury (1801–85)

16th May

To the angel of the church in Laodicea write: These are the words of the Amen, the faithful and true witness, the ruler of God's creation. I know your deeds, that you are neither cold nor hot. I wish you were either one or the other! So, because you are lukewarm – neither hot nor cold – I am about to spit you out of my mouth. You say, "I am rich; I have acquired wealth and do not need a thing." But you do not realise that you are wretched, pitiful, poor, blind and naked. I counsel you to buy from me gold refined in the fire, so that you can become rich; and white clothes to wear, so that you can cover your shameful nakedness; and salve to put on your eyes, so that you can see.

(Revelation 3:14–18)

Methodism (so called), any man of understanding may easily discern . . . is only plain, scriptural religion, guarded by a few prudential regulations. The essence of it is holiness of heart and life.

It nearly concerns us to understand how the case stands with us at present. I fear, wherever riches have increased (exceeding few are the exceptions), the essence of religion, the mind that was in Christ, has decreased in the same proportion. Therefore do I not see how it is possible, in the nature of things, for revival of true religion to continue long. For religion must necessarily produce both industry and frugality; and these cannot but produce riches. But as riches increase so will pride, anger, and love of the world in all its branches.

How, then, is it possible that Methodism, that is, the religion of the heart, though it flourishes now as a green baytree, should continue in this state? For the Methodists in every place grow diligent and frugal; consequently, they increase in goods. Hence they proportionably increase in pride, in anger, in the desire of the flesh, the desire of the eyes, and the pride of life. So, although the form of religion remains, the spirit is swiftly vanishing away.

Is there no way to prevent this? this continual declension of pure religion? We ought not to forbid people to be diligent and frugal: We must exhort all Christians to gain all they can, and to save all they can; that is, in effect, to grow rich! What way, then (I ask again), can we take, that our money may not sink us to the nethermost hell? There is one way, and there is no other under heaven. If those who "gain all they can", and "save all they can", will likewise "give all they can"; then, the more they gain, the more they will grow in grace, and the more treasure they will lay up in heaven.

London, August 4, 1786

John Wesley (1703–91)

17th May

Remember this: Whoever sows sparingly will also reap sparingly, and whoever sows generously will also reap generously. Each man should give as he has decided in his heart to give, not reluctantly or under compulsion, for God loves a cheerful giver.

(2 Corinthians 9:6–7)

These modern Christians refuse to *give their substance* to carry on the war. You see war is impossible without money. I wish it were not so, but I cannot help it. This war is as impossible as any other without money. Men and women must eat to live, however little they manage with. And travelling expenses, rent of buildings, announcements, working expenses, prosecutions, breakdowns through sickness, etc., must be met. This war, I say, must have money, AND THE MORE WAR THE MORE MONEY IS WANTED. How many of these mongrel Christians, when faced with the needs of the war-chest, exclaim, "Money again! always begging."

Now contrast the feelings of these same people when there is any great popular national war on foot. Then, what do they say in their newspapers, in their public meetings? They say to their statesmen: "You must ask for grants; you must stick fast for money. We must win. John Bull must not be beaten for the sake of a few millions!" Ah, ah! their *hearts* are in *this warfare*! The women would sell their ornaments, and the men would hand over their balances, rather than England's freedom or greatness should be sacrificed.

Now then, I say that if the Christians of this London and this England of ours had the true war spirit, the spirit which says, "I want this world for Christ Jesus: I want my King to reign over the hearts of men: He shall win, be it at the cost of money or blood, or all else," – if this spirit possessed them, instead of begruding and reckoning how little they could give, and how much they would save appearances, they would try how far they could deny themselves, and how much they could give. Oh is this not true? Can you contradict it? Then, what am I to think of a band of professed soldiers, who are always grumbling about having to give their money to extend the reign of their king, whom they profess to love more than all else besides!

Catherine Booth (1829–90)

18th May

Large crowds were travelling with Jesus, and turning to them he said: "If anyone comes to me and does not hate his father and mother, his wife and children, his brothers and sisters – yes, even his own life – he cannot be my disciple. And anyone who does not carry his cross and follow me cannot be my disciple."

(Luke 14:25–7)

[Continued from yesterday.]

Further, these modern Christians refuse to give *themselves or their children* to the propogation of the kingdom. They studiously bring their children from three to four years of age to eighteen or twenty, grinding it into them every day of their lives, for six or eight hours a day, how to get on and up in this world; but when Jesus Christ wants one of them – especially if he or she happens to be clever – to do any unpopular, or in the eyes of the world, vulgar work for Him – any work that will bring a cross – they consider it absolutely throwing that child away.

All the ordinary silly, sickly circles of gossip, and croquet, and drawing-room occupations, are considered most respectable and satisfactory in the case of young girls, alongside of any one of them giving herself up to seek and to save the lost. I heard a young lady say of a large circle of Christian friends: "When I was in frivolity and sin they left me alone; I never had a letter, that I remember, from any of them about my soul; but as soon as they found that I had given myself to work among the poor and the lost, then they all woke up to deep concern about my future, and I was flooded with letters from these *Christian friends*!" Oh!, what do you think Jesus Christ would say to such people? Would He not say, as He said of their representatives, the Pharisees, "Well hath Esaias prophesied of you hypocrites, as it is written, This people honoureth Me with their lips, but their heart is far from Me."

Why should that daughter be thought thrown away who comes out and chooses voluntary poverty and humility, and becomes a Salvation Army officer to win poor lost men and women, for whom you say Jesus Christ shed His blood? If they were worth His blood surely, they are worth your daughter's respectability! Then why, because she chooses to sacrifice it, should she be put at a disadvantage compared with her elder or younger sisters, who spend their time in the frivolities of the world? Answer all ye parents, professed followers of the despised Nazarene!

Catherine Booth (1829–90)

19th May

Obey your leaders and submit to their authority. They keep watch over you as men who must give an account. Obey them so that their work will be a joy, not a burden, for that would be of no advantage to you.

(Hebrews 13:17)

Be ready to aid your minister in carrying out his plans for doing good. When the minister is wise to devise plans for usefulness, and the Church is ready to carry them out, they may carry all before them. But when the members hang back from every enterprise until they are actually dragged into it – when they are opposing every proposal, because it will *cost something*, they are a dead weight on the minister.

I was once attending a "protracted meeting", where we were embarrassed because there were no lamps to the building. I urged the people to get them, but they thought the expense would be too much. I then proposed to get them myself, and was about to do it, but found that it would give offence, and we went without. But the blessing did not come to any great extent. How could it? The Church began by calculating to a nicety how much it would cost, and they would not go beyond that exact figure to save souls from hell.

So, where a minister appoints such a meeting, such people object, because it will cost something. If they can offer unto the Lord that which costs nothing, they will do it. Miserable helpers they are! Such a people can have no revival. A minister might as well have a millstone round his neck, as such a Church. He had better leave them, if he cannot teach them better, and go where he will not be so hampered.

Charles G. Finney (1792–1875)

20th May

You shall not steal.

(Exodus 20:15)

How a man gets property – and by property of course I mean whatever he can call his own, whether it be much or little, – is one of the surest tests of what he is. If he gets it by fair means and by fair means only, if he resists every temptation to get it illegitimately, the habits of honesty and the love of it are strengthened, and many of the meaner passions and tendancies are suppressed. Men are under a constant temptation to steal – to get what belongs to others without giving them the return for it which they are led to expect. To break into a house and carry off the plate, to rob a till, to pick a pocket, are very coarse modes of theft. For a clerk to forge a signature to a bill, for a trustee to appropriate and employ for his own purposes the money which has been placed in his keeping, are modes of theft only a little less gross. Whoever gets into his possession what belongs to another man, on false pretences, without giving what he led or permitted that other to expect, is guilty of the same crime, though in a less flagrant form.

If a manufacturer charges you Twenty Pounds for a hundred yards of cloth and sends you only half the quantity, he as really steals Ten Pounds as though he broke open your cash box and took a Ten Pound note. If he engages to send you cloth of a certain quantity and charges you for it, and then sends you cloth which is worth in the market only two-thirds the price, he is just as much a thief as though he stood behind you in a crowd and robbed you of your purse. No one disputes this.

The same principle holds in every business transaction. To give short weight or short measure, is to steal. To supply an article of inferior quality to that which it is understood that the buyer expects, is to steal. To take a Government contract and send to Weedon or Portsmouth articles which you know will be worthless, or which you know are of a worse kind than it was understood that you would furnish, is to steal. To take advantage of your superior knowledge in order to pass off on any man articles for which he would never pay the price that he pays for them but for his confidence in your integrity, is to steal. To start a company and to induce people to take shares in it by false representations of the amount of the subscribed capital and of its probable success, is to steal. But during the last ten or fifteen years so much has been said and written about commercial immorality, that one has become weary of speaking of it.

R. W. Dale (1829–95)

21st May

Therefore let all Israel be assured of this: God has made this Jesus, whom you crucified, both Lord and Christ.

(Acts 2:36)

In order that He might set the human race free from the bonds of deadly transgression, He hid the power of His majesty from the raging devil, and opposed him with our frail and humble nature. For if the cruel and proud foe could have known the counsel of God's mercy, he would have aimed at soothing the Jews' minds into gentleness rather than firing them with unrighteous hatred, lest he lose the thraldom of all his captives in assailing the liberty of One Who owed him nought.

Thus he was foiled by his own malice: he inflicted a punishment on the Son of God, which was turned to the healing of all the sons of men. He shed righteous Blood, which became the ransom and the drink for the world's atonement. The Lord undertook that which He chose according to the purpose of His own will. He permitted mad-men to lay their wicked hands upon Him: hands which, in ministering to their own doom, were of service to the Redeemer's work.

And yet so great was His loving compassion for even His murderers, that He prayed to the Father on the cross and begged not for His own vengeance, but for their forgiveness, saying, "Father, forgive them, for they know not what they do." And such was the power of that prayer, that the hearts of many who had said, "His blood be upon us and on our sons," were turned to penitence by the Apostle Peter's preaching, and on one day there were baptised about 3,000 Jews: and they all were "of one heart and of one soul", being ready now to die for Him, whose crucifixion they had demanded.

Leo the Great (c. 400–461)

22nd May

When the day of Pentecost came, they were all together in one place. Suddenly a sound like the blowing of a violent wind came from heaven and filled the whole house where they were sitting.
(Acts 2:1–2)

Pause then for a moment and think what Whitsunday was, the first Whitsunday. We read the story of the miracle. We hear the rushing of the mighty wind and see the cloven tongues of fire quivering above the heads of the apostles. Perhaps we cannot understand it. It seems natural enough that when Jesus is born the sky should open and the angels sing; that when Jesus dies the skies should darken and the rocks should break. The great events were worthy of those miracles or greater. But here at Pentecost what was there to call out such prodigies? . . . It was the coming back of God into man. It was the promise in these typical men of how near God would be to every man henceforth. It was the manifestation of the God Inspirer as distinct from and yet one with the God Creator and the God Redeemer. It was primarily the entrance of God into man and so, in consequence, the entrance of His spirit and full meaning into every truth that man could know. It was the blossom-day of humanity, full of the promise of unmeasured fruit.

And what that first Whitsunday was to all the world, one certain day becomes to any man, the day when the Holy Spirit comes to him. God enters into him and he sees all things with God's vision. Truths which were dead spring into life and are as real to him as they are to God. He is filled with the Spirit and straightway he believes; not as he used to, coldly holding the outside of things. He has looked right into their hearts. His belief in Jesus is all afire with love. His belief in immortality is eager with anticipation. Can any day in all his life compare with that day? If it were to break forth into flames of fire and tremble with sudden and mysterious wind, would it seem strange to him – the day when he first knew how near God was and how true truth was, and how deep Christ was?

O have we known that day? O, careless, easy, cold believers! if one should come and ask you, "Have you received the Holy Ghost since you believed?" dare you, could you, answer him, "Yes"?

Phillips Brooks (1835–93)

23rd May

They saw what seemed to be tongues of fire that separated and came to rest on each of them. All of them were filled with the Holy Spirit and began to speak in other tongues as the Spirit enabled them.

(Acts 2:3–4)

For ten days the one hundred and twenty loyal souls had been awaiting the gift of spiritual power as the Lord had promised. Each day as it passed witnessed the same absorbed expectancy. "Not many days," the Lord had said, and therefore any day might be the one on which His gift might be poured forth. For the world's sake and for their own they had continued to claim the fulfilment of the promise and to rid themselves of any conceivable obstacle to its reception.

It would appear that on this special day, when, in the temple, the priest presented the first loaves of the new harvest to the Almighty, they had risen from their knees and were sitting in an expectant attitude. Then, suddenly, they saw tongue-like flames distributing themselves, one resting on the head of each, and they were all similarly anointed and filled with the Holy Spirit. The same experience befell them as had befallen their Divine leader when he was baptised. That had been His Pentecost, as this became their Baptism. Each looked at the rest, admiring their halos of fire, not daring to suppose that he or she had been similarly blessed.

From the beginning the Holy Spirit had brooded over the chaos of the elements and the ordering of human society; but, now, for the first time . . . He created the nucleus of the Body of Christ, and laid the foundations of the one holy mystical Church! This was according to Christ's word: "I will build My Church, and the gates of Hades shall not prevail against it."

F. B. Meyer (1847–1929)

24th May

Now there were staying in Jerusalem God-fearing Jews from every nation under heaven. When they heard this sound, a crowd came together in bewilderment, because each one heard them speaking in his own language.

(Acts 2:5–6)

["This is that which was spoken by the prophet Joel."] But we sorrowfully confess today that *"This" is not "That"*. The professing Church as we know it, is far removed from her Pentecostal prototype. *"That"* was united; *"This"* is divided into an infinite number of sects. *"That"* was full of triumphant joy; whilst *"This"* gets choirs and choristers to sing for her. *"That"* made little of material wealth; *"This"* pays court to it. *"That"* was characterised by simplicity of method, as each member said to neighbour and brother, "Know the Lord"; whilst *"This"* substitutes paid agents to perform the work of evangelisation and soul-winning. *"That"* was a commonwealth of mutual helpfulness; in *"This"* class distinctions are permitted and observed. No greater contrast between *"That"* and *"This* could be adduced than between the brief sentences which describe the Church's infancy, when the Lord added to her *daily* those who were being saved, and the endeavour of modern Christian communities to attract audiences by an ornate ritual or popular orations of the topics of the day, or adventitious attractions which savour of the dancing academy or the club.

When at Colombo, I read an extract from a Buddhist paper in which a correspondent cited such things as "the ruses" adopted in a Christian country to induce people to attend church. There are vast numbers of significant exceptions, where the buildings are crowded, and the Gospel is still proved to be the power of God to salvation; but, speaking generally, with the facts of Church decline before us, we are sorrowfully compelled to confess that *"This" is not "That"*.

F. B. Meyer (1847–1929)

25th May

Therefore, since we have a great high priest who has gone through the heavens, Jesus the Son of God, let us hold firmly to the faith we possess.

(Hebrews 4:14)

Immanuel is God with us, God in our nature still. He suffered as a man, and as a man he now reigns on the throne of glory; exercising all power and authority, and receiving all spiritual worship both in heaven and upon earth. He is the head of all principalities and powers, thrones and dominions. Thus man is not only saved, but unspeakably honoured and ennobled. He is brought into the nearest relation to him, who is over all blessed together.

The angels adore him; but only redeemed sinners can say: "He loved us, and gave himself for us; he has washed us from our sins in his own blood" (Galatians 2:20, Revelation 1:5). He is our Saviour, our shepherd, our friend, our "Immanuel, God with us" . . .

What a cold assent is paid to the doctrine of the Godhead of Christ by many who profess and receive it as a truth! They have received from education, from books or ministers, what is called an orthodox scheme of religious sentiments, and with this they are contented. They have not been accustomed to doubt of it, and therefore take for granted that they really believe it. But . . . it is so contrary to our natural apprehensions, that no man can, from his heart, say that "Jesus Christ is Lord," unless he be taught of God. And a cordial belief of this point will and must produce great and abiding effects.

They who know the Saviour's name, will so trust in him, as to renounce every other ground of confidence. They will trust him supremely, and forsake every thing that stands in competition with his favour. They will glory in his cross, they will espouse his cause, and devote themselves to his service. They will make continual application to him, that they may receive out of his fulness, grace according to their need. They will obey his precepts, and walk in his Spirit.

John Newton (1725–1807)

26th May

"Therefore let all Israel be assured of this: God has made this Jesus, whom you crucified, both Lord and Christ." When the people heard this, they were cut to the heart and said to Peter and the other apostles, "Brothers, what shall we do?" Peter replied, "Repent and be baptised, every one of you, in the name of Jesus Christ for the forgiveness of your sins. And you will receive the gift of the Holy Spirit. The promise is for you and your children and for all who are far off – for all whom the Lord our God will call."

(Acts 2:36–9)

Men who trade enter into commercial intercourse for exchange of things. For ancient commerce was only an exchange of things. A man gave what he had, and received what he had not. For example, he had wheat, but had no barley; another had barley, but no wheat; the former gave the wheat which he had, and received the barley which he had not. How simple it was that the larger quantity should make up for the cheaper sort! So then another man gives barley, to receive wheat; lastly, another gives lead, to receive silver, only he gives much lead against a little silver; another gives wool, to receive a ready-made garment. And who can enumerate all these exchanges?

But no one gives life to receive death. Not in vain then was the voice of the Physician as He hung upon the tree. For in order that He might die for us because the Word could not die, "The Word was made flesh and dwelt among us". He hung upon the Cross, but in the flesh. There was the meanness which the Jews despised; there the dearness, by which the Jews were delivered. For them was it said, "Father forgive them, for they know not what they do." And that voice was not in vain. He died, was buried, rose again, having passed forty days with his disciples, He ascended into heaven, He sent the Holy Ghost on them, who waited for the promise. They were filled with the Holy Ghost, Whom they had received, and began to speak with the tongues of all nations.

Then the Jews who were present, amazed that unlearned and ignorant men, whom they had known as brought up among them with one tongue, should in the name of Christ speak in all tongues, were in astonishment, and learnt from Peter's words whence this gift came. He gave it, Who hung upon the tree. He gave it, Who was derided as He hung upon the tree, that from His seat in heaven He might give the Holy Spirit. They of whom he had said, "Father, forgive them, for they know not what they do", heard, believed. They believed, were baptised, and their conversion was effected. What conversion? In faith they drank the Blood of Christ, which in fury they had shed.

Augustine of Hippo (354–430)

27th May

With many other words he warned them; and he pleaded with them, "Save yourselves from this corrupt generation." Those who accepted his message were baptised, and about three thousand were added to their number that day.

(Acts 2:40–41)

Young converts should, ordinarily, offer themselves for admission to some Church of Christ immediately. By "immediately" I mean that they should do it the first opportunity they have. They should not wait. If they set out in religion by waiting, most likely they will always be waiting, and never do anything to much purpose. If they are taught to wait under conviction, before they give themselves to Christ; or if they are taught to wait after conversion, before, by joining the Church, they give themselves publicly to God, they will probably go halting and stumbling through life. The first thing they should always be taught is; NEVER WAIT, WHERE GOD HAS POINTED OUT YOUR DUTY. We profess to have given up the waiting system; let us carry it through and be consistent.

While I say it is the duty of young converts to offer themselves to the Church immediately, I do not say that, in all cases, they should be received immediately. The Church has an undoubted right to assume the responsibility of receiving them immediately or not. If the Church is not satisfied in the case, it has the power to bid candidates wait till inquiries can be made as to their character and sincerity. This is more necessary in large cities than it is in the country, because so many applications are received from persons who are entire strangers.

But if the Church thinks it necessary to postpone an applicant, the responsibility is not his. He has not postponed obedience to the dying command of Christ, and so he has not grieved the Spirit, and so may not be essentially injured if he is faithful in other respects. Whereas, if he had neglected the duty voluntarily, he would soon have got into the dark, and would likely have backslidden.

Charles G. Finney (1792–1875)

28th May

But you will receive power when the Holy Spirit comes on you; and you will be my witnesses in Jerusalem, and in all Judea and Samaria, and to the ends of the earth.

(Acts 1:8)

About the same time, the school of the faithful was governed by a man most distinguised for his learning, whose name was Pantaenus. As there had been a school of sacred learning established there from ancient times, which has continued down to our times, and which we have understood was held by men able in eloquence, and the study of divine things. For the tradition is, that this philosopher was then in great eminence, as he had been first disciplined in the philosophical principles of those so called stoics.

But he is said to have displayed such ardour, and so zealous a disposition, respecting the divine word, that he was constituted a herald of the gospel of Christ to the nations of the east, and advanced as far as India. There were even there yet many evangelists of the word, who were ardently striving to employ their inspired zeal after the apostolic example, to increase and build up the divine word. Of these Pantaenus is said to have been one, and to have come as far as the Indies.

And the report is, that he there found his own arrival anticipated by some who were there acquainted with the gospel of Matthew, to whom Bartholomew, one of the apostles, had preached, and had left them the gospel of Matthew in Hebrew, which was also preserved until this time.

Pantaenus, after many praiseworthy deeds, was finally at the head of the Alexandrian school, commenting on the treasures of divine truth, both orally and in his writings.

Eusebius (c. 260–c. 340)

29th May

Through Jesus, therefore, let us continually offer to God a sacrifice of praise – the fruit of lips that confess his name. And do not forget to do good and to share with others, for with such sacrifices God is pleased.

(Hebrews 13:15–16)

It is very observable, that there is not one command in all the Gospel for public worship; and perhaps it is a duty that is least insisted upon in Scripture of any other. The frequent attendance at it is never so much mentioned in all the New Testament. Whereas that religion or devotion which is to govern the ordinary actions of life is to be found in almost every verse of Scripture.

Our blessed Saviour and His Apostles are wholly taken up in doctrines that relate to common life. They call us to renounce the world, and differ in every temper and way of life, from the spirit and the way of the world; to renounce all its goods, to fear none of its evils, to reject its joys, and have no value for its happiness: to be as new-born babes, that are born into a new state of things: to live as pilgrims in spiritual watching, in holy fear, and heavenly aspiring after another life: to take up our daily cross, to deny ourselves, to profess the blessedness of mourning, to seek after poverty of spirit: to forsake the pride and vanity of riches, to take no thought for the morrow, to live in the profoundest state of humility, to rejoice in worldly sufferings: to reject the lust of the flesh, the lust of the eyes, and the pride of life: to bear injuries, to forgive and bless our enemies, and to love mankind as God loved them: to give up our whole heart and afflictions to God, and strive to enter through the strait gate into a life of eternal glory.

This is the common devotion which our blessed Saviour taught, in order to make it the common life of all Christians. Is it not therefore exceeding strange, that people should place so much piety in the attendance upon public worship, concerning which there is not one precept of our Lord's to be found, and yet neglect these common duties of our ordinary life, which are commanded in every page of the Gospel? I call these duties the devotion of our common life, because if they are to be practised, they must be made parts of our common life; they can have no place anywhere else.

William Law (1686–1761)

30th May

Let us not give up meeting together, as some are in the habit of doing, but let us encourage one another – and all the more as you see the Day approaching.

(Hebrews 10::25)

MY DEAR SISTER

The more I consider your case, the more I am convinced that you are in the school of God, and that the Lord loveth whom he chasteneth. From the time you omitted meeting your class or band [the small groups of Methodism], you grieved the Holy Spirit of God, and he gave a commission to Satan to buffet you: Nor will that commission ever be revoked, till you begin to meet again. Why were you not a mother in Israel? a repairer of the waste places? – a guide to the blind? – a healer of the sick? – a lifter up of hands that hung down? Wherever you came, God was with you, and shone upon your path. Many daughters had done virtuously: But thou excelledst them all. Woman, remember the faith! In the name of God, set out again, and do the first works! I exhort you, for my sake (who tenderly love you), for God's sake, for the sake of your own soul, begin again without delay. The day after you receive this, go and meet a class or band. Sick or well, go! If you cannot speak a word go; and God will go with you. You sink under the sin of omission! My friend, my sister, go! Go, whether you can or not. Break through! Take up your cross. I say again, do the first works, and God will restore your first love! and you will be a comfort, not a grief, to

   Yours most affectionately
   John Wesley

John Wesley (1703–91)

31st May

For we were all baptised by one Spirit into one body – whether Jews or Greeks, slave or free – and we are all given the one Spirit to drink.

(1 Corinthians 12:13)

Personality does not come into the world with us ready made, but it has a history and a growth. Education is not merely its training, it is its creation. In all of us the personality is incomplete; and it misleads us in the most grave way when we use it as an analogy for the ever complete and holy personality of God. We are but persons in the making.

Personality is created by social influences, and finds itself only in these. We complete our personality only as we fall into place and service in the vital movement of the society in which we live. Isolation means arrested development. The aggressive egoist is working his own moral destruction by stunting and shrinking his true personality. Social life, duty, and sympathy, are the only conditions under which a true personality can be shaped.

And if it be asked how a society so crude, imperfect, unmoral, and even immoral as that in which we live is to mould personality, it is here that Christ comes to the rescue with the gift to faith of an active Spirit and a society complete in Himself, which in Him is none of these evil things, the society of the Kingdom of God ... We are saved only in a salvation which set up a kingdom, and did not merely set it upon foot. We have the Kingdom not with Christ but in Christ. Do not leave Christ out of the Kingdom, as if He were detachable from it like any common king. The individual is saved only in this social salvation. And the more you insist that a soul can only be saved, and a personality secured, by Christ's finished work, the more you must contend that the Kingdom of God is not merely coming but is come, and is active in the Spirit among us now.

P. T. Forsyth (1848–1921)

June

1st June

We must go through many hardships to enter the kingdom of God.
(Acts 14:22b)

So long as we live in this world we cannot be without tribulation and temptation.

As it is written in the book of Job, "Is there not a warfare to man upon the earth?"

Every one ought therefore to be careful about his temptations, and watch unto prayer, lest the devil find an advantage to deceive him; who never sleepeth, but goeth about seeking whom he may devour.

No man is so perfect and holy, but that he hath sometimes temptations; and altogether without them he cannot be.

Nevertheless temptations are very often very profitable to us, though they may seem troublesome and grievous; for in them a man is humbled, purified and instructed.

All the Saints passed through many tribulations and temptations and profited thereby.

Thomas à Kempis (c. 1380–1471)

2nd June

Who shall separate us from the love of Christ? Shall trouble or hardship or persecution or famine or nakedness or danger or sword?

(Romans 8:35)

A dull, uneasy, complaining spirit, which is sometimes the spirit of those most careful of religion, is yet, of all tempers, the most contrary to religion; for it disowns that God whom it pretends to adore. For he sufficiently disowns God, who does not adore Him as a Being of infinite goodness.

If a man does not believe that all the world is as God's family, where nothing happens by chance, but all is guided and directed by the care and providence of a Being that is all love and goodness to all His creatures, he cannot be said to truly believe in God. And yet he that has this faith, has faith to overcome the world, and always be thankful to God. For he that believes that everything happens to him for the best, cannot possibly complain for the want of something that is better.

If, therefore, you live in murmurings, accusing all the accidents of life, it is not because you are a weak, infirm creature, but it is because you lack the first principle of religion – a right belief in God. For as thankfulness is an express acknowledgement of the goodness of God towards you, so repinings and complaints are plain accusations of God's lack of goodness towards you.

On the other hand, would you know who is the greatest saint in the world? It is not he who prays most or fasts most; it is not he who gives alms, or is most most eminent for temperance, chastity or justice; but it is he who is always thankful to God, who wills everything that God willeth, who receives everything as an instance of God's goodness, and has a heart always ready to praise God for it.

All prayer and devotion, fastings and repentance, meditation and retirement, all Sacraments and ordinances, are but so many means to render the soul thus Divine, and comfortable to the will of God, and to fill it with thankfulness and praise for everything that comes from God. This is the perfection of all virtues; and all virtues that do not tend to it, or proceed from it, are but so many false ornaments of a soul not converted unto God.

You need not, therefore, now wonder that I lay so much stress upon singing a Psalm at all your devotions, since you see it is to form your spirit to such joy and thankfulness to God as is the highest perfection of a Divine and holy life.

William Law (1686–1761)

3rd June

Then he said to them, "The Sabbath was made for man, not man for the Sabbath. So the Son of Man is Lord even of the Sabbath."
(Mark 2:27–8)

The Christian Sunday and the Jewish Sabbath are absolutely different institutions, different in almost every particular that constitutes a characteristic of either . . .

The Sabbath was founded on a specific Divine command. We can plead no such special command for the obligation to observe Sunday.

The Sabbath was to be observed on a particular day which was determined by Divine authority; the Jews were commanded to keep "holy" the seventh day of the week. Among us the seventh is a common day, and it is the first day of the week that we celebrate as a religious festival.

The purpose of the Sabbath was to commemorate the manifestation of God's power in the creation of all things, and of His goodness in redeeming the Jews from their misery in Egypt. The Christian Sunday commemorates the resurrection of Christ from the dead.

Obedience to the law of the Sabbath required physical rest and nothing more; neither public nor private worship constituted any part of the obligation which was imposed upon the Jews by the Fourth Commandment. The great object for which the Christian Sunday is set apart from other days is to secure opportunity for religious thought, for thanksgiving and prayer.

The penalty for breaking the Sabbath was Death. There is not a single sentence in the New Testament to suggest that we incur any penalty by violating the supposed sanctity of Sunday.

The only similarity between the Lord's Day and the Sabbath is that both recur once a week, and that both are religious festivals. But if you change the day of a festival, change the Facts which it commemorates, and change the Manner of celebrating it, if one festival is instituted by the immediate authority of God and the other not, if one is protected by the Penalty of Death and the other by no Penalty at all, it is difficult to see how the two can be regarded as identical.

R. W. Dale (1829–95)

4th June

The law is only a shadow of the good things that are coming – not the realities themselves.

(Hebrews 10:1)

[Continued from yesterday.]

It was the grim custom of some of the old Nonconformists to celebrate the thirtieth of January, the anniversary of the beheading of King Charles, by a dinner. Suppose now that a man had directed in his will that this day should be kept by his children according to the traditions of Nonconformity. And suppose that his children in their old age, had given up the dinner on the thirtieth of January in commemoration of the beheading of King Charles I, and instead had gone to church on the twenty-ninth of May to thank God for the return of King Charles II – thus changing the day of the festival, changing the event which the day commemorated, and changed the manner of celebrating it, – do you think that the mere fact that in both cases a day was kept as an annual holiday, and as a holiday in the celebration of a great national event, would have made the two days in any rational sense, the same? Could they have appealed to their father's authority, which required them to celebrate the first day as a sanction for their celebration of the second?

Now I do not mean to say that the spirit and idea of the Christian Sunday are as absolutely different from the spirit and idea of the Jewish Sabbath, as was the thanksgiving service at church for the return of Charles II from the Nonconformist dinner in commemoration of the beheading of Charles I, but I do say that between the two religious institutions as such, the differences are not less flagrant. Their direct origin is different; they are kept on different days; they are kept in a different manner; they commemorate different things.

R. W. Dale (1829–95)

5th June

May the God of peace, who through the blood of the eternal covenant brought back from the dead our Lord Jesus, that great Shepherd of the sheep, equip you with everything good for doing his will, and may he work in us what is pleasing to him, through Jesus Christ, to whom be glory for ever and ever. Amen.

(Hebrews 13:20–21)

[Jan Hus is writing to the people of Pilsen.]

To the good – perseverance in virtue; and to the evil – a holy knowledge of our Lord Jesus Christ!

Dear lords and brothers in God's grace, I hear to my great grief that there is a difference and dissension among you concerning divine truth, and that you who began well are doing badly, vexing God, losing your souls, showing a bad example to others, flinging away your integrity, and for the insignificant gain of this world are holding of small moment the life eternal. Why do you not recall our Saviour's words: "What does it profit a man if he gain the whole world but suffer the loss of his soul? and what shall a man give in exchange for his soul?" Why do you not recall that you were a good example to all Bohemia by your goodly concord, your attention to God's word and the restraint you exercised over a wrong spirit? Oh! how strangely you have forgotten that it was your holy union in that which is good that defended you from your enemies, enriched you, and marked you out before God and man! The devil,

God's enemy, saw this, and took it so much to heart that he aroused the members of Antichrist and himself to drive divine grace and goodwill out of you. And now the unclean spirit has returned to the house from which he had been driven out. Taking seven spirits more wicked than himself, he has come back; and the last state is made worse than the first. He hath swept out of you the divine word, and restored to you frivolities, gambling, and other sins! Where is the Shepherd of your souls? How does He guide you? Your wound hath not been pointed out. There is none to have pity on you, to "pour in oil and wine and to bind up the wound" inflicted on you by the thieves. Methinks you are attended by those who administer poison to you by making light of Holy Writ, and who pour in the oil, not of true love, but of flattery. You do not understand that the smooth-tongued flatterer is an enemy, while he that chastises is a lover and a healer of wounds, although the sick man is angry and murmurs at the chastisement.

Jan Hus (1373–1415)

6th June

Because there is one loaf, we, who are many, are one body, for we all partake of the one loaf.

(1 Corinthians 10:17)

The body of Christ is the faithful community of Christ. Whoever eats of this bread in the Supper of the Lord, testifies that he desires to have fellowship with and to participate in all things with the body of Christ. That is he commits himself to the community in all things, in love and suffering, wealth and poverty, honour and dishonour, sorrow and joy, death and life, indeed that he is ready to give life and limb for the brothers, as Christ gave himself for him. Similarly with the cup in the blood of Christ: whoever drinks of this cup has first surrendered himself and testifies with it that he is prepared to pour out his blood for the sake of Christ and his church insofar as faith and the test of love demands it.

Whoever gives his body and pours out his blood as indicated, he does not give his own life or spill his own blood, but rather the body and blood of Christ. For we are members of his body, indeed of his flesh and bone says Paul. For this reason also Christ said to Paul, when he called him on the way to persecuting Christians: Saul, Saul, why do you persecute me? It is as if the Lord had said: why do you kill my body and spill my blood? Thus it is among true Christians. If one among them suffers, they all suffer since they are all members of one another and of Christ the head. Thus the head always suffers the most. Thus the Lamb has been slain from the beginning of the world and will be persecuted and killed. For as many of us as partake of the one bread and the one cup are all one bread and one body.

This is the test in which a man must persevere. Is he ready to be thus minded toward Christ the head and all his brothers and sisters as his members? Is he ready to be one member of this body and to remain and persevere to the end in all things that concern this body?

And this means discerning the body of Christ. But whoever eats and drinks alone has fellowship with Judas who also ate and drank with the other disciples from the bread and cup of the Lord. But he did not wish to participate in the common brotherly love but went and sought his own gain and sold the Lord.

Hans Schlaffer (d. 1528)

7th June

Then, leaving her water jar, the woman went back to the town and said to the people, "Come, see a man who told me everything I ever did. Could this be the Christ?"

(John 4:28-9)

We can imagine the speed with which she went her way into the city with her new found joy. She had been their sport, now she was their evangelist! The spring had overflowed in her heart and demanded expression. She cherished no grudge against those men, some of whom may have helped to her downfall! Those who are one with Christ through the Spirit find themselves filled with a love that kindles a revival in other hearts as well as their own. It was because

of the love that glowed in this wondrously transformed soul that
the Samaritans came to Christ, and invited Him to tarry with them.
The love of God glowed in her heart, because she had put away her
sin, and the spring of eternal love had began to rise within.

In a large mining centre, during the Welsh Revival, the evening
meeting was commencing in the crowded chapel an hour before the
advertised time. Some were praying, some giving their experience,
many were singing or reciting texts of Scripture. In the midst of the
excitement, Evans Roberts entered, passed to his chair in the pulpit,
and knelt for a time in silent prayer. His sensitive nature soon
became aware that the meeting was stirred more by emotion than
by the love and power of God. So he rose, silenced the hubbub, and
for a whole half hour made the great congregation remain hushed
beneath the searching light of the Holy Spirit.

At the end of that period, one of the best-known mineowners of
the neighbourhood rose from his seat, and extended his hand to
another mineowner, and the two men, professing Christians, who
had been at feud for years, were reconciled. Instantly, the entire
atmosphere of the meeting was changed. The keynote was Calvary,
and the power was that of Pentecost. Scores were born into the
kingdom of God, and all were conscious of the overshadowing
presence of the Saviour. Like one vast choir, the people sang a new
song, and to those two men the blessed consciousness of God's love
came at full tide. You must get right with God if you would have
springing-water.

F. B. Meyer (1847–1929)

8th June

*What business is it of mine to judge those outside the church? Are
you not to judge those inside? God will judge those outside "Expel
the wicked man from among you."*

(1 Corinthians 5:12–13)

The last part of discipline, is the excluding from the communion of
the church, those who after sufficient trial, remain impenitent.
Exclusion from church communion, commonly called Excom-

munication, is of different kinds or degrees, which are not to be confounded; but that which is commonly to be practised among us, is, only to remove an impenitent sinner from our communion, till it shall please the Lord to give him repentance.

In this exclusion or removal, the minister or governors of the church are authoritatively to charge the people, in the name of the Lord, to have no communion with him, and to pronounce him one of whose communion the church is bound to avoid. It is the people's duty carefully to avoid him, provided the pastor's charge contradict not the word of God.

We must, however, pray for the repentance and restoration even of the excommunicated; and if God shall give them repentance, we must be happy to receive them again into the communion of the church.

Richard Baxter (1615–91)

9th June

A young man ran and told Moses, "Eldad and Medad are prophesying in the camp." Joshua son of Nun, who had been Moses' assistant since youth, spoke up and said, "Moses, my lord, stop them." But Moses replied, "Are you jealous for my sake? I wish that all the Lord's people were prophets and that the Lord would put his Spirit on them!"

(Numbers 11:27–9)

There is no more searching test than this. Am I as eager for God's kingdom to come through others as through myself? In my private intercessions can I pray as heartily and earnestly for the success of my competitors as for my own? Can I see with equanimity other and younger men coming to the front, and showing themselves possessed of gifts which I always considered to be my special province? Am I conscious of the rising of jealousy or envy when my leadership is subordinated to the claims of rivals? Should I be willing that the will of God should be done through another, if he suited God's purpose better than myself? Few of us could answer these questions without the sense of almost insuperable difficulty in assuming the position taken up by Moses when he heard that Eldad and Medad prophesied in the camp.

And yet, in so far as we fall short of that position, do we not betray the earthly ingredients which have mingled, and mingle still, in our holy service? Yes; it is ourselves that we serve – our schemes, and plans, and selfhood. And if we were to eliminate from Christian service all that has emanated from these sources, what a scanty handful of gold-dust would be left! Oh, when we are able to say, "Would that all the Lord's people were prophets," and view with thankful joy the levelling up of all Christians to the table-land of our gifts and grace?

This can never come till we have learnt to spend long hours with God; till we have been taken into his secret place; till we have come to care for his honour more than for our own; till we have become absorbed in the one consuming passion to see Him glorified in his saints and admired in all that believe. "The zeal of thine house has eaten me up." Thus does the herald star, which on the fringe of night has told weary eyes that the dawn is near, sink contentedly into a very ocean of light; though not itself less bright because every inch of space is illuminated with a lustre like its own.

F. B. Meyer (1847–1929)

10th June

He must become greater; I must become less.

(John 3:30)

There was a day of Pentecost in Israel as Moses grew old, when the Spirit of the Lord fell on seventy of the elders of Israel in order to fit them to be Moses' assessors and assistants in ruling and in teaching the refractory people. And as God would have it, over and above the selected seventy, there were two exceptional men on whom the Spirit fell also, till Joshua grudged and fretted at the way the people's eyes were drawn off his master and turned to Eldad and Medad as they prophesied in the camp. "Forbid them, my Lord!" said Joshua, in his jealousy for Moses. To which speech of Joshua Moses made the golden answer: "Enviest thou for my sake?

Would God that all the Lord's people were prophets, and the Lord would put His Spirit upon them!" . . . And when we turn to John's gospel we find this fine parallel passage: "A man can receive nothing," said the Baptist, "except it be given from heaven. Ye yourselves bear witness that I said, I am not the Christ. The Christ must increase, but I must decrease."

It is beautiful to see Moses' best disciple so jealous of other gifted men, and all out of pure honour and love to his great master; and it is beautiful to see the same mistaken loyalty in John's disciples. But both Moses and John shine splendidly to all time in their rebukes to their disciples, and show themselves to be the true masters of such deserving disciples in their never-to-be-forgotten answers and lessons and reproofs. Moses, and John, and Paedaritus of Sparta, Moses' contemporary, who, when he was passed over and left out in the election of the Three Hundred, went home beaming with happiness, it did him much good to see that there were many men in Sparta who were better men than himself.

Alexander Whyte (1836–1921)

11th June

Clothe yourselves with humility towards one another, because, "God opposes the proud but gives grace to the humble."

(1 Peter 5:5b)

One of our most heinous and palpable sins is PRIDE. This is a sin that hath too much interest in the best of us; but which is more hateful and inexcusable in us [ministers] than in other men. Yet is it so prevalent in some of us, that it endeth our discourses, it chooseth our company, it formeth our countenances, it putteth the accent and emphasis upon our words. It fills some men's minds with aspiring desires and designs: it possesseth them with envious and bitter thoughts against those who stand in their light, or who by any means eclipse their glory, or hinder the progress of their reputation.

O what a constant companion, what a tyrannical commander, what a sly and subtle insinuating enemy is this sin of pride! It goes with men to the draper, the mercer, the tailor; it chooseth them their cloth, their trimming, and their fashion. Fewer ministers would ruffle it out in the fashion in hair and habit, if it were not for the command of this tyrant.

And I would that this were all, or the worst. But alas! how frequently doth it go with us to our study, and there sit with us when we do our work? How oft doth it choose our subject; and, more frequently still, our words and ornaments. God commandeth us to be as plain as we can, that we may inform the ignorant; and as convincing and serious as we are able, that we might melt and change their hardened hearts. But pride stands by and contradicteth all, and produceth its toys and trifles.

Richard Baxter (1615–91)

12th June

Take my yoke upon you and learn from me, for I am gentle and humble in heart, and you will find rest for your souls.
(Matthew 11:29)

There is no harder lesson to learn than the lesson of humility. It is not taught in the schools of men, only in the school of Christ. It is the rarest of all gifts. Very rarely do we find a man or a woman who is following closely the footsteps of the Master in meekness and in humility. I believe that it is the hardest lesson which Jesus Christ had to teach his disciples while He was here on earth. He said: "Learn of Me, for I am meek and lowly of heart." It looked at first as though He had failed to teach it to the twelve men who had been with Him almost constantly for three years . . .

Did you notice the reason that Christ gave for learning of Him? He might have said: "Learn of Me, because I am the most advanced thinker of the age. I have performed miracles that no man has performed. I have shown my supernatural power in a thousand ways." But no: the reason He gave was that He was "meek and lowly of heart".

We read of the three men in Scripture whose faces shone, and all three were noted for their meekness and humility. We are told that the face of Christ shone at his transfiguration; Moses, after he had been in the mount for forty days, came down from his communion with God with a shining face; and when Stephen stood before the Sanhedrin on the day of his death, his face was lighted up with glory. If our faces are to shine we must get into the valley of humility; we must go down in the dust before God.

Bunyan says that it is hard to get down into the valley of humiliation, the descent into it is steep and rugged; but that it is very fruitful and fertile and beautiful when once we get there. I think that no one will dispute that; almost every man, even the ungodly, admires meekness.

Someone once asked Augustine, what was the first of the religious graces, and he said "Humility". He asked him what was the second, and he replied, "Humility." He asked him the third, and he said, "Humility." I think that if we are humble, we have all the graces.

D. L. Moody (1837–99)

13th June

When Moses came down from Mount Sinai with the two tablets of the Testimony in his hands, he was not aware that his face was radiant because he had spoken with the Lord.

(Exodus 34:29)

There is a law known to medical men as Holland's law; which affirms that whenever attention is directed specially to any one organ of the body, the action of that organ is more or less disturbed. If, for instance, we begin to think of our heart counting its beats, and listening to its throbs, we disturb its rhythmic action. There are few who can let the physician feel their pulse with perfect composure; and he is generally obliged to make some allowances for the effect of this self-consciousness. So with the functions of digestion, and respiration and thought. These great and vital processes of the body go on most healthily and satisfactorily when they are not made direct subjects of attention. And in these respects we may trace a close analogy between the physical and spiritual life of man. A counterpoint of Holland's law pervades the physiology of the spiritual life. We shall do best, and make the quickest progress, when we know it not.

True Christian excellence is as unconscious of its beauty as Moses was; whenever it becomes self-conscious it loses its charm. Beware of the man who talks about his graces. There is such a thing as being proud of humility, and making capital out of our nothingness. The man who boasts of a shining face is a counterfeit and a cheat. The possessor of the genuine article never talks about it, never thinks about it; and would be almost overwhelmed to hear of any such thing ascribed to him. The charm of a little child is its utter unconsciousness of self; and that is the charm in true God-likeness. It is like the bloom on a peach, the dew-jewels on the morning lawn, or the stillness of the surface of a mountain pool.

F. B. Meyer (1847–1929)

14th June

Dear friend, do not imitate what is evil but what is good.

(3 John 11)

The spirit of Christian long-suffering and meekness is commended to us by the example of the saints. The example of Christ alone might be and is sufficient; since it is the example of him who is our head, and Lord and master, whose followers we profess to be, and whose example we believe to be perfect. And yet some may be ready to say with regard to the example of Christ, that he was sinless, and had no corruption in his heart, and that it cannot be expected of us that we should do in all things as he did.

Now, though this is no reasonable objection, yet the example of the saints, who were man of like passion with ourselves, is not without its special use, and may in some respects have a peculiar influence. Many of the saints have set bright examples of this long-suffering that has been recommended. With that meekness, for instance, did David bear the injurious treatment that he received from Saul, when he hunted him as a partridge on the mountains, and pursued with the most unreasonable envy and malice, and with murderous designs, though he had ever behaved himself dutifully toward him.

And when he had the opportunity put into his hands of cutting him off, and at once delivering himself from his power, and others around him were ready to think it very lawful and commendable to do so yet as Saul was the Lord's anointed, he chose rather to commit himself and all his interests to God, and venture his life in his hands, and suffer his enemy still to live. And when, after this, he saw that his forbearance and goodness did not overcome Saul, but that he still pursued him, and when again he had the opportunity of destroying him, he chose rather to go out as a wanderer, and an outcast, than to injure the one that would have destroyed him.

Another example is that of Stephen, of whom we are told (Acts 7:60), that, when his persecutors were venting their rage upon him, by stoning him to death, "he kneeled down, and cried with a loud voice, Lord lay not this sin to their charge."

Jonathan Edwards (1703–58)

15th June

Remember this: Whoever sows sparingly will also reap sparingly, and whoever sows generously will also reap generously. Each man should give what he has decided in his heart to give, not reluctantly or under compulsion, for God loves a cheerful giver.
(2 Corinthians 9:6–7)

In respect to contributions for defraying the expenses [of World Mission], money will doubtless be wanting; and suppose the rich were to use a portion of that wealth over which God has made them stewards in this important undertaking, perhaps there are few ways that would turn to a better account at last. Nor ought it to be confined to the rich; if persons of more moderate circumstances were to devote a portion, suppose a tenth of their annual increase to the Lord, it would not only correspond with the practice of the Israelites, who lived under the Mosaic economy, but of the patriarchs Abraham, Isaac, and Jacob, before that dispensation commenced. Most of our eminent forefathers amongst the Puritans followed that practice; if that were but attended to now, there would not only be enough to support the ministry of the gospel at home, and to encourage village preaching in our respective neighbourhoods, but to defray the expenses of carrying the gospel into the heathen world.

If congregations were to open subscriptions of one penny or more per week, according to their circumstances, and deposit it as a fund for the propagation of the gospel into most of the villages in England; where, though men are placed whose business it is to give light to those who sit in darkness, it is well known that they have it not. Where there was no person to open his house for the reception of the gospel, some other building might be procured for a small sum, and even then something considerable may be spared for the Baptist or other committees for propagating the gospel among the heathen.

Many persons have of late left off the use of West Indian sugar on account of the iniquitous manner in which it is obtained [through slaves and the slave trade]. Those families who have done so, and have not substituted anything in its place, have not only cleansed their hands of blood, but have made a saving to their families, some of six pence and some of a shilling a week. If this or a part of this were appropriated to uses before mentioned, it would abundantly suffice. We have only to keep the end in view, and have our hearts thoroughly engaged in the pursuit of it, and means will not be very difficult.

William Carey (1761–1834)

16th June

Devote yourselves to prayer, being watchful and thankful.
(Colossians 4:2)

To cultivate the ceaseless spirit of prayer, use more frequent acts of prayer. To learn to pray with freedom, force yourself to pray. The great liberty begins in necessity.

Do not say, "I cannot pray. I am not in the spirit." Pray till you are in the spirit. Think of the analogies from lower levels.

Sometimes when you need rest most you are too restless to lie down and take it. Then compel yourself to lie down, and to lie still. Often in ten minutes the compulsion fades into consent, and you sleep, and rise a new man.

Again, it is often hard enough to take up the task which in half an hour you enjoy. It is often against the grain to turn out of an evening to meet the friends you promised. But once you are in their midst you are in your element.

Sometimes, again, you say, "I will not go to church. I do not feel that way." That is where the habit of an ordered religious comes in aid. Religion is the last region for chance desires. Do it as a duty and it may open out into a blessing. Omit it, and you may miss the one thing that would have made an eternal difference. You stroll instead, and return with nothing but an appetite – when you might have come back with an inspiration. Compel yourself to meet your God as you would meet your promises, your obligations to your fellow men.

So if you are averse to pray, pray the more. Do not call it lip-service. That is not the lip-service God disowns. It is His Spirit acting in your self-coercive will, only not yet in your heart. What is unwelcome to God is lip-service which is untroubled at not being more. As appetite comes with eating, so prayer with praying. Our hearts learn the language of lips.

Compel yourself often to shape on your lips the detailed needs of your soul. It is not needful to inform God, but to inform yourself before God, to enrich that intimacy with yourself which is so necessary to answer the intimacy of God ... Love loves to be told what it knows already. Every lover knows that. It wants to be asked for what it longs to give. And that is the principle of prayer to the all-knowing Love. As God knows all, you may reckon that your brief humble prayer will be understood (Matthew 6:8).

P. T. Forsyth (1848–1921)

17th June

Suppose one of you wants to build a tower. Will he not first sit down and estimate the cost to see if he has enough money to complete it? For if he lays the foundation and is not able to finish it, everyone who sees it will ridicule him, saying, "This fellow began to build and was not able to finish."

(Luke 14:28–30)

The sufferings that are in the way of our duty, are among the difficulties that attend religion. They are part of the cost of being religious. He, therefore, that is not willing to meet this cost, never complies with the terms of religion. He is like the man that wishes his house to be built, but is not willing to meet the cost of building it; and so, in effect, refuses to build it. He that does not receive the gospel with all its difficulties, does not receive it as it is proposed to him. He that does not receive Christ with his cross as well as his crown, does not receive him at all.

It is true that Christ invites us to come to him and find rest, and to buy wine and milk; but then he also invites us to come and take up the cross, and that daily, that we may follow him. If we come only to accept the former, we do not in truth accept the offer of the gospel, for both go together, the rest and the yoke, the cross and the crown: and it will signify nothing, that, in accepting only the one, we accept what God never offered to us.

They that receive only the easy part of Christianity, and not the difficult, at best are almost Christians; while they that are wholly Christians receive the whole of Christianity, and thus shall be accepted and honoured, and not cast out with shame, at the last day.

Jonathan Edwards (1703–58)

18th June

The brother in humble circumstances ought to take pride in his high position.

(James 1:9)

What a different life Christian men and women would live throughout the week if they kept in their thoughts the palaces which are to be their homes, the crowns which they are to wear, the dignity which belongs to them already, and the greater dignity which they may win by gentle speech, by the courteous manners, the gracious temper, the truthfulness, the uprightness, the industry, the purity which should distinguish them as the sons and daughters of God, – if they would think of all the wealth and glory that are theirs, however humble may be their earthly condition.

I was returning yesterday from Church Stretton, where I had been for a few days rest. It was a brilliant afternoon, and as we came through Shropshire and North Staffordshire the country seemed perfectly beautiful. When we reached Wolverhampton there was a great contrast. You know the country – huge masses of cinder and black waste upon mounds; dreary workshops, rows of mean houses, foul with dirt and smoke; the very grass, where it would grow at all, unlovely and dingy. I said, "What a change!" but then I lifted my eyes, and above all that dreary waste there was a divine glory. In the west the sun was sinking in a sea of flame. The heavy clouds were of rich purple, fringed with fire; lighter clouds touched with the sun, were of brilliant orange. It was a vision of transcendent splendour.

And that may be a true type of your life. Your earthly condition may be poor, mean, ignoble. But over you too God's heaven is hanging. It is always there, – the sun in its splendour by day, the shining hosts of stars by night; these are the heritage of the brother of low degree, as well of the rich and the great. Every promise of divine love, every gift of the divine grace, every dignity that belongs to the children of the Most High, every immortal hope, – they are all yours. Live like men whom God has so greatly blessed. "Glory in your high estate."

R. W. Dale (1829–95)

19th June

You are the light of the world. A city on a hill cannot be hidden. Neither do people light a lamp and put it under a bowl. Instead they put it on its stand, and it gives light to everyone in the house.
(Matthew 5:14–15)

By these words He trains them to strictness of life, teaching them to be earnest in their endeavours, as set before the eyes of all men, and contending in the midst of the amphitheatre of the world. For, "look not to this," He saith, "that we are sitting here, that we are in a small portion of one corner. For ye shall be as conspicuous to all as a city set on the ridge of a hill, as a candle in a house on the candlestick, giving light."

Where now are they who persevere in disbelieving in the power of Christ? Let them hear these things, and let them adore His might, amazed at the power of the prophecy. For consider how great things he promised to them, who were not known even in their own country; that earth and sea should know them, and that they should by their fame reach the limits of the inhabited world; or rather, not by their fame, but by the working of the good they wrought. For it was not fame that bearing them everywhere made them conspicuous, but also the actual demonstration by their works. Since, as though they had wings, more vehemently than the sunbeam did they overrun the whole earth, sowing the light of godliness.

But here He seems to me to be also training them to boldness of speech. For to say, "A city on a hill cannot be hidden" is to speak as declaring His own powers. For as that city can by no means be hidden, so it was impossible that what they preached, should sink into silence and obscurity. Thus since He had spoken of persecutions and calumnies, of plots and wars, for fear they might think that these would have power to stop their mouths; to encourage them, He saith, that so far from being hid, it should overshine the whole world; and that on this very account they should be illustrious and renowned.

John Chrysostom (c. 344/345–407)

20th June

And this gospel of the kingdom will be preached in the whole world as a testimony to all nations, and then the end will come.
(Matthew 24:14)

When a trading company have obtained their charter they usually go to its utmost limits; and their stocks, their ships, their officers and men are so chosen and regulated as to be likely to answer their purpose; but they do not stop here, for encouraged by the prospect of success, they use every effort, cast their bread upon the waters, cultivate friendship with everyone from whose information they expect the least advantage. They cross the widest and most tempestuous seas and encounter the most unfavourable climates. They introduce themselves into the most barbarous nations, and sometimes undergo the most affecting hardships. Their minds continue in a state of anxiety, and suspense, and a longer delay than usual in the arrival of a vessel agitates them with a thousand changeful thoughts, and foreboding apprehensions, which continue till the rich returns are safe arrived in port. But why these fears? Whence all these disquietudes and this labour? Is it not because their souls enter into the spirit of the project and their happiness in a manner depends on its success?

Christians are a body whose truest interest lies in the exaltation of the Messiah's kingdom. Their charter is extensive, their encouragements exceeding great, and the returns infinitely superior to all the gains of the most lucrative company. Let everyone in his position in life consider himself as bound to act with all his might and in every way possible for God.

Suppose a company of serious Christians, ministers and private persons, were to form themselves into a society, and make a number of rules respecting the regulation of the plan, and the persons who are to be employed as missionaries, the means of defraying the expense etc., etc. This society must consist of persons whose hearts are in the work, men of serious religion, and possessing a spirit of perseverance; there must be a determination not to admit any person who is not of this description, or to retain him who no longer answers to it.

From such a society a committee might be appointed, whose business it should be to procure all the information they could upon the subject, to receive contributions, to enquire into the tempers, abilities and religious views of the missionaries, and also to provide them with the necessities for their undertakings.

William Carey (1761–1834)

21st June

Consider it pure joy, my brothers, whenever you face trials of many kinds, because you know that the testing of your faith develops perseverance.

(James 1:2–3)

Saturday night had brought us to a point some thirty miles off the land; but during the Sunday morning service, which was held on deck, I could not fail to notice that the captain looked troubled, and frequently went over to the side of the ship. When the service was ended, I learnt from him the cause – a four-knot current was carrying us rapidly towards some sunken reefs, and we were already so near that it seemed improbable that we should get through the afternoon in safety. After dinner the long-boat was put out, and all hands endeavoured, without success, to turn the ship's head from the shore.

After standing together on the deck for some time in silence, the captain said to me, "Well, we have done everything that can be done; we can only await the result." A thought occurred to me, and I replied, "No, there is one thing we have not done yet." "What is it?" he queried. "Four of us on board are Christians," I answered (the Swedish carpenter and our coloured steward, with the captain and myself); "let us each retire to his own cabin, and in agreed prayer ask the Lord to give us immediately a breeze. He can as easily send it now as at sunset."

The captain complied with this proposal . . . The first officer, a godless man, was in charge. I went over and asked him to let down the clews or corners of the mainsail, which had been drawn up in order to lessen the useless flapping of the sail against the rigging. He answered. "What would be the good of that?" I told him we had been asking for a wind from God, that it was coming immediately, and we were so near the reef by this time that there was not a minute to lose. With a look of incredulity and contempt, he said with an oath that he would rather see a wind than hear of it! But while he was speaking I watched his eye, and followed it up to the royal (the topmost sail), and there, sure enough, the corner of the sail was beginning to tremble in the coming breeze. "Don't you see the wind is coming? Look at the royal!" I exclaimed. "No, it is only a cat's-paw," he rejoined (a mere puff of wind). "Cat's-paw or not," I cried, "pray let down the mainsail, and let us have the benefit!"

This he was not slow to do. In another minute the heavy tread of the men on the deck brought up the captain from his cabin to see what was the matter; and he saw that the breeze had indeed come. In a few minutes we were ploughing our way at six or seven knots an hour through the water. We were soon out of danger; and though the wind was sometimes unsteady, we did not altogether lose it until after passing the Pelew Islands.

Thus God encouraged me, ere landing on China's shores, to bring every variety of need to Him in prayer, and *to expect that He would honour the Name* of the LORD JESUS, and give the help which each emergency required.

James Hudson Taylor (1832–1905)

22nd June

Crowds gathered also from the towns around Jerusalem, bringing their sick and those tormented by evil spirits, and all of them were healed.

(Acts 5:16)

I rode to Everton, having been there some months before. On Sunday afternoon God was eminently present with us, though to comfort rather than to convince. But I observed a remarkable difference since I was there, as to the manner of the work: None now were in trances, none cried out, none fell down, or were convulsed; only some trembled exceedingly, a low murmur was heard, and many were refreshed with the multitude of peace. The danger *was* to regard such extraordinary circumstances too much, such as outcries, convulsions, visions, trances, as if they were essential to the inward work, so that it could not go on without them. Perhaps the danger *is*, to regard them too little; to condemn them altogether; to imagine they had nothing of God in them; yea, were a hindrance to the work.

Whereas, the truth is, (1) God suddenly and strongly convinced many that they were undone, lost sinners; the natural consequences whereof were sudden outcries, and strong bodily convulsions. (2) To strengthen and encourage them that believed, and to make the work more apparent, He favoured several of them with divine dreams; others with trances and visions. (3) In some of these instances, after a time, nature mixed with grace. (4) Satan likewise mimicked this part of the work of God, in order to discredit the whole work: And yet it is not wise to give up this part, any more than to give up the whole. At first, it was doubtless wholly from God: It is partly so at this day; and He will enable us to discern how far in every case the work is pure, and how far mixed.

John Wesley (1703–91)

23rd June

Jesus declared, "I tell you the truth, no-one can see the kingdom of God unless he is born again."

(John 3:3)

Do not I hear someone say, "I trust I am a Christian; I believe I have experienced a great change of heart; but I do not remember the time?" Beloved friend, there is an old legal maxim that "possession is nine points of the law"; and as long as you have Christ, I am not going to raise questions about when you got him. Surely, if the hold you have be equivalent to nine points of the law, it represents *all* the points of the gospel. If you have Christ he will never be taken away from you. If you are resting on his blood and righteousness, it is well enough; and if you are producing the fruits of the Spirit, and your life is what it should be, by your fruits you are to be known. We shall ask no more questions.

"But I should like to know exactly when you were converted," saith one. Well, I do not wonder that you should; but suppose you do not know, and cannot ascertain, what then? Suppose there is a person here who does not know exactly his age, and he wants to find the register of his birth and he had tried and cannot find it. Now, what is the inference that he draws from his not being able to tell the day of his birth? Well, I do not know what the inference might be, but I will tell you of one inference he does *not* draw. He does not say, therefore, "I am not alive." If he did, he would be an idiot, for if the man is alive he is alive, whether he knows his birthday or not. And if a man really trusts in Jesus, and is alive from the dead, he is a saved soul, whether he knows exactly when and where he was saved or not.

At the same time, do not let me be understood. "Ye *must* be born again." There is, and must be, in every man that will enter heaven, a time – a point and a place, too – in which he did pass out of the kingdom of Satan into the kingdom of God's dear Son. I believe that in many cases it is not easy to tell the precise point, for with them it is like the rising of the sun. Sometimes the sun is up before you know whether he has risen or not, because a long morning twilight precedes his actual appearance above the horizon. So it may be that spiritual life begins by slow degrees, before we quite perceive it there; but there *is* a time when it begins: there is a point – there is a place – in which the unsaved becomes saved, and unregenerate becomes regenerate; and there is a broad line between the two characters. A great gulf, indeed, is fixed between them, which only the supernatural grace of God can enable anyone to cross.

C. H. Spurgeon (1834–92)

24th June

The man said, "The woman you put here with me – she gave me some fruit from the tree, and I ate it." Then the Lord God said to the woman, "What is this you have done?" The woman said, "The serpent deceived me, and I ate."

(Genesis 3:12–13)

The tendency in human nature to excuse sin, to put forward pleas in extenuation and defence, to provide in the constitution or education or environment of the sinner explanations which neutralise his guilt, is instinctive and almost ineradicable. Few sayings are more popular with the morally feeble, than that to understand everything is to pardon everything. To be reconciled to God through faith in Christ, who died bearing our sin, is death to this tendency.

It means that we enter into the mind of Christ in relation to sin, that we see it in its truth as he saw it, that we sorrow over it as He sorrowed, that we repel it henceforth as He repelled it; all of which is part at least of what is meant by repentance. There is no salvation except in and through the truth, and to take our sin as what it truly is – as what in the Passion of Jesus it has been revealed really to be – is to enter into the truth through which salvation is realised.

Repentance in this sense is not a condition preliminary to salvation; it is part of the experience of being saved. It is not something which we produce out of our resources and bring to God, in the assurance that now of course He will forgive us; it is something which is only produced in us by the sense that there is already forgiveness with Him; it is a saving grace begotten in our hearts by that passion of love in which Jesus made our sins His own. It is not a substitute for the atonement, or something that makes it unnecessary; it is the fruit of the atonement and of nothing else.

James Denney (1856–1917)

25th June

Godly sorrow brings repentance that leads to salvation and leaves no regret, but wordly sorrow brings death.

(2 Corinthians 7:10)

Sorrow is overmuch when it is fed by a mistaken cause. All is too much where none is due. And great sorrow is too much when the cause requireth but less.

If a man thinketh that somewhat is a duty, which is no duty, and then sorrow for omitting it, such sorrow is all too much, because it is undue and caused by error. Many I have known who have been greatly troubled, because they could not bring themselves to that length or order of meditation, for which they had neither the ability or the time; and many, because they could not reprove sin in others, when prudent instruction and intimation was more suitable than reproof. And many are troubled, because in their shops and calling they think of anything but God, as if our outward business must have no thoughts.

Superstition always breeds such sorrows, when men make themselves religious duties which God never made them, and then come short in the performance of them. Many dark souls are assaulted by the erroneous, and told that they are in a wrong way; and they must take some error as a necessary truth, and so are cast into perplexing difficulties, and perhaps repent of the truth which they before owned. Many fearful Christians are troubled about every meal that they eat, about their clothes, their thoughts, thinking or fearing that all is sinful which is lawful, and that unavoidable infirmities are heinous sins. All such as these are troubles and sorrows without cause and therefore overmuch.

Sorrow is overmuch when it hurteth and overwhelmeth nature itself, and destroyeth bodily health or understanding. Grace is the due qualification of nature, and duty is the right employment of it, but neither of them must destroy it. As civil, and ecclesiastic, and domestic government are for edification and not for destruction, so also is personal self-government. God will have mercy and not sacrifice; and he that would not have us to kill or hurt our neighbour on pretence of religion, would not have us destroy or hurt ourselves, being bound to love our neighbour but as ourselves. As fasting is a duty no further than it tendeth to some good, as to express or exercise true humiliation, or to mortify some fleshly lust etc., so it is with sorrow for sin: it is too much when it doth more hurt than good.

Richard Baxter (1615–91)

26th June

Finally, brothers, whatever is true, whatever is noble, whatever is right, whatever is pure, whatever is lovely, whatever is admirable – if anything is excellent or praiseworthy – think about such things.
(Philippians 4:8)

[Continued from yesterday.]

The passions of grief and trouble of mind to oft overthrow the sober and sound use of reason, so that a man's judgement is corrupted and perverted by it, and is not in that case to be trusted. As a man in raging anger, so one in fear or great trouble of mind thinks not of things as they are, but as his passion represents them, about God and religion, and about his own soul, and his actions, or about his friends or enemies, his judgement is perverted, and usually false, and like an inflamed eye, thinks all things of the colour which is like itself. When it perverteth reason it is overmuch.

Overmuch sorrow disableth man to govern his thoughts; and ungoverned thoughts must needs be both sinful and very troublesome: grief carrieth them away as in a torrent. You may almost as easily keep the leaves of the trees in quietness and order in a blustering wind as the thoughts of one in troubling passions. If reason would stop them from perplexing subjects, or turn them to better or sweeter things, it cannot do it; it hath no power against the stream of troubling passions.

Overmuch sorrow would swallow up faith itself, and greatly hindereth its exercise. They are matters of unspeakable joy which the gospel calleth us to believe: and it is wonderful hard for a grieved, troubled, soul to believe anything that is matter of joy, much less of so great joy as pardon and salvation are. Though it dare not flatly give God the lie, it hardly believes his free and full promises, and the expressions of his readiness to receive all penitent, returning sinners. Passionate grief serves only to feel somewhat countrary to the grace and promises of the gospel, and that feeling hinders faith.

Richard Baxter (1615–91)

27th June

This grace was given us in Christ Jesus before the beginning of time, but it has now been revealed through the appearing of our Saviour, Christ Jesus, who has destroyed death and has brought life and immortality to light through the gospel.

(2 Timothy 1:9b–10)

The Cross is the sign of Christian devotion, the inspiration of Christian service; but the crucifix is no adequate symbol of the Christian faith. Christ was crucified through weakness; but He lives by the power of God, and we must not forget His life. Sometimes people do. They look at Christ on the Cross as if that exhausted the truth about Him, or even the truth about His relation to sin. They forget that He is not on the Cross, but on the throne; that He has ascended above all heavens, separate from sinners, inaccessible to sin. They forget that the keynote of the Christian life as it is related to the Ascended Christ is one of victory and triumph . . .

The exalted Christ is through His Spirit the author and giver of our life as Christians, and the life which He communicates is His own. It is essentialy a victorious, triumphant, joyous life. It is as such we see it in the apostolic writings, and as such we ought to see it everywhere.

Christianity has been named, sometimes patronisingly, sometimes sentimentally, sometimes honestly enough, the Religion of Sorrow; but there never was a more complete misnomer. It is not the religion of sorrow, but the religion which, because it is inspired by One who lives and *was* dead, gives the victory over every sorrow, even the crowning sorrows of death and sin. There is not in the New Testament from beginning to end, in the record of the original and genuine Christian life, a single word of despondency or gloom. It is the most buoyant, exhilarating, and joyful book in the world. The men who write it have indeed all that is hard and painful in the world to encounter; but they are of good courage, because Christ has overcome the world, and when the hour of conflict comes, they descend crowned into the arena.

James Denney (1856–1917)

28th June

The man who enters by the gate is the shepherd of his sheep. The watchman opens the gate for him, and the sheep listen to his voice. He calls his own sheep by name and leads them out.
(John 10:2–3)

A friend of mine was in Syria, and he found a shepherd that kept up the old custom of naming his sheep. My friend said he wouldn't believe that the sheep knew him when he called them by name. So he said to the shepherd: "I wish that you would call one or two."

The shepherd said, "Carl." The sheep stopped eating and looked up. The shepherd called out, "Come here." The sheep came and stood looking up into his face. He called another and another, and there they stood looking up at the shepherd.

"How can you tell them apart?"

"Oh, there are no two alike. See, that sheep toes in a little; this sheep is a little squint eyed; that sheep has a black spot on its nose."

My friend found that he knew every one of his sheep by their failings. He didn't have a perfect one in his flock.

I suppose that is the way the Lord knows you and me. There is a man who is covetous; he wants to grasp the whole world. He wants a shepherd to keep down that spirit. There is a woman down there who has an awful tongue; she keeps the whole neighbourhood stirred up. There is a woman over there who is deceitful, terribly so. She needs the care of a shepherd to keep her from deceit, for she will ruin her children; they will all turn out like their mother. There is a father over there who wouldn't swear for all the world before his children, but sometimes he gets provoked in his business and swears before he knows it. Doesn't he need a shepherd's care?

I would like to know if there is a man or woman on earth who doesn't need the care of a shepherd. Haven't we all got failings? If you really want to know what your failings are, you can find someone who can point them out. God would never have sent Christ into the world if we didn't need His care. We are as weak and foolish as sheep.

D. L. Moody (1837–99)

29th June

Therefore, the Lord himself will give you a sign: The virgin will be with child and will give birth to a son, and will call him Immanuel.
(Isaiah 7:14)

There is a signature of wisdom and power impressed upon the works of God, which evidently distinguishes them from the feeble imitations of men. Not only the splendour of the sun, but the glimmering of the glow-worm, proclaims his glory. The structure and growth of a blade of grass, are the effects of the same power which produced the fabric of the heavens and the earth. In his word likewise he is inimitable. He has a style and manner peculiarly his own. What he is pleased to declare of himself by the prophet, may be prefixed as a proper motto to the whole revelation of his will in the Bible. "My thoughts are not your thoughts, neither are your ways my ways, saith the Lord. For as the heavens are higher than the earth, so are my ways higher than your ways, and my thoughts than your thoughts." (Isaiah 55:8–9)

This superiority of his thoughts to ours, causes a proportionable difference in his manner of operation. His ways are above our conceptions, and often contrary to them. He sometimes produces great effects, by means, which, to us, appear unsuitable and weak. Thus he gave Gideon a complete victory, not by providing him an army equal to that of his enemy, but by three hundred men furnished with earthen pitchers and lamps (Judges 7:19–20). At other times, the greatness of the preparations, intimates that there are difficulties in the case, insuperable to any power but his own, where our narrow apprehensions, until enlightened and enlarged by his teaching, can scarcely perceive any difficulty.

It is eminently so with respect to the restoration of fallen man to his favour. We have but slight thoughts of his holiness, and therefore are but slightly affected by the evil of sin. But though he be rich in mercy, no wisdom but his own, could have proposed an expedient, whereby the exercise of his mercy towards sinners might be made to correspond with his justice and truth, and with the honour of his moral government. His gospel reveals this expedient, and points out a way in which mercy and truth meet together, and his inflexible righteousness is displayed, in perfect harmony with the peace of sinners who submit to his appointment; and thus God appears not only gracious but just, in receiving them to favour.

This is the greatest of all his works, and exhibits the most glorious discovery of his character and perfections. The means are answerable to the grandeur of the design and are summarily expressed in the text [from Isaiah].

John Newton (1725–1807)

30th June

"For my thoughts are not your thoughts, neither are your ways my ways," declares the Lord. "As the heavens are higher than the earth, so are my ways higher than your ways and my thoughts than your thoughts."

(Isaiah 55:8–9)

How true are these words! When the Lord is bringing great blessing in the best possible way, how oftentimes our unbelieving hearts are feeling, if not saying, like Jacob of old, "All these things are against me." Or we are filled with fear, as were the disciples when the Lord, walking on the waters, drew near to quiet the troubled sea, and to bring them quickly to their desired haven. And yet mere common sense ought to tell us that He whose way is perfect, can make no mistakes; that He who has promised to "perfect that which concerneth" us, and whose minute care counts the very hair of our heads, and forms for us our circumstances, *must* know better than we the way to forward our truest interests and to glorify His own Name.

> *Blind unbelief is sure to err*
> *And scan His work in vain;*
> *God is His own interpreter,*
> *And he will make it plain.*

To me it seemed a great calamity that failure of health compelled my relinquishing work for God in China, just when it was more fruitful than ever before; and to leave the little band of Christians in Ningpo, needing much care and teaching, was a great sorrow. Nor was the sorrow lessened when, on reaching England, medical testimony assured me that return to China, at least for years to come, was impossible. Little did I then realise that the long separation from China was a necessary step towards the formation of a work which God would bless as He has blessed the CHINA INLAND MISSION. While in the field, the pressure of the claims immediately around me were so great that I could not think much of the still greater need of the regions farther inland; and if they were thought of, could do nothing for them. But while detained for some years in England, daily viewing the whole country on the large map on the wall of my study, I was as near to the vast regions of Inland China as to the smallest districts in which I had laboured personally for God; and prayer was often the only resource by which the burdened heart could gain any relief.

As a long absence from China now appeared inevitable, the next question was how to serve China, while in England, and this led to my engaging for several years . . . in the revision of a version of the New Testament in the colloquial of Ningpo . . . In undertaking this work, in my short-sightedness, I saw nothing beyond the use that the Book, and the marginal references, would be to the native Christians; but I have often seen since that, without those months of feeding and fasting on the Word of God, I should have been quite unprepared to form, on its present basis, a mission like the CHINA INLAND MISSION.

James Hudson Taylor (1832–1905)

July

1st July

Wine is a mocker and beer a brawler; whoever is led astray by them is not wise.

(Proverbs 20:1)

They were going to have a great celebration at the opening of a saloon and billiard hall in Chicago, in the northern part of the city where I lived. It was to be a gateway to death and hell, one of the worst places in Chicago. As a joke they sent me an invitation to go to the opening. I took the invitation, and went down and saw the two men who had the saloon, and I said, "Is that a genuine invitation?" They said it was. "Thank you," I said, "I will be around, and if there is anything here I don't like I may have something to say about it." They said, "You are not going to *preach*, are you?"

"I may."

"We don't want you. We won't let you in."

"How are you going to keep me out?" I asked. "There is an invitation."

"We will put a policeman at the door."

"What is that policeman going to do with the invitation?"

"We won't let you in."

"Well," I said, "I will be there."

I gave them a good scare, and then I said, "I will compromise the matter; if you two men will get down here and let me pray with you, I will let you off."

I got those two rum-sellers down on their knees, one on one side of me and the other on the other side, and I prayed to God to save their souls, and smite their business. One of them had a Christian mother, and he seemed to have some conscience left. After I had prayed, I said, "How can you do business? How can you throw this place open to ruin the young men of Chicago?"

Within three months the whole thing smashed up, and one of them was converted shortly afterward. I have never been invited to a saloon since.

D. L. Moody (1837–99)

2nd July

"No razor may be used on his head, because the boy is to be a Nazirite, set apart to God from birth, and he will begin the deliverance of Israel from the hands of the Philistines." . . . The woman gave birth to a boy and named him Samson. He grew and the Lord blessed him.

(Judges 13:5, 24)

We shall set it down to Samson's credit that, with all his license and with all his riot, he never became a drunkard. But then it always comes into my heart when I read of Samson's total abstinence –

> *What boots it at one gate to make defence*
> *And at another to let in the foe?*

You are making a gallant defence at one gate, but what about all the other gates; and especially, what about the gates on the other side of the city? You keep with all diligence, this and that gate of the body, but what about the more deadly gate of the soul? Plutarch tells us of a great Roman who was very brave; but, then, he was envious of other brave men, and his envy did himself and them and the state more mischief than if he had been a coward.

You work hard for God at your books and your visiting as a

Sabbath-school teacher, but you restrain prayer. You stand up for use and wont in public worship, and in pulpit and in published doctrine; but, then, you hate and hunt down the men who innovate upon you in these things. You go out, like Samson, against the enemies of God and His Church, but all the time you make your campaign on occasion for your own passions, piques, retaliations, and revenges. You do not touch wine, but how do you stand to all Samson's other sins? Death and hell will come still more surely into your hearts through the gates of envy, and ill-will, and hatred, and pride, and revenge, and malice, and unbelief, and neglect of God in prayer, than at those more yawning gates that all decently living men make a defence at. What avails this "temperance not complete"?

Alexander Whyte (1836–1921)

3rd July

As obedient children, do not conform to the evil desires you had when you lived in ignorance. But just as He who called you is holy, so be holy in all you do; for it is written: "Be holy, because I am holy."

(1 Peter 1:14–16)

People all over the land are astounded at our poor, weak, illiterate Salvation Army Soldiers. A gentleman, in a meeting on Easter Monday, a leading man of thought and experience in the holiness world, who was there all day – when my daughter said, "Why don't you speak?" said, "One feels as if one can't speak in these meetings" Why? These people have such unction from the Holy One that they are wiser than their teachers. Another gentleman, of considerable position too, in the religious world, said, "I feel like getting down at their feet. I feel as if they could teach me."

How is it that they have such power – these babes in intellect and intelligence? All over the land people say this to me. People who talk and go ahead in other meetings, when they get into our meeting say, "I can't. They are so far ahead of me that, to tell you the truth, I have nothing to say." I say, the Lord have mercy upon you, and make haste and come up after them. Only get down from your high mightiness as low as these people, and you will get it. It is not because they *are* poor and illiterate that they have power, but because they are babes in spirit. Even as Christ said, "I thank thee, oh! Father, that Thou hast hid these things from the wise and prudent, and hast revealed them unto babes."

The simple spirit, the teachable believing soul – oh! how much more it learns of God, in one hour's precious communion, than Doctors of Divinity learn in weeks of close study, who have not got it, because it is the SPIRIT that teaches the things of God. This union with Jesus that bringeth forth fruit unto God, and oh! the wonderful things it enables us to bring forth.

Catherine Booth (1829–90)

4th July

Consider it pure joy, my brothers, when you face trials of many kinds, because you know that the testing of your faith develops perseverance. Perseverance must finish its work so that you may be mature and complete, not lacking anything. If any of you lacks wisdom, he should ask God, who gives generously to all without finding fault, and it will be given to him.

(James 1:2–5)

This, I say, is stern doctrine. To count it all joy when suffering comes upon us, and suffering that tests our faith, how is this possible? It is only possible when we come to think of righteousness as being infinitely more precious than comfort, happiness or peace; when we come to see that the great thing for us in this life is not to enjoy ease and prosperity, to get rich, to rise in the world, but to become better men. For this we require wisdom, – a true estimate of the nature and ends of human life.

"If any of you lacketh wisdom let him ask of God." Wisdom was a great word among the Jews, especially during the centuries immediately before Christ. There was a distinct class of Jewish literature, represented by the Book of Proverbs, and the Book of Ecclesiastes, and the Book of Job. "The wise men", says Professor

Driver, "took for granted the main postulates of Israel's creed, and applied themselves rather to the observation of human character as such, seeking to analyse conduct, studying action in its consequences, and establishing morality, upon the basis of principles common to humanity at large ... They have been termed ... The Humanists of Israel. Their teaching had a practical aim." It related to conduct and education. And further, "the observation of human nature ... naturally leads on to reflection on the problems it presents." The inequalities among men, the apparent vanity of human pursuits, – these problems are discussed in Job and Ecclesiastes.

And so when James speaks of wisdom, he means a true understanding of human life, and of the moral order of the world – the power and habit of forming a just judgement on wealth and poverty, joy and sorrow, ease and pain, public honour and public dishonour, and all the incidents of human experience, – a clear vision of the laws which should regulate conduct, of the principles which should form character. It is, as someone has said, a living insight into Christian duty; it is the art of Christian conduct. "If any man lack this wisdom let him ask of God."

R. W. Dale (1829–95)

5th July

This, then, is how you should pray: Our Father in heaven, hallowed be your name.

(Matthew 6:9)

First of all, the Teacher of peace and Master of unity would not have men pray singly and severally, since, when any prays, he is not to pray for himself only. For we say not, "My Father, which art in heaven;" nor "Give me this day my bread;" nor does each individual pray that his own debt only should be forgiven, or ask for himself alone, not to be led into temptation, or to be delivered from evil. Our prayer is general and for all; and when we pray, we pray not for one person but for us all, because we all are one.

God, the Master of peace and concord, so willed that one should pray for all, according as Himself in one did bear us all. This rule of prayer the Three Children shut up in the fiery furnace kept, being in unison in prayer, and being concordant in an agreement of spirit. They spake as out of one mouth, though Christ had not yet taught them to pray. Hence in prayer their words were availing and effectual, because the Lord was gained by peaceable and simple and spiritual praying.

It was thus, too, that we find the Apostles and disciples prayed, after the Ascension of the Lord; "They all", we are told, "continued with one accord in prayer with the women, and Mary the Mother of Jesus, and His brethren." They continued with one accord in prayer, manifesting at the same time the instancy of their praying, and the agreement. Because God "who maketh men to be of one mind in an house", admits into the house divine and eternal those only among whom is unanimous prayer.

Cyprian (c. 201/210–258)

6th July

And lead us not into temptation, but deliver us from the evil one.
(Matthew 6:13)

A steamboat was stranded in the Mississippi River, and the captain could not get her off. Eventually a hard-looking fellow came on board, and said: "Captain, I understand you want a pilot to take you out of this difficulty?"

The captain said, "Are you a pilot?"

"Well they call me one."

"Do you know where the snags and sand-bars are?"

"No, sir."

"Well, how can you expect to take me out of here if you don't know where the snags and sand-bars are?"

"I know where they ain't!" was the reply.

Beware of temptations. "Lead us not into temptation," our Lord taught us to pray; and again He said, "Watch and pray, lest ye enter into temptation." We are weak and sinful by nature, and it is a good deal better for us to pray for deliverance rather than to run into temptation and then pray for strength to resist.

D. L. Moody (1837–99)

7th July

You are not your own; you were bought at a price. Therefore honour God with your body.

(1 Corinthians 6:19b–20)

> "Not your own!" but His ye are,
> Who paid a price untold
> For your life, exceeding far
> All earth's store of gems and gold.
> With the precious blood of Christ,
> Ransom treasure all unpriced,
> Full redemption is procured,
> Full salvation is assured.
>
> "Not your own!" but His by right,
> His peculiar treasure now,
> Fair and precious in His sight,
> Purchased jewels for His brow.
> He will keep what thus he sought,
> Safely guard the dearly bought,
> Cherish that which He did choose.
> Always love and never lose.
>
> "Not your own!" but His, the King,
> His the Lord of earth and sky,
> His, to whom archangels bring
> Homage deep and praises high.
> What can royal birth bestow?
> Or the proudest titles show?
> Can such dignity be known
> As the glorious name, "His own!"

"Not your own!" To Him ye owe
All your life and all your love;
Live, that ye His praise may show,
Who is yet all praise above.
Every day and every hour,
Every gift and every power,
Consecrate to Him alone,
Who hath claimed you for His own.

Teach us, Master, how to give
All we have and are to Thee;
Grant us, Saviour, while we live,
Wholly only Thine to be.
Henceforth be our calling high
Thee to serve and glorify;
Ours no longer, but Thine own,
Thine for ever, Thine alone!

Frances Ridley Havergal (1836–79)

8th July

He came and preached peace to you who were far away and peace to those who were near.

(Ephesians 2:17)

There is much about reconciliation which experience does not demonstrate, because experience is never complete. A man may be assured that the reconciliation to God which he owes to Christ is final and absolute, yet have much to learn about the consequences of sin. All he knows about these consequences to begin with is that, be what they may, they can and do negate reconciliation. But he has to learn by further experience how the healing power of reconciliation works in a sin-stricken nature, and, though he can never be reconciled to sin, whether there are not by the will of God painful and disabling consequences of sin to which in the meantime he must resign himself as patiently and unmurmuringly as he can.

He has to learn what the standing temper of the reconciled life will be in his own case. It may be determined in part by his natural temperament, in part by his past life, in part by the completeness with which he had received the reconciliation; it may be triumphant or more subdued . . . but it does not affect the reconciliation itself. Most men after they receive the gospel have much to learn of the scope of reconciliation. They do not realise how much God covers, and that reconciliation to Him has not had its perfect work, until we are reconciled also to our fellows, to the order of providence, and to the inexorable laws of the spiritual world.

Of one thing, however, there is never any question: the place of Jesus in the reconciliation. *He* is our Peace.

James Denney (1856–1917)

9th July

If you love me, you will obey what I command.

(John 14:15)

In the little country district where I went to school there were two parties. One party said that boys could not possibly be controlled without the cane, and they kept a schoolmaster who acted on their plan; the other party said they should be controlled by love. The struggle went on, and at last, on one election day, the first party was put out, and the other ruled in their stead. I happened to be at school at the time, and we said to each other that we were going to have a grand time that winter. There would be no more corporal punishment, and we were going to be ruled by love.

The new teacher was a lady, and she opened the school with prayer. We hadn't seen it before, and we were impressed, especially when she prayed that she might have grace and strength to rule the school with love. The school went on for several weeks, and we saw no cane.

I was one of the first to break the rules of the school. The teacher asked me to stay behind. I thought that the cane was coming out again and I was in fighting mood. She took me alone. She sat down and began to talk to me kindly. That was worse than the cane; I did not like it. She said –

"I have made up my mind that if I cannot control the school by love. I will give it up. I will have no punishment. If you love me, try to keep the rules of the school."

I felt something rise in my throat, and never gave her any more trouble. She just put me under grace. And that is what God does. God is love, and He wants us all to love Him.

D. L. Moody (1837–99)

10th July

If I speak in the tongues of men and of angels, but have not love, I am only a resounding gong or a clanging cymbal. If I have the gift of prophecy and can fathom all mysteries and all knowledge, and if I have a faith that can move mountains, but have not love, I am nothing. If I give all I possess to the poor and surrender my body to the flames, but have not love, I gain nothing.

(1 Corinthians 13:1–3)

MY DEAR SISTER,

I know not that ever you asked me a question which I did not readily answer. I never heard any one mention anything concerning you on that account; but I myself was jealous over you. Perhaps I shall find faults in you that others do not; for I survey you on every side. I mark your very motion and temper; because I long for you to be without spot or blemish.

What I have seen in London occasioned the first caution I gave you. George Bell, William Green, and many others, then full of love, were favoured with extraordinary revelations and manifestations from God. But by this very thing Satan beguiled them from the simplicity that is in Christ. By insensible degrees they were led to value these extraordinary gifts more than the ordinary grace of God; and I could not convince them that a grain of humble love was better than all these gifts put together. This, my dear friend, was what made me fear for you. This makes me remind you again and again. Faith and hope are glorious gifts, and so is every ray of eternity let into the soul. But still these are but means: The end of all, and the greatest of all is love. May the Lord just now pour it into your heart as he never has done before.

By all means spend an hour every other day in the labour of love, even though you cannot help them as you would. Commending you to Him who is able to make you perfect in every good word and work.

I am
Yours affectionately.
John Wesley

John Wesley (1703–91)

11th July

And now these three remain: faith, hope and love. But the greatest of these is love.

(1 Corinthians 13:13)

Let him who has love in Christ keep the commandments of Christ. Who can describe the blessed bond of the love of God? What man is able to tell the excellence of its beauty as it ought to be told? The height to which love exalts is not capable of description. Love unites to God. Love covers a multitude of sins. Love beareth all things, is long-suffering in all things. There is nothing base, nothing arrogant in love. Love admits of no schisms: love gives rise to no seditions: love does all things in harmony. By love have all the elect of God been made perfect; without love nothing is well-pleasing to God. In love has the Lord taken us to Himself. On account of the Love he bore us, Jesus Christ our Lord gave His blood for us by the will of God; His flesh for our flesh, and His soul for our souls.

Ye see, beloved, how great and wonderful is love, and that there is no declaring its perfection. Who is fit to be found in it, except such as God has vouchsafed to render so? Let us pray, therefore, and implore of His mercy, that we may live blameless in love, free from human partialities for one above another.

Clement of Rome (fl. c. 90–100)

12th July

Then David and all the men with him took hold of their clothes and tore them. They mourned and wept and fasted till evening for Saul and his son Jonathan, and for the army of the Lord and the house of Israel, because they had fallen by the sword.

(2 Samuel 1:11–12)

What can be a proof of greater kindness of heart than the lament of David over that man, who had always thirsted for his death, and that he bore with so much regret the death of him, whom he succeeded in the kingdom? . . . Assuredly a kindliness of heart so great was an infallible mark of an abundant measure of this best of perfumes. Therefore, also he addressed with confidence his prayer to God; remember David and all his kindness of heart (Psalm 132:1).

All these holy persons such as David had this best of perfumes, of which fragrant odours are spread through all the Churches even at the present day. And not only they, but all those also who, during this life, have shown themselves to be benevolent and charitable, who have striven so to live humanely among men as not to keep for their own advantage, but to use for the common benefit of all, every grace they possessed, regarding themselves as debtors, alike to enemies and friends, to the wise and to the unwise. As they were useful to all, humble in all circumstances, and before all things showed themselves to be dear to God and to men; so their fragrance is held in pious memory.

As many, I repeat, of those who have gone before, who have been in character such as this, were of good report as of sweet perfume in their own days, and their sweetness remains at the present time. Thus also with you, my brother, whosoever you are, if you shall willingly share with us, who are your companions, the gift which you have received from on high. If you show yourself always helpful, sympathetic, kindly, tractable, humble, then you, too, will have from all of us a similar testimony that you are fragrant with the richest perfumes.

Bernard of Clairvaux (1090–1153)

13th July

This is my command: Love each other.

(John 15:17)

You may have heard of the boy whose home was in a wood. One day he thought he heard the voice of another boy not far off. He shouted, "Hallo, there!" and the voice shouted back, "Hallo, there!" He did not know that it was an echo of his own voice, and he shouted again, "You are a mean boy!" Again the cry came back, "You are a mean boy!"

After some more of the same kind of thing he went into the house and told his mother that there was a bad boy in the wood. His mother who understood how it was, said to him –

"Oh, no! You speak kindly to him, and see if he does not speak kindly to you."

He went into the wood again and shouted, "Hallo, there!"

"Hallo, there!" "You are a good boy." Of course the reply came, "You are a good boy," "I love you." "I love you," said the other voice.

This little story explains the secret of the whole thing. Some of you perhaps think you have bad and disagreeable neighbours; most likely the trouble is with yourself. If you love your neighbours they will love you. Love begets love.

D. L. Moody (1837–99)

14th July

Put to death, therefore, whatever belongs to your earthly nature: sexual immorality, impurity, lust, evil desires and greed, which is idolatry.

(Colossians 3:5)

Man's habits have so long applied themselves to . . . admiration of money, that no one is thought worthy of honour unless he is rich. This is no new habit. Nay, this vice (and that makes the matter worse) grew long years ago in the heart of men. When the city of

Jericho fell at the sound of the priests' trumpets, and Joshua the son of Nun gained the victory, he knew that the valour of the people was weakened through love of money and desire for gold. For when Achan had taken a garment of gold and two hundred shekels of silver and a gold ingot from the spoils of the ruined city, he was brought before the Lord and could not deny the theft, but owned it.

Love of money, then, is an old, an ancient vice, which showed itself even at the declaration of the divine law; for a law was given to check it (Exodus 20:17). On account of love of money Balak thought that Balaam could be tempted by rewards to curse the people of our fathers (Numbers 22:17). Love of money would have won the day too, had not God bidden him hold back from cursing.

Overcome by love of money Achan led to destruction all the people of the fathers. So Joshua the son of Nun, who could stay the sun from setting, could not keep the love of money in man from creeping on. At the sound of his voice the sun stood still, but love of money stayed not. When the sun stood still Joshua completed his triumph, but when the love of money went on, he almost lost the victory.

Ambrose of Milan (c. 339–397)

15th July

The rulers of the Philistines went to her and said, "See if you can lure him into showing you the secret of his great strength and how we can overpower him so that we may tie him up and subdue him. Each one of us will give you eleven hundred shekels of silver." So Delilah said to Samson, "Tell me the secret of your great strength and how you can be tied up and subdued."

(Judges 16:5–6)

[Continued from yesterday.]

Did not the woman Delilah's love of money deceive Samson, the bravest man of all? So he who had torn asunder the roaring lion with his hands; who, when bound and handed over to his enemies, alone, without help, burst his bonds and slew a thousand of them;

who broke the cords interwoven with sinews as they were slight threads of a net; he, I say, having laid his head on the woman's knee, was robbed of the decoration of his victory – bringing hair, that which gave him his might. Money flowed into the lap of the woman, and the favour of God forsook the man.

Love of money, then, is deadly. Seductive is money, whilst it also defiles those who have it, and helps not those who have it not. Supposing that money sometimes is a help, yet it is only help to a poor man who makes his wants known. What good is it to him who does not long for it, nor seek it; who does not need its help, and is not turned aside by the pursuit of it? What good is it to others, if he who has it is alone the richer for it? Is he therefore more honourable because he has that whereby honour is often lost, because he has what he must guard rather than possess? We possess what we use, but what is beyond our use brings us no fruit of possession, but only the danger of watching.

Ambrose of Milan (c. 339–397)

16th July

I am not saying this because I am in need, for I have learned to be content whatever the circumstances ... I can do everything through him who gives me strength.

(Philippians 4:11, 13)

It is no test of faith when we are full and abound. The test comes when the scarcity comes; then can be seen the faithful and the others. The faithful take the five loaves and two small fish and give God thanks. The others begin to grouse at Peter for maladministration, as though they had contracted with Peter instead of with Jesus ...

There are no funds. It may be God is answering our prayers in one of His higher ways. These people know much of the facts of the gospel but they imbibe little. They know all about the cross but have never seen it: may it not be that God is going to put the cross visibly across our lives so that they may realise the Cross of Jesus, and so then their "chest stones" become hearts, and so their lives change? Anyway we are willing for it. We are not going to let Shadrach and Co. outstrip us. "We know that our God can deliver." If it is a fiery oven we will walk in it with HIM. If it is starvation camp we will abide with Him there till the gates open to Glory. We have often shouted "hallelujah for the cross" when we saw none visible. Now we see the cross coming here. Let us meet it with a welcoming shout of triumph and display it with the glory of our King. I was rather amused a few days ago to hear one member pray for those who have financial responsibilities at home. This is the first time I have heard anyone pray to God on God's behalf! None but God is responsible for us financially . . .

"Why does God permit shortage?" He may be teaching us to fast as well as pray, that the devil may be exorcised from these people. It may be we have erred, or somebody else has done so, as with Achan [Joshua 7]. If it is a *thing*, let us put it away. If it is a man, let us leave God to settle with him. It may be God sees the fight in front of us and is training us to endure by these very easy ways.

C. T. Studd (1862–1931)

17th July

We rejoice in our sufferings, because we know that suffering produces perseverance; perseverance character; and character, hope. And hope does not disappoint us, because God has poured out his love into our hearts by the Holy Spirit, whom he has given us.

(Romans 5:3–5)

It is good that we have sometime troubles and crosses; for they often make a man enter into himself, and consider that he is here in banishment, and ought not to place his trust in any worldly thing.

It is good that we sometimes be contradicted, and that there be evil or a lessening conceit had of us; and this though we do and intend well.

These things help often to the attaining of humility, and defend us from vain glory; for then we chiefly seek God for our inward witness, when outwardly we be condemned by men, and when there is no credit given unto us.

And therefore a man should settle himself so fully in God, that he need not to seek many comforts of men.

When a good man is afflicted, tempted, or troubled with evil thoughts; then he understandeth better the great need he hath of God, without whom he perceiveth he can do nothing that is good.

Then also he sorroweth, lamenteth, and prayeth, by reason of the miseries he suffereth.

Then he is weary of living longer, and wisheth that death would come, that he might be dissolved and be with Christ.

Then also he well perceiveth, that perfect security and full peace cannot be had in this world.

Thomas à Kempis (c. 1380–1471)

18th July

The spiritual man makes judgments about all things, but he himself is not subject to any man's judgment. "For who has known the mind of the Lord, that he may instruct him?" But we have the mind of Christ.

(1 Corinthians 2:15–16)

If a gentleman should fancy that the moon is no bigger than it appears to the eye, that it shines with its own light, that all of the stars are only so many spots of light; if, after reading books of astronomy, he should continue in the same opinion, most people would think that he had but a poor apprehension. But if the same person should think it better to provide for short life here, than to prepare of a glorious eternity hereafter: that it was better to be rich, than to be eminent in piety, his ignorance and dullness would be too great to be compared to anything else.

There is no knowledge that deserves so much the name of it, but that which we call judgement. And that is the most clear and improved understanding, which judges best of the value and worth of things. All the rest is but the capacity of an animal, it is but mere seeing and hearing. And there is no excellence of any knowledge in us, till we exercise our judgement, and judge well of the value and worth of things.

If a man had eyes that could see beyond the stars, or pierce into the heart of the earth, but could not see the things that were before him, or discern anything that was serviceable to him, we should reckon that he had nothing but a very bad sight.

In like manner, if a man has a memory that can retain a great many things; if he has a wit that is sharp and acute in the arts and sciences, or an imagination that can wander agreeably in fictions, but has a dull, poor apprehension of his duty and relation to God, of the value of piety, or of the worth of moral virtue, he may justly be reckoned to have a bad understanding. He is but like the man, that can only see and hear such things as are of no benefit to him.

As certain therefore as piety, virtue, and eternal happiness are of most concern to man; as certain as the immortality of our nature; so certain is it, that he who dwells most in contemplation of them, whose heart is most affected with them, who sees farthest into them, who best judges all wordly attainments to be mere bubbles and shadows in comparison of them, proves himself to have, of all others, the finest understanding and the strongest judgement.

William Law (1686–1761)

19th July

After David had finished talking with Saul, Jonathan became one in spirit with David, and he loved him as himself.

(1 Samuel 18:1)

When he woke up to find how truly he loved David, a new difficulty entered his life. Not outwardly, because, though Saul eyed David with jealousy, there was no open rupture. David went in and out of the palace, was in a position of trust, and was constantly at hand for the intercourse for which each yearned. But when the flames of hostility, long smouldering in Saul's heart broke forth, the true anguish of his life began. On one hand, his duty as son and subject held him to his father, though he knew his father was doomed, and that union with him meant disaster to himself; on the other hand, all his heart cried out for David.

His love for David made him eager to promote reconciliation between his father and his friend. It was only when repeated failure had proved the fruitlessness of his dream that he abandoned it; and then the thought must have suggested itself to him: Why not extricate yourself from this sinking ship whilst there is time? Why not join your fortunes with his whom God hath chosen? The new fair kingdom of the future is growing up around him – identify yourself with it, though it be against your father.

The temptation was specious and masterful, but it fell blunt and ineffectual at his feet. Stronger than the ties of human love were those of duty, sonship, loyalty to God's anointed king; and in some supreme moment he turned his back on the appeal of his heart, and elected to stand by his father. From that choice he never flinched . . . When Saul finally started for his last battle with the Philistines, Jonathan fought beside him, though he knew that David was somehow involved in alliance with them . . .

Conflicts like these await us all – when the appointment of God says one thing, and the choice of the heart says another; when the wind sets in from one quarter, and the tide from the opposite one. Whenever this befalls thee, may God's grace enable thee to follow as straight a course, as true to the loftiest dictates of conscience, as Jonathan, the son of Saul!

F. B. Meyer (1847–1929)

20th July

When Solomon had finished all these prayers and supplications to the Lord, he rose from before the altar of the Lord, where he had been kneeling with his hands spread out towards heaven. He stood and blessed the whole assembly of Israel.

(1 Kings 8:54–55)

Solomon "blessed the congregation" when, in their name, he lifted his voice to bless the Lord, prayed that God would incline their hearts to keep His law, and would maintain their cause, and exhorted them to keep their hearts perfect with Him. We bless each other when we ask God to bless, and when we draw each other nearer Him.

Standing there in the new Temple, with a united nation before him, the cloud filling the house, and peace resting on all his land to it farthest border, the king looks back on the long road from Sinai and the desert, and sums up the whole history in one sentence. The end has vindicated the methods. There had been many a dark time when the enemies had oppressed, and many a hard-fought field had been stained with Israel's blood; but all had tended to this calm hour, when Israel's multitudes were gathered in worship, and their unguarded homes were safe. There had been many heroes in the long line. "Time would fail" him "to tell of Gideon, Barak, Samson, Jephthah; of David and Samuel . . . who . . . turned to flight armies of aliens."

One name alone is worthy to be named, – the name of the true Deliverer and Monarch. It is the Lord who "hath given rest to His people". We look on the past most wisely when we see in it all the working of one mighty Hand, and pass beyond the great names of history or the dear names which have made light of our homes, to the ever-living God, who works through changing instruments; and "the help that is done on earth, He doeth it Himself". We read the past most truly when we see in all its vicissitudes God's unchanging faithfulness, and recognise that the foes and sorrows which often pressed sore upon us were no breach of His faithful promises, but either His loving chastisement for our faithlessness, or His loving discipline meant to perfect our characters.

We read the past best from the vantage-ground of the Temple. From its height we understand the lie of the land. Communion with God explains much which is else inexplicable. Solomon's judgement of Israel's checkered history will be our judgement of our own when we stand in the higher courts of the heavenly home, and look from that height upon all the way the Lord God hath led us.

Alexander Maclaren (1826–1910)

21st July

Are not all angels ministering spirits sent to serve those who will inherit salvation?

(Hebrews 1:14)

On the ladder Jacob saw the angels of God ascending and descending (Genesis 28:12); what is that for? to show that they are ministering spirits sent forth to minister to them that shall be the heirs of salvation. Therefore we find them attending upon Christ. We do not hear much of them after the canon of scripture was closed, but as soon as ever Christ was born, the angels sang. Up until then we can never hear of their singing below as far as I can judge, since creation. Then the sons of God shouted for joy; but when Eve reached out her hand to pluck the fatal apple, and gave it to Adam, earth groaned, and the angels hung, as it were, their harps on the willows. But when Christ, the second Adam, was born, the angels sang at midnight, Glory to God in the highest. I pray to God we may all die singing that anthem, and sing it to all eternity.

After Christ's temptations, they came and ministered to him, as some think, food for his body, and wished him joy and comfort in his soul. In his agonies in the garden, an angel strengthened him. After his resurrection two appeared again, one at the head and another at the foot of his tomb . . . When our Lord departed, a cloud received him out of their sight, which probably was a cloud of angels; having led his disciples out of the city he blessed them, and then went away to heaven: may that blessing rest upon you and your children!

This shows us that God makes use of angels to attend his people, especially when they are departing into eternity: perhaps part of our entertainment in heaven will be, to hear the angels declare how many millions of times they have assisted and helped us.

George Whitefield (1714–70)

22nd July

"Look", he said, "I see heaven open and the Son of Man standing at the right hand of God."

(Acts 7:56)

[Continued from yesterday.]

Our Lord says, angels there do behold the face of the Father of the little ones (Matthew 18:10); therefore I love to talk to the lambs of the flock, and why should I not talk to them whom angels think it their honour to guard . . .

What gave the greatest comfort to Jacob was, that the Lord was on top of the ladder, which I do not know whether it would have been so, if Jacob had not seen God there. It comforts me, I assure you, to think, that whenever God shall call for me, I shall be carried by angels into Abraham's bosom. I have often thought that whenever that time comes, that blessed, long longed-for moment comes, as soon as ever they will have called upon me, my first question will be to them, where is my dear master? where is Jesus? where is that dear Immanuel, who has loved me with an everlasting love, and has called me by his grace, and have sent you to fetch me home to see his face?

But I believe you and I shall have no occasion to ask where he is, for he will come to meet us. He will stand at the top of his ladder, to take his pilgrims in.

George Whitefield (1714–70)

23rd July

See that you do not look down on one of these little ones. For I tell you that their angels in heaven always see the face of my Father in heaven.

(Matthew 18:10)

On the 6th June [1848] Shaftesbury brought forward in the House of Commons a motion, "That it is expedient that means be annually provided for the voluntary emigration to some of her Majesty's colonies of certain number of young persons of both sexes, who have been educated in the schools ordinarily called 'Ragged Schools' in and about the metropolis." . . .

"Til very recently the few children that came to our notice in the streets and places of public traffic were considered to be chance vagrants, beggars, or pilferers, who, by a little exercise of magisterial authority, might be either extinguished or reformed. It is only of late been discovered that they constitute a numerous class, having habits, pursuits, feelings, customs, and interests of their own; living as a class, though shifting as individuals, in the same resorts; perpetuating and multiplying their filthy numbers. For the knowledge of these details we are mainly indebted to the London City Mission. It is owing to their deep, anxious, and constant research; it is owing to the zeal with which their agents have fathomed the recesses of human misery, and penetrated into places repulsive to every sense, moral and physical; it is owing to such exertions, aided by the piety, self-denial, and devotion of Sunday-school teachers, that we have advanced thus far. Certain excellent persons, who gave their energies to Sabbath training, were the first to observe these miserable outcasts, and hoping, by the influence of the Gospel, to effect some amendment, opened schools in destitute places, to which children were invited, not coerced . . .

"[Of 1600 studied] 162 confessed that they had been in prison not once or twice – many of them several times; 116 had run away from their homes, the result, in many instances of ill-treatment; 170 slept in lodging houses – nests of every abomination that the mind of man can conceive; 253 confessed that they lived altogether by begging; 216 had neither shoes or stockings; 280 had no caps, hats, bonnets, or head covering; 101 had no linen; 219 never slept in beds – many had no recollection of having ever tasted that luxury; 68 were children of convicts; 125 had step-mothers, to whom may be chased much of the misery that drives the children of the poor to the commission of crime; 306 had lost either one or both parents, a large proportion having lost both."

Lord Shaftesbury (1801–85)

24th July

For our struggle is not against flesh and blood, but against the rulers, against the authorities, against the power of this dark world and against the spiritual forces of evil in the heavenly realms.
(Ephesians 6:12)

In looking at the requirements of the King, and at the history of the early apostles and disciples, I charge it on modern Christianity, that its professors do not even *comprehend the first principles of this warfare*, much less do they set themselves to carry it on to the ends of the earth.

The service rendered to the King and to the kingdom in these days is, alas, with few exceptions, of a very milk-and-watery type, of a very short weight character, and the great effort of the majority of its teachers, judging from their writings, and from what we see and know of their public services and of their private lives, seems to be intended to make things comfortable all round. "Peace, peace," is the continual cry, when there is no peace. As one of the bishops said a little while ago, "We hear a great deal about Church defence; we ought to be hearing about Church aggression." Yes, alas! in the great mass of instances when these modern Christians do fight, it is over opinions and ceremonies with their own children, inside their own walls, instead of with the enemy outside. They are far more valiant in defending some ceremonial of the Church, than they are in defending the cross of Christ in the presence of its adversaries. They are far more concerned in propagating their "ism" than the kingdom of righteousness, peace, and joy in the Holy Ghost. Alas, that it should be so; but such is the fact, and it is patent to every enlightened observer.

Jesus Christ did not call us to fight each other, but He called us to present one bold front to the enemy. He bade us go and take captive the hearts and souls of men, and not merely to change their *opinions*. Get a man's heart right, and his opinions will soon follow. But you may be tinkering at his intellect till the hour of his death and he will not be a whit nearer heaven, but perchance nearer hell, than if he had been left alone.

Catherine Booth (1829–90)

25th July

Therefore put on the full armour of God, so that when the day of evil comes, you may be able to stand your ground, and after you have done everything, to stand.

(Ephesians 6:13)

In ancient warfare battles were lost or won very largely according to the weight of the masses of men that were hurled against each other; and the heavier men, with firmer footing were likely to be the victors. Our modern way of fighting is different from that. But in the old time the one thing needful was that a man should stand firm and resist the shock of the enemies that rushed upon him. Unless our footing is good we shall be tumbled over by the onset of some unexpected antagonist. And for good footing there are two things necessary.

One is a good, solid piece of ground to stand on, that is not slippery or muddy, and the other is a good strong pair of soldier's boots, that will take hold on the ground and help the wearer to steady himself. Christ has set our feet on the rock, and so the first requisite is secured. If we, for our part, will keep near to the Gospel which brings peace into our hearts, the peace that it brings will make us able to stand and bear unmoved any force that may be hurled against us. If we are to be "steadfast, unmovable," we can only be so when our feet are shod with the preparedness of the Gospel of peace.

The most of your temptations, most of the things that would pluck you away from Jesus Christ, and upset you in your standing will come down upon you unexpectedly. Nothing happens in this world except the unexpected; and it is the sudden assaults that we were not looking for that work most disastrously against us. A man may be aware of some special weakness in his character, and have given himself carefully and patiently to try and fortify himself against it, and, lo! all at once a temptation springs up from the opposite side; the enemy was lying in hiding there, and whilst his face was turned to face one foe, a foe that he knew nothing about came storming behind him.

There is only one way to stand, and that is not merely by cultivating watchfulness against our weaknesses, but by keeping fast hold of Jesus Christ manifested to us in His Gospel. Then the peace that comes from that communion will itself guard us.

Alexander Maclaren (1826–1910)

26th July

Stand firm then, with the belt of truth buckled round your waist, with the breastplate of righteousness in place.
(Ephesians 6:14)

In the conflicts of the Christian life we are safe only while we practise every personal and private virtue, and discharge with fidelity every duty to man and to God. "Righteousness" is the defence and guarantee of righteousness. The honest man is not touched by temptations to dishonesty; the truthful man is not touched by temptations to falsehood; habits of industry are a firm defence against temptations to indolence; a pure heart resents with disgust the first approaches of temptation to impurity.

The separate virtues of perfect character are necessary to each other, and through a single vicious habit or tendency we may be betrayed into many kinds of sin. Vanity and cowardice makes us accessible to temptations to untruthfulness; covetousness on the one hand and reckless extravagance on the other may be the means of destroying our integrity; intemperance may lead to violence and licentiousness.

The practical obedience to Christ which is possible to us through the power of His Spirit is a protection against temptations which might destroy our very life. It is like the "breastplate" which the soldier wore to protect the vital parts of his body. In anticipation of the fierce assault of the "spiritual hosts of wickedness" we are to arm ourselves with perfect conformity to all the precepts of Christ; we are to "stand . . . having put on the breastplate of righteousness."

R. W. Dale (1829–95)

27th July

Since we belong to the day, let us be self-controlled, putting on faith and love as a breastplate, and the hope of salvation as a helmet. For God did not appoint us to suffer wrath, but to receive salvation through our Lord Jesus Christ.

(1 Thessalonians 5:8–9)

Upton Lane, First Month 28th, 1833. – It has been a serious time to the country, the cholera prevailing nearly throughout England and Ireland. We were frequently where it was on our journey, but were favoured to escape unhurt. A great stir in the elections for the new Reform Parliament. Joseph Pease, a Friend [Quaker], admitted; this opens a new door for our Society – to what it leads is doubtful. A war for a short time with Holland. Much stirring in the world generally, religiously and politically – great variety of sentiments.

Notwithstanding all these things, it appears to me, that the kingdom of God is spreading its pure, blessed, and peaceful influence, and that the partition walls that have been built up between Christians generally, are breaking down. The suppression of Slavery – the diminution of Capital Punishment – the Improvement in Prisons, and the state of the poor prisoners – the spread of the Scriptures, also of the Gospel to distant lands – the increase of education and knowledge generally, and many other things, are truly encouraging.

I do thankfully believe that there is a great and glorious work going on, promoting the advancement of that day, when the knowledge of God and His glory, will cover the earth as the waters cover the sea. For Thine own name's sake, gracious Lord, hasten this day, when all flesh may see and rejoice in Thy salvation!

Elizabeth Fry (1780–1845)

28th July

I urge you, brothers, to watch out for those who cause divisions and put obstacles in your way that are contrary to the teaching you have learned.

(Romans 16:17)

Love is the great and new commandment, that is, the last which Christ would leave, at his departure, to his disciples. O could we learn of the Lord of love, and Him, who calleth himself love itself, to love our enemies, to bless them that curse us, and do good to the evil, and pray for them that hurt and persecute us, we should prove that we are genuine Christians, the children of our heavenly father (Matthew 5:44–5), but should heap coals of fire on our enemies' heads and melt them into compassion and some remorse, if not a holy love.

I tell you it is the Christian who doth truly love his neighbour as himself; who loveth the godly as his co-heirs of heaven, and loveth the ungodly with a desire to make them truly godly; who loveth a friend as a friend, and an enemy as a man that is capable of holiness and salvation. It is he that liveth, walketh, speaketh, converseth, yea, suffereth, which is the great difficulty in love, and is, as it were, turned by the love of God shed abroad upon his heart, into love itself; who doth glorify God in the world, and glorify his religion and really rebuke the blasphemer, that derideth the Spirit in believers, as if it were but a fanatical dream.

And it is he that by tyranny, cruelty, contempt of others, and needless, proud singularities and separations, magisterially condemning and vilifying all that walk not in his fashion, and pray not in his fashion, and are not of his opinion, where it is not like enough he is himself mistaken, that is the scandalous Christian who doth as much against God and religion, and the church and men's souls, as he doth against love.

And though it be Satan's way, as an angel of light and his ministers' way, as ministers of righteousness, to destroy Christ's interest by dividing it, and separating things that God will have conjoined, and so to pretend the love of truth, and love of order, as the love of godliness, or discipline, against the love of souls, to use even the name of love itself against love, to justify all their cruelties, or censures, and alienations; yet God will keep up that sacred fire in the hearts of the sound Christians which live and conquer these temptations.

Richard Baxter (1615–91)

29th July

Also a dispute arose among them as to which of them was considered to be greatest.

(Luke 22:24)

Envy may be defined to be a spirit of dissatisfaction with, and opposition to, the prosperity and happiness of others as compared with our own. The thing that the envious person is opposed to, and dislikes, is, the comparative superiority of the state of honour, or prosperity or happiness, that another may enjoy, over that which he possesses. And this spirit is especially called envy, when we dislike and are opposed to another's honour or prosperity, because in general, it is greater than our own, or because, in particular, they have some honour and enjoyment that we have not.

It is a disposition natural in men, that they love to be uppermost; and this disposition is directly crossed when they see others above them. And it is from this spirit that men dislike and are opposed to the prosperity of others, because they think it makes them who possess it superior in some respect, to themselves. And from this same disposition, a person may dislike another's being equal to himself in honour or happiness, or in having the same sources of enjoyments that he has; for as men very commonly are, they cannot bear a rival much, if any, better than a superior, for they love to be singular and alone in their eminence and advancement.

Such a spirit is called envy in the Scriptures. Thus Moses speaks of Joshua's envying for his sake, when Eldad and Medad were admitted to the same privilege with himself in having the spirit of prophecy given them, saying (Numbers 11:29), "Enviest thou for my sake? Would that all the Lord's people were prophets, and that the Lord would put his Spirit upon them!"

Jonathan Edwards (1703–58)

30th July

For where you have envy and selfish ambition, there you find disorder and every evil practice. But the wisdom that comes from heaven is first of all pure; then peace-loving, considerate, submissive, full of mercy and good fruit, impartial and sincere. Peacemakers who sow in peace raise a harvest of righteousness.

(James 3:16–18)

The genuine Christian hath an humble and cautelous understanding; sensible when he knoweth most how little he knoweth, and how much he is still unacquainted with, in the great mysterious matters of God. His ignorance is his daily grief and burden, and he is still longing and looking for some clearer light. Not a new word of revelation from God, but a clearer understanding of his word. He knoweth how weak and slippery man's understanding is, and he is humbly conscious of the darkness of his own. Therefore he is not conceitedly wise, not a boaster of his knowledge; but saith, as Paul (1 Corinthians 8:2), "If any man think that he knoweth anything (that is, is proudly conceited of his knowledge), he knoweth nothing yet as he ought to know."

And hence it is that though he daily grow in the firmer apprehension of necessary truths, yet he is never confident and peremptory about uncertain, doubtful things; and therefore he is not apt to be quarrelsome and contentious, nor yet censorious against those that differ from him in matters of no greater moment.

And hence it is that he runneth not into sects, nor burneth with the feverish dividing zeal, nor yet is scandalously mutable in his opinions; because, as one that is conscious of his ignorance, he doth not rashly receive things which he understands not, but suspendeth his judgement till evidence make him fit to judge; and joineth with neither of the contending parties, till he is sure to know indeed, which of them is right: and thus he avoideth that dishonouring of religion which the scandalous Christian is woefully guilty of; who, with an unhumbled understanding, groweth confident upon quick and insufficient information, and judgeth before he understandeth the case, and before he hath heard or read, and considered, what on both sides may be said, and what is necessary to a true understanding.

And thus, either by audacious prating of what he never understood, or reviling and censuring men wiser than himself, or by making himself a judge where he hath to be many years a learner, or making a religion of his own mistakes, and setting up dividing sects to propagate them, or else by shameful mutability and unsettledness he becometh a scandal to harden unbelievers; and a disease to the church and a shame to his profession . . . Conceited wisdom kindleth a contentious zeal, and is not of God, but from beneath.

Richard Baxter (1615–91)

31st July

Through him we both have access to the Father by one Spirit.
(Ephesians 2:18)

I do not think the New Testament contemplates the existence of unattached Christians – persons who have accepted the Christian salvation, and embraced the Christian ideal and vocation – but who are not members of a church. The Christian end can never be attained for ourselves or for others, except by the mutual action and reaction, the reciprocal giving and receiving, of all who are in fellowship with Christ.

What the brethren have is indispensible to us; what we have is indispensible to them . . . It is the recognition of this truth on which the vital unity of the Church depends. The Church is united, it is *one* Church, because it is the body of Christ, and because every member is necessary to all the rest. It is united, because to *every* member grace has been given according to the measure of Christ; because to *every* one the manifestation of the Spirit is given, not for his private satisfaction, but to profit withal; in other words, for the furtherance of the common good.

It is not united by offices, nor even by officials; it is not united by a documentary constitution or creed; it is not united by a uniform and all-embracing government – none of these things is mentioned by the apostles. Christ's gifts to it for the maintenance and furtherance of its unity are not offices or officials, but spiritually endowed men; it is not in the fellowship of a priestly or episcopal order – much less in the fellowship of a Pope – that it is one; it is one in the fellowship of the Holy Ghost.

James Denney (1856–1917)

August

1st August

Awake, awake! Clothe yourself with strength, O arm of the Lord; awake as in days gone by, as in generations of old . . . Awake, awake, O Zion, clothe yourselves with strength.

(Isaiah 51:9, 52:1)

We have here a common principle underlying both the clauses of our text, to which I must briefly call attention, namely the occurrence in the Church's history of successive periods of energy and languor.

It is freely admitted that such alternation is not the highest ideal of growth, either in the individual or in the community. Our Lord's own parables set forth a more excellent way – the way of uninterrupted increase, whereof the type is the springing corn, which puts forth "first the blade, then the ear, after that the full corn in the ear," and passes through all the stages from the tender green spikelets that gleam over the fields in the spring-tide to the yellow abundance of autumn, in one unbroken season of genial months. So would our growth be best, healthiest, happiest. So *might* our growth be, if the mysterious life in the seed met no checks. But as a matter of fact, the Church has not thus grown. Rather at the best, its emblem is not to be looked for in corn, but in forest trees – the very rings in whose trunk tell of recurring seasons when the sap has risen at the call of spring, and sunk again before the frowns of winter. I have not now to do with the causes of this ... Nor am I saying that such a manner of growth is inevitable. I am only pointing out a fact, capable of verification and familiar to us all. Our years have summer and winter. The evening and the morning have completed all the days since the first.

We know it only too well. In our own hearts we have known such time, when some cold clinging mist wrapped us round and hid all the heaven of God's love and the starry lights of His truth; when the visible was the only real, and He seemed far away and shadowy; when there was neither confidence in our belief, nor heat in our love, nor enthusiasm in our service; when the shackles of conventionalism bound our souls, and the fetters of the frost imprisoned all their springs.

And we have seen a like palsy smite whole regions and ages of the Church of God, so that even the sensation of impotence was dead like all the rest, and the very tradition of spiritual power had faded away.

Alexander Maclaren (1826–1910)

2nd August

Repent, then, and turn to God, so that your sins may be wiped out, that times of refreshing may come from the Lord.

(Acts 3:19)

[Continued from yesterday.]

If then there are such recurring seasons of languor, they must either go on deepening till sleep becomes death, or they must be broken by a new outburst of vigorous life. It would be better if we did not need the latter. The uninterrupted growth would be best; but if that has not been attained, then the ending of winter by spring, and the suppling of the dry branches, and the resumption of the arrested growth, is the next best, and the only alternative to rotting away.

And it is by such times that the Kingdom of Christ always has grown. Its history has been one of successive impulses gradually exhausted, as by friction and gravity, and mercifully repeated just at the moment when it was ceasing to advance and had begun to slide backwards. And in such manner of progress, the Church's history has been in full analogy with that of all other forms of human association and activity. It is not in religion alone that there are "revivals." to use that word of which some people have such a dread. You see analagous phenomena in the field of literature, arts, social and political life. In them all, there come times of awakened interest in long-neglected principles. Truths which for many years had been left unheeded, save by a faithful few watchers of the beacon, flame up all at once as the guiding pillar of a nation's march, and a whole people strike their tents and follow where they lead. A mysterious quickening thrills through society. A contagion of enthusiasm spreads like fire, fusing all hearts in one. The air is electric with change. Some great advance is secured at a stride; and before and after that supreme effort are years of comparative quiescence; those before being times of preparation, those after being times of fruition and exhaustion – but slow and languid compared with the joyous energy of that moment. One day may be as a thousand years in the history of a people, and a nation may be born in a day.

So also is the history of the Church. And thank God it be so, for if it had not been for the dawning of these times of refreshing, the steady operation of the Church's worldliness would have killed it long ago. Surely dear brethren, we ought to desire a merciful interruption of the sad continuity of our languor and decay. The surest sign of its coming would be a widespread desire and expectation of its coming, joined with a penitent consciousness of our heavy and sinful slumber.

Alexander Maclaren (1826–1910)

3rd August

Many deceivers, who do not acknowledge Jesus Christ as coming in the flesh, have gone out into the world. Any such person is the deceiver and the antichrist. Watch out that you do not lose what you have worked for, but that you may be rewarded fully. Anyone who runs ahead and does not continue in the teaching of Christ does not have God; whoever continues in the teaching has both the Father and the Son.

(2 John 7–9)

We must be warned then, dearest brethren, not only against things open and manifest, but also against those which deceive us, through the guile of craft and fraud. What now can be more crafty, or what more artful, than for this enemy, detected and downfallen by the advent of Christ to rear his head? Light has come to the nations, and the beams of salvation shine to the health of man so that the deaf may hear the sound of spiritual grace, and the blind may open their eyes upon God. The sick regain the strength of an eternal healing, the lame run to church, and the dumb lift on high their voices to speak and worship. The enemy, thus seeing his idols left, his seats and temples deserted by the manifold congregation of believers, invents the new deceit to carry the incautious into error, while retaining the name of the Christian profession.

He has made heresies and schisms, with which to subvert faith, to corrupt truth, and rend unity. Those whom he cannot detain in the blindness of the old way, he compasses and deceives by misleading them on their new journey. He snatches men from out of the Church itself, and while they think themselves come to the light, and escaped from the night of this world, he secretly gathers fresh shadows upon them. Standing neither with the Gospel of Christ, nor with His ordinances, nor with His law, they yet call themselves Christians. They walk among darkness, thinking that they have light. Meanwhile the foe flatters and misleads, transforms himself, according to the word of the Apostle, into "an Angel of light"; and garbs his ministers like ministers of righteousness.

These are the maintainers of night for day, of death for salvation, giving despair while they proffer hope, faithlessness clothed as faith, Antichrist under the name of Christ. By putting false things under an appearance of true, they with subtlety impede the truth.

Cyprian (c. 201/210–258)

4th August

Speak to one another with psalms, hymns and spiritual songs. Sing and make music in your heart to the Lord, always giving thanks to God the Father for everything, in the name of our Lord Jesus Christ. Submit to one another out of reverence for Christ.
(Ephesians 5:19–21)

In regard to the order of public worship ... difficulties have been met in the effecting of every change, because the professing Christians have felt as if God had established just the *mode which they were used to*.

Formerly it was customary to sing the Psalms. By and by there was introduced a version of the Psalms in rhyme. This was "very bad," to be sure. When ministers tried to introduce them, the Churches were distracted, the people displayed violent opposition, and great trouble was created by the innovation. But the new measure triumphed.

Yet when another version was brought forward, in a better style of poetry, its introduction was opposed as yet a further new measure. Finally came Watts's version, which is still opposed in many Churches. No longer ago than 1828, when I was in Philadelphia, I was told that a minister there was preaching a course of lectures on Psalmody, to his congregation, for the purpose of bringing them to use a better version of psalms and hymns than the one they were accustomed to.

And even now, in a great many congregations, there are people who will rise and leave, if a psalm or hymn is given out from a new book. If Watts's version of the Psalms should be adopted, they would secede and form a new congregation, rather than tolerate such an innovation!

Charles G. Finney (1792–1875)

5th August

I liken you, my darling, to a mare harnessed to one of the chariots of Pharaoh.

(Song of Songs 1:9)

It will be remembered that horses originally came out of Egypt, and that the pure breed still found in Arabia was during Solomon's reign brought by his merchants for all the kings of the East. Those selected for Pharaoh's own chariot would not only be of the purest blood and perfect in proportion and symmetry, but also perfect in training, docile and obedient; they would know no will but that of the charioteer, and the only object of their existence would be to carry the king whithersoever he would go. So should it be with the Church of Christ; one body with many members, indwelt and guided by one SPIRIT; holding the HEAD, and knowing no will but HIS; her rapid and harmonious movement should cause His kingdom to progress throughout the world.

Many years ago a beloved friend, returning from the East by the overland route, made the journey from Suez to Cairo in the cumbrous diligence then in use. The passengers on landing took their places, about a dozen wild young horses were harnessed with ropes to the vehicle, the driver took his seat and cracked his whip, and the horses dashed off, some to the right, some to the left, and others forward, causing the coach to start with a bound, and as suddenly stop, with effect of first throwing those sitting in the front seat into the laps of those sitting behind, and then of reversing the operation. With the aid of sufficient Arabs running in each side to keep these wild animals progressing in the right direction the passengers were jerked and jolted, bruised and shaken, until, on reaching their destination, they were too wearied and sore to take the rest they so much needed.

Is not the Church of God today more like these untrained steeds than a company of horses in Pharaoh's chariot? And while self-will and disunion are apparent in the Church, can we wonder that the world still lieth in the wicked one, and that the great heathen nations are barely touched?

James Hudson Taylor (1832–1905)

6th August

Now a man came up to Jesus and asked, "Teacher, what good thing must I do to get eternal life?"

(Matthew 19:16)

One day a young man came to Jesus. He had seen some glimpse of Jesus' idea. He dreamed that he might be a son of God. "What shall I do that I might reach eternal life?" he said. And Jesus lifted his finger and pointed out to him the long line of milestones that marked the way to celestial aspiration – humanity, purity, honesty, brotherly love. They did not satisfy the youth. He knew them all, yet he did not get what he wanted, what he dreamed of. "All these have I done. What lack I yet?"

His soul was like a boat tied fast, but tied up with a long rope. It was able to struggle up the channel, past headland and light and buoy that marked the way; but always something held it back from perfectly laying itself at rest beside the golden shore. "What lack I yet? What lack I yet?" And then said Jesus, "Go and sell all that thou hast and thou shalt have treasure in heaven and come and follow Me." He did not say, "You do not deserve wealth." He did not say, "It is wicked to be rich." He only said, "You will be free if you are poor, and then I can lead you to the Father, in whom you shall find yourself." He went back, past the buoys and headlands, down to the bay where the rope was tied, and cut the boat loose from its anchorage.

The sadness with which the young man went away one would fain believe was the sadness of the rescued slave, who misses and mourns for the familiar fetter, even while his heart begins already to open to the embrace of the new life of liberty that spreads bewilderingly, almost awfully before him.

Phillips Brooks (1835–93)

7th August

Jesus looked at him and said, "How hard it is for the rich to enter the kingdom of God!"

(Luke 18:24)

"The criminal classes" is another of the cant phrases of modern Christianity, which thus brands every poor lad who steals, because he is hungry, but stands, hat in hand, before the rich man whose trade is well known to be a system of wholesale cheatery.

It is never convenient for ministers or responsible churchwardens or deacons to ask how Mr Money-maker gets the golden sovereigns or crisp notes which look so well in the collection. He may be the most "accursed sweater" who ever waxed fat on that murderous cheap needlework system, which is slowly destroying the bodies and ruining the souls of thousands of poor women, both in this and other "civilised" countries. He may keep scores of employees standing wearily sixteen hours per day behind the counter, across which they dare not speak the truth, and on salaries so small that all hope of marriage and home is denied to them. Or he may trade in some damning thing which robs men of all that is good in the world and all hope for the next, such as opium or intoxicating drinks; but if you were simple enough to suppose that modern Christianity would object to him on account of any of these things, – in fact, that you were alluding to such as he, in the phrase "criminal classes," – how respectable Christians would open their eyes, and, in fact, suspect that you had recently made your escape from some lunatic asylum, and ought to be hastened back there as soon as possible. If any one should dare to cast any reflections upon any of these Christian money-makers, the representatives of the churches would say, "hush, hush, my dear sir, Mr So-and-so is the great man at our place, you know; they would be glad enough of him at the church opposite, but he likes our minister, and we mean to propose him as a deacon at the next church meeting." So the wholesale and successful thief is glossed over and called by all manner of respectable names by the representatives of a bastard Christianity. It is ready enough to cry, "Stop, thief," when some poor fellow who has been out of work for perhaps months, gets desperate at the sight of children crying for bread, and makes a bungling attempt at getting what is not his own in order to satisfy them; or when it hears that such men, left helplessly to their own devices, take to living together, and bringing up a generation of thieves, it cries out vigorously against the criminals. Sure, it may suggest a mission to them, and even set about it in a helpless patronising sort of way, wondering if really it is of any use to try to help "such men", as though they were of different flesh and blood to themselves. Verily such Christianity *is* of different blood from Him who preferred talking to a thief in His own last moments, to holding conversation with any priest or white-washed temple worshipper standing around.

Catherine Booth (1829–90)

8th August

When they came to the place called the Skull, there they crucified him, along with the criminals – one on his right, the other on his left.

(Luke 23:33)

My first active co-operation [with the London City Missioner, Thomas Jackson] was in consequence of a speech I had made in the House of Commons on the subject of emigration. I received under cover of a letter from Jackson, a round robin, signed by about forty of the principal thieves and burglars in London, praying me in most respectful terms to meet them in a place appointed in the south of London, and give them my opinion and advice as to their means of obtaining relief from their present mode of life by transplantation to some distant and happier region. I had no hesitation in complying with their request.

I went to them at the stated time, and found Jackson in the room with close upon 400 men of every appearance, from the swell mob in black coats and white neckcloths, to the most fierce-looking, rough, half-dressed savages I ever beheld. I took the chair of the meeting.

The meeting opened with reading the Scriptures, Jackson taking for his commencement the history of the thieves on the Cross. We then proceeded to offer up prayer (the whole assembly on their knees), and the most devout of congregations could not have surpassed them in stillness, and external reverence.

We then proceeded to address them, but our object was mainly to hear the unhappy men speak for themselves; and so they did. I cannot go into a tenth part of the interesting details; but we gathered this truth from them all, that they were miserable, that they hated their mode of life, but they saw no means of escape from it. They implored our assistance. Well, we promised to do what we could; and then one man, on behalf of the rest, exclaimed, "But will you ever come back and see us again?" "Yes," I replied, "whenever you send for me." The low, deep, murmur of gratitude was very touching.

Great efforts were immediately begun, and in a short time not a few of them were disposed of in various ways, but mostly by emigration. We were very anxious and inquisitive to know the issue of our enterprise, but Jackson could not, after frequent investigation, make out that more than fifty had returned to their former occupation. Everyone may learn from this event that the worst classes are utterly wretched in their career, and that many are corrigible, but it is only by change of scene, and still more by change of association. Some there are no doubt, and some there will ever be, in whom the spirit of dash, and the necessity of excitement are so strong that they cannot live without perpetually affronting hazard, and are ready to jeopardise their whole existence on a single venture.

Lord Shaftesbury (1801–85)

9th August

I am not ashamed of the gospel, because it is the power of God for the salvation of everyone who believes: first for the Jew, then for the Gentile.

(Romans 1:16)

On February the 17th [1818] two women were executed for forgery, Charlotte Newman and Mary Ann James. The morning of their execution, Newman addressed the following letter to Mrs [Elizabeth] Fry; and James wrote one to her fellow-prisoners; these letters found their way into the public print . . .

Honoured Madam,

As the only way of expressing my gratitude to you for your very great attention to the care of my poor soul; I feel I may have appeared more silent than perhaps some would have been on so melancholy an event; but believe me, my dear madam, I have felt most acutely the awful situation I have been in. The mercies of God are boundless, and I trust through His grace this affliction is sanctified to me, and through the Saviour's blood my sins will be washed away. I have much to be thankful for. I feel such serenity of mind and fortitude. God, of His infinite mercy, grant I may feel as I do now in the last moments. Pray, madam, present my most grateful thanks to the worthy Dr Cotton and Mr Baker, and all our kind friends the ladies, and Mrs Guy. It was a feeling I had to my own unworthiness, made me more diffident of speaking so brief as was perhaps looked for. I once more return you my grateful thanks. It is now past six o'clock, I have not one moment to spare; I must devote the remainder to the service of my offended God.

    With respect, your humble servant,
      (signed) CHARLOTTE NEWMAN

Tuesday morning, six o'clock, February 17th, 1818, James joins with me, and feels all I have expressed, I hope.

                              Elizabeth Fry (1780–1845)

10th August

For in the gospel a righteousness from God is revealed, a righteousness that is by faith from first to last, just as it is written: "The righteous will live by faith."

(Romans 1:17)

[Continued from yesterday.]

Condemned Cell.

My dear fellow-prisoners,

Impressed with the deepest sense of your feelings for me under my awful situation, I am sure was I to ask anything of you it would be granted. Then was I to ask one particular favour of you all, I would flatter myself, as my last dying word, it would be granted. I would impress on your minds the true interest of the Gospel, and, by informing you how I found an interest in Christ; in the first place, God gave me the spirit of humility, you must feel a love and affection for those that so kindly visit this prison. Then pray to the Lord to give you the grace of His Holy Spirit, and I am sure our beloved friends, will acquaint you by what way that is to be found. I was dark when I first came into these walls, and what must you all suppose the love, the gratitude I feel now, I am going but a short time before you. God can call you in a moment. Then pray, I entreat you, do not neglect the great work.

"Go up stairs rejoicing as if to a bridal feast." Keep every rule. Oh, should the Lord deliver you from these walls, think on me and remember that the end of sin is death. You have all my prayers. Oh, lay hold of Jesus. He is my refuge and my strength. Look up to Him; and may the Lord be with you and keep you all. Tomorrow morning I shall be with my heavenly Father in Paradise.

I am your fellow-prisoner,
  Wishing every blessing, your affectionate,
    (Signed) MARY ANN JAMES.

Elizabeth Fry (1780–1845)

11th August

After they had mocked him, they took off the robe and put his own clothes on him. Then they led him away to crucify him.

(Matthew 27:31)

So the Lord was handed over to their savage wishes, and in mockery of His kingly state, ordered to be the bearer of His own instrument of death, that what Isaiah the prophet foresaw might be fulfilled, saying, "Behold a Child is born, and a Son is given to us whose government is upon His shoulders."

When, therefore, the Lord carried the wood of the cross which should turn for Him into the sceptre of power, it was indeed in the eyes of the wicked a mighty mockery. But to the faithful a mighty mystery was set forth, seeing that He, the glorious vanquisher of the Devil, and the strong defeater of the powers that were against Him, was carrying in noble sort the trophy of His triumph, and on the shoulders of His unconquered patience bore into all realms the adorable sign of salvation: as if then to confirm all His followers by this mere symbol of His work, and say, "He that taketh not his cross and followeth Me, is not worthy of Me."

Leo the Great (c. 400–461)

12th August

Who has believed our message and to whom has the arm of the Lord been revealed?

(Isaiah 53:1)

The words of the text stand in closest connection with the great picture of the Suffering Servant which follows, and the pathetic figure portrayed there is the revealing arm of the Lord. The closest bringing together of the ideas of majesty and power and of humiliation, suffering, and weakness, would be a paradox to the first hearers of the prophecy. Its solution lies in the historical manifestation of Jesus.

Looking on Him, we see that the growing up of that root out of a dry ground was the revelation of the great power of God. In Jesus' low humanity God's power is made perfect in man's weakness, in another and not less true sense than that in which the apostle spoke (1 Corinthians 1). There we see divine power in its noblest form, in its grandest operation, in its widest sweep, in its loftiest purpose. That humble man, lowly and poor, despised and rejected in life, hanging faint and pallid on the Roman cross, and dying in the dark, seems a strange manifestation of the "glory" of God, but the Cross is indeed His throne, and sublime as are the other forms in which Omnipotence clothes itself, this is, to human eyes and hearts, the highest of them all.

In Jesus the arm of the Lord is revealed in its grandest operation. Creation and the continual sustaining of the universe are great, but redemption is greater.

Alexander Maclaren (1826–1910)

13th August

God made him who had no sin to be sin for us, so that in him we might become the righteousness of God.

(2 Corinthians 5:21)

Let us flee the amateur notion that in the Cross there is no ultimate ethical issue involved, that it is a simple religious appeal to the heart. The pulpit is doomed to futility if it appeals to the heart in any sense that discredits the final conscience. I mean it is doomed if it keeps declaring that, with such a Father as Christ's, forgiveness is a matter of course; the only difficulty being to insert it into men's hearty belief. There is no doubt that it is a very popular notion. "How natural for God to forgive. It is just like Him." Whereas the real truth is that it is only like the God familiar to us from the Cross, and not from our natural expectation. Real forgiveness is not natural. Nor is it natural and easy to be content to be forgiven.

The more quick our moral sensibility is the more slow we are to accept forgiveness. And not through pride always, but often through the exact opposite – through shame, and the inability to forgive oneself. Is it Newman who says that the good man never forgives himself? I wish a good many more said it. We should then have a better hold on the forgiveness of God. We should realise how far from a matter of course forgiveness was for a holy, and justly angry, God, for all His love. A free forgiveness flows from moral strength, but an easy forgiveness only means moral weakness.

How natural it is for God to forgive! Nay, if there is one thing in the world for ever supernatural it is real forgiveness – especially on the scale of redemption. It is only natural to the Supernatural. The natural man does not forgive. He resents and revenges. His wrath smoulders till it flash. And the man who forgives easily, jauntily, and thoughtlessly, when it is a real offence, is neither natural nor supernatural but subnatural. He is not only less than God he is less than man.

P. T. Forsyth (1848–1921)

14th August

For it is by grace you have been saved, through faith – and this not from yourselves, it is the gift of God – nor by works, so that no-one can boast. For we are God's workmanship, created in Christ Jesus to do good works, which God prepared in advance for us to do.
(Ephesians 2:8–10)

Nothing is more intensely real than the sense of guilt; it is as real as the eternal distinction between right and wrong in which it is rooted. And nothing is more intensely real than the sense of release from guilt which comes from the discovery and assurance of the remission of sins. The evil things which a man has done cannot be undone; but when they have been forgiven through Christ, the iron chain which so bound him to them as to make the guilt of them eternally his has been broken; before God and his own conscience he is no longer guilty of them.

This is the Christian mystery of justification, which according to Paul – and his words have been confirmed in the experience of millions of Christian men – is "the power of God unto salvation to everyone that believeth." It changes light into darkness; despair into victorious hope; prostration into buoyancy and vigour. It is one of the supreme motives to Christian living, and it makes Christian living possible. The man who received this great deliverance is no longer a convict, painfully observing all prison rules without the hope of shortening his sentence, but a child in the home of God.

R. W. Dale (1829–95)

15th August

If we walk in the light, as he is in the light, we have fellowship with one another, and the blood of Jesus, his Son, purifies us from all sin.
(1 John 1:7)

"If we confess our sins, He is faithful and just to forgive us our sins, and to cleanse us from all unrighteousness." That is the difference between a believer and a non-believer. If we have confessed our sins, it is distrusting God not to believe that they are put away.

Suppose that I have a little boy, and when I go home he comes to me and says, "Papa, I did that naughty thing that you told me not to do."

I see there are signs of contrition, and say, "I am sorry you did it; but I am thankful you confessed it. I forgive you."

He goes off lightly. He has been forgiven. But the next day he comes and says –

"Papa, do you know that yesterday, while you were away, I did that naughty thing that you told me not to do. I am very sorry. Won't you forgive me?"

I say, "My son, was not that forgiven yesterday?"

"Well," he says, "I wish you would forgive me again."

Don't you see how dishonouring it is? It is very disheartening to a father to have his child act in that way. And it is distrusting God, and dishonouring Him for us to be constantly raking up the past. If God has forgiven us, that is the end of it. "Who shall lay anything to the charge of God's elect? It is God that justifieth" [Romans 8:33]. If God has justified me, will He lay any charge against me? But dear friend, if you are not already forgiven, do not sleep until you are. Have this question of sin for ever settled for time and eternity. God wants to forgive you, and He will, if you confess your sins and ask His pardon.

D. L. Moody (1837–99)

16th August

I have no greater joy than to hear that my children are walking in the truth.

(3 John 4)

Another class of converts that need our special help, are those who labour under some particular corruption, which keeps under their graces, and makes them a trouble to others, and a burden to themselves. Alas! there are too many such persons. Some are particularly addicted to pride, and others to worldly-mindedness; some to sensual desires, and others to perverseness, or other evil passions.

Now it is our duty to give assistance to all these; and partly by dissuasions, and clear discoveries of the odiousness of the sin, and partly by suitable directions about the remedy, to help them to a more complete conquest of their corruptions. We are leaders of Christ's army against the powers of hell, and must resist all the works of darkness wherever we find them, even it should be in the children of light. We must be no more tender of the sins of the godly, than of the ungodly, nor any more befriend them, or favour them. By how much more we love their persons, by so much the more must we manifest it, by making opposition to their sins.

And yet we must expect to meet with some tender persons here, especially when iniquity hath got any head, and made a party, and many have fallen in love with it. They will be as pettish and as impatient of reproof as some worse men, and perhaps will interest even piety itself in their faults. But the ministers of Christ must do their duty, notwithstanding their peevishness; and must not so far hate their brother, as to forbear rebuking him, or suffer sin to lie upon his soul. It must, no doubt, be done with much prudence, yet done it must be.

Richard Baxter (1615–91)

17th August

Then Nathan said to David, "You are the man!"
(2 Samuel 12:7)

Nathan's advent on the scene must have been a positive relief. One day while statesmen and soldiers were crowding the outer corridor of the cedar palace, the prophet, by right of old acquaintance made his way to them, and sought a private audience. He told what seemed to be a great and pathetic story of high-handed wrong; and David's anger was greatly kindled against the man who had perpetuated it. Then, as a flash of lightning on a dark night suddenly reveals to the traveller the precipice, on the void of which he is about to place his foot, the brief awful stunning sentence, "Thou art the man!" revealed David to himself in the mirror of his own judgement, and brought him to his knees. Nathan reminded him of the past, and dwelt especially on the unstinted goodness of God. It was a sunny background, the sombre hues of which made recent events look the darker . . .

"I have sinned against the Lord," was David's only answer – a confession followed by a flood of hot tears – and instantly his scorched heart found relief. Oh, blessed showers that visit parched souls and parched lands!

When Nathan had gone, he beat out that chief confession into Psalm 51, dedicated to the chief musician, that all the world might use it, setting it to music if they would. The one sin and the many transgressions; the evil done against God, as though Uriah might not be named in the same breath; the confession of inbred evil; the ache of broken bones; the consciousness of the unclean heart; the loss of joy; the fear of forfeiting the Holy Spirit; the broken and contrite heart – thus the surcharged waters of the inner lake broke forth turbid and dark. Ah, those cries for the multitude of God's tender mercy! nothing less could erase the dark legend from the book of remembrance, or rub out the stains from his robe, or make the leprous flesh sweet and whole. To be clean, because purged with hyssop; to be whiter than snow, because washed; to sing aloud once more, because delivered from blood guiltiness; to be infilled with a steadfast, a willing, and a holy spirit; to be able to point transgressors to the Father's heart – these were the petitions which that weak, sin-weary heart laid upon the altar of God, sweeter than the burnt-offering or fragrant incense.

But long before this pathetic prayer was uttered, immediately on his acknowledgement of sin, without the interposition of a moment's interval before his confession and the assurance, Nathan had said, "The Lord hath put away thy sin." . . . Sin is dark, dangerous and damnable: but it cannot staunch the love of God; it cannot change the love that is not of yesterday, but dates from eternity itself. The one thing that can really hurt the soul is to keep the confession pent within itself.

F. B. Meyer (1847–1929)

18th August

The Lord is my shepherd, I shall not be in want.

(Psalm 23:1)

David did many other services, both intended and executed, both in the field, and on the throne, and in the house of God; but by far and away David's greatest service was his Psalms. The temple was built and built again, and built again; but for two thousand years now not one stone of that so sacred and so stately structure has stood upon another. The very foundations of the temple have been razed out, sown with salt, and for ever lost. But the Psalms of David shine to this day with greater splendour than on the first day they were first sung. And long after the foundations of this whole earth have been ploughed up and removed out of their place, David's songs will be sounding out for ever beside the song of the Moses and the Lamb . . .

What a service David has done, not knowing he was doing it; and not to his nation only, but to the whole Israel of God. And not to Israel only, but to the God of Israel, and to the Redeemer of Israel. "I have found David my servant, with My holy oil have I anointed him. I have exalted one chosen out of the people."

I have said that David did a great service to the Redeemer of Israel, and I intended to say it. When I think of that service, all the other services that David has done by his Psalms shine out in a far diviner glory. I bless David's name for the blessing my own soul gets out of his Psalms every day I live. But when I trace that blessing up to its true source, I find that true and grace-gushing source in Jesus of Nazareth, whom I see growing in grace every day he goes about in Galilee with David's Psalms never out of His hands. Think people of God, of the honour to David, higher far than all thrones on earth and heaven – the unparalleled and immortal honour of being able to teach Jesus Christ to sing and pray. For when the Holy Child said to Mary, "Mother, teach Me to sing and pray," what did Mary do, hiding all that in her heart, but put into her child's hands David's golden Psalm beginning thus: The Lord is my shepherd, I shall not want.

Alexander Whyte (1836–1921)

19th August

Rejoice in the lord always. I will say it again: Rejoice!
(Philippians 4:4)

Paul says, "Sing and make melody in your heart to the lord, with psalms and hymns and spiritual songs" (Ephesians 5:19). For this reason we say that to sing spiritual songs is good and pleasing to God if we sing in the right way, that is attentively, in the fear of God and as inspired by the Spirit of Christ.

For it is for this reason that they are called spiritual songs: namely, that they are inspired and made and composed by the urge of the Spirit, and also attract and move men to blessedness. Therefore, since they are composed and made by the inspiration and urge of the Spirit of Christ, they must also be sung as inspired by the same Spirit, if they are to be sung aright and to be of service to men.

Where this is not the case, and one sings only for carnal joy or for the sweet sound or for some other reason, one misuses them, changing them into what is carnal and worldly, and does not sing songs of the Spirit, but of the letter. Likewise also, he who enjoys listening for the music's sake – he hears it in the letter and not in the Spirit, so with him also it is without fruit; and because they are not used, sung and heard aright, he that does so sins greatly against God; for he uses his word, which was given for his salvation and as an urge to blessedness, as leading to the lust of the flesh and to sin. Thus, it is changed by him into harm, for though the song itself is spiritual, yet it is to that man no longer a spiritual song. It is a worldly song, for it is not sung in the Spirit.

He, however, who sings in the Spirit, considers diligently every word, how far and where it goes, why it has been used and how it may serve to his betterment. He who does this sings to the Lord's praise, to the betterment of both himself and others and as an instigation to a godly life. This is to sing well; to sing in any other way is in vain. Thus, we allow it not among us that other than spiritual songs are sung.

Peter Riedeman (1506–56)

20th August

Sing to him, sing praise to him; tell of all his wonderful acts. Glory in his holy name; let the hearts of those who seek the Lord rejoice.
(Psalm 105:2–3)

I do delight in these commands that tell us to do just what everything in us makes us want to do. The musical want to make music, so, "Sweep the strings to Jehovah," "Make ye music to him," "Play skilfully." The singers want to sing, so "Sing ye to him," "O let your songs be of him." And all his lovers want to tell of the loving things he is continually doing, so "Let your talking be of him."

We see a rose, and our first instinct is to smell it and enjoy its loveliness. Suppose the Maker of the rose became suddenly visible standing beside the rose bush, and said, "Do smell it and enjoy it." It is like that.

"Go and see what Tommy is doing and say *Don't*." This is the wrong way to bring up a child. It is not our Father's way. His is much nicer. He makes us want to do happy things and then He says, "Do them." Dullness, restraint, nervousness, fear – these things are simply not in the picture. Psalmist and apostle (and often in the Psalms it is the Lord Jesus speaking) pile up words of joy to show the light and the liberty of the sons of God – the happy God.

This does not cross out discipline or inner sensitiveness, but it is the life of the Christian in flower. Our Bible shows life whole. It is not always dwelling on the root underground (which must be if there is to be this flower in sunshine), it goes on to flower and fruit.

"In your presence is fullness of joy" – *there* and *here*. "At your right hand there are pleasures for evermore." Don't let us postpone the joy and the pleasures as if they belonged only to the life further on. They are for today as well as for tomorrow.

So today's word is, "Let the heart of them rejoice that seek the Lord." "Joy is the grace we say to God."

Amy Carmichael (1867–1951)

21st August

For whoever wants to save his life will lose it, but whoever loses his life for me and for the gospel will save it. What good is it for a man to gain the whole world, yet forfeit his soul? Or what can a man give in exchange for his soul?

(Mark 8:35–7)

As one looks around the community today, how clear the problem of unhappy lives appears. Do we not all know men for whom it is just as clear as daylight that that is what they need, the sacrifice of themselves for other people? Rich men who with all their wealth are weary and wretched; learned men whose learning only makes them querulous and jealous; believing men whose faith is always souring into bigotry and envy – every one knows what these men need; just something which shall make them let themselves go out into the open ocean of a complete self-sacrifice. They are rubbing and fretting and chaffing against the wooden wharves of their own interests to which they are tied. Sometime or other a great slow, quiet tide or a great strong, furious storm must come and break every rope that binds them, and carry them out to sea; and then they will for the first time know the true, manly joy for which a man was made, as a ship for the first time knows the full joy for which a ship was made, when she trusts herself to the open sea and, with the wharf left far behind, feels the winds over her and the waters under her, and recognises her true life.

Only, the trust to the great ocean must be complete. No trial trip will do. No ship can tempt the sea and learn its glory, so long as she goes moored by any rope, however long, by which she means to be drawn back again if the sea grows too rough. The soul that trifles and toys with self-sacrifice never can get its true joy and power. Only the soul that with an overwhelming impulse and a perfect trust gives itself up forever to the life of other men, finds the delight and peace which complete self-surrender has to give.

Phillips Brooks (1835–93)

22nd August

As the offering began, singing to the Lord began also, accompanied by trumpets and the instruments of David king of Israel.
(2 Chronicles 29:27)

[Continued from yesterday.]

One would not seem to be so foolish as to say that self-sacrifice does not bring pain. Indeed it does. The life of Christ must be our teacher there. He carried the song and trumpet always in his heart. That life, marking its way with drops of blood, on which the pity of the world has dwelt more tenderly than over any other life it knows, has yet always seemed to the world's best standards to be a true triumphant march, radiant with splendour all along the way, and closing on true victory at last. Indeed I think that one of the brightest insights which we ever get into the human heart and its essential breadth and justice, and its power, when it is working at its best, to hold what seem contradictory ideas in their true spiritual harmony, is given to us when we see how men have been able to see together both sides of the life of Jesus, to pity His sorrow and to glory in His happiness, and yet to blend both of these two thoughts of Him into one single idea of one single self consistent Christ.

It is a sort of witness of how truly men, in that highest mood into which they are drawn when they try to study Christ, easily see the real truth with regard to human life, which is that in it joy and pain, so far from being inconsistent with and contradictory to one another, are, in some true sense, each others' complements and neither alone, but both together, make the true sum of human life.

There is a conceivable world where pure, unclouded joy can come, just as there are countries where the mountains are very lofty and all nature is on so grand a scale that it can bear a pure, unclouded sky, and in its unveiled splendour perfectly satisfy the eye. But there are other lands whose inferior grandeur needs for its perfect beauty the effects of mist and cloud that give its lower mountains the mystery and poetry which they could not have in themselves. So one may compare the Swiss and the Scotch landscapes. And something of this sort is true about this world and marks its inferiority, proves that it is not yet the perfect state of being. It needs the pain of life to emphasise its joy. Its joy is not high or perfect enough to do without the emphasis of pain. And so . . . it is not strange that that which is the necessary condition of joy in this human life – namely, self sacrifice – should also be associated with suffering and pain.

Phillips Brooks (1835–93)

23rd August

Do you not know that your body is a temple of the Holy Spirit, who is in you, whom you have received from God? You are not your own; you were bought at a price. Therefore honour God with your body.

(1 Corinthians 6:19–20)

A Christian minister is a person who in a peculiar sense is "not his own"; he is the "servant" of God, and therefore ought to be wholly devoted to him. By entering on that sacred office he solemnly undertakes to be always engaged as much as possible in the Lord's work, and not to choose his own pleasure, or employment, or pursue his ministry as a something that is to subserve his own interests, or as a kind of bye-work. He engages to go where God pleases, and to do, or endure what he sees fit to command, or call him to, in the exercise of his function.

He virtually bids farewell to friends, pleasures, and comforts, and stands in readiness to endure the greatest sufferings in the work of his Lord and Master. It is inconsistent for ministers to please themselves with thoughts of a numerous congregation, cordial friends, a civilised country, legal protection, affluence, splendour, or even a sufficient income. The slights and hatred of men, and even pretended friends, gloomy prisons, and tortures, the society of barbarians of uncouth speech, miserable accommodations in wretched wildernesses, hunger and thirst, nakedness, weariness, and pains, hard work, and but little worldly encouragement, should rather be the object of their expectation.

Thus the apostles acted in primitive times, and endured hardness, as good soldiers of Jesus Christ; and though we living in a civilised country where Christianity is protected by law, are not called to suffer these things while we continue here, yet I question whether all are justified in living here, while so many are perishing without the means of grace in other lands. Sure I am that it is entirely contrary to the spirit of the gospel, for its ministers to enter upon it from selfish motives, or with great worldly expections. On the contrary the commission [Matthew 28:18–20] is a sufficient call to them to venture all, and like the primitive Christians, go everywhere preaching the gospel.

William Carey (1761–1834)

24th August

Therefore I urge you to imitate me. For this reason I am sending to you Timothy, my son whom I love, who is faithful in the Lord. He will remind you of my way of life in Christ Jesus, which agrees with what I teach everywhere in every church.

(1 Corinthians 4:16–17)

[John Fountain (1767–1800) has been sent to India to join William Carey.]

After getting a boat to Calcutta, and other necessary things, I left it on the 24th September [1796], and arrived at Mudnabatty on the 10th of October. Brother Carey most kindly received me. When I entered, his Pundit stood by him, teaching him Sanskrit. He labours in the translation of the Scriptures, and has nearly finished the New Testament, being somewhere in the middle of Revelation.

He keeps the grand end in view, which first induced him to leave his country, and those Christian friends whom he still dearly loves. He reads a chapter and expounds, every morning, to twelve or sixteen persons. On a Sabbath morning he also expounds, and preaches twice in the day besides, to forty or fifty persons; after which, he often goes into some village in the evening. In the intervals of preaching to the natives, we have worship in English.

He indeed appears to be the character he describes in his publication [The Enquiry], where he says, "A Christian minister is a person who, in a peculiar sense, is not his own; he is the servant of God, and therefore ought to be wholly devoted to him."

William Carey (1761–1834)

25th August

For I resolved to know nothing while I was with you except Jesus Christ and him crucified.

(1 Corinthians 2:2)

The whole of the life of faith . . . in all its manifoldness, and in all its universalness and his own full assurance of everlasting life, – all that, and much more than all that, Paul, by his splendid genius, and it all so splendidly sanctified and inspired, drew out of the cross of Christ. Take away the cross of Christ and he is as weak as any man. Paul has nothing left to preach if you take him away from the cross of Christ. His mouth is shut. His pulpit is in ruins. His arm is broken. He is of all men most miserable. But let God reveal the cross of Christ in Paul, and, straightway he can both do, and endure, all things. Paul is henceforth debtor both to the Greeks and to the Barbarians; both to the wise, and the unwise. Once reveal the cross of Christ in Paul, and you thereby lay a life-long necessity upon him. Yea, woe is unto him, ever after, if he preaches not the Gospel of the cross of Christ.

We preach not ourselves, Paul asserts with a good conscience in another sermon of his. And yet at the same time, he introduces himself into almost every sermon he preaches. Paul simply cannot preach the cross of Christ as he must preach it, without boldly bringing himself in, as both the best pattern and the best proof of what the cross of Christ can do. Paul's salvation – the absolute graciousness of Paul's salvation, and his absolute assurance of it, – these things are the infallible marks of their authenticity that Paul prints upon every Epistle of his. The cross of Christ, and Paul's salvation by that cross, are the two constant, and complementary, topics of Paul's pulpit; they are but the two sides of Paul's shield of salvation.

Alexander Whyte (1836–1921)

26th August

Jesus said to the woman, "Your faith has saved you; go in peace."
(Luke 7:50)

The evangelist who records the Pharisaic sneer – "This man receiveth sinners" – is rich in illustrations of it which enable us to see what reconciliation to God through Christ implies. One is the story in Luke 7:36–50 of the woman who was a sinner. Apparently she was a sinner in the city, one of that unhappy class who walk the streets and live by sin. There are none in the world more friendless, none from whom the passers-by more instinctively turn aside, none whom ordinary society would be so determined not to receive; in a word, none so hopeless.

But one day this woman heard Jesus, and His holiness and love overcame her. She was drawn irresistibly to Him, and not long after, as He sat at meat in the Pharisee's house, she made her way in, and standing beside Him, wet His feet with tears, wiped them with the hair of her head, kissed them over and over again, and anointed them with ointment.

"What an extraordinary demonstration!" we are tempted to say. Was it hysterics, the weakness of a breaking wave? No it was not hysterics, it was regeneration. It was the new birth of faith and hope and love, evoked and welcomed by Jesus: it was the passionate sinner's reconciliation to God. Such a thing is possible for we here actually see it. Jesus did not shrink from the sinful woman: He received her. He took her part against the Pharisee. He spoke great and gracious words in her defence. "Her sins are forgiven, for she loved much." "Thy faith hast saved thee; go in peace." And as she went, she knew that friendless as she had been before she now had a friend with God; it is not too much to say, she knew that God Himself was her friend.

We see from this incident what a profound, thrilling and far-reaching experience reconciliation is. It is something which moves nature in all its depths, which melts it and casts it into a new mould. It regenerates the soul which passes through it, and it is accomplished with the sense of an infinite debt to Jesus. How this last is to be explained we are not explicitly told, but it was not for nothing that the sinful woman restored to God poured out her gratitude at Jesus' feet.

James Denney (1856–1917)

27th August

Just as Moses lifted up the snake in the desert, so the Son of Man must be lifted up, that everyone who believes in him may have eternal life.

(John 3:14–15)

Your letter shows me what I was most anxious to hear, that you are growing in self-knowledge; and it therefore opens to me a fit opportunity of declaring to you what have been my fears respecting you from the very beginning. You have always appeared to me to be sincere. But your views of Christianity seemed to be essentially defective. You have always appeared to admire Christianity *as a system*; but you never seemd to have views of Christianity as a remedy; you have never seemed to possess self-knowledge, or to know the evil of your own heart. I never saw in you any deep contrition, much less anything of a tender self-loathing and self-abhorrence. This always made me jealous over you with a godly jealousy; and never till this moment have I had my fears for your ultimate state removed. I beheld in you somewhat of a child-like simplicity; and I well know that, *if it be associated with contrition*, it is a virtue of the sublimest quality; but if contrition be wanting, the disposition which assumes that form differs but little from childishness.

You may conceive the brazen serpent which Moses erected in the wilderness to have been exquisitely formed, and you may suppose persons to have greatly admired the workmanship, and the contrivance of erecting it upon a pole for the benefit of all who should behold it; but the meanest person in the whole camp, who had but the most indistinct view of it, if he beheld it with a sense of his own dying condition, and with an experience of its efficacy to heal his wounds, would have an incomparably better view of it than the virtuoso, however much he might admire it.

This hint will show you what in my judgement you *were*, and what I hope you *will* be. Christianity is a personal matter, not to be commended merely to others, but to be experienced in your own soul: and though you may confound your opponents by your arguments, you will never do any essential good, and much less will you reap any saving benefit to your own soul, till you can say, "What mine eyes have seen, mine ears have heard, and mine hands have handled of the word of life, that same declare I unto you."

Charles Simeon (1759–1836)

28th August

Therefore, since we have been justified through faith, we have peace with God through our Lord Jesus Christ, through whom we have gained access by faith into this grace in which we now stand.

(Romans 5:1–2)

Wednesday, 24 May: In the evening I went very unwillingly to a society in Aldersgate-street, where one was reading Luther's preface to the Epistle to the Romans. About a quarter before nine, while he was describing the change which God works in the heart through faith in Christ, *I felt my heart strangely warmed*. I felt I did trust in Christ, Christ alone, for salvation: and an assurance was given me, that he had taken away my sins, even mine, and saved me from the law of sin and death.

I began to pray with all my might for those who had in a more especial manner despitefully used me and persecuted me. I then testified to all openly there, what I first felt in my heart. But it was not long before the enemy suggested, "This cannot be faith; for where is thy joy?" Then was I taught, that peace and victory over sin are essential to faith in the Captain of our salvation; but that, as to transports of joy that usually attend the beginning of it, especially in those who have mourned deeply, God sometimes giveth, sometimes withholdeth them, according to the counsels of his own will.

After my return home, I was much besetted with temptations; but cried out, and they fled away. They returned again and again. I as often lifted my eyes, and he "sent me help from his holy place". And herein I found the difference between this and my former state chiefly consisted. I was striving, yea, fighting with all my might under the law, as well as under grace. But then I was sometimes, if not often, conquered; now, I was always conqueror.

Thursday 25: The moment I awaked, "Jesus Master," was in my heart and mouth; and I found all my strength lay in my keeping my eye fixed upon him, and my soul waiting on him continually.

John Wesley (1703–91)

29th August

So the churches were strengthened in the faith and grew daily in numbers.

(Acts 16:5)

Of those who flourished in these times, Quadratus is said to have been distinguished for his prophetical gifts. There were many others, also, noted in these times, who held first rank in the apostolic succession. These, as the holy disciple of such men, also built up the churches where foundations had been previously laid in every place by the apostles. They augmented the means of promulgating the gospel more and more, and spread the seeds of salvation throughout the world far and wide.

For most of the disciples at that time, animated by a fervent love of the divine word, had first fulfilled the Saviour's precept by distributing their substance to the needy.

Afterwards leaving their country, they performed the office of evangelist to those who had not yet heard the faith, whilst with a noble ambition to proclaim Christ, they had also delivered to them the book of the holy gospels. After laying the foundation of the faith in foreign parts as the particular object of their mission, and after appointing others as shepherds of the flocks, and committing to these care of those that had recently been introduced, they went again to other regions and nations, with the grace and co-operation of God.

The Holy Spirit also, wrought many wonders as yet through them, so that as soon as the gospel was heard, men voluntarily in crowds, and eagerly, embraced the true faith with their whole minds. As it is impossible for us to give the numbers of individuals that became pastors or evangelists, during the immediate succession from the apostles in churches throughout the world, we have recorded only those by name in our history, of whom we have received the traditional account as it is delivered in the various comments on the apostolic doctrine, still extant.

Eusebius (c. 260–c. 340)

30th August

A man ought to examine himself before he eats of the bread and drinks of the cup.

(1 Corinthians 11:28)

Now concerning the Eucharist, thus give thanks; first concerning the cup: We thank Thee, our Father, for the holy vine of David thy servant which Thou hast made known to us through Jesus, Thy servant; to Thee be glory forever. And concerning the broken bread: We thank Thee, our Father, for the life and knowledge which Thou hast made known to us through Jesus Thy servant; to Thee be the glory forever. Just as this broken bread was scattered over the hills and having been gathered together became one, so let Thy church be gathered together from the ends of the earth into Thy kingsom. But let no one eat and drink of your Eucharist, except those baptised in the Lord's name; for in regard to this the Lord hath said: Give not that which is holy to the dogs.

We thank Thee, holy Father, for Thy holy name, which Thou hast caused to dwell in our hearts, and for the knowledge and of faith and immortality which Thou has made known to us through Jesus Thy servant; to Thee be glory forever. Thou, Almighty Master didst create all things for Thy name's sake; both food and drink Thou gives to men for enjoyment, in order that we may give thanks to Thee; but to us Thou hast graciously given spiritual food and drink and eternal life through Thy servant.

Before all things, we thank Thee that Thou art powerful; to Thee be glory forever. Remember, Lord, Thy Church, to deliver it from every evil, and to make it perfect in Thy love, and gather it from the four winds, it, the sactified, into Thy kingdom, which Thou hast prepared for it; for thine is the power and the glory forever. Let grace come and let this world pass away. Hosanna to the Son of David! Whoever is holy, let him come; whoever is not, let him repent. Marantha. Amen. But permit the prophets to give thanks as much as they will.

The Didache (1st–3rd century)

31st August

Dear friends, you are faithful in what you are doing for the brothers, even though they are strangers to you.

(3 John 5)

[Continued from yesterday.]

Now whoever cometh and teacheth you all these things, before spoken, receive him; but if the teacher himself turn aside and teach another teaching so as to overthrow this, do not hear him; but if he teach so as to promote righteousness and knowledge of the Lord, receive him as the Lord.

But, in regard to the apostles and prophets, according to the ordinance of the gospel, so do ye. And every apostle who cometh to you, let him be received as the Lord; but he shall not remain more than one day; if, however there be need then the next day; but if he remain three days he is a false prophet. But when the prophet departeth, let him take nothing except bread enough till he lodge again; but if he ask money, he is a false prophet.

And every prophet who speaketh in the spirit, ye shall not judge; for every sin shall be forgiven, but this sin shall not be forgiven. But not everyone that speaketh in the spirit is a prophet, but only if he have the was of the Lord. So from their ways shall the false prophet and the prophet be known.

And no prophet who orders a meal, in the spirit, eateth of it, unless he indeed he is a false prophet. But every prophet, proved true, acting with a view to the mystery of the church on earth, but not teaching others to do all that himself doeth, shall not be judged among you; for with God, he hath his judgement; for so did the ancient prophets also.

The Didache (1st–3rd century)

September

1st September

I know whom I have believed, and am convinced that he is able to guard what I have entrusted to him for that day.

(2 Timothy 1:12)

Suppose you are sick almost unto death. A friend brings you a testimony concerning some wonderful physician who has cured many such cases, and is fully able and willing to take yours. Now, you may receive the record of your friend concerning the skill and successes of this physician's treatment, and you may *fully believe* it, and yet there may be some reason why you shrink from putting yourself in his hands and trusting him with your life. You may believe all that is said *about* him, and yet fail so to trust *in his person* as to give yourself up fully into his power. Just so there are numbers who believe God's testimony concerning His Son, that Jesus has atoned for their sin, and that His treatment would cure them of its disease, who dare not trust Him to do it for them – no, not for a single moment. Here is the difference between a dead and a living faith; between a faith that lies useless on the shelves of the intellect, or bubbles up on the waves of mere emotion, and that which renews the soul in righteousness, and makes it the abode of an indwelling Christ.

The term faith is used in several different senses in the Scripture, but when used to designate that act through which the soul is justified before God, and renewed by His Spirit, it always signifies trust in, or committal to, a living Saviour. The word used to signify this trust is sometimes rendered "commit" as in John 2:24: "But Jesus did not commit Himself unto them, because He knew all men." He did not believe in them, or *trust* them with His person – He did not commit himself into their power. That is just what God requires the sinner to do in order to be saved – to *commit himself* to the faithfulness and power of Jesus.

Catherine Booth (1829–90)

2nd September

By faith Moses, when he had grown up, refused to be known as the son of Pharaoh's daughter. He chose to be ill-treated along with the people of God rather than to enjoy the pleasures of sin for a short time. He regarded disgrace for the sake of Christ as of greater value than the treasures of Egypt, because he was looking ahead to his reward.

(Hebrews 11:24–6)

Moses believed God's promise to Abraham, that after four hundred years of bondage his people would come out; and he knew that that period had nearly expired. He cherished a fervent belief in that promise made to the chosen people, that from their ranks the true deliverer would arise – a shadowy belief in the coming Messiah, which, notwithstanding its vagueness, he dared not forfeit. He believed that there was a destiny waiting for the chosen people in the long future, which would throw into shadow all the pomp and splendour of the magnificent Pharaoh. He believed that there was a recompense of reward awaiting them beyond the bourne and limit of Egypt, more glorious than the dazzling splendour of its highest rewards and honours. He evidently believed, what he expected his brethren to believe, that God will deliver them by his hand. And it was this that determined him.

Had he simply acted on what he saw, he would never have left Pharaoh's palace. But his faith told him of things hidden from his co-temporaries; and these altered his course, and led him to act in a way which to them was perfectly incomprehensible.

He did not simply close his eyes to the claims of Egypt, and steel his nerves against the threats of Pharaoh, isolating himself with the exclusiveness of a cynic: that might have been dictated by a strong and wise policy. But he did what he did, because he saw by faith what eye had not seen, or ear heard, or the heart conceived; and these things – that wealth and that reward – being so much better than anything Egypt could offer, he cheerfully took the path of affliction, or self-denial and reproach, which led to them.

See, child of God, what is within thy reach, if only thou wilt dare to deny thyself and take up thy cross! Send the spies into the Land of Promise. Climb the delectable mountains, and put the telescope to thine eyes. And as the far more exceeding and eternal weight of glory breaks on thy vision, thou wilt be prepared to count all things else, which had seemed to be gain, to be loss and dung, and not worthy to be mentioned in comparison. Is the renunciation hard? Do not forget that Christ is suffering with you in it all. His steps lie along this road.

F. B. Meyer (1846–1929)

3rd September

By faith Abraham, even though he was past age – and Sarah herself was barren – was enabled to become a father because he considered him faithful who had made the promise.

(Hebrews 11:11)

Sometimes, beloved, holy scripture has its well near to the troubled heart, not so much in the form of doctrine, as in the form of promise. There never was a trouble yet in human experience among God's people, but what there was a promise to meet it. You have only to look long enough, and you will find the counterfoil; you shall discover that God has in his book that which exactly meets your case.

"Oh," said the Christian, in Bunyan's *Pilgrim*, "what a thousand fools have I been to lie rotting in this stinking dungeon all these weeks, when I have a key in my bosom which, I am persuaded, would fit the locks of all the doors in Doubting Castle. Come, good brother, let us try it." And Christian plucked up courage, and he found his key of promise, though it grated a little: and Bunyan says that one of the doors went, as he put it in his old edition, "damnably hard". He did not know how to put it strong enough until he has used that word.

Yet the key did open every single door, and even the iron gate itself, the external gate of the castle by the help of that key. O dear hearts, some of you have laid fretting and worrying about things which God has dealt with already in his own word. You have said, "Would God he would do that!" and he has done it. You have asked him to give you something, and you have got it. I have used sometimes the simile of a man in the dark dying of hunger, and yet he is shut up in a pantry. There is food all around him, if he could only put out his hand and take it. Did he know it to be there, and would he grasp it, there is just what he wants.

I am persuaded, beloved, if you search the scriptures well, there is not a child of God here that need despair of finding that the Master has opened a well of promise for him.

C. H. Spurgeon (1834–92)

4th September

When Abraham was ninety-nine years old, the Lord appeared to him and said, "I am God Almighty; walk before me and be blameless. I will confirm my covenant between me and you and will greatly increase your numbers."

(Genesis 17:1–2)

"*Walk* before me." Not merely "think before me," and "pray before me," but "*walk* before me." I know that many find it easy to cultivate a sense of God's presence in their own study, or in the room where they are accustomed to pray, but this is the point – to feel it in business, and in the details of every-day life. God's eye is upon me when I am weighing out or measuring the goods, when I am engrossed with transactions with my fellow merchants, or when

I, as a servant, am sweeping the hearth or minding the household duties.

This you should distinctly recognise and act upon. You are to live in the little things of life, knowing that God is always with you, and always looking at you – doing your work just as will please him. Oh, how we smart ourselves up if there is somebody calling to see us. How we adjust our dress in the presence of those we admire. I have sometimes thought I have seen working men proceeding very slowly at their tasks alone, but when the master comes by they quicken their pace wonderfully. That is all wrong. It is eye-service, the custom of a man-pleaser, but not the habit of one who would please the Lord.

We should feel, "God is always looking at me." There is many a word we should not say if we remembered that he would hear it, and many an act we dare not do if we remembered that he would register it. Yes, there is the believer's true place, – my God is God Almighty, and I am always in his presence. A person might do fifty things in a certain place, which he would not think of doing if he were at court and had just presented a petition to the queen; there is a decorousness of manner which we all observe when we are in such conditions: and, therefore, the reasoning is cogent when I ask you before the King of kings what manner of people you ought to be! We are always in Jehovah's courts, and under his royal gaze: "Walk before me."

C. H. Spurgeon (1834–92)

5th September

Who shall separate us from the love of Christ? Shall trouble or hardship or persecution or famine or nakedness or danger or sword?

(Romans 8:35)

As the greatest manifestation of God to the world was by suffering, so the most influential revelation of His people to the world has been by suffering. They are seen to the best advantage in the furnace. The blood of the martyrs has ever been the seed of the

Church. The patience, meekness, firmness, and happiness of God's people in circumstances of suffering, persecution and death, have paved the way for the gospel in almost all lands and ages. A baptism of blood has prepared the hard and sterile soil of humanity for the good seed of the kingdom, and made it doubly fruitful. The exhibition of the meek and loving spirit of Christianity under suffering has doubtless won thousands of hearts to its Divine Author, and tamed and awed many a savage persecutor, besides Saul of Tarsus . . .

Patient suffering, cheerful acquiescence in affliction and anguish, mental or physical, is the most convincing proof of the Divine in man which it is possible for humanity to give. "Truly this was the Son of God," said those who stood by the cross when they saw how He suffered. And how many who have been thoroughly sceptical as to the professions of their converted kindred, and have most bitterly persecuted them, and withstood every argument and entreaty advanced in health and activity; have yielded almost without a word before the patience and peace with which the billows of suffering and death have been braved, nay, welcomed! Such evidence is too mighty, such proof too positive to be resisted, even by persecutors and blasphemers.

Abraham might have written a book and preached all his life long, as doubtless he did, but the whole, ten times told, would not have convinced his family, his contemporaries and posterity, of the depth and fervency of his love to God, as did that holy calm surrender of the best loved of his soul to the requirements of God. Job might have been the upright benevolent, righteousness man he was, but probably we should never have heard of him, but for his wonderful submission, patience, and faith, under suffering. It is this which lifts him up as an example and a teacher to all succeeding generations. It was when sitting on the dunghill, apparently forsaken by God and man, and suffering the direst physical agony which Satan could inflict, that Job attained to his greatest victory and made that wonderful exhibition of trust in God which has been the comfort and admiration of God's people from that day to this.

Catherine Booth (1829–90)

6th September

As the body without the spirit is dead, so faith without deeds is dead.

(James 2:26)

You believe that God in His infinite love sent the Lord Jesus Christ to be the Saviour of men; what proof is there in your life of the reality of your belief? Does the wonder which this immense manifestation of the love of God should create, or the gratitude, or the joy, show itself in your spirit and conduct? You believe that Christ is the Lord of Life: what do you do that you would not do if you did not believe it? You believe that Christ came to save all men: what effect does that faith have upon your actions? What sympathy do you show with Christ's great purpose? What are you doing that men may know what Christ has done for and endured for them?

You believe in the Judgement to come: do you? From what sin does it restrain you? To what duty that would be otherwise neglected does it impel you? Have you avoided a single sinful habit or a single sinful act through the dread of that final account? You believe that God is your Father: do you? Be honest with yourself, and ask what difference it would make, – not in the sentiment of your life, but in your actual conduct, – if you ceased to believe it. Your children, I suppose, could tell you of a dozen things they did or left undone last week because they respect your authority. How many things have you done, or left undone, last week because you respect God's authority?

You believe that there is heaven on the other side of death: do you? Does that belief make any difference to you? Does it make you more patient in trouble? Does your heart quiet when you suffer injustice? Does it enable you to bear losses with less agitation? Does it lead you to place an altogether different estimate on wealth, and all that wealth can purchase, from that which other men place who do not believe in heaven? Does it make you less eager for social position and public honour? Are you doing anything to make your place in heaven sure beyond all doubt? Does the bare possibility of missing heaven fill you with dismay and distress?

Paul, James – either of them – might ask these questions. I entreat every one of you to endeavour to answer them honestly, and to remember that if a man say he hath faith and have not works – works which are the clear result of his faith – that faith cannot save him.

R. W. Dale (1829–95)

7th September

This is the covenant I will make with the house of Israel after that time, declares the Lord. I will put my laws in their minds and write them on their hearts. I will be their God, and they will be my people. No longer will a man teach his neighbour, or a man his brother saying, "Know the Lord," because they will all know me, from the least of them to the greatest. For I will forgive their wickedness and will remember their sins no more.

(Hebrews 8:10–12)

Knowledge is as powerless as ignorance. A man is not a whit nearer to God, or more like Christ, because he has his head crammed with this Word. In fact, some I have known who have been best acquainted with the Word, have been the greatest slaves of sin, and even ministers of Jesus Christ have confessed to me that they have been bond slaves of some besetting sin. It is not in knowledge, and God is raising up thousands of witnesses to this fact, that it is not in knowledge – it is in union with Him, and the little child in intellect and intelligence, who has the real vital union with Jesus, has more power in his little finger than the most cultivated theologian has in his whole body without Christ.

The things of God can only be understood by those who have the Spirit of God. The world by wisdom knows not God any more now than it did in days of old. The things of the Spirit are only spiritually comprehended. Hence this beautiful union cannot be explained, but I only know that it is spoken of all through the Bible, both in the Old Testament and in the New, as *knowing God*. After God has summed up the failures of His people, He gives them a promise, and says, "I will betroth thee unto Me in righteousness for ever, and thou shalt *know* the Lord," as though that were the end of the whole matter, coming really and truly to know Him.

When they come to that living union of soul with Him, it brings the vital sap like the branch of the tree – another of his beautiful illustrations. "Abide in me, and I in you. As the branch cannot bear fruit of itself, except it abide in the vine; no more can ye, except ye abide in me." You know what the branch is when it is broken off. It is a branch. It retains the form of a branch, and, for a while, the beauty and the greenness of a branch but it is broken off. Suppose it could maintain that form. Alas! human branches often do, and maintain those green leaves fragrant in beauty, as when it was first lopped off. It can never bear fruit. Why? Because the communication is cut off between itself and the vine, and there is no sap in its fibre. It is cut off. Now, my friends, you can see why a soul who has never been truly united to Christ in living spiritual marriage cannot bear fruit unto God.

Catherine Booth (1829–90)

8th September

Just as Moses lifted up the snake in the desert, so the Son of Man must be lifted up.

(John 3:14)

Self sacrifice is rightly recognised as the supreme trait of a noble character. Take, for instance, the spirit of Abraham Lincoln's address to his friends and neighbours, as he left home to become the President of the United States:

"My friends, no one, not in my situation, can appreciate the feelings of sadness that come over me at this parting. To you and to the kindness of this people I owe everything. Here I have lived for a quarter of a century, and have passed from a young to an old man. I now leave you – not knowing when or whether I shall ever return – with a task before me greater than that which rested upon Washington. Without the aid of that Divine Being who ever attended him, I cannot succeed. With His assistance, I cannot fail. Trusting in Him, who can go with *me* and remain with *you*, let us confidently hope 'that all may be well'. To His care commending you, as I hope in your prayers you will commend me, I bid you an affectionate farewell."

As he was about to choose his cabinet, he said: "We have a great task on our hands, and it seems the heaviest load has fallen on my poor shoulders. We must save this Union, not only for ourselves and our children, but for the world. I must get the best men that I can to help me. If . . . can help to save this Union, it does not matter how he treats me."

Nobler words than these can have seldom been uttered; and when he had finished the task that was allotted to him, he was cut down by an assassin; but even this heroic life pales in glory, when we see Jesus facing Calvary.

F. B. Meyer (1847–1929)

9th September

I have a baptism to undergo, and how distressed I am until it is completed!

(Luke 12:50)

[Continued from yesterday.]

[Jesus] knew that He would tread the winepress alone!

He knew that though He loved the race, and desired to save every item of it, that the majority would repudiate Him.

He knew that He would stand before unfallen worlds and ranks of beings, as identified with a world's sin.

He knew that His Father's face would be hidden from Him, as by an eclipse.

He knew that the conflict would break His heart and force the sweat of blood on His forehead.

He knew that the Serpent of hell would bruise His heel, and that He would appear as a Lamb that had been slain.

He knew that those whom He had chosen out of the world would deny Him and flee.

Yet – He slackened not His pace, but laying aside the insignia of

His glory, He became obedient unto death, even the death of the Cross!

Looking at this stupendous act, shall we not catch the infection of His self-giving? Shall we not follow Him as far as we can? "Christ," says the apostle, "has left us an example that we should follow in His steps." It is not what we get, but what we give; not our own pleasure, but the uplift of the fallen, and the extrication of those who are slipping into the pit; not ridding ourselves of burdens, but bearing the burden of others. This is the path of true blessedness, the path trodden by all the saints, the path which led Christ to Gethsemane and Calvary, but has ended in the throne! Follow that path, and life will become transcendently useful and blessed!

But there is an infinite chasm between our highest attainments and the divine self-giving of our Saviour to redeem and save us. He trod that winepress alone, and of all the people there were none with Him! So far as we know, Gethsemane and Calvary have no equivalents throughout God's universe. They are the wonders into which angels desire to look, and the theme of the untiring song of the redeemed.

F. B. Meyer (1847–1929)

10th September

"Now then," said Joshua, "throw away the foreign gods that are among you and yield your hearts to the Lord, the God of Israel." And the people said to Joshua, "We will serve the Lord our God and obey him." On that day Joshua made a covenant for the people, and there at Shechem he drew up for them decrees and laws.

(Joshua 24:23–5)

It was fitting that the transition from the nomad stage to that of the settled abode in the land should be marked by the solemn renewal of the covenant, which is thus declared to be the willingly accepted law for the future national life. We have here the closing scene of that solemn assembly set before us.

The narrative carries us to Shechem, the lovely valley in the heart of the land, already consecrated by many patriarchal associations, and by that picturesque scene (Joshua 8:30–35), when the gathered nation, ranged on the slopes of Ebal and Gezirim, listened to Joshua reading "all that Moses had commanded". There, too, the coffin of Joseph, which had been reverently carried all through the desert and the war, was laid in the ground that Jacob had bought five hundred years ago, and which now had fallen to Joseph's descendants, the tribe of Ephraim.

There was another reason for the selection of Shechem for this renewal of the covenant. The gathered representatives of Israel stood, at Shechem, on the very soil where, long ago, Abram had made his first resting place as a stranger in the land and had received the first divine pledge, "unto thy seed I give this land," and had piled beneath the oak of Moreh his first altar (of which the weathered stone might still be there), "to the Lord who appeared unto him". It was fitting that this cradle of the nation should witness their vow, as it witnessed the fulfilment of God's promise. What Plymouth Rock is to one side of the Atlantic, or Hastings Field to the other, Shechem was to Israel. Vows sworn there had sanctity added by the place.

Nor did these remembrances exhaust the appropriateness of the site. The oak, which had waved down green above Abram's altar, had looked down on another significant incident in the life of Jacob, when in preparation for his journey to Bethel, he had made a clean sweep of the idols of his household, and buried them "under the oak which was by Shechem" (Genesis 35:2–4). His very words are quoted by Joshua in his command in verse 23, and it is impossible to overlook the intention to parallel the two events. The spot which had seen the earlier act of purification from idolatry was for that reason chosen for the latter.

Alexander Maclaren (1826–1910)

11th September

Joshua said to the people, "You are not able to serve the Lord. He is a holy God; he is a jealous God. He will not forgive your rebellion and your sins. If you forsake the Lord and serve foreign gods, he will turn and bring disaster on you and make an end of you, after he has been good to you. But the people said to Joshua, "No! we will serve the Lord."

(Joshua 24:19–21)

[Continued from yesterday.]

"Jealousy" is an ugly word, with repulsive associations, and its application to God has sometimes been explained in ugly fashion, and has actually repelled men. But, rightly looked at, what does it mean but that God desires our whole hearts for His own, and loves us so much, and is so desirous to pour His love into us, that He will have no rivals for our love? The metaphor of marriage, which puts His love to men in its tenderest form, underlies this word, so harsh on the surface, but so gracious at the core.

There is still abundant need for Joshua's warning. We rejoice that it takes so little to be a Christian that the feeblest and simplest act of faith knits the soul to the all-forgiving Christ. But let us not forget that, on the other hand, it is hard to be a Christian indeed; for it means "forsaking all that we have", and loving God with all our powers. The measure of His love is the measure of His "jealousy", and He loves us no less than He did Israel. Unless our conceptions of His service are based on the recognition of His holiness and demand for our all, we, too, "cannot serve the Lord".

The other half of Joshua's warnings refers to the penalties of broken vows. These are put with extraordinary force. The declaration that the sins of the servants would not be forgiven is not, of course, to be taken so as to contradict the whole teachings of scripture, but as meaning that the sins of His people cannot be left unpunished. The closer relation between God and them made retribution certain . . . "You only have I known of all the families of the earth: therefore I will punish you for all your iniquities" (Amos 3:2)...

Thus on the spot made sacred by so many ancient memories, the people ended their wandering and homeless life, and passed into the possession of their inheritance, through the portal of this fresh acceptance of the covenant, proclaiming thereby that they held the land on condition of serving God, and writing their own sentence in case of unfaithfulness. It was the last act of the assembled people, and the crown and close of Joshua's career.

Alexander Maclaren (1826–1910)

12th September

We know that an idol is nothing at all in the world and that there is no God but one.

(1 Corinthians 8:4)

When did men begin to desert the worshipping of idols, save since the true God and Word of God has come among men? Or when have the oracles, among the Greeks and everywhere, ceased and become empty, save when the Saviour has manifested himself upon earth? Or when did those who are called gods and heroes in the poets begin to be convicted of being merely mortal men, save since the Lord effected his conquest of death, and preserved incorruptible the body he had taken, raising it from the dead? Or when did the deceitfulness and madness of demons fall into contempt, save when the Power of God, the Word, the Master of all these as well, condescending because of man's weakness, appeared on earth? Or when did the art and the schools of magic begin to be trodden down, save when the divine manifestation of the Word took place among men? And in a word, at what time has the Wisdom of the Greeks become foolish, save when the true Wisdom of god manifested itself on earth? For formerly the whole world and every place was led astray by the worshipping of idols, and men regarded nothing else but the idols as gods. But now all the world over men are deserting the superstition of the idols, and taking refuge with Christ; and worshipping him as God, are by his means coming to know the Father also, whom they knew not.

Athanasius (c. 296–373)

13th September

And you see and hear how this fellow Paul has convinced and led astray large numbers of people here in Ephesus and in practically the whole province of Asia. He says that man-made gods are no gods at all.

(Acts 19:26)

And whereas formerly every place was full of the deceit of the oracles, and the oracles at Delphi and Dodona, and in Boeotia and Lycia and Libya and Egypt and those of the Cabiri, and the Pythoness, were held in repute by men's imagination, now, since Christ has begun to be preached everywhere, their madness also has ceased and there is none among them to divine anymore. And whereas formerly demons used to deceive men's fancy, occupying springs or rivers, trees or stones, and thus imposed upon the simple by their juggleries; now, after the divine visitation of the Word, their deception has ceased. For by the sign of the Cross, though a man but use it, he drives out their deceits.

And while formerly men held to be gods the Zeus and Cronos and Apollo and the heroes mentioned in the poets, and went astray in honouring them; now that the Saviour has appeared among men, those others have been exposed as mortal men, and Christ alone has been recognised among men as the true God, the Word of God. And what is one to say of the magic esteemed among them? That before the word sojourned among us this was strong and active among Egyptians, and Chaldees, and Indians, and inspired awe in those who saw it; but that by the presence of the Truth and the appearing of the Word, it has been thoroughly confuted, and brought wholly to nought.

Athanasius (c. 296–373)

14th September

Then I heard a voice from heaven say, "Write: Blessed are the dead who die in the Lord from now on."

(Revelation 14:13)

A great crowd was collected early; at Sexti, as the Proconsul commanded. And the same day Cyprian was brought before him as he sat for judgement in the court called Sauciolum. The Proconsul demanded, "Are you Thascius Cyprianus?" Cyprian Bishop answered, "I am he." Galerius Maximus Proconsul said, "The most sacred Emperors have commanded you to conform to the Roman rites." Cyprian Bishop said, "I refuse to do so." Galerius: "Take heed for yourself." Cyprian: "Execute the Emperor's orders; in a matter so manifest I may not deliberate."

Galerius, after briefly conferring with his judicial council, with much reluctance pronounced the following sentence. "You have long lived an irreligious life, and have drawn together a number of men bound by an unlawful association, and professed yourself an open enemy to the gods and the religion of Rome. The pious, most sacred, and august Empeors, Valerian and Gallienus, and the most noble Caesar Valerian, have endeavoured in vain to bring you back to conformity with their religious observances. Since you have been apprehended as principal and ringleader in these infamous crimes, you shall be made an example to those whom you have wickedly associated with you: the authority of the law shall be ratified in your blood."

He then read the sentence of the court from written tablet. "It is the will of this court, that Thascius Cyprianus be immediately beheaded." Cyprian Bishop said, "Thanks be to God." After sentence was pronounced, the whole of the assembled brethren cried out, "We will be beheaded with him." A great tumult arose among the brethren, and a crowd followed to the place of execution. He was brought forth into the field near Sexti, where having laid aside his upper garment, he kneeled down, and addressed himself in prayer to the Lord.

Then stripping himself of his dalmatic and giving it to the

Deacons, he stood in his linen tunic, and awaited the executioner, to whom when he came Cyprian bade five and twenty pieces of gold be given. The brethren, meanwhile, spread linen cloths and napkins on the ground before him. Being unable to tie the sleeve of his robe at the wrist, Julian Presbyter and Julian Subdeacon performed this office for him. Then the blessed Cyprian covered his eyes with his hands, and so suffered.

His body was exposed in a place nearby, to gratify the curiosity of the heathen. But in the course of the night it was removed, and transported with prayers and great pomp, with wax tapers and funeral torches to the burying ground of Macrobius Candidianus the Procurator, near the fish ponds in the Mappalian way. A few days after, Galerius Maximus the Proconsul died.

Cyprian (c. 201/210–258)

15th September

For they themselves report what kind of reception you gave us. They tell how you turned to God from idols to serve the living and true God.

(1 Thessalonians 1:9)

In 627, Edwin the king, hearing these words, answered, that he was both willing and bound to receive the faith which he taught; but that he would confer about it with his principal friends and counsellors, to the end that if they also were of his opinion they might all together be cleansed in Christ the fountain of Life. Paulinus consenting, the king did as he said; for, holding a council with the wise men, he asked of everyone in particular what he thought of the new doctrine, and the new worship that was preached? To which the chief of his own priests, Coifi, immediately answered, "O king consider what this is which is now preached to us; for I verily declare to you, that the religion which we have hitherto professed has, as far as I can learn, no virtue in it. For none of your people has applied himself more diligently to the worship of our gods than I; and yet there are many who receive greater favours from you, and are more preferred than I, and are more prosperous in all their undertakings. Now if the gods were good for any thing, they would rather forward me, who have been more careful to serve them. It remains, therefore, that if upon examination you find those new doctrines, which are now preached to us, better and more efficacious, we immediately receive them without delay."

Another of the king's chief men, approving of his words and exhortations, presently added: "The present life of man, O king, seems to me, in comparison of that time which is unknown to us, like to the swift flight of a sparrow through the room wherein you sit at supper in winter, with your commanders and ministers, and a good fire in the midst, whilst the storms of rain and snow prevail abroad: the sparrow, I say, flying in at one door, and immediately out at another, whilst he is within, is safe from the wintry storm; but after a short space of fair weather, he immediately vanishes out of your sight, into the dark winter from which he had emerged. So this life of man appears for a short space, but of what went before, or what is to follow, we are utterly ignorant. If, therefore, this new doctrine contains something more certain, it seems justly to deserve to be followed." The other elders and kings's counsellors, by Divine inspiration, spoke to the same effect.

The Venerable Bede (c. 673–735)

16th September

I am the Lord; that is my name! I will not give my glory to another or my praise to idols.

(Isaiah 42:8)

[Continued from yesterday.]

But Coifi added, that he wished more attentively to hear Paulinus discourse concerning the God whom he preached; which he having by the king's command performed, Coifi hearing his words, cried out, "I have long since been sensible that there was nothing in that which we worshipped; because the more diligently I sought after truth in that worship, the less I found it. But now I freely confess, that such truth evidently appears in this preaching as can confer on us the gifts of life, of salvation, and of eternal happiness. For which reason I advise, O king, that we instantly abjure and set fire to those temples and altars which we have consecrated without reaping any benefit from them." In short, the king publicly gave his licence to Paulinus to preach the Gospel, and renouncing idolatry, declared that he received the faith of Christ: and when he inquired of the high priest who should first profane the altars and temples of their idols, with the enclosures that were about them, he answered, "I; for who can more properly than myself destroy these things which I worshipped through ignorance, for an example to all others, through the wisdom which has been given me by the true God?"

Then immediately, in contempt of his former superstitions, he desired the king to furnish him with arms and a stallion; and mounting the same, he set out to destroy the idols; for it was not lawful before for the high priest either to carry arms, or to ride on any but a mare. Having, therefore, girt a sword about him, with a spear in his hand, he mounted the king's stallion and proceeded to the idols. The multitude, beholding it, concluded he was distracted; but he lost no time, for as soon as he drew near the temple he profaned the same, casting into it the spear which he held; and rejoicing in the knowledge of the worship of the true God, he commanded his companions to destroy the temple, with all its enclosures, by fire.

This place where the idols were is still shown, not far from York, to the eastward, beyond the river Derwent, and is now called Godmundingham, where the high priest, by the inspiration of the true God, profaned and destroyed the altars which he had himself consecrated.

The Venerable Bede (c. 673–735)

17th September

Jesus replied, "No-one who puts his hand to the plough and looks back is fit for service in the kingdom of God."

(Luke 9:62)

"But the Lord looks on the heart," is another of the pet doctrines of

popular Christianity. True, terribly true in the right sense – for God is not to be mocked with lip service or the formality of worship in which the heart has no share – but false ruinously false, when it means, as it generally does, that all sorts of wrongs may be passed over and excused, if people only say they mean to do right . . .

Friend, let me ask you, did you really worship and serve God last Sunday? Had you any convictions as to what He wished you to do, not only on that day but throughout the following week? If so, have you acted on them, have you honestly tried to carry them out? If not, do not I beseech you, try to pacify your conscience with any nonsense about the Lord looking on the heart.

He has plainly told us over and over again in the New Testament, and in the very last book of it, that He will judge every man according to *his works*, and, moreover, He has laid down the same rule of judgement for us. "By their fruits ye shall know them." "Little children, let no man deceive you; he that doeth righteousness is righteous." I fear there are thousands of professed Christians excusing themselves from the performance of the most manifest duty by this excuse; for instance, when a prayer meeting is announced, there are a certain number of people who make an effort to be present, but a much larger number of so-called Christians who deliberately choose to keep away. It is quite allowable to apply the doctrine of the Lord's looking at the heart to the poor mother who would fain be there, were she not detained by the inexorable claims of half a dozen little children; but to cloak over with the same excuse, the constant indifference, nay positive irreligion, in the great majority, is only to refuse to come to the light because it would condemn you. People who mean well, where there is no physical impossibility, *do well*; but those who fail to do well, will fare ill when the great reckoning day comes.

Catherine Booth (1829–90)

18th September

Never be lacking in zeal, but keep your spiritual fervour, serving the Lord.

(Romans 12:11)

One of the first things that young converts should be taught is to distinguish between emotion and principle in religion. I want you to get hold of the words and have them fixed in your mind; to have you distinguish between emotion and principle.

By emotion, I mean that state of mind of which we are conscious, and which we call "feeling" – an involuntary state of mind, that arises, of course, when we are in certain circumstances, or under certain influences. There may be high-wrought feelings, or they may subside into tranquillity, or disappear entirely. But these emotions should be carefully distinguished from religious principle. By principle, I do not mean any substance or root or seed or sprout implanted in the soul. But I mean the voluntary decision of the mind, the firm determination to fulfil duty and to obey the will of God, by which a Christian should always be governed.

When a man is fully determined to obey God, because it is RIGHT that he should obey God, I call that principle. Whether he feels any lively religious emotion at the time or not, he will do his duty cheerfully, readily, and heartily, whatever may be the state of his feelings. This is acting upon principle, and not from emotion. Many young converts hold mistaken views upon this subject, and depend almost entirely on the state of their feelings to go forward in duty. Some will not lead a prayer meeting, unless they feel as if they could make an eloquent prayer. Multitudes are influenced almost entirely by their emotions, and they give way to this, as if they thought themselves under no obligation to duty, unless urged on by some strong emotion. They will be very zealous in religion when they feel like it, when their emotions are warm and lively, but they will not act out religion consistently and carry it into all concerns of life. They are religious only as they are impelled by a gush of feeling. But this is not true religion.

Young converts should be carefully taught that when their duty is before them they are to do it. However dull their feelings may be, if duty calls, DO IT. Do not wait for feeling, but DO IT. Most likely the emotions for which you would wait will be called into exercise when you begin to do your duty. If the duty be prayer, for instance, and you have not the feelings you would wish, do not wait for emotions before you pray, but pray, and "open thy mouth wide" (Psalm 81:10); and in doing it, you are most likely to have the emotions for which you were inclined to wait, and which constitute the conscious happiness of religion.

Charles G. Finney (1792–1875)

19th September

Here is a trustworthy saying: If anyone sets his heart on being an overseer, he desires a noble task. Now the overseer must be above reproach, the husband of but one wife, temperate, self-controlled, respectable, hospitable, able to teach.

(1 Timothy 3:1–2)

Take heed to yourselves, because the tempter will make his first and sharpest onset upon you. If you will be the leaders against him, he will spare you no further than God restraineth him. He beareth you the greatest malice that are engaged to do him the greatest mischief. As he hateth Christ more than any of us, because He is the General of the field and the Captain of our salvation, and doth more than all the world besides the kingdom of darkness; so doth he hate the leaders under Him more than the common soldiers: he knows what a rout he may make against the rest if the leaders fall before their eyes. He hath long tried that way of fighting, neither against great or small comparatively, but of smiting the shepherds that he may scatter the flock: and so great hath been his success this way he will follow it on as far as he is able.

Take heed, therefore, brethren, for the enemy hath a special eye upon you. You shall have his most subtle insinuations and incessant solicitations and violent assaults. As wise and learned as you are, take heed to yourselves lest he overwit you. The devil is a greater scholar than you, and a nimbler disputant: he can transform himself into an angel of light to deceive: he will get within you and trip up your heel before you are aware: he will play the juggler with you undiscerned, and cheat you of your faith and innocency, and you shall not know that you have lost it; nay, he will make you believe it is multiplied or increased when it is lost. You shall see neither hook nor line, much less the subtle angler himself, while he is offering you his bait. And his bait shall be so fitted to your temper and disposition, that he will be sure to find advantages within you, and make your own principles and inclinations betray you. Oh what a conquest will he think he hath got, if he can make a minister lazy and unfaithful, if he can tempt a minister into covetousness or scandal.

Richard Baxter (1615–91)

20th September

Be shepherds of God's flock that is under your care, serving as overseers — not because you must, but because you are willing, as God wants you to be; not greedy for money, but eager to serve.

(1 Peter 5:2)

Follow the example of the Lord; being firm and immutable in the faith, lovers of the brotherhood, lovers of one another; companions together in the truth, being kind and gentle towards each other, despising none. When it is in your power to do good, defer it not; for "charity delivereth from death". "Be all of you subject to one another, having your behaviour honest among the Gentiles"; that, by your good works, both ye yourselves may receive praise and the Lord may not "be blasphemed through you". But woe to him by whom the name of the Lord is blasphemed. Therefore teach all men sobriety, in which do ye also exercise yourselves.

I am greatly afflicted for Valens, who was once a presbyter among you, that he should so little understand the place that was given him in the church. Wherefore I admonish you that ye abstain from covetousness, and that ye be chaste and true of speech. "Keep yourselves from all evil." For he that in these things cannot govern himself, how shall he be able to prescribe them to another? If a man does not keep himself from covetousness, he shall be polluted with idolatry, and be judged as if he were a Gentile. But who of you are ignorant of the judgement of God? "Do ye not know that the saints shall judge the world," as Paul teaches? But I have neither perceived or heard anything of this kind in you [in Philippi] among whom the blessed Paul laboured, and who are named at the beginning of this letter: for he glories of you in all the churches, who then only knew God; for we did not then know him. Wherefore, my brethren, I am exceedingly sorry both for him and for his wife, to whom God a true repentance.

And be ye also moderate upon this occasion, and look not upon such as enemies, that ye may save your whole body; for by doing so ye shall edify your own selves.

Polycarp (c. 70–155/160)

21st September

But Ruth replied, "Don't urge me to leave you or to turn back from you. Where you go I will go, and where you stay I will stay. Your people will be my people and your God my God." . . . So Naomi returned from Moab accompanied by Ruth the Moabitess, her daughter-in-law, arriving in Bethlehem as the barley harvest was beginning.

(Ruth 1:16, 22)

The question has often been asked, what the purpose of the *Book of Ruth* is, and various answers have been given. The genealogical table at the end, showing David's descent from her, the example which it supplies of the reception of a Gentile into Israel, and other reasons for its presence in Scripture have been alleged, and, no doubt, correctly. But the Bible is a very human book, just because it is a divine one; and surely it would be no unworthy object to enshrine in its pages a picture of the noble working of that human love that makes so much of human life.

The hallowing of the family is a distinct purpose of the Old Testament, and the beautiful example which this narrative gives of the elevating influence of domestic affection entitles it to a place in the canon. How many hearts, since Ruth spoke her vow, have found in it the words that fitted their love best! How often they have been repeated by quivering lips, and heard as music by loving ears! How solemn, and even awful, is that perennial freshness of words which came hot and broken by tears, from lips that have long ago mouldered into dust! What has made them thus "enduring for ever", is that they express most purely the self-sacrifice which is essential to all noble love.

The very inmost longing of love is to give itself away to the object loved. It is not so much a desire to acquire as to bestow, or rather, the antithesis of giving and receiving melts into one action which has a two fold motion – one outwards to give; one inwards, to receive. To love is to give one's self away, therefore all lesser givings are its food and delight; and, when Ruth threw herself on Naomi's withered breast, and sobbed out her passionate resolve, she was speaking the eternal language of love, and claiming Naomi for her own, in the very act of giving herself to Naomi.

Human love should be the parent of all self-sacrificing love as of all heroic virtues; and in our homes we do not live in love, as we ought, unless it leads us to the daily exercise of self-suppression and surrender, which is not felt to be loss, but the natural expression of our love, which it would be a crime against it, and a pain to ourselves to withhold.

Alexander Maclaren (1826–1910)

22nd September

So Boaz took Ruth and she became his wife. Then he went to her, and the Lord enabled her to conceive, and she gave birth to a son. The women said to Naomi: "Praise be to the Lord, who this day has not left you without a kinsman-redeemer. May he become famous throughout Israel!"

(Ruth 4:13–14)

Boaz is a splendid pattern to be set before all landowners, and farmers, and masters, and employers of labour. Courteous, solicitous, affectionate, devout, bountiful; Boaz greets his reapers in the harvest field as if they had been his sons and daughters. He meets them in the morning with a benediction, as if he had been a priest . . . Just, honourable, and upright in the market and in the gate, he is kind, generous and hospitable at home. He eats and drinks with a merry heart in the harvest season; but with it all he is at all times and in all places both temperate and chaste . . . Altogether a husband worthy of Naomi's dear daughter Ruth . . .

From gleaning in his fields, and from falling at his feet, until she sat at his table and lay in his bosom, – Ruth from first to last had nothing in her heart but pride, and respect, and love for Boaz . . . A happy pair, with a romantic history behind them, and with a future before them that it had not entered into their sweetest dreams to dream.

With all that, it is not at all to be wondered at that the Church of Christ with such a dash of romance and mysticism in her heart, should have seen in Ruth's husband, Boaz, a far-off figure of her own husband, Jesus Christ. For she, like Naomi and Ruth, was disinherited, disconsolate, despised, forgotten, and without kinsman-redeemer in her famine and all her deep distress, when His eye and His heart fell on her in the field. And how well He has performed a kinsman's part all the world has read in a Book that for truth and beauty far outstrips the Book of Ruth. How He has not only redeemed her, but has given her rest in His own house, in His Father's house, and His own heart – what written book can ever fully tell? Boaz the Bethlehemite and Ruth the Moabitess made a noble marriage, and a noble race sprang out of that marriage. Obed, and Jesse, and David, and Solomon, and Joseph and Mary, and Jesus Christ – my Kinsman-Redeemer, and yours.

Alexander Whyte (1836–1921)

23rd September

So Boaz took Ruth and she became his wife. Then he went to her, and the Lord enabled her to conceive, and she gave birth to a son . . . And they named him Obed. He was the father of Jesse, the father of David.

(Ruth 4:13, 17)

We may see in Ruth's entrance into the religion of Israel, a picture of what was intended to be the effect of Israel's relation with the Gentile world. The household of Elimelech emigrated to Moab in a famine, and, whether that were right or wrong, they were there among heathens as Jehovah worshippers. They were meant to be missionaries, and in Ruth's case, the purpose was fulfilled. She became the "first-fruits of the Gentiles"; and one aim of the book, no doubt, is to show how the believing Gentile was to be incorporated into Israel.

Boaz rejoices over her, and especially over her conversion... She is married to him, and becomes the ancestress of David, and through him, of the Messiah. All this is a beautiful completion to the other side of the picture which the fierce fighting in Judges makes prominent, and teaches that Israel's relation to the nations around, was not to be one of mere antagonism, but that they had another mission than destruction, and were set in their land, as the candlestick in the Tabernacle, that light may stream out into the darkness of the desert.

The story of the Moabitess, whose blood flowed in David's veins, was a standing protest against the later narrow exclusiveness which called Gentiles "dogs", and prided itself on outward connection with the nation, in the exact degree in which it lost real union with the nation's God, and real understanding of the nation's mission.

Alexander Maclaren (1826–1910)

24th September

Leaving that place, Jesus withdrew to the region of Tyre and Sidon. A Canaanite woman from that vicinity came to him, crying out, "Lord, Son of David, have mercy on me! My daughter is suffering terribly from demon-possession." Jesus did not answer a word. So his disciples came to him and urged him, "Send her away, for she keeps crying out after us."

(Matthew 15:21–3)

Take the case of the Syrophenecian woman. When she called to the Master, it seemed for a time as He were deaf to her request. The disciples wanted her to be sent away. Although they were with Christ for three years, and sat at His feet, yet they did not know how full of grace His heart was. Think of Christ sending away a poor sinner who had come to Him for mercy! Can you conceive such a thing? Never once did it occur. This poor woman put herself in the place of her child. "Lord, help me!" she said. I think that when we get so far as that in earnest desire to have our friends blessed – when we put ourselves in their place – God will soon hear our prayer.

I remember, a number of years ago at a meeting, I asked all those who wished to be prayed for to come forward and kneel or take seats in front. Among those who came was a woman. I thought by her looks that she must be a Christian; but she knelt down with the others. I said: "You are a Christian, are you not?" She said she had been one for so many years. "Did you not understand the invitation? I asked those only who wanted to become Christians." I shall never forget the look on her face as she replied. "I have got a son who has gone far away; I thought that I would take his place today, and see if God would not bless him." Thank God for a mother such as that!

The Syrophenecian woman did the same thing – "Lord, help *me*!" It was a short prayer, but it went right to the heart of the Son of God. He tried her faith, however. He said: "It is not meet to take the children's bread and cast it to dogs." She replied: "Truth, Lord; yet the dogs eat the crumbs which fall from their master's table." "O woman, great is thy faith!" What a eulogy He paid her! Her story will not be forgotten as long as the Church is on the earth. He honoured her faith and gave her all she asked for. Everyone here can say, "Lord help me!" We all need help. As Christians we need more grace, more love, more purity of life, more righteousness. Are we not hungering and thirsting after righteousness? Then let us make this our prayer today. I want God to help me to preach better and live better, to be more like the Son of God. The golden chains of faith link us right to the throne of God, and the grace of heaven flows down into our souls.

D. L. Moody (1837–99)

25th September

He answered, "I was sent only to the lost sheep of Israel." The woman came and knelt before him. "Lord, help me!" she said. He replied, "It is not right to take the children's bread and toss it to their dogs." "Yes, Lord," she said, "but even the dogs eat the crumbs that fall from their master's table." Then Jesus answered, "Woman, you have great faith! Your request is granted." And her daughter was healed from that very hour.

(Matthew 15:24–8)

[Continued from yesterday.]

I do not know but that woman was a great sinner; still, the Lord heard her cry. It may be that up to this hour some of you have been living in sin; but if you will cry, "Lord, help me!" He will answer your prayer, if it is an honest one. Very often when we cry to God we do not really mean anything. You mothers understand that. Your children have two voices. When they ask you for anything you can soon tell if the cry is a make-believe one or not. If it is, you do not give any heed to it; but if it is a real cry for help, how quickly you respond! The cry of distress always brings relief. Your child is playing around, and it says, "Mamma, I want some bread;" but it goes on playing. You know that it is not very hungry, so you let it alone. But by and by, the child drops the toys, and comes tugging at your dress. "Mamma, I am so hungry." Then you know that the cry is a real one; you soon go to the pantry, and get some bread. When we are in earnest for the bread of heaven, we will get it. This woman was terribly in earnest, therefore her petition was answered.

I remember hearing of a boy brought up in one of your almshouses. He had never learned to read or write except that he could read the letters of the alphabet. One day a man of God came there and told the children that if they prayed to God in their trouble, He would send them help. After a time this boy was apprenticed to a farmer. One day he was sent out into the fields to look after some sheep. He was having a rather hard time, so he remembered what the preacher had said, and he thought that he would pray to God about it. Someone going by the field heard a voice behind the hedge. They looked to see whose it was, and saw the little fellow on his knees, saying, "A, B, C, D," and so on. The man said, "My boy, what are you doing?" He looked up, and said that he was praying. "Why that is not praying; it is only saying the alphabet." He said he did not know just how to pray, but a man came to the poor-house, who told them that if they called upon God He would help them. So he thought that if he named the letters of the alphabet, God would take them and put them together into a prayer, and give him what he wanted.

The little fellow was really praying. Sometimes, when your child talks, your friends cannot understand what he says; but the mother understands very well. So if our prayer comes from the heart, God understands our language. It is a delusion of the devil to think that we cannot pray; we can if we really want anything . . . When this poor Gentile woman cried out, "Lord help me!" the cry flashed over the divine wires and the blessing came. So you can pray if you will; it is the desire, the wish of the heart, that God delights to hear and to answer.

D. L. Moody (1837–99)

26th September

Our people must learn to devote themselves to doing what is good, in order that they may provide for daily necessities and not live unproductive lives.

(Titus 3:14)

But whoever [of the apostles or prophets], in the spirit, says, Give me money, or something else, ye shall not hear him; but if for others in need, he bids *you* give, let no one judge him.

But let everyone that cometh in the Lord's name be received, but afterward ye shall test and know him; for ye shall have understanding, right and left. If he who comes is a traveller, help him as much as ye can; but he shall not remain with you, unless for two or three days, if there be necessity. But if he will take up his abode among you, being an artisan, let him work and so eat; but if he has no trade, provide, according to your understanding, that no idler live with you as a Christian. But if he will not act according to this, he is one who makes gain out of Christ; beware of such.

But every true prophet who will settle among you is worthy of his support. Likewise a true teacher, he also is worthy like the workman, of his support. Every first fruit, then, of the products of wine-press and threshing floor, of oxen and of sheep, thou shalt take and give to the prophets; for they are your high priests. But if ye have no prophet, give it to the poor. If thou makest a baking of bread, take the first of it and give according to the commandment. In like manner when thou openest a jar of wine or oil, take the first of it and give it to the prophets; and of money and clothing and every possession take the first, as seems right to thee, and give according to the commandment.

The Didache (1st–3rd century)

27th September

Until we all reach unity in the faith and in the knowledge of the Son of God and become mature, attaining to the whole measure of the fulness of Christ.

(Ephesians 4:13)

It is not proof that a person grows in grace because he thinks he is doing so. One may be very favourably impressed with regard to his own progress in religion, when it is evident to others that he is not only making no progress but is, in fact, declining. An individual who is growing worse and worse, is not ordinarily aware of the fact. It is not uncommon for both impenitent sinners and Christians to think that they are growing better, when they are growing no better.

This results from the very nature of the case. If any person is growing worse, his conscience will, for the time being, become more seared, and his mind more and more dark, as he stifles conscience and resists the light. Then he may imagine he is growing better, because he has less sense of sin; and while his conscience continues to sleep he may continue under the fatal delusion. A man will judge of his own spiritual state as he compares himself with a high or a low standard. If he keeps Christ before him, in His fulness, as his standard, he will doubtless always, at least in this state of existence, have but a lower estimate of his own attainments. While at the same time, if he sets before himself the Church, or any member of the Church, as a standard, he will very likely to form a high estimate of his progress in religion, and be well satisfied with himself.

This is the reason why there is such a difference in people's views of their own state and of the state of the Church. They compare the state of the Church with different standards. Hence, one takes a very humbling view of his own state, and complains of that of the Church; another thinks such complaints of the Church censorious, for him the Church appears not to be doing very well. The reason why he does not think the Church cold and in a low state, is that Christ is not the standard of comparison. If a man shuts his eyes, he will not see the defilement on him, and may think that he is clean, while to all around he appears loathesome.

Charles G. Finney (1792–1875)

28th September

Blessed is the man who perseveres under trial, because when he has stood the test, he will receive the crown of life that God has promised to those who love him.

(James 1:12)

What painter would have the courage and endurance to devote several months of his life to a painting, in which his genius was to reveal all its splendour, if he knew that at the moment the work was finished, when the last brush of varnish had been laid on, it would be destroyed by fire, leaving only the remembrance of it to survive in the minds of those who had visited his studio and seen it in the successive stages of its progress? And if every palace, every temple, when it was completed, when the last stroke of the chisel had been given to the carving, when it had been enriched with all beautiful and precious things, were destined to be destroyed by earthquake or scattered by storm, – if from this doom there were no escape, – what architect, what prince, what church, would care to spend its genius and treasure in erecting it?

And if the moral nobleness and beauty which require a patience and suffering beyond what any artist ever had to consecrate to the expression of his imagination on canvas, which impose a severer strain on the moral energies of men, and involve a greater cost, than the erection of the most stately buildings that have ever commanded the wonder and veneration of mankind, – if these were to perish as soon as they were perfected, the moral courage of most men would be paralysed, and they would be content to live a life of compromise and ease.

Desperate indeed would be our condition if the great hope were not ours. When the elastic energy of youth declines, – and with some it declines very soon, – when the passion and energy which make hardship itself exhilarating, begin to sink, many a man would renounce the attempt to achieve a perfect righteousness, unless he knew that the righteousness would be eternal. For some of you life is a very troubled sea; storm after storm breaks upon you; the winds are fierce, the waves run high; and if it were certain that sooner or later the ship would run upon an iron-bound coast at night, or be destroyed in mid-ocean by the fury of the tempest, struck by lightning, shattered by heavy seas, I do not know what heart or courage you would have to fight the winds and the waves any longer.

It is the port which, by the divine help, you are sure of making; it is the land of eternal sunlight and peace to which at last, through God's defence, you are sure to come, that makes it supremely worth while to oppose to all difficulties a stubborn and invincible endurance.

R. W. Dale (1829–95)

29th September

We loved you so much that we were delighted to share with you not only the gospel of God but our lives as well, because you had become so dear to us.

(1 Thessalonians 2:8)

As soon as they entered the dwelling place assigned them, they began to imitate the course of life practised in the primitive church; applying themselves to frequent prayer, watching and fasting; preaching the word of life to as many as they could; despising all worldly things, as not belonging to them; receiving only their necessary food from those they taught; living themselves in all respects conformably to what they prescribed to others, and being always disposed to suffer any adversity, and even to die for that truth which they preached. In short, several believed and were baptised, admiring the simplicity of their innocent life, and the sweetness of their heavenly doctrine. There was on the east side of the city, a church dedicated to the honour of St Martin, built whilst the Romans were still in the island, wherein the queen, who, as has been said before, was a Christian, used to pray. In this they first began to meet, to sing, to pray, to say mass, to preach, and to baptise, till the king, being converted to the faith, allowed them to preach openly, and build or repair churches in all places.

When he, among the rest, induced by the unspotted life of these holy men, and their delightful promises, which, by many miracles, they proved to be most certain, believed and was baptised, greater numbers began daily to flock together to hear the word, and, forsaking their heathen rites, to associate themselves, by believing, to the unity of the church of Christ. Their conversion the king so far encouraged, as that he compelled none to embrace Christianity, but only showed more affection to the believers, as to his fellow citizens in the heavenly kingdom. For he had learned from his instructors and leaders to salvation, that the service of Christ ought to be voluntary, not by compulsion. Nor was it long before he gave his teachers a settled residence in his metropolis of Canterbury, with such possessions of different kinds as were necessary for their subsistence.

The Venerable Bede (c. 673–735)

30th September

I only know that in every city the Holy Spirit warns me that prison and hardships are facing me. However, I consider my life worth nothing to me, if only I may finish the race and complete the task the Lord Jesus has given me – the task of testifying to the gospel of God's grace.

(Acts 20:23–4)

[A pioneer missionary on his way to the country from which he never came home.]

Nov. 9, 1793 . . . For near a month we have been within two hundred miles of Bengal, but the violence of the currents set us back when we have been at the very door. I hope I have learned the necessity of bearing up in the things of God against wind and tide, when there is occasion, as we have done in our voyage. We have had our port in view all along, and there has been every attention paid to ascertain our situation by solar and lunar observations: no opportunity occurred that was neglected. Oh that I was but as attentive to the evidence of my state, as they to their situation! A ship sails within six points of the wind; that is, if the wind blow from the North, a ship will sail E.N.E. upon one tack, and W.N.W. upon the other; if our course is North, we must therefore go E.N.E. upon one tack, and W.N.W. upon the other; if our course is North, we must therefore go E.N.E. for a considerable way, then W.N.W; and if the wind shifts a point, the advantage is immediately taken. Now, though this is a tiresome work, and (especially if a current sets against us) we scarcely make any way; nay sometimes, in spite of all that we can do, we go backwards instead of forwards; yet it is absolutely necessary to keep working up, if we ever mean to arrive at our port. So in the Christian life, we often have to work against wind and currents; but we must do it if we expect ever to make port.

William Carey (1761–1834)

October

1st October

To this you were called, because Christ suffered for you, leaving you an example, that you should follow in his steps. "He committed no sin, and no deceit was found in his mouth." When they hurled their insults at him, he did not retaliate; when he suffered, he made no threats. Instead, he entrusted himself to him who judges justly.

(1 Peter 2:21–3)

"Oh!" people say, "the world is different in these days from what it was in the days of Jesus Christ and Paul." Is it? Try it on the *same lines*, and you will soon find out how far different it is. The very essence of the spirit of the age is antagonistic to the spirit of good. Good and evil are as diametrically opposed to each other as ever; therefore they can never be brought into contact without conflict, without war, and sometimes of the most deadly kind, ending in the death and martyrdom of the saints.

I was amused with the exemplification of this some weeks ago. As one of our female [Salvation Army] officers was walking up Clapton, a band of lads were hooting after her, "Hallelujah!" "Jesus Christ!" "Salvation!" and other beautiful names; for in whatever voice they hissed out, they cannot make such words ugly. They were hissing these names at her, as she walked meekly and quietly along. At length she suddenly turned on them and said: "What are you doing this for? I have never done you any harm. I am walking peaceably along the road; why are you shouting after me?" They were all so taken aback that they stood breathless for a moment, then one of them I suppose a little bolder than the rest, and at least an honest lad, said, "It is because you are good and we are bad."

Ah! that was the truth for once. That was the expression, in his rough way, of the eternal principle, that there will always be conflict between good and evil; and the greater good you bring in conflict with evil, the more evil will rage and try for the mastery. Hence, the world treated Him who was the very personification of the Father's holiness, worse than it ever treated any other human being, because He was the concentration of goodness, and therefore the devil did his worst on Him; and just as we approximate to His character will the devil do his worst on us.

Catherine Booth (1829–90)

2nd October

In the beginning was the Word, and the Word was with God and the Word was God. He was with God in the beginning.
(John 1:1–2)

We read the four Gospels. We know that they were received as trustworthy and authoritative by Christian Churches at the close of the first century, when in every part of the world, large numbers of Christian people were still living who had heard the story of our Lord's life and teaching and wonderful works, the story of his death and resurrection, from the original apostles, and from others who had known Him during His earthly ministry. Whether we read Matthew, Mark, Luke or John, we receive the same complex impression. About the reality of our Lord's humanity there can be no doubt. His body was no phantom; He grew from childhood to youth, and from youth to manhood; He suffered weariness and pain; at last He was nailed to the cross, and buried in Joseph's new tomb. His intellect was subject to human limitations. He felt the same emotions that we feel – surprise, anger, fear, indignation, joy.

He had His human friendships. He was tempted and He prayed. He was deeply moved by all forms of human suffering. And yet He is not as other men. This, I say, is the impression which we receive from the representation of our Lord in the four gospels.

Nor is it merely from His contemporaries that He is separated; while we read we are conscious that He is separated from ourselves. The story of no other life – whether the life of hero, saint, reformer, or prophet, impresses us in the same way. Moses, Elijah, Paul, Francis of Assisi, Luther, Wesley – they reached heights of power that we cannot reach, but they do not impress us as belonging to an order of life different from our own. Christ does impress in that way. He speaks our common language, but with an accent of His own. He has a regal manner which appears native to Him, and which the humble conditions of His life cannot conceal.

How this impression of the distance which separates Him from us is produced we may be unable to tell; but we are conscious of it; and it is deepened, year after year, as we become more familiar with the contents of the Gospels. He stands apart from other men and above them.

R. W. Dale (1829–95)

3rd October

And if Christ has not been raised, your faith is futile; you are still in your sins.

(1 Corinthians 15:17)

When we speak of the difference between a dead faith and a living, what we really mean is a difference in the *object* of our faith more than its kind. The object determines the kind. The great fundamental difference is between a dead Christ and a living. Living faith is faith in a living Christ. It is only a living Christ that calls out a living faith, a faith with stay and power – especially power.

Do not fret yourself examining your faith, trying its limbs, feeling its pulse, watching its colour, measuring its work. See rather that it is set on a living Christ. Care for that Christ and He will care for your faith. Realise a living Christ, and He will produce in you a living faith. Visit His holy sepulchre in Scripture, and as you pore and wait He will surprise you from behind with his immortal life (John 20:14). A living faith, a living Christianity, a living Christendom, means a living Christ. Christianity is more than Christendom, but Christ is more than Christianity. The truth of Christ is more than its appreciation by any age of the Christian Church. But Christ himself is more than Christianity. He is more than any truth that can be told about Him, any principle He embodies, or deeds done in His name. Faith in Christ is faith neither in Christendom (or a Church) nor in Christianity (or a system of creed or conduct). But it is faith in the practical reality of His unseen Person, now living, reigning, guiding from His unseen throne the history and hearts of men to the Kingdom of God.

He acts in many ways. He acts by His historic character. He acts by His historic Church. But still more He acts by His Eternal Person and Holy Ghost. This living Lord is invisible, invincible, and immortal; He is royal, and at the last irresistible; He is infinitely patient because of infinite power and grace; He acts not only on the large course of human events, but directly on living souls and wills, whether humble or refractory; and He rejoices alike in the love of His Father and the love of His Redeemed, and in the communion of both.

P. T. Forsyth (1848–1921)

4th October

What do you think about the Christ?

(Matthew 22:42)

I suppose there is no one here who has not thought, more or less about Christ. You have heard about Him, and read about Him, and heard men preach about Him. For eighteen hundred years men have been talking about Him, and thinking about Him; and some have made up their minds about who He is, and doubtless some have not. And although all these years have rolled away, this question comes up, addressed to each of us, today, "What think ye of Christ?"

I do not know why it should not be thought a proper question for one man to put to another. If I were to ask you what you think of any of your prominent men, you would already have your mind made up about him. If I were to ask you what you think of your noble Queen [Victoria], you would speak right out and tell me your opinion in a minute. If I were to ask about your prime minister, you would tell me freely what you had for or against him. And why should not people make up their minds about the Lord Jesus Christ, and take their stand for or against Him? If you think well of Him, why not speak well of Him, and range yourselves on his side? And if you think ill of Him, and believe Him to be an imposter, and that He did not die to save the world, why not lift up your voice, and say you are against Him? It would be a happy day for Christianity if men would just take sides – if we could know positively who was really for Him, and who was against Him.

It is of very little importance what the world thinks of any one else. The Queen and the statesmen, the peers and the princes, must soon be gone. Yes: it matters little, comparatively, what we think of them. Their lives only interest a few; but every living soul on the face of the earth is concerned with this Man. The question for the world is, "What think ye of Christ?" . . .

I should like to ask, Was He really the Son of God – the great God-man? Did He leave heaven and come down to this world for a purpose? Was it really to seek and to save? I should like to begin with the manger, and follow Him up through the thirty-three years He was here on earth. I should ask you what you think of his coming into this world, and being born in a manger when it might have been a palace; why He left the grandeur and the glory of heaven, and the royal retinue of angels; why He passed by palaces and crowns and dominions and came down here alone?

> D. L. Moody (1837–99)

5th October

So then, just as you received Christ Jesus as Lord, continue to live in him, rooted and built up in him, strengthened in the faith as you were taught, and overflowing with thankfulness.

(Colossians 2:6–7)

All the events, then, of Christ's crucifixion, of His burial, of His resurrection the third day, of His ascension into heaven, of His sitting down at the right hand of the Father, were so ordered, that the life which the Christian leads here might be modelled upon them, not merely in a mystical sense, but in reality. For in reference to His crucifixion it is said: "They that are Christ's have crucified the flesh, with the affections and lusts." And in reference to His burial: "We are buried with Him by baptism into death." In reference to His resurrection: "That, like as Christ was raised up from the dead by the glory of the Father, even so we also should walk in the newness of life." And in reference to His ascension into heaven and sitting down at the right hand of the Father: "If ye then be risen with Christ, seek those things which are above, where Christ sitteth on the right hand of God. Set your affection on things above, not on things on the earth. For ye are dead, and your life is hid with Christ in God."

Augustine of Hippo (354–430)

6th October

I want to know Christ and the power of his resurrection and the fellowship of sharing in his sufferings, becoming like him in his death, and so, somehow, to attain to the resurrection from the dead.

(Philippians 3:10–11)

To conquer the emmity of death you must live by faith in Jesus Christ; as men that are emptied of themselves, and ransomed from his hands that had the power of death, and as men are redeemed from the curse, and are now made heirs of the grace of life, being made his members, who is the Lord of life, even the second Adam, who is a quickening Spirit. The serious, believing study of his design and office (to destroy sin and death, and to bring many sons to glory), and also of his voluntary suffering, and his obedience to the death of the cross, may raise us above the fears of death.

When we live by faith as branches of this blessed vine, are righteous with his righteousness, justified by his blood and merits, and sanctified by his word and Spirit, and find that we are united to him, we may then be sure that death cannot conquer us, and nothing take us out of his hands, for our life being hid with Christ in God, we know that we shall live, because he liveth (Colossians 3:3, John 14:19), and that when Christ who is our life, appeareth, we shall also appear with him in glory (Colossians 3:4), and that he will "change our vile bodies, and make them like unto his glorious body, by his mighty power by which he is able to subdue all things unto himself" (Philippians 3:21).

In our own strength we dare not stand the charge of death, and with it the charge of the law, and of our consciences. How dreadfully should we then be foiled and nonplussed if we must be found in no other righteousness but what we have received from the first Adam, and have wrought by the strength received from him. But being gathered under the wings of Christ, as the chicken under the wings of the hen (Matthew 23:37), and being found in him, having the righteousness which is of God by faith, we may boldly answer to all that can be charged to our terror.

Richard Baxter (1615–91)

7th October

Bless those who persecute you; bless and do not curse.
(Romans 12:14)

He did not say, be not spiteful or revengeful, but required something far better. For that a man that was wise might do, but this is quite an angel's part. And after saying "bless", he proceeds, and "do not curse", lest we should do both the one and the other, and not the former only. For they that persecute us are purveyors of a reward to us. But if thou art sober minded, there will be another reward after that one, which thou will gain thyself. For he will yield thee that for persecution, but thou wilt yield thyself the one from the blessing of another, in that thou bringest forth a very great sign of love to Christ. For he that curseth his persecutor, sheweth that he is not much pleased at suffering this for Christ, thus he that blesseth sheweth a great love. Do not then abuse him, that thou thyself mayest gain the greater reward, and mayest teach him that the thing is matter of inclination, not of necessity, of holiday and feast, not of calamity and dejection.

For this cause Christ Himself said, "Rejoice when men speak all kind of evil against you falsely." Hence too it was the apostles returned with joy not from having been evil spoken of only, but also at having been scourged. For besides what I mentioned, there will be another gain, and that no small one, that you will make, both the abashing of your adversaries hereby, and instructing of them by your actions that you are travelling to another life; for if he sees thee joyous and elevated, from suffering ill, he will see clearly from the actions that thou hast hopes greater than those of this life.

John Chrysostom (c. 344/345–407)

8th October

Dear children, keep yourselves from idols.

(1 John 5:21)

If you are selfish, and make yourself and your own private interests your idol, God will leave you to yourself, and let you promote your own interests as well as you can. But if you do not selfishly seek your own, but do seek the things that are Jesus Christ's and things of your fellow-beings, then God will make your interest and happiness his own charge, and he is infinitely more able to provide for and promote it than you are. The resources of the universe move at his own bidding, and he can easily command them all to subserve your welfare. So that, not to see your own, in the selfish sense, is the best way of seeing your own in the better sense. It is the directest course you can take to secure your own highest happiness.

When you are required not to be selfish, you are not required, as has been observed, not to love and seek your own happiness, but only not to seek mainly your own private and confined interests. But if you place your happiness in God, in glorifying him, and in serving him by doing good, – in this way, above all others, will you promote your wealth, and honour and pleasure here below, and obtain hereafter a crown of unfading glory, and pleasures for evermore at God's right hand. If you seek, in the spirit of selfishness, to grasp all as your own, you shall lose all, and be driven out of the world at last, naked and forlorn, to everlasting poverty and contempt.

But if you seek not your own, but the things of Christ, and the good of your fellow-men, God himself will be yours, and Christ yours, and the Holy Spirit yours, and all things yours (1 Corinthians 3:21–2)

Let these things, then, incline us to be less selfish than we are, and to seek more of the contrary most excellent spirit. Selfishness is a principle native to us, and, indeed, all the corruption of our nature does radically consist in it; but considering the knowledge that we have of Christianity, and how numerous and powerful the motives it presents, we ought to be less selfish than we are, and less ready to seek our own interests and these only.

Jonathan Edwards (1703–58)

9th October

Very early in the morning, while it was still dark, Jesus got up, left the house and went off to a solitary place, where he prayed.
(Mark 1:35)

You must not consider how small a crime it is to rise late, but you must consider how great a misery it is to want the spirit of religion, to have a heart not right affected by prayer; and to live in such softness and idleness, as makes you incapable of the most fundamental duties of a truly Christian and spiritual life. This is the right way of judging the crime of wasting great part of your time in bed. You must not consider the thing barely in itself, but what it proceeds from; what virtues it shows to be wanting; what vices it naturally strengthens. For every habit of this kind discovers the state of the soul, and plainly shows the whole turn of your mind.

If our blessed Lord used to pray early before day; if He spent whole nights in prayer; if the devout Anna was day and night in the temple [Luke 2:36–7]; if St Paul and Silas at midnight sang praises unto God; if the primitive Christians, for several hundred years, beside their hours of prayer in the daytime, met publicly in the churches at midnight, to join in psalms and prayers; is it not certain that these practices showed the state of their heart? Are they not so many plain proofs of the whole turn of their minds?

And if you live in a contrary state, wasting great part of every day in sleep, thinking any time soon enough to be at your prayers; is it not equally certain, that this practice as much shows the state of your heart, and the whole turn of your mind?

So if this indulgence is your way of life, you have as much reason to believe yourself destitute of the true spirit of devotion, as you have to believe the Apostles and saints of the primitive Church were truly devout. For as their way of life was a demonstration of their devotion, so a contrary way of life is as strong a proof of a want of devotion.

William Law (1686–1761)

10th October

Besides everything else, I face daily the pressure of my concern for all the churches.
(2 Corinthians 11:28)

[June 12th, 1806, in the life of a pioneer missionary in India.]

I rose this morning at a quarter before six, read a chapter of the Hebrew Bible, and spent the time till seven in private addresses to God, and then attended family prayer with the servants in Bengali. While tea was getting ready, I read a little in Persian with a moonshi who was waiting when I left my bedroom; and also before breakfast a portion of the Scriptures in the Hindusthani. The moment breakfast was over, sat down to the translation of the Ramayana from Sanskrit, with a pundit who was also waiting, and continued this translation till ten o'clock, at which time I went to College and attended duties there till between one and two o'clock. When I returned home I examined a proof-sheet of the Bengali translation of Jeremiah, which took till dinner-time. I always when down in Calcutta, dine at Mr Rolt's, which is near.

After dinner, translated with the assistance of the chief pundit of the college, the greatest part of the eighth chapter of Matthew into Sanskrit. This employed me till six o'clock. After six, sat down with a Telinga pundit to learn that language. At seven I began to collect a few previous thoughts into the form of a sermon, and preached at half past seven. About forty persons present, and among them one of the Puisne Judges of the Sudder Dewany Adawalt. After sermon I got a subscription from him for five hundred rupies towards erecting our new place of worship; he is an exceedingly friendly man. Preaching was over and the congregation gone by nine o'clock. I then sat down and translated the eleventh of Ezekiel into Bengali, and this lasted till near eleven; and now I sit down to write to you.

William Carey (1761–1834)

11th October

And Joshua set up at Gilgal the twelve stones they had taken out of the Jordan. He said to the Israelites, "In the future when your descendants ask their fathers, 'What do these stones mean?' tell them, 'Israel crossed the Jordan on dry ground.'"

(Joshua 4:20–22)

Gilgal, the first encampment, lay defenceless in the open plain, and the first thing to be done would be to throw up some earthwork around the camp. It seems to have been the resting-place of the ark and probably of the non-combatants during the conquest, and to have derived a sacredness which long clung to it, and finally led, singularly enough, to its becoming a centre of idolatrous worship. The rude circle of unhewn stones without inscription was, no doubt, exactly like the many prehistoric monuments found all over the world, which forgotten races have raised to keep in everlasting remembrance forgotten fights and heroes. It was a comparatively small thing; for each stone was but a load for one man, and it would seem mean enough by the side of Stonehenge or Carnac, just as Israel's history is on a small scale, as compared with the world-embracing empires of old. Size is not greatness; and Joshua's little circle told a more wonderful story than its taller kindred, or Egyptian obelisks or colossi.

These grey stones preached at once the duty of remembering, and the danger of forgetting, the past mercies of God. When they were reared, they would seem needless; but the deepest impressions get filled up by degrees, as the river of time deposits its sands on them. We do not forget pain as quickly as joy, and most men have a longer and keener remembrance of their injurers than of their benefactors, human or divine.

The stones were set up because Israel remembered, but also lest Israel should forget. We often think of the Jews as monsters of ingratitude; but we should more truly learn the lesson of their history, if we regarded them as fair, average men, and asked ourselves whether our recollection of God's goodness to us is more vivid than theirs. Unless we make distinct and frequent efforts to recall, we shall certainly forget "all his benefits". The cultivation of thankful remembrance is a very large part of practical religion; and it is not by accident that the Psalmist puts it in the middle, between hope and obedience, when he says, "that they might set their hope in God, and not forget the works of God, but keep His commandments" (Psalm 78:7)

Alexander Maclaren (1826–1910)

12th October

Paul and his companions travelled throughout the region of Phrygia and Galatia, having been kept by the Holy Spirit from preaching the word in the province of Asia. When they came to the border of Mysia, they tried to enter Bithynia, but the Spirit of Jesus would not allow them to. So they passed by Mysia and went down to Troas. During the night Paul had a vision of a man of Macedonia standing and begging him, "Come over to Macedonia and help us." After Paul had seen the vision, we got ready at once to leave for Macedonia, concluding that God had called us to preach the gospel to them.

(Acts 16:6–10)

There are three tests which I have found help.

1. Is what appears to me guidance, in line with the general tenor of Scripture?

2. Have I some word that I can recognise as my Lord's to me?

3. When I am nearest God is there peace in my heart about it, and a quiet sureness?

The Scriptures teach us that personal desires don't count. We follow a crucified Saviour, so that anything that has I in it cannot be guidance. In community life one cannot act apart from others; each has to consider the other (Galatians 6:2; Philippians 2:4). How will this, that I think of as guidance, affect others?

Test yourself by this question: "If I am mistaken, am I as glad to yield as I would be to go forward?" If not, "This persuasion does not come from him who calls you" (Galatians 5:8 NKJ).

If the word is His, He will so deal with circumstances that I can obey it. Sometimes the way opens as the Red Sea did before the children of Israel so that they went over dry shod. Sometimes it is as it was later, when the waters of Jordan did not divide till the feet of the priests were dipped in the brim of the water. What is certain is that sooner or later, if He is leading on, He deals with my circumstances so that all is clear.

"If in doubt, do nou't (nothing)" is a Cumberland saying which often helps. If the peace of God does not fill your heart and mind, if there is an up-and-down feeling, a question mark over the matter, don't move.

Amy Carmichael (1867–1951)

13th October

My father David had it in his heart to build a temple for the Name of the Lord, the God of Israel. But the Lord said to my father David, "Because it was in your heart to build a temple for my Name, you did well to have this in your heart."

(2 Chronicles 6:7–8)

David was a better man because he had given expression to the noble purpose. Its gleam left a permanent glow on his life. The rejected candidate to the missionary society stands upon a higher moral platform than those who were never touched by the glow of missionary enthusiasm. For a woman to have loved passionately, even though the dark waters may have engulfed her love before it was consummated, leaves her ever after richer, deeper, than if she had never loved and been loved in return. That a plant should have dreamt in some dark night of the possibility of flowering into matchless beauty, stamps it as belonging to a higher family than the moss that clings to the stump. "Thou didst well that it was in thine heart."

The martyrs in the apocalyptic vision behold a day when their wrongs will be avenged; but they are told to wait, since God's time had not come: in the meanwhile white robes were given them. Their ideal was not yet, but it purified them, and bound them close to the Christ.

God will credit us with what we would have been if we might. He that has the missionary's heart, though he be tied to an office-stool, is reckoned as one of that noble band; the woman at Zarephath, who did nothing more than share her last meal with the prophet [Elijah], shall have the prophet's reward; the soul that thrills with the loftiest impulses, which the cares of a widowed mother, or dependant relatives, stay in fulfilment, will be surprised one day to find itself credited with the harvest which would have been reaped, had those seed-germs been cast on more propitious soil. In the glory David will find himself credited with the building of the temple on Mount Zion.

F. B. Meyer (1847–1929)

14th October

Nevertheless, you are not the one to build the temple, but your son, who is your own flesh and blood – he is the one who will build the temple for my Name.

(2 Chronicles 6:9)

[Continued from yesterday.]

The energy which would have been expended in building the temple wrought itself out in gathering materials for its construction. "I have prepared with all my might for the house of my God . . ." (1 Chronicles 29:2, etc.). If you cannot have what you hoped, do not sit down in despair and allow the energies of your life to go to waste; but arise, and gird yourself to help others to achieve. If you may not build, you may gather materials for him that shall. If you may not go down the mine, you can hold the ropes.

There is a fact in nature known as the law of the conservation of force. The force of the accumulating velocity of the falling stone passes into heat, of which some is retained by the stone, the rest passes into the atmosphere. No true ideals are fruitless; somehow they help the world of men. No tears are wept, no prayers uttered, no conceptions honestly entertained in vain.

Somehow God makes up to us. He stooped over David's life in blessing. The promise made through Nathan was threefold: (1) That David's house should reign for ever; (2) that David's seed should build the temple; (3) that the kingdom of Israel should be made sure. As we read the glowing words [2 Samuel 7], we feel that they could only be realised in Him who Peter declares David foresaw. There is only One of the sons of men whose reign can be permanent, and his Kingdom without end, who can bring rest to the weary sons of men, and build the true temple of God (Acts 2:30). But how great the honour that He should be David's Son!

F. B. Meyer (1847–1929)

15th October

So you too should be glad and rejoice with me.

(Philippians 2:18)

"I believe the Word of God. But if I could speak alone to you, I would like to tell you my excuse. The fact is, I love the world very much, and if I became a Christian, I shall have to give up all pleasure and go through the world with a long face and never smile again. My joy will be for ever gone!" Well, I want to say here, that no greater lie was ever forged than that. The devil started it away back in Eden; but there is not one word of truth in it; it is a libel on Christianity. It does not make a man gloomy to become a child of God.

See! there is a man going to execution. In a few moments he will be launched into eternity. But, flashing over the wires, comes a message from the Queen. She sends a reprieve. I run in haste to the man. I shout, "Good news! good news! You are *not* going to die!" Does that make him gloomy? No! no! no!

Young men, young women, old and young, don't believe Satan's lies any longer. It is the *want of* Christ that makes men gloomy. Take a man who is really thirsty, dying for want of water, and you go and give him water. Is that going to make him gloomy? That is what Christ is – water to the thirsty soul. If a man is dying for want of bread, and you give him bread, is that going to make him gloomy? That is what Christ is to the soul – the bread of life. You will never have true pleasure or peace or joy or comfort until you have found Christ.

The idea that a man cannot have peace and joy in this world, if he is a Christian, is all folly. That used to be my difficulty. But I want to tell you that I had more joy and solid comfort and peace the first year after I was converted, than I had in all my previous life put together, and I have never heard of any young convert who would not testify the same thing.

D. L. Moody (1837–99)

16th October

Rejoice with those who rejoice; mourn with those who mourn.
(Romans 12:15)

Since it is possible to bless and not to curse, and yet not to do this out of love, he wishes us to be penetrated with warmth of friendship throughout. And this is why he goes on in these words, that we are not only to bless, but even feel compassion for their pains and sufferings, whenever we happen to see them fallen into trouble. Yes, it will be said, but to join in the sorrow of mourners one can see why he ordered them, but why did he ever command them the other thing, when it is no great matter? Aye, but that requires more of a high Christian temper, to rejoice with them that do rejoice, than to weep with them that weep.

For this nature itself fulfils perfectly: and there is none so hard-hearted as not to weep over him that is in calamity: but the other requires a very noble soul, so as not only to keep from envying, but even to feel pleasure with the person who is in esteem. And that is why he placed it first. For there is nothing that ties love so firmly as sharing both joy and pain one with another. Do not then, because thou art far from difficulties thyself, remain aloof from sympathising too. For when thy neighbour is ill-treated, thou oughtest to make the calamity thine own. Take share then in his tears, that thou mayest lighten his low spirits. Take share in his joy, that thou mayest make the joy strike deep root, and fix the love firmly, and be of service to thyself rather than to him in so doing, by weeping rendering thyself merciful, and by feeling his pleasure, purging thyself of envy and grudging.

And let me draw attention to St Paul's considerateness. For he does not say, Put an end to the calamity, lest thou shouldst say in many cases that it is impossible: but he has enjoined the easier task and that which thou hast in thy power. For even if thou art not able to remove the evil, yet contribute tears, and thou wilt take the worst half away. And if thou be not able to increase a man's prosperity, contribute joy, and thou wilt have made a great addition to it. Therefore it is not abstaining from envy only, but what is the much greater thing that he exhorts us to, namely, joining in the pleasure. For this is a much greater thing than not envying.

John Chrysostom (c. 344/345–407)

17th October

The heavens declare the glory of God, the skies proclaim the work of his hands.

(Psalm 19:1)

The heavens, revolving under His government, are subject to Him in peace. Day and night run their course appointed by Him, in no wise hindering one another. The sun and moon, with the company of the stars, roll on in harmony according to His command within their prescribed limits, and without deviations. The fruitful earth, according to His will, brings forth food in abundance, at the proper seasons, for man and beast and all living beings upon it, never hesitating, never changing any of the ordinances which He has fixed.

The unsearchable places of abysses and the indescribable arrangements of the lower world, are restrained by the same laws. The vast unmeasurable sea, gathered together by His working into various basins, never passes beyond the bounds placed around it . . . The ocean, impassable to man, and the worlds beyond it, are regulated by the same enactments of the Lord. The seasons of spring, summer, autumn, and winter, peacefully give place to one another. The winds in their several quarters, fulfil, at the proper time, their service without hinderance . . .

The very smallest of living beings meet together in peace and concord. All these the great Creator and Lord of all has appointed to exist in peace and harmony; while He does good to all, but most abundantly to us who have fled for refuge to His compassions through Jesus Christ our Lord, to whom be glory and majesty for ever and ever. Amen.

Clement of Rome (fl. c. 90–100)

18th October

Therefore, since I myself have carefully investigated everything from the beginning, it seemed good also to me to write an orderly account for you, most excellent Theophilus, so that you may know the certainty of the things you have been taught.

(Luke 1:3–4)

The eighteenth day of October has long been kept in the Church as the Festival of the Evangelist, Saint Luke. Once every year upon this day, the Church has chosen to remind us that the third Gospel did not drop down from the stars, and did not spring up out of the earth; but that it is the description of the life of Jesus through a special human medium; and that it is good for us, in our sense of the preciousness of the Gospel, to remember and study and be grateful to the man who wrote it.

No doubt the institution of a Saint Luke's day was meant to be a special commemoration of the evangelist. It is as the author of the Gospel that the Church is mostly interested in Saint Luke. That book is one of the four golden columns on which rest the Christian history. It is one of the four golden trumpets on which has been blown the summons of Christ to the sons of men. And besides being one of four, it has also its own peculiar character. The reader of the Gospel of Saint Luke, if he has been intelligent and sympathetic, has always felt a sort of human breadth and richness in it which, in kind at least was peculiarly its own. It was not so Jewish as the others. The very fact that it is the gospel in which we have most fully told the story of the Lord's nativity, and in which alone occurs the Parable of the Prodigal Son, is enough to show how well the Church does in commemorating always the man who wrote it.

Phillips Brooks (1835–93)

19th October

Our dear friend Luke, the doctor, and Demas send greetings.
(Colossians 4:14)

[Continued from yesterday.]

As he [Luke] and Paul are seen travelling on together over land and sea, those two figures taken together represent in a broad way the total care of man for man. Paul is distinctively a man of the soul, a man of the spiritual life. We know him only in his spiritual labours. If he turns aside to tent making, it is not for the sake of the tents which he can make, but simply that, earning his own living, he may be in true relations to the men whose souls he wants to save. Luke, on the other hand, is physical. His care is for the body. The two together, then, as we watch their figures, climbing side by side over mountains, sleeping side by side on the decks of little Mediterranean boats, standing side by side in the midst of little groups of hard won disciples, – may we not say of them that they may be considered as recognising and representing between them the double nature and the double need of man? Body and soul as man is, the ministry that would redeem him and relieve him must have a word to speak to, and a hand to lay upon, both soul and body. The two missionaries together make a sort of composite copy of the picture which Saint Matthew gives us of Jesus going "about all Galilee, teaching in their synagogues and preaching the Gospel of the Kingdom, and healing all manner of disease among the people." . . .

The figures of Paul and Luke walking together through history as the ministers of Christ, – the images of theology and medicine labouring in harmony for the redemption of man, for the saving of the body, soul, and spirit, – become very sacred and impressive. May their fellowship become more generous and hearty as the years go on! May each gain greater honour for the other, and both become more humbly and transparently the ministers of Christ! Thus may the two together, working as if they were but one, grow to be more and more a worthy channel through which the helpfulness of God may flow forth to the neediness of man.

Phillips Brooks (1835–93)

20th October

He took a little child and had him stand among them. Taking him in his arms, he said to them, "Whoever welcomes one of these little children in my name welcomes me; and whoever welcomes me does not welcome me but the one who sent me."

(Mark 9:36–7)

Oct 9th, 1872 – Yesterday stirred after a long interval, by my poor [chimney] climbing boys. One suffocated in a flue in Staffordshire. The Act which forbids the practice, intentionally made the evidence difficult. Years of oppression and cruelty have rolled on and now a death has given me the power of one more appeal to the public through the *Times*.

March 20th, 1873 – Then to the House of Lords to move for report of coroner's inquest on a poor little chimney-sweeper, seven and half years old, killed in a flue in Washington, in county of Durham. So much for my labour on behalf of the climbing-boys! But, by God's mercy, good may have come out of evil.

April 28th, 1875 – Again on the rescue of the climbing boys. One's soul is torn by their misery and degradation. Have prepared a Bill; the second reading stands for May 11th. God in His mercy, grace, and love, be with me. Shall I have, after the manner of men, to contend with beasts? One hundred and two years have elapsed since the good Jonas Hanway brought the brutal iniquity before the public, yet in many parts of England and Ireland it still prevails, with the full knowledge and consent of thousands of all classes.

May 12th – Last night Chimney Sweepers' Bill in the House of Lords. It was under God, a success in its issue, though I did not think it, or feel it, at the time. Was much disheartened at the onset. House very inattentive – had twice to implore their "condescension to hear me". At least, they listened, and so far as their undemonstrative natures would allow, applauded me . . . Yet by His grace I have stirred the country. The *Times*, may the paper be blessed, has assisted me gloriously.

June 4th – By God's blessing, Chimney Sweepers' Bill passed through Committee of the House of Lords in the twinkling of an eye – not a syllable uttered.

June 12th – Cross, Secretary of State for Home Department, has consented to take up the Chimney Sweepers' Bill in House of Commons.

Lord Shaftesbury (1801–85)

21st October

This is the message you heard from the beginning: We should love one another.

(1 John 3:11)

Give me a man who, before all things, loves God with all his being; who loves both himself and his neighbour in the same degree in which each loves God; who loves his enemy as one who may perhaps at some time in the future turn to the love of God; who loves his relatives according to the flesh very tenderly, on account of nature, but his spiritual parents, that is, those who have instructed him, more abundantly on account of grace, and thus his love for all other things whatsoever is regulated by his love for God. Give me one who despises the earth and looks upward to the heaven; who uses this world as not abusing it, and knows how to distinguish, by a certain inward faculty of soul, between things which are to be chosen and loved, and those to be merely used. Things transitory are made use of as they pass for temporary need, and as long as the need requires, while things eternally enduring are embraced with lasting joy. Show me a man such as this, and I will boldly pronounce him wise . . .

O Wisdom, whose powerful guidance extendest from the beginning to the end of all things, establishing and controlling them; who disposest all with admirable gentleness, ordering, blessing, and gladdening all affections, direct our actions, according to our needs within time and dispose our affections as thy eternal truth demands ... For thou art the power of God, and the Wisdom of God, Jesus Christ our Lord, the Bridegroom of the Church, God above all, Blessed for ever. Amen.

Bernard of Clairvaux (1090–1153)

22nd October

For everything God created is good, and nothing is to be rejected if it is received with thanksgiving, because it is consecrated by the word of God and prayer.

(1 Timothy 4:4–5)

Eating is one of the lowest actions of our lives. It is common to us with mere animals; yet we see that the piety of all ages of the world has turned this ordinary action of animal life into a piety to God, by making every action to begin and end with devotion.

We see yet some remains of this custom in most Christian families, some such little formality as shows you, that people used to call upon God at the beginning and end of their meals. But, indeed, it is now generally performed, as to look more like a mockery upon devotion, than any solemn application of the mind unto God. In one house you may perhaps see the head of the family just pulling off his hat; in another, half getting up from his seat; another shall, it may be, proceed so far as to make as if he said something; but, however, these little attempts are the remains of some devotion, that was formerly used at such time, and are proofs that religion formerly belonged to this part of common life.

But to such a pass are we now come, that though the custom is yet preserved, yet we can hardly bear with him that seems to perform it with any degree of seriousness, and look upon it as a sign of fanatical temper, if a man has not done as soon as he begins.

I would not be thought to plead for the necessity of long prayers at these times; but thus much I think may be said, that if prayer is proper at these times, we ought to oblige ourselves to use such a form of words, as should show we solemnly appeal to God for such graces and blessings as are then proper to the occasion. Otherwise the mock ceremony, instead of blessing our victuals, does but accustom us to trifle with devotions and give us a habit of being unaffected with our prayers.

William Law (1686–1761)

23rd October

So God created man in his own image, in the image of God he created him; male and female he created them.

(Genesis 1:27)

[At the age of 88 John Wesley writes his last letter. It is to William Wilberforce to encourage him in his fight against the slave trade.]

24 February, 1791
Balam, England

Dear Sir:

Unless the divine power has raised you up to be as "Athanasius against the world", I see not how you can go through your glorious enterprise in opposing that execrable villainy, which is the scandal of England, and of human nature. Unless God has raised you up for this very thing, you will be worn out by the opposition of men and devils. But if God be for you, who can be against you? Are all of them stronger than God? O be not weary of well doing! Go on, in the name of God and the power of His might, till even American slavery (the vilest that ever saw the sun) shall vanish away before it.

Reading this morning a tract by a poor African [former slave Gustavus Vassa], I was especially struck by the circumstance, that a man who has a black skin, being wronged or outraged by a white man, can have no redress; it being a LAW in all our colonies that the OATH of a black man against a white goes for nothing. What villainy is this!

That He who has guided you from youth up may continue to strengthen you in this and all things is the prayer of, dear sir,

    Your affectionate servant,
      John Wesley

John Wesley (1703–91)

24th October

We are bringing you good news, telling you to turn from these worthless things to the living God, who made heaven and earth and sea and everything in them. In the past, he let all nations go their own way. Yet he has not left himself without testimony: He has shown kindness by giving you rain from heaven and crops in their seasons; he provides you with plenty of food and fills your heart with joy.

(Acts 14:15–17)

When the Lord says, "Thou shalt love the Lord thy God, from all thy heart and mind: and thou shalt love thy neighbour as thyself," let the faithful soul put on the unfading love of its Author and Ruler, and subject itself also entirely to His will in Whose works and judgements true justice and tender-hearted compassion never fail. For although a man be wearied out with labours and many misfortunes, there is good reason for him to endure all in the knowledge that adversity will either prove him good or make him better. But this godly love cannot be perfect unless a man love his neighbour also. Under which name must be included not only those who are connected with us by friendship or neighbourhood, but absolutely all men, with whom we have a common nature, whether they be foes or allies, slaves or free.

For the One Maker fashioned us, the One Creator breathed life into us; we all enjoy the same sky and air, the same days and nights. Though some be good, others bad, some righteous, others unrighteous, yet God is bountiful to all, kind to all . . .

But the wide extent of Christian grace had given us yet greater reasons for loving our neighbour, which, reaching to all parts of the whole world, looks down on no one, and teaches that no one is to be neglected. And full rightly does He command us to love our enemies, and to pray to Him for our persecutors, who, daily grafting shoots of the wild olive from among all nations upon the holy branches of His own olive, makes men reconciled instead of enemies, adopted sons instead of strangers, just instead of the ungodly, "that every knee may bow of things in heaven, of things on earth, and of things under the earth, and every tongue confess that the Lord Jesus Christ is in the glory of God the Father."

Leo the Great (c. 400–461)

25th October

Do not offer the parts of your body to sin, as instruments of wickedness, but rather offer yourselves to God, as those who have been brought from death to life; and offer the parts of your body to be instruments of righteousness.

(Romans 6:13)

The religion of Christ does not teach us to despise even the mortal body. We are taught that Christ himself – "without whom was not anything made that was made" – formed man of the dust of the earth. By him every limb was moulded; he traced the winding course of nerve, and artery, and vein; he gave to the hand its possibilities of skill, to the eye its vision, to the ear its susceptibility to sound. The simplest of our physical pleasures, the slightest of our physical pains; every kind of liability to physical injury from excessive toil, from mental suffering, from mere changes of temperature and accidental imprudence, he provided for, and rendered possible in the original plan and design of our nature. The body, therefore, is a sacred thing; the very handiwork of Christ, though sadly marred and spoiled.

By his incarnation a new sacredness has been added to it. Strange, almost incredible, and yet most certain fact! God was made flesh, and dwelt among us! He heard the sounds and saw the sights with which we are familiar. Sweet music and the voices of dear friends were pleasant to him as they are to us; the glowing outlines of the mountains of Galilee, the wildflowers that grew in the valley of Judea, the sunset and sunrise of yonder eastern land were as beautiful to him as to other men. There can be nothing mean, nothing contemptible in the pleasures which yielded joy or refreshment to the heart of Christ; nor can that body in which he revealed the brightness of the Father's glory, and the express image of his person, justly be thought of as an insuperable hindrance to human nobleness. The instrument whose strings could be made to express the sublime and awful harmonies of a Divine perfection, cannot be too poor and feeble for the lowlier music of the virtue and holiness proper to humanity.

R. W. Dale (1829–95)

26th October

Therefore, my dear brothers, stand firm. Let nothing move you. Always give yourselves fully to the work of the Lord, because you know that your labour in the Lord is not in vain.
(1 Corinthians 15:58)

I have long been taunted with narrow and exclusive attention to the children in the factories alone; I have been told, in language and writing, that there were other cases fully as grievous, and not less numerous; that I was unjust and inconsiderate in my denouncement of the one and omission of the other. I have, however long contemplated this effort which I am now making; I had long resolved that, as soon as I could see the factory children, as it were, safe in harbour, I would undertake a new task. The Committee of this [Parliamentary] Session on Mills and Factories, having fully substantiated the necessity, and rendered certain amendment of the law, I am now endeavouring to obtain an inquiry into the actual circumstances and condition of another part of our juvenile population . . .

Now, whatever may be done or proposed in time to come, we have, I think, a right to know the state of our juvenile population; the House has a right, the country has a right. How is it possible to address ourselves to the remedy of evils which we all feel, unless we have previously ascertained both the nature and the cause of them? The first step towards a cure is knowledge of the disorder. We have asserted these truths in our Factory Legislation, I have on my side the authority of all civilised nations of modern times; the practice of this House; the common-sense of the thing; and the justice of the principle . . .

My first grand object is to bring these [exploited] children within the reach of education; it will then be time enough to fight about the mode. Only let us exhibit these evils – there is wit and experience enough, activity enough, and principle enough in this country, to devise some remedy. I am sure that the exhibition of the peril will terrify even the most sluggish and the most reluctant, into some attempt at amendment; but I hope for far better motives. For my own part I will say, though possibly I may be charged with cant and hypocrisy, that I have been bold enough to undertake this task, because I regard the objects of it as beings created, as ourselves, by the same Maker, redeemed by the same Saviour, and destined to the same immortality; and it is, therefore, in this spirit, and with the same sentiments, which, I am sure are participated in by all who hear me, that I now venture to entreat the countenance of this House, and the co-operation of her Majesty's Ministers, first to investigate, and ultimately to remove, these sad evils, which press so deeply and so extensively on such a large and interesting portion of the human race.

Lord Shaftesbury (1801–85)

27th October

The reason the Son of God appeared was to destroy the devil's work.

(1 John 3:8b)

If we consider the Christian scheme of doctrine, we shall find that it tends strongly to enforce the precepts which we have considered; for all of it, from beginning to end, strongly tends to the contrary of an envious spirit. In all its bearings and teachings, the Christian form of doctrine militates against a spirit of envy. The things it teaches as to God are exceeding contrary to it; for there we are told how far God was from begrudging us the most exceeding honour and blessedness, and how he has withheld nothing as too much to be done for us, or as too great or good to be given us.

He has not begrudged us his only-begotten Son, who was dearer to him than anything else beside; nor hath he begrudged us the highest honour and blessedness in and through him. The doctrines of the gospel also teach us how far Christ was from begrudging us anything that he could do for or give us. He did not begrudge us a life spent in labour and suffering, or his own precious blood which he shed for us on the cross; nor will he begrudge us a throne of glory with him in the heavens, where we shall live and reign with him for ever.

The Christian scheme of doctrine teaches us how Christ came into the world to deliver us from the power of Satan's envy towards us; for the devil, with miserable baseness, envied mankind the happiness that they first had, and could not bear to see them in their happy state in Eden, and therefore exerted himself to the utmost for their ruin, which he accomplished. And the gospel also teaches how Christ came into the world to destroy the works of the devil, and deliver us from the misery which his envy brought us, and to purify our natures from every trace of the same spirit, that we may be fitted for heaven.

Jonathan Edwards (1703–58)

28th October

David said to the Philistine, "You have come against me with sword and spear and javelin, but I come against you in the name of the Lord Almighty, the God of the armies of Israel, whom you have defied.

(1 Samuel 17:45)

Throughout the Scriptures, a name is not simply, as with us, a label; it is a revelation of character. It catches up and enshrines some moral or physical peculiarity in which its owner differs from other men, or which constitutes his special gift and force. The names which Adam gave the animals that were brought to him were founded on characteristics which struck his notice. And the names which the Second Adam gave to the apostles either expressed qualities which lay deep within them, and which He intended to evolve, or unfolded some great purpose for which they were being fitted.

Thus the Name of God, as used so frequently by the heroes and saints of sacred history, stands for those Divine attributes and qualities which combine to make Him what He is. In the history of the early Church *the Name* was a kind of summary of all that Jesus had revealed of the nature and heart of God ... There was no need to specify whose name it was – there was none other Name by which men could be saved, none other Name that could be compared with that, or mentioned on the same page. Stars die out and become invisible when the sun appears. That Name is above every name, and in it every knee shall bow and tongue confess; because that it embodies under one all-sufficient designation everything that any single soul, or the whole race, can require, or imagine, or attain in the conceiving of God.

F. B. Meyer (1847–1929)

29th October

God made the wild animals according to their kinds, the livestock according to their kinds, and all the creatures that move along the ground according to their kinds. And God saw that it was good.
(Genesis 1:25)

Lord Shaftesbury, who was president of the Society for the Prevention of Cruelty to Animals, had taken a deep interest in the costermongers' donkeys. It was proverbial, at one time, that both the donkeys and ponies were shamefully ill-used; but by education and exhortation, by the institution of donkey shows and prizes, and a variety of other means, the men of Golden Lane had come to take pride in their animals, and had found that kind and just treatment was the wisest policy. With twenty four hours's rest on Sunday, they would do thirty miles a day without exhaustion; whereas, without it, they did not do an average of more than fifteen.

In recognition of his kind services, the costers invited Lord Shaftesbury to meet them in their Hall to receive a presentation. Over a thousand costers, with their friends were there, and the platform was graced by many ladies and gentlemen, when a handsome donkey, profusely decorated with ribands, was led on the platform and presented as a token of esteem to the chairman.

Lord Shaftesbury good humouredly vacated the chair and made way for the new arrival, and then, putting his arm round the animal's neck, returned thanks in a short speech, in which, however, there was a ring of pathos, as he said, "When I have passed away from this life I desire to have no more said of me than that I have done my duty, as the poor donkey has done his, with patience and unmurmuring resignation." The donkey was led down the steps of the platform, and Lord Shaftesbury remarked, "I hope the reporters of the press will state that, the donkey having vacated the chair, the place was taken by Lord Shaftesbury."

Lord Shaftesbury (1801–85)

30th October

For just as through the disobedience of the one man the many were made sinners, so also through the obedience of the one man the many will be made righteous.

(Romans 5:19)

Had not MESSIAH engaged for us and appeared in our nature, a case would have occurred, which I think we may warrantably deem incongruous to the Divine Wisdom. I mean, that while fire and hail, snow and vapour, and the stormy wind fulfil the will of God; while the brutes are faithful to the instincts implanted in them by their Maker, a whole species of intelligent beings would have fallen short of the original law and design of their creation, and indeed have acted in direct and continual opposition to it.

For the duty of man, to love, serve, and trust God with all his heart and mind, and to love his neighbour as himself, is founded on the very nature and constitution of things, and necessarily results from his relation to God, and his absolute dependence on him as a creature. Such a disposition must undoubtedly have been as *natural* to man before his fall, as it is for a bird to fly, or a fish to swim. The prohibitory form of the law delivered to Israel from Mount Sinai, is a sufficient intimation that it was designed for *sinners*. Surely our first parents, while in a state of innocence, could not stand in need of warnings and threatenings to restrain them from worshipping idols, or profaning the name of the great God whom they loved. Nor would it be necessary to forbid murder, adultery, or injustice, if his posterity had continued under the law of their creation, the law of love. But the first act of disobedience, degraded and disabled man, detached him from his proper centre, if I may so speak, and incapacitated him for both his duty and his happiness.

After his fall, it became impossible for either Adam or his posterity to obey the law of God. But MESSIAH fulfilled it, exactly as a man; and the principles of it are renewed, by the power of his grace, in all who believe on him. And though their best endeavours fall short, *his* obedience to it is accepted on their behalf; and he will at length perfectly restore them to their primitive order and honour. When they see him as he is, they will be like him, and all their powers and faculties will be perfectly conformed to his image.

John Newton (1725–1807)

31st October

He himself bore our sins in his body on the tree, so that we might die to sins and live for righteousness; by his wounds you have been healed.

(1 Peter 2:24)

We offer no injury or reproach to God, but thanking Him with all our hearts, we praise and proclaim the ineffable depth of His mercy. For the more marvellous and contrary to all expectation it was that He should deliver us from such great and deserved evils, in which we were involved and restore us to the enjoyment of such great and undeserved blessings, the greater was the love and kindness He showed to us. For if they would carefully consider how fitting it was that man's restoration should be procured in this way, they would join us in praising the wise beneficence of God. For it was fitting that as by man's disobedience death entered the human race so by a man's obedience should life be restored. And just as sin, which was the cause of our condemnation, had its beginning from a woman, so should the author of our righteousness and salvation be born of a woman. And as the devil had conquered man by the tasting of a tree, to which he persuaded him, so by the suffering endured on a tree which he inflicted, should he, by a man, be conquered. There are many other things also which, when carefully considered, show a certain ineffable beauty in our redemption having been procured in this way.

Anselm of Canterbury (c. 1033–1109)

November

1st November

Brothers, we do not want you to be ignorant about those who fall asleep, or to grieve like the rest of men, who have no hope.
(1 Thessalonians 4:13)

[A missionary in China writes to a friend in England.]

It is Sunday evening. I am writing from Mr White's bungalow. The cool air, the mellow autumn beauty of the scene, the magnificent Yangtze – with Silver Island, beautifully wooded, reposing as it were, on its bosom – combine to make one feel as if it were a vision of dreamland rather than actual reality. And my feelings accord. But a few months ago my home was full, now so silent and lonely – Samuel, Noel, my precious wife with Jesus; the elder children far, far away, and even little T'ien-pao in Yang-Chow. Often, of late years, has duty called me from my loved ones, but I have returned, and so warm the welcome! Now I am alone. Can it be that there is no return from this journey, no home-coming to look forward to! Is it real and not a sorrowful dream, that those dearest to me lie beneath the cold sod? Ah it is indeed true! But not more so, than there is a home-coming awaiting me, which no parting shall break into, no tears mar . . . Love gave the blow that for a little while makes the desert more dreary, but heaven more home-like. "I go to prepare a place for you": and is not our part of it peopling it with those we love?

And the same loving Hand that makes heaven more home-like is the while loosening ties that bind us to this world, thus helping our earth-cleaving spirits to sit looser, awaiting our own summons, whether personally to be "present with the Lord", or at "the glorious appearing of our great God and Saviour". "Even so, come, Lord Jesus," come quickly! But if He tarry – if for the rescue of some still scattered on the mountains He can wait the full joy of having all His loved ones gathered to Himself – surely we too, should be content, nay thankful, a little while longer to bear the cross and unfurl the banner of salvation. Poor China, how great her need! Let us seek to occupy a little while longer.

I have been very ill since I last wrote to you, through a severe attack of dysentery. My strength does not return rapidly. I feel like a little child . . . But with weakness of a child I have *the rest of a child*. I know my Father reigns: this meets questions of every kind. I have heard today that war has broken out in Europe, between France and Prussia; it is rumoured that England joins the former and Russia the latter. If so fearful doings may be expected; but, "the Lord reigneth".

James Hudson Taylor (1832–1905)

2nd November

But the angel said to them, "Do not be afraid. I bring you good news of great joy that will be for all the people. Today in the town of David a Saviour has been born to you; he is Christ the Lord.
(Luke 2:10–11)

A man born blind can have no more conception of light and colours, than we have of what passes in the world of spirits. And a nation of blind men, if there were such a nation, would probably treat a seeing person as a visionary madman, if he spoke to them of what he saw. But he would be sure of his own perceptions, though he could not satisfy the enquiries and cavails of the blind. Our senses are accommodated to our present state; but there may be a multitude of real objects, as real in themselves, and as near to us, as any that we behold with our eyes; of which we, for want of suitable faculties, can have no idea. To deny this, and to make our senses the criteria of the existence of things which are not within their reach, is exactly such an absurdity, as a blind man would be guilty of, who should deny the possibility of a rainbow, because he had never heard it or felt it.

However, "Faith is the evidence of things not seen." And they who believe the word of God, cannot doubt of the existence of an invisible state and invisible agents. The barrier between the inhabitants of that state and us, is too strong to be passed; for the will of the Creator seems to be the barrier. Otherwise it is probable they should easily surprise us, since, upon special occasions, they have been permitted to discover themselves. We have a natural dread of such visitants, even though they should appear to us, as they did to the shepherds, as messengers of peace and mercy from God.

Yet we must shortly mingle with them. Death will introduce us into the world of spirits; and what shall we then meet with, what Beings will be ready to accost us upon our first entrance into that unknown, unchangeable state, who can say? It deserves our serious thought. We are now encompassed by the objects of sense, but we must soon be separated from them all. We live in a crowd, but we must die alone. Happy are they who, like Stephen (Acts 7:59), shall be able to commend their departing spirits into the hand of Jesus! He is Lord of all worlds, and has the key of the invisible state.

John Newton (1725–1807)

3rd November

I have fought the good fight, I have finished the race, I have kept the faith. Now there is in store for me the crown of righteousness, which the Lord, the righteous Judge, will award to me on that day – and not only to me, but also to all who have longed for his appearing.

(2 Timothy 4:7–8)

When Mr Stand-fast had thus set things in order, and the time being come for him to haste him away, he also went down to the river. Now there was a great calm at that time in the river; wherefore Mr Stand-fast, when he was about half-way in, he stood awhile and talked to his companions that had waited upon him thither. And he said, "This river has been a terror to many; yea the thoughts of it have often frightened me. But now, methinks, I stand easy. My foot is fixed upon that upon which the feet of the priests that bare the ark of the covenant stood while Israel went over this Jordan. The waters indeed are to the palate bitter and to the stomach cold. Yet the thoughts of what I am going to, and of the conduct that waits me on the other side, doth lie as a glowing coal at my heart. I see myself now at the end of my journey; my toilsome days are ended. I am now going to see that head that was crowned with thorns, and that face that was spit upon for me. I have formerly lived by hearsay and faith, but now I go where I shall live by sight, and shall be with him in whose company I delight myself.

I have loved to hear my Lord spoken of, and wherever I have seen the print of his shoe on earth, there I have coveted to set my foot too. His name has been to me as a civet-box, yea, sweeter than all perfumes. His voice to me has been more sweet, and his countenance I have more desired than they that have most desired the light of the sun. His Word I did use to gather for my food and for antidotes against my faintings. He has held me, and I have kept me from my iniquities. Yea, my steps have been strengthened in his way."

Now while he was thus in discourse his countenance changed, his strong men bowed under him, and after he had said, "Take me, for I come unto thee," he ceased to be seen of them.

But glorious it was to see how the open region was filled with horses and chariots, with trumpeters and pipers, with singers and players on stringed instruments, to welcome pilgrims as they went up and followed one another in at the beautiful gate of the city.

John Bunyan (1628–88)

4th November

Jesus replied: "A certain man was preparing a great banquet and invited many guests. At the time of the banquet he sent his servant to tell those who had been invited, 'Come, for everything is now ready.' But they all alike began to make excuses."

(Luke 14:16–18)

No sooner does anyone begin to preach the Gospel than men and women begin "to make excuses". It is the old story. There is not an unsaved person here, but has got some excuse. If I were to go to each of you and ask why you do not accept God's invitation to the Gospel feast, you would have an excuse ready on the end of your tongue; and if you had not one ready, the devil would be there to help you to make one. And if they could be answered, he is ready to make new ones. He has had six thousand years experience, and he is very good at it; he can give you as many as you want.

Do you know the origin of excuses? You will find it away back in Eden. When Adam had sinned, he tried to excuse himself. "The woman *whom Thou gavest* to be with me, she gave me of the tree and I did eat." He tried to lay the blame on God, Eve tried to lay it on the serpent; and down to the present time, men and women, with one consent begin to make excuse.

Remember that these men Luke tells us about were not invited to a funeral, or to hear some dry, stupid lecture or sermon; they were not invited to visit an hospital, or a prison, or a madhouse; to witness some terrible scene or execution – something that would have pained them. It was to go to a feast. The Gospel is represented in the Bible as a feast . . .

Not only was this a feast, but it was *a royal feast*. If you had the honour of an invitation from Windsor Castle – if Her Majesty the Queen [Victoria] invited you to some great banquet got up in honour of her son, there is not a man or woman here but would accept the invitation. You would want it put in the papers, to show how you had been honoured. But here is something worth more than that. Here is an invitation from the King of kings, the Lord of lords, God's only Son.

By and by He will take his bride into the bridal chamber. The marriage supper of the Lamb is hastening on. He has gone on to prepare new mansions for his bride; the old mansions are not good enough; and He will come by and by to take her to Himself. The invitations are going out now to every corner of the earth. There is not one here who is not invited.

D. L. Moody (1837–99)

5th November

They made their lives bitter with hard labour in brick and mortar and with all kinds of work in the fields; in all their hard labour the Egyptians used them ruthlessly.

(Exodus 1:14)

Lord Shaftesbury moved an Address on the subject [of children employed in brickfields] in the House of Lords. He stated that there were about 3,000 brickyards in the country, and that the number employed in them amounted to nearly 30,000, their ages varying from 3½ to 17 . . .

"I went down to a brickfield and made a considerable inspection. On approaching, I first saw, at a distance, what appeared like eight or ten pillars of clay, which, I thought, were placed there in order to indicate how deep the clay had been worked. On walking up, I found to my astonishment that these pillars were living beings.

"They were so like the ground on which they stood, their features were so indistinguishable, their dress so besoiled and covered with clay, their flesh so like their dress, that, until I approached and saw them move, I believed them to be the products of the earth. When I approached, they were so scared at seeing anything not like themselves, they ran away screaming as though something satanic were approaching . . . I saw little children, three parts naked, tottering under the weight of wet clay, some of it on their heads, and some on their shoulders, and little girls with large masses of wet, cold, and dripping clay pressing on their abdomens. Moreover, the unhappy children were exposed to the most sudden transitions of heat and cold; for, after carrying their burdens of wet clay, they had to endure the heat of the kiln, and to enter places where the heat was so fierce, that I was not myself able to remain more than two or three minutes.

"Can it be denied that in these brickfields, men, women and children, especially poor female children, are brought down to a point of degradation and suffering lower than the beasts of the field? No man with a sense of humanity, or with the aspirations of a Christian, could go through these places and not feel that what he saw was a disgrace to the country, and ought not for a moment be allowed to continue. Therefore my lords, I hope that not a day will be permitted to pass, until an Address is sent up to the Queen praying Her Majesty, to take the condition of these poor people into her gracious consideration, in order that such abominations may be brought speedily to an end."

The prayer was granted, and children in brickfields at length came under the beneficent protection of the law.

Lord Shaftesbury (1801–85)

6th November

"So now, go. I am sending you to Pharaoh to bring my people the Israelites out of Egypt." But Moses said to God, "Who am I, that I should go to Pharaoh and bring the Israelites out of Egypt?"
(Exodus 3:10–11)

In the first blush of youthful enthusiasm Moses had been impetuous enough to attempt the emancipation of his people by the blows of his right hand (Exodus 2:11–15). But now that God proposes to send him to lead an Exodus, he starts back in dismay almost petrified at the proposal. But how true this is to nature! The student, as a precocious schoolboy, thinks that he knows all that can be acquired of a certain branch of science; but twenty years after he feels as if he had not mastered its elements, though he had never ceased to study. The believer who began by speaking of himself as "the least of the saints" ends by calling himself "the chief of sinners". And Moses, who had run before God in feverish impatience, now lags faint-hearted behind Him.

At first he expostulated: "Who am I, that I should go to Pharaoh?" There was something more than humility here; there was a tone of self-depreciation, which was inconsistent with a true faith in God's selection and appointment. Surely it is God's business to choose his special instruments; and when we are persuaded that we are in the line of his purpose, we have no right to question the wisdom of his appointment. To do so is to depreciate his wisdom, or to doubt his power and willingness to become the complement of our need.

"And God said, Certainly I will be with thee." . . . What an assurance was here! And yet something of this kind is said to each of us when we are called to undertake any new charge. We have been called into the fellowship of the Son of God. "He died for us, that whether we wake or sleep, we should live together with Him." He is with us all our days, even until the end of the age. He will never leave us, neither forsake us. "Fear not", he seems to say; "I am with thee: I who change not, and without whom no sparrow falls to the ground. All power is given unto me in heaven and earth. Not an hour without my companionship; not a difficulty without my co-operation; not a Red Sea without my right arm; not a mile of wilderness journeying without the Angel of my Presence."

Days break very differently on us. Sometimes we open the door to a flood of sunshine, sometimes a sky laden with black, dull clouds; now a funeral, and then a marriage; hours in which it is a luxury to live, and others which pass with leaden-footed pace; but nothing can part us from our Divine Companion – nothing but needless worry or permitted sin.

F. B. Meyer (1847–1929)

7th November

And God said, "I will be with you."

(Exodus 3:12)

Self-confidence is not the temper which God uses for His instruments. He works with "bruised reeds", and breathes His strength into them. It is when a man says "I can do nothing," that he is fit for God to employ. "When I am weak, then I am strong." Moses remembered enough of Egypt to know that it was no slight peril to front Egypt, and enough of Israel not to be particularly eager to have the task of leading them. But mark there is no refusal of the charge, though there is a profound consciousness of inadequacy.

If we have reason to believe that any duty, great or small, is laid upon us by God, it is wholesome that we should drive home to ourselves our own weaknesses, but not that we should try to shuffle out of the duty because we are weak. Moses' answer was more of a prayer for help than of a remonstrance, and it was answered accordingly.

God deals very gently with conscious weakness. "Certainly I will be with thee." Moses' estimate of himself is quite correct, and it is the condition of his obtaining God's help. If he had been self-confident, he would have had no longing for, and no promise of God's presence. In all our little tasks we may have the same assurance, and, whenever we feel that they are too great for us, the strength of that promise may be ours. God sends no man on errands which He does not give him power to do. So Moses had not to calculate the difference between his feebleness and the strength of a kingdom. Such arithmetic left out one element, which made all the difference in the sum total. "Pharaoh *versus* Moses" did not look a very hopeful cause, but "Pharaoh *versus* Moses and Another" – that other being God – was a very different matter. God and I are always stronger than any antagonists. It was needless to discuss whether Moses was able to cope with the king. That was not the right way of putting the problem. The right way was, Is God able to do it?

Alexander Maclaren (1826–1910)

8th November

During the night Pharaoh summoned Moses and Aaron and said, "Up! Leave my people, you and the Israelites! Go, worship the Lord as you have requested. Take your flocks and herds, as you have said, and go. And also bless me."

(Exodus 12:31–2)

It is related as a memorial deed of a Roman general, that when the physician of a hostile king came to him and promised to give him poison, he sent him back bound to the enemy. In truth, it is a noble thing for a man to refuse to gain the victory by foul acts, after he has entered on the struggle for power. He did not consider virtue to lie in victory, but declared that to be a shameful victory unless it was gained with honour . . .

The king of Egypt would not let the people of our fathers go. Then Moses bade the priest Aaron to stretch his rod over the waters of Egypt. Aaron stretched it out and the water of the river turned into blood. None could drink the water, and all the Egyptians were perishing for thirst; but there was pure water flowing in abundance for the fathers. They sprinkled ashes towards heaven, and sores, and burning boils, came down upon man and beast. They brought down hail mingled with flaming fire, and all things were destroyed upon the land. Moses prayed, and all things were restored to their former beauty. The hail ceased, the sores were healed, the rivers gave their wonted draught.

Then, again, the land was covered with thick darkness, because Moses raised his hand and spread out the darkness. All the firstborn of Egypt died, whilst the offspring of the Hebrews was left unharmed. Moses was asked to put an end to the horrors and he prayed and obtained his request . . . He was indeed, as it is written, gentle and meek. He knew that the king would not keep true to his promises, yet he thought it right and good to pray when asked to do so, to bless when wronged, to forgive when besought.

He cast down his rod and it became a serpent which devoured the serpents of Egypt [Exodus 7:10–12]; this signifying that the Word should become flesh to destroy the poison of the dread serpent by the forgiveness and pardon of sins ... He Who was the Son of God begotten of the Father became the Son of man born of a woman, and lifted like the serpent on the cross, poured His healing medicine on the wounds of man. Wherefore the Lord himself says: "As Moses lifted up the serpent in the wilderness, so must the Son of Man be lifted up."

Ambrose of Milan (c. 339–397)

9th November

"Don't be angry, my lord," Aaron answered. "You know how prone these people are to evil. They said to me, 'Make us gods who will go before us. As for this fellow Moses who brought us out of Egypt, we don't know what has happened to him.' So I told them, 'Whoever has any gold jewellery, take it off.' Then they gave me the gold, and I threw it into the fire, and out came this calf!"

(Exodus 32:22–4)

Was he simply telling a lie to Moses and trying to hide the truth from his brother whom he dreaded, when he said, "I cast the earrings into the fire, and this calf came out"? Or was he in some dim degree, in some half-conscious way deceiving himself? Was he allowing himself to attribute some power to the furnace in the making of the calf? Perhaps as we read Exodus 32:4 in which it is distinctly said that Aaron fashioned the idol with a graving tool, any such supposition seems incredible. But yet I cannot but think that some degree, however dim, of self-deception was in Aaron's heart. The fire was mysterious. He was a priest. Who could say that some strange creative power had not been at work there in the heart of the furnace which had done for him what he seemed to do for himself. There was a human heart under that ancient ephod, and it is hard to think that Aaron did not succeed in bringing himself to be somewhat imposed upon by his own words and in hiding his responsibility in the heart of the hot furnace.

However it may have been with Aaron, there can be no doubt that in almost all cases this is so. Very rarely indeed does a man excuse himself to other men and yet remain absolutely unexcused in his own eyes. When Pilate stands washing the responsibility of Christ's murder from his hands before the people, was he not feeling himself as if his hands grew cleaner while he washed?

When Shakespeare paints Macbeth with the guilty ambition that was to be his ruin first rising in his heart, you remember how he makes him hide his newborn purpose to be king even from himself. He pretends that he believes that he is willing to accept the kingdom only if it shall come out of the working of things, for which he is not responsible, without an effort of his own.

> *If chance will have me king,*
> *Why, chance may crown me,*
> *Without my stir.*

That was the first stage of the growing crime which finally became murder.

Phillips Brooks (1835–93)

10th November

The heart is deceitful above all things and beyond cure. Who can understand it?

(Jeremiah 17:9)

[Continued from yesterday.]

Suppose one of the Israelites who stood by had spoken up on Aaron's behalf and said to Moses, "Oh, he did not do it. It was not his act. He only cast the gold into the fire, and there came out this calf." Must not Aaron as he listened have felt the wretchedness of such a telling of the story, and been ashamed, and even cried out and claimed his responsibility and his sin? Very often it is good for us to imagine someone saying aloud on our behalf what we are saying to ourselves in self-apology. We see its thinness when another holds it up against the sun, and we stand off and look at it.

If I might turn again to Shakespeare and his wonderful treasury of human character, there is a scene in *Hamlet* that illustrates exactly what I mean. The king has determined that Hamlet must die, and he is just sending him off upon the voyage from which he means that he is never to return. The king has fully explained the act to his own conscience, and accepted the crime as a necessity. Then he meets the courtiers, Rosencrantz and Guildenstern, who are to have the execution of the base commission. And they, as courtiers do, try to repeat to the king the arguments with which he has convinced himself . . . But when they come to him from these other lips, he will have none of them. He cuts them short. He cannot hear from others what he has said over and over to himself.

Arm you, I pray you, to this speedy voyage.

So he cried out and interrupts them. Let the deed be done, but let not these echoes of his self-excuse parade before him the way he is trifling with his own soul . . .

The only hope for any of us is in a perfectly honest manliness to claim our sins. "I did it, I did it," let me say of all my wickedness. Let me refuse to listen to one moment to any voice which would make my sins less mine. It is the only honest and hopeful way, the only way to know and be ourselves. When we have done that, then we are ready for the gospel, ready for all that Christ wants to show us that we may become, and for all the powerful grace by which He wants to make us be it perfectly.

Phillips Brooks (1835–93)

11th November

From then on, Pilate tried to set Jesus free, but the Jews kept shouting, "If you let this man go, you are no friend of Caesar. Anyone who claims to be a king opposes Caesar."

(John 19:12)

The world has drawn a distinction (though I know not by what right or on what ground) between the principles which regulate our public, and those which regulate our private life. A man, it seems by their admissions, may be treacherous politically, and yet faithful socially; selfish, ambitious, and dishonest towards the State, and yet disinterested, moderate, and upright towards his friends.

Undoubtedly for this there is no sanction in the Divine law; and it is difficult to ascertain the precise fallacy by which it is permitted in the human.

Assuredly the Almighty gave us a different rule when he said (Genesis 18:17, 19) "Shall I hide from Abraham that thing which I do? for I know him, that he will command his children and his household after him, that they shall keep the way of the Lord, to do justice and judgement; that the Lord may bring upon Abraham that which he hath spoken of him." Here the private excellence of the Patriarch is taken by the Almighty as the ground of public trust, of the revelation of the future, the skilful conjecture of which is regarded among men as political wisdom. The good rule of a family is held to be an earnest of the good rule of a State; and God then invested him with power and wealth and command and great responsibility.

We, however, while we affix a stain to moral turpitude, only censure or rebuke political dishonour (and it is a great thing if we do even that). The most fiery votaries of the "code of honour", however jealous and ready and sensitive on all occasions, are amply satisfied when, after some charge or reflection on their characters, they receive an assurance that the remark was not *personal*. "I speak *politically*," says the explainant, and then all goes well! Now wherefore? – no, I see the wherefore, but, by what authority, do they make such distinctions? Do selfishness, truth, honour, ambition, pride, and disinterestedness change their nature; or do we change our language on them? Are the vices and the virtues of the human mind less so than when applied to affairs of a family or a circle? Do the principles of morality in a public business flow from a different source and into another receptacle? Were the law of Mount Sinai and the sermons of our Saviour, for the instruction of householders and private persons only, the rule of public life being arbitrary deduction and single interpretation? No, as surely as there is but "one Lord, one faith, one baptism," so is there for the government of our actions but one truth, one law, and one responsibility.

Lord Shaftesbury (1801–85)

12th November

You shall not covet your neighbour's house. You shall not covet your neighbour's wife, or his manservant or maidservant, his ox or donkey, or anything that belongs to your neighbour.

(Exodus 20:17)

"Thou shalt not covet." The violations of this law may assume many forms. As it was given in the first instance to a nation, it is natural to consider some of the ways in which a nation can violate it.

The history of the world is stained and darkened by the crimes to which nations have been driven by the spirit of covetousness. A great and prosperous people with a beautiful country rich in all the material resources which contribute to national wealth and splendour, cannot endure that the cornfields, and the vineyards, and the noble river which can be seen from its frontiers should belong to the neighbouring power. Or an inland state with hardly any sea-board looks upon the indented coast of some insignificant and feeble neighbour, and dreams of the formidable navies which could ride in safety in those secure harbours, of the vast commercial cities which might be built if these convenient sea-ports were its own. Or a strong and masculine and enterprising race speculates on the wealth it might win if it could appropriate by policy or by force rich and fertile territories on the other side of the world, governed by a decaying empire and possessed by an unwarlike and imperfectly civilised people.

Sooner or later, it is almost certain that in every case this national covetousness will end in a war of aggression and conquest. Some pretext will found for a quarrel; there will be an insult to avenge; or an ancient wrong to redress, or a frontier to rectify; or the idea of national unity to vindicate; or punishment to inflict and compensation to claim for the violation of a commercial treaty; by some means or other there will be a justification discovered or created for seizing by force of arms, what the heart of the nation has longed for.

But I repeat that it is the covetousness itself which this

commandment forbids; and the covetousness is forbidden not merely to prevent the miseries, and horrors, and crimes of aggressive war, but to train the spirit of the nations to the recognition of God's own idea of their relations to each other.

R. W. Dale (1829–95)

13th November

This is how you should pray: "Our Father in heaven, hallowed be your name, your kingdom come, your will be done on earth as it is in heaven."

(Matthew 6:9–10)

Prayer is doing God's will. It is letting Him pray in us. We look for answer because His fullness is completely equal to His own prayers. Father and Son are perfectly adequate to each other. That is the Holy Spirit and self-sufficiency of the Godhead.

If God's will is to be done on earth as it is in heaven, prayer begins with *adoration*. Of course, it is thanks and petition; but before we give even our prayer we must first receive. The answerer provides the very prayer. What we do here rests on what God has done. What we offer is drawn from us by what He offers. Our self-oblation stands on His; and the spirit of prayer flows from the gift of the Holy Ghost, the Great Intercessor. Hence praise and adoration of His work in itself comes before even our thanks-giving for blessings to us. At the height of prayer, if not at its beginning, we are preoccupied with the great and glorious thing God has done for His own holy name in Redemption, apart from its immediate and particular blessing to us. We are blind for the time to ourselves. We cover our faces with our wings and cry "Holy, holy, holy is the Lord God of hosts; the fullness of the earth is His glory" (Isaiah 6:2–3). Our full hearts glorify. We magnify His name. His perfections take precedence of our occasions. We pray for victory in the present war [the First World War] for instance, and for deliverance from all war, for the sake of God's kingdom – in a spirit of adoration for the deliverance there that is not destroyed, or foiled, even by a devilry like this. If the kingdom of God not only got over the murder of Christ, but made it its great lever, there is nothing than it cannot get over, and nothing it cannot turn to eternal blessing and to the glory of the holy name. But to the perspective of this faith, and to its vision of values so alien to human standards, we can rise only in prayer.

But it would be unreal prayer which was adoration only, with no reference to special bonds or human needs. That would be as if God recognised no life but His own – which is a very undivine egoism, and its collective form is the religion of mere nationalism. In true prayer we do two things. We go out of ourselves, being lost in wonder, love and praise; but also, and in the same act, we go in on ourselves. We stir up *all that is within us* to bless and hallow God's name.

P. T. Forsyth (1848–1921)

14th November

Endure hardship with us like a good soldier of Christ Jesus. No-one serving as soldier gets involved in civilian affairs – he wants to please his commanding officer.

(2 Timothy 2:3–4)

A soldier in France [in the First World War] was in the first trench and throwing bombs against the enemy. One slipped from his hands and rolled back into the trench. In a moment it would explode and kill his fellow soldiers. He could not bear his mistake to cause them suffering or loss of life so he threw himself on the bomb, covering it with his body till it burst. It killed him, but he saved his friends. I think this is a wonderful story. He got the V.C. and I came across a soldier who knew him. He might easily have excused himself but his mistake brought him an imperishable memorial in the hall of heroes: one minute a nobody and the next minute a hero. That's the whole beautiful religion of Jesus Christ, as Paul said: "To die is gain." That's the only supremely happy way for a Christian . . .

In the South African war General Hart found a soldier, unwounded, coming back from the front and enquired why. He was told, "I am so short sighted that I couldn't see so I gave my place to another man." "Ah, dear me," said the General. "Come along with me." He took him to the thickest part of the battle saying, "My good man, it's a great shame you should have been so mishandled. Here you cannot possibly miss." The position of the churches gets blacker in my view every day. Jesus said, "Love one another as I have loved you." Now look at the delightful passionate obedience of Christ's followers today and the glorious impotent results! The fact is, the Church has got a chronic attack of hiccups. They make a thundering noise (and all the world looks on and laughs) and in between times they roll their eyes and denounce us who would give them a warning dose of ginger. If they would only take it, it would turn them into an army of lions of Judah. As it is they sit in their corner like Jack Horner eating their Christian pie.

C. T. Studd (1862–1931)

15th November

If it is possible, as far as it depends on you, live at peace with everyone.

(Romans 12:18)

Now since Christ, the Prince of Peace, has prepared and won himself a kingdom, that is a church, through his own blood; in this same kingdom all worldly warfare has an end, as was promised aforetime, "The law will go out of Zion, the word of the Lord from Jerusalem. He will judge between the nations and will settle disputes for many peoples. They will beat their swords into ploughshares and their spears into pruning hooks. Nation will not take up sword against nation, nor will they train for war any more" (Isaiah 2:3–4 NIV).

Therefore a Christian neither wages war nor wields the worldly sword to practise vengeance, as Paul also exhorts us saying, "Do not take revenge, my friends, but leave room for God's wrath, for it is written: 'It is mine to avenge; I will repay,' says the Lord" (Romans 12:19 NIV). Now if vengeance is God's and not ours, it ought to be left to him and not practised or exercised by ourselves.

For since we are Christ's disciples, we must show forth the nature of him who, though, he could indeed, have done so, repaid not evil with evil. For he could, indeed, have protected himself against his enemies, the Jews, by striking down with a single word all who wanted to take him captive.

But though he might have done this, he did not himself and would not permit others to do so. Therefore he said to Peter, "Put your sword back in its place" (Matthew 26:52 NIV). Here we can see how our King sets out with a powerful host against his enemy; how he defeats the enemy and how he takes vengeance: in that he takes Malchus' ear, that had been struck off, and puts it on again. And he who did this says, "Who ever will be my disciple, let him take his cross upon him and follow me."

Now therefore, Christ desires that we should act even as he did, so he commands us, saying, "You have heard that it was said, 'Eye for eye, and tooth for tooth,' But I tell you, Do not resist an evil person. If someone strikes you on the right cheek, turn to him the other also" (Matthew 5:38–9 NIV). Here it is clearly to be seen that one ought neither to avenge oneself nor go to war, but rather offer his back to the strikers and his cheeks to them that pluck off his hair – that is, suffer with patience and wait upon God, who is righteous, and who will repay it.

Peter Riedeman (1506–56)

16th November

They also will answer, "Lord, when did we see you hungry or thirsty or a stranger or needing clothes or sick or in prison, and did not help you?" He will reply, "I tell you the truth, whatever you did not do for one of the least of these, you did not do for me."
(Matthew 25:44–5)

Oct. 11th 1857. Read in afternoon Matt 25. What a revelation of the future judgement on the largest portion of the human race! Those on the left hand are condemned, not for murder, robbery, debauchery, not for breaches of the Decalogue, or for the open blasphemy, not for sins they have *committed*, but for duties they have *omitted*. And is not this the state of the great mass of mankind? The great mass do not commit any great crimes; did they so, society would fall to pieces in the twinkling of an eye; but they go on day after day to their life's end, thinking of themselves, very little of others, and nothing of God . . . "I have done no harm", "I am not worse than my neighbours", "I have merely used my own", etc, etc; all these are the pleas, the hopes, the justifications of the "innocent" world. But while man takes one view, God takes another. "Have you done good?" "Have you attempted it?" "Have you sought to advance my Name?" "Have you laboured for the physical and spiritual welfare of your fellow sinners?" St James (4:17) condenses the spirit of our Lord's words, "Therefore to him that knoweth to do good and doeth it not, to him it is sin."

Lord Shaftesbury (1801–85)

17th November

Let us not become weary in doing good, for at the proper time we will reap a harvest if we do not give up. Therefore, as we have opportunity, let us do good to all people, especially to those who belong to the family of believers.

(Galatians 6:9–10)

I believe that the mutual hostility which separates class from class, the envy with which the poor too often regard the rich, the contempt or the indifference with which the rich too often regard the poor, will never by subdued but by a common sense of brotherhood in Him. In Christ, Jew and Gentile, Greek and Barbarian, forgot the hatred of centuries; in Christ, and in Christ alone, will the social alienations which are the peril of our country be healed.

Nor do I know where we can find the courage, and the hope, and the enthusiasm which are necessary to sustain us in the attempt to solve any of the graver problems suggested by our social condition except in Him. But for Christ, I should despair of the civilisation of the modern world and the future of the human race. How the struggle between labour and captial, now just beginning, is to end, I cannot tell. How the fever and excitement of unscrupulous commercial competition are to be cooled and quieted, and all the immorality and misery it occasions prevented, I cannot tell. How that army of crime, which has encamped in the very heart of all our wealth and greatness, and whose ravages no force of law seems able to repress, is to be swept away, I cannot tell. How that hereditary pauperism, which no changes in our commercial policy, no manufacturing prosperity, no reforms in administering relief, no schemes of emigration, seem able to remove, is to disappear, I cannot tell.

We are confused and bewildered by the schemes of social reformers. We are disheartened by repeated failure. I am afraid of the indifference which comes from despair. But there is hope in this, that Christ came to save the world, and He will surely save it. And while this is a reason for hope it is also a stimulus for exertion. It fires enthusiasm. It transforms the work of common philanthropy into a religious duty. It elevates our war against poverty, and ignorance and crime, into a crusade.

R. W. Dale (1829–95)

18th November

For though we live in the world, we do not wage war as the world does. The weapons we fight with are not the weapons of the world. On the contrary, they have divine power to demolish strongholds. We demolish arguments and every pretention that sets itself up against the knowledge of God, and we take captive every thought to make it obedient to Christ.

(2 Corinthians 10:3–5)

We must cultivate reality by preaching to the social situation, to social sin. It is impossible to preach with reality to an age like this and ignore the social crisis and demand. We must face the questions put to the Gospel by a time which is passing from one social epoch to another. It is to the Gospel these questions are put, though they are addressed to the care of the Church. I hope the Church will see that they reach their destination.

We are at the junction of two ages – the Capitalist and the Socialist. And we who live in the supreme society of the Church, and who possess the word of moral power for every age, must not be unprepared with a relevant word, even if we have not yet the final word. It is a work to be done with the greatest judgement. And it is not honestly done without due knowledge. We must know the ethic of the Gospel on one hand, and the economics of the age on the other. You [preachers] will not be so ill-advised as to make this the staple of your pulpit. Some should not touch it there at all. It is not for every preacher and not for the preacher alone, but for the preacher co-operating with the men of affairs who will add his knowledge to their own.

Neither the preacher alone nor the lay-men alone makes the Church, but both do. But the Church, as the great collective preacher, should have some social word that deserves public attention and respect, even if it cannot secure immediate belief. The realism of the Gospel and of the age alike require that.

P. T. Forsyth (1848–1921)

19th November

The sins of some men are obvious, reaching the place of judgement ahead of them; the sins of others trail behind them. In the same way, good deeds are obvious, and even those that are not cannot be hidden.

(1 Timothy 5:24–5)

[The condition of children in Factories] was a great political, moral and religious question; it was political because it would decide whether thousands would be left in discontent, aye and just discontent; it was moral because it would decide whether the rising generation should learn to distinguish between good and evil – be raised above the enjoyment of mere brutal sensualities, and be no longer, as they then were, degraded from the dignity of thinking beings. It was a great religious question; for it involved the means to thousands and tens of thousands being brought up in the fear and faith of God that had created them. [Shaftesbury] had read of those who had sacrificed their children to Moloch; but they were a merciful people compared with Englishmen in the nineteenth century. He had heard of the infanticide of the Indians, but they, too, were a merciful people compared with Englishmen in the nineteenth century. For those nations destroyed at once their wretched offspring, and prevented a long career of suffering and crime; but we, having sucked out every energy of body and soul, tossed them on the world, a mass of skin and bone, incapable of exertion, brutalised in their understandings, and disqualified for immortality. He feared that in the House of Commons they would have to encounter great and formidable opposition, but it was gratifying to think that all masters were not against them, neither were they without numerous and cordial supporters in the House; but it behoved those who were out of doors to use their best and most strenuous exertions to guard against the possible failure of the Bill.

There was one consideration to which he particularly wished to call their attention – namely, that before publication of the evidence, the people of England had nothing like the responsibility which since rested upon their heads. So long as these horrid facts remained unknown, the guilt attached to the perpetrators only; but, if this terrible system were permitted to continue any longer, the guilt would descend upon the whole nation. As for himself he assured them that he would not give way a single moment on the question of the Ten Hours; he would persevere in the cause he had adopted. He had taken up the measure as a matter of conscience, and as such he was determined to carry it through. If the House would not adopt the Bill, they must drive him from it, as he would not concede a single step. He must positively declare that as long as he had a seat in that House; as long as God gave him health and a sound mind, no efforts, no exertions, should be wanted on his part to establish the success of the measure. If defeated in the present Session, he would bring it forward in the next, and so on in every succeeding Session till his success was complete.

Lord Shaftesbury (1801–85)

20th November

I urge, then, first of all, that requests, prayers, intercession and thanksgiving be made for everyone – for kings and all those who live in authority, that we may live peaceful and quiet lives in all godliness and holiness. This is good and praises God our Saviour, who wants all men to be saved and to come to a knowledge of the truth.

(1 Timothy 2:1–4)

A frequent intercession with God, earnestly beseeching Him to forgive the sins of all mankind, to bless them with His providence, enlighten them with His Spirit, and bring them to everlasting happiness, is the divinest exercise that the heart of man can be engaged in.

Be daily, therefore, on your knees, in a solemn, deliberate performance of this devotion, praying for others in such forms, with such length, importunity, and earnestness, as you use for yourself; and you will find all little, ill-natured passions die away, your heart grows great and generous, delighting in the common happiness of others, as you used to delight in your own.

For he that daily prays to God, that all men may be happy in heaven, takes the likeliest way to make him wish for, and delight in their happiness on earth. And it is hardly possible for you to beseech and entreat God to make anyone happy in the highest enjoyments of His glory to all eternity, and yet be troubled to see him enjoy the much smaller gifts of God in this short and low state of human life. For how strange and unnatural it would be, to pray to God to grant health and a longer life to a sick man, and at the same time to envy him the poor pleasures of agreeable medicines!

Yet this would be no more strange or unnatural than to pray to God that your neighbour may enjoy the highest degrees of His mercy and favour, and yet at the same time to envy him the little credit and figure he hath amongst his fellow-creatures.

When therefore you have once habituated your heart to a serious performance of this one holy intercession, you have done a great deal to render it incapable of spite and envy, and to make it naturally delight in the happiness of all mankind.

William Law (1686–1761)

21st November

Pray in the Spirit on all occasions with all kinds of prayers and requests. With this in mind, be alert and always keep on praying for all the saints.

(Ephesians 6:18)

Young converts should be taught to pray without ceasing. That is, they should always keep a watch over their minds, and be all the time in a prayerful spirit. They should be taught to pray always, whatever may take place. For the want of right instruction on this point many young converts suffer loss and get far away from God. For instance, sometimes it happens that a young convert will fall into some sin, and then he feels as if he could not pray, and instead of overcoming this he feels so distressed that he waits for the keen edge of his distress to pass away. Instead of going right to Jesus Christ in the midst of his agony, and confessing his sin out of the fulness of his heart, and getting a renewed pardon, and peace restored, he waits till all the keenness of his feelings has subsided; and then, his repentance, if he does repent, is cold and half-hearted. Let me tell you, beloved, never to do this; but when your conscience presses you, go then to Christ, confess your sin fully, and pour out your heart to God.

Sometimes people will neglect to pray because they are in the dark, and feel no desire to pray. But that is the very time when they need prayer. That is the very reason why they ought to pray. You should go right to God and confess your coldness and darkness of mind. Tell him just how you feel. Tell Him: "O Lord, I have no desire to pray." And immediately the Spirit may come and lead your heart out in prayer, and all the dark clouds will pass away.

Charles G. Finney (1792–1875)

22nd November

Now when Daniel learned that the decree had been published, he went home to his upstairs room where the windows opened towards Jerusalem. Three times a day he got down on his knees and prayed, giving thanks to God, just as he had done before.
(Daniel 6:10)

How many men there are who are ashamed to be caught on their knees! Many a man, if found upon his knees by the wife of his bosom, would jump right up and walk round the room as if he had no particular object in view. How many young men there are who come up from the country and enter upon city life, and have not the moral courage to go down on their knees before their room-mates! How many young men say, "Don't ask me to get down on my knees at this prayer-meeting." Men have not the moral courage to be seen praying. They lack moral courage. Ah! thousands of men have been lost for lack of moral courage; have been lost because at some critical moment they shrank from going on their knees, and being seen and known as being worshippers of God – as being on the Lord's side. Ah, the fact is – we are a pack of cowards: that is what we are. Shame on the Christianity of the nineteenth century! it is a weak and sickly thing. Would to God that we had a host of men like Daniel living today!

I can picture that aged man, with his grey hairs upon him, listening to the words of those "miserable counsellors", who would tempt him to "trim", and "hedge" and shift – to "save his skin", as men say, at the cost of his conscience. And their counsel falls flat and dead. I can fancy how Daniel would receive a suggestion that he should even seemingly be ashamed of the God of his fathers. Will he be ashamed or afraid? Not likely! You know he will not; and I know he will not . . .

True as steel, that old man goes to his room three times a day. Mark you, he had time to pray. There is many a business man today who will tell you he has no time to pray: his business is so pressing that he cannot call his family around him, and ask God to bless them. He is so busy that he cannot ask God to keep him and them from the temptations of the present life – the temptations of every day. "Business is so pressing." I am reminded of the words of an old Methodist minister: "If you have so much business to attend to that you have no time to pray, depend upon it you have more business on hand than God ever intended you should have." But look at this man. He had the whole, or nearly whole, of the king's business to attend to. He was Prime Minister, Secretary of State, and Chancellor of the Exchequer, all in one. He had to attend to all his work; and to give an eye to the work of lots of men. And yet he found time to pray; not just now and then, nor once in a way, not just when he happened to have a few moments to spare, mark you – but "three times a day".

D. L. Moody (1837–99)

23rd November

While they were worshipping the Lord and fasting, the Holy Spirit said, "Set apart for me Barnabas and Saul for the work to which I have called them." So after they had fasted and prayed, they placed their hands on them and sent them off.

(Acts 13:2–3)

If the prophecies concerning the increase of Christ's kingdom be true, and if what has been said concerning the commission (Matthew 28:16–20) given by him to his disciples being obligatory on us, be just, it must be inferred that all Christians ought to heartily concur with God in promoting his glorious designs, for "he who unites himself with the Lord is one with him in spirit" (1 Corinthians 6:17).

One of the first and most important duties which are incumbent upon us is fervent and united prayer. However the influence of the Holy Spirit may be set at nought and run down by many, it will be found upon trial, that all means we can use without it, will be ineffectual. If a temple will be raised for God in the heathen world, it will not be "by might nor by power", nor by the authority of the magistrate, or by the eloquence of the orator; "but by my spirit, saith the Lord of Hosts" (Zechariah 4:6). We must therefore be in real earnest in seeking his blessing upon our labours . . .

The most glorious works of grace that have ever taken place have been in answer to prayer; and it is in this way, we have the greatest reason to suppose, that the glorious outpouring of the Spirit which we expect at last will be bestowed.

With respect to our own immediate connections, we within these few years have been favoured with some tokens for good, granted in answer to prayer, which should encourage us to persist, and increase in that important duty. I trust that our monthly prayer-meetings for the success of the gospel have not been in vain. It is true that a want of importunity too generally attends our prayers; yet importunate, and feeble as they have been, it is to be believed that God has heard, and in a measure answered them. The churches that have engaged in this practice have in general since that time been evidently on the increase; some controversies that which have long perplexed and divided the church are more clearly stated than ever; there are calls to preach the gospel in many places where it has not been usually published; yea, a glorious door is opened, and is likely to be opened wider and wider, by the spread of civil and religious liberty, accompanied also by a diminuation of a spirit of popery; a noble effort has been made to abolish the inhuman Slave Trade, and though at present it has not been so successful as might be wished, yet it is to be hoped that it will be persevered in till it is accomplished.

William Carey (1761–1834)

24th November

He said to them, "Go into all the world and preach the good news to all creation. Whoever believes and is baptised will be saved, but whoever does not believe will be condemned.

(Mark 16:15–16)

I am persuaded that I need not inform this congregation, that when ambassadors are sent to a prince, or when judges go to their respective circuits, it is always customary for them to show their credentials, to open and read their commission, by which they act in his Majesty's name. The same is absolutely necessary for those who are ambassadors of the Son of God, as they would be faithful to their Lord ... Here it is written with the King's own hand, by the finger of the ever-blessed God and sealed with the signet of his eternal Spirit, with his broad seal annexed to it. The commission is short, but very extensive; and it is remarkable, it was given out just before the Redeemer went to heaven; he reserved it in his infinite wisdom for his last blessing, to appoint and employ viceregents to carry on his work on earth ...

Go ye, poor fishermen, ye that the letter-learned doctors will look upon as illiterate men; Go ye, that hitherto have been dreaming of temporal preferments, quarrelling "who should sit on my right hand and on my left hand in my kingdom". Go ye, not stay till the people come to you, but imitate the conduct of your Master ...

Go therefore: where? into all the world; there is a commission for you; there never was such a commission on earth; there was never any like this. Go into all the world, that is, into the Gentile as well as the Jewish world. Hitherto my gospel has been confined to the Jews; I once told you, you must not go to the Gentiles; I once told a poor woman that came to me, it is not right to take children's bread and give it to the dogs. But now the partition wall is broken down, and the veil of the temple is rent in two, he gave them a universal command; Go ye, therefore, into all the world.

George Whitefield (1714–70)

25th November

His purpose was to create in himself one new man out of the two, thus making peace, and in this one body to reconcile both of them to God through the cross, by which he put to death their hostility.
(Ephesians 2:15b–16)

Though the primary form of reconciliation is the sinner's reconciliation to God, this carries with it other modes of reconciliation to which Paul in particular directs attention. Thus it involves the reconciliation of Jew and Gentile, or rather of all races of men to each other. It is when men are not right with God that they are most apt to fall out with each other, and in coming into right relationships to God they discover that they are at one, in all that is deepest in their nature and interests, with multitudes of whom they have been ignorant or from whom they have been estranged by prejudice or suspicion.

The apostle regards this as an important truth. Through Christ we all have our access by one Spirit unto the Father: our reconciliation to God includes our gathering together as one body in Christ. The reconciliation of individuals creates the Church (Ephesians 2:14ff). It is not so much the carrying of this process further, in the way of experience, as a characteristic assertion of the uniqueness of Christianity, when we find Paul declaring to the Colossians, that it pleased the Father through Christ "to reconcile all things to Himself . . . whether they be things on earth or in heaven."

The reconciliation achieved in Christ is so transcendent and wonderful, that there is no limit to its scope. Wherever we have to think of reconciliation, in the seen world or the unseen, in Him lie the love and power by which it must be achieved. Though we cannot tell precisely what Paul had in his mind when he spoke of things in heaven needing reconciliation, we can understand his feeling; there is no problem of reconciliation too hard for the love which bore our sins at the cross.

James Denney (1856–1917)

26th November

For whenever you eat this bread and drink this cup, you proclaim the Lord's death until he comes.

(1 Corinthians 11:26)

> Thou art coming! At Thy table
> We are witnesses for this,
> While remembering hearts Thou meetest,
> In communion clearest, sweetest,
> Earnest of our coming bliss.

Showing not Thy death alone,
And Thy love exceeding great,
But Thy coming and Thy throne,
All for which we long and wait.

Thou are coming! We are waiting
With a hope that cannot fail;
Asking not the day or hour,
Resting on Thy word of power
Anchored safe within the veil.
Time appointed may be long,
But the vision must be sure:
Certainty shall make us strong,
Joyful patience can endure!

Oh, the joy to see Thee reigning,
Thee, my own beloved Lord!
Every tongue Thy name confessing,
Worship, honour, glory, blessing,
Brought to Thee with glad accord!
Thee, my Master and my Friend,
Vindicated and enthroned!
Unto earth's remotest end
Glorified, adored, and owned!

Frances Ridley Havergal (1836–79)

27th November

Look, he is coming with the clouds, and every eye will see him, even those who pierced him; and all the peoples of the earth will mourn because of him. So shall it be! Amen.

(Revelation 1:7)

I have been greatly stirred by reading Revelation. The chief lesson that I learned is that as Christ died for the world, so also must we, His Body, do the same. The tortures and deaths inflicted on Christians will evidently be of such a nature that no human being could endure them unless he was indwelt by God's Spirit. So the test will be a perfect one and only those who come through as victors who can do the impossible, endure the unendurable, being specially enabled and indwelt by the Spirit of God. Thus shall God be perfectly justified in His anger and judgement when He comes to deal with a world which tortured and killed His Son Who came to save it, and did the same to His Body, the true Church who followed His only Son. Who indeed shall be able to stand? Holy Ghost-possessed men, women and children and none else! . . .

How small things look in the light of eternity, or of the Great Tribulation (Revelation 7:14). Who can go through it? The meek can, and lots of others. But I? There's the real question. I know I can't unless God's mighty power possesses me and chloroforms me . . .

We now use the word "hallelujah" instead of "amen" at the conclusion of prayer. "Amen" was a sleepy affair, something like the last moans of a dying cow. I fancy even the angels must have screwed up their faces. Our "hallelujah" lends itself to enthusiasm and is something like the triumphant shout of a herd of hefty bulls of Bashan. Nobody can remain asleep long, for he is obliged to wake up at the end of each prayer. We have also adopted an improved form of finale after the benediction. I ask the people, "is it not true that God *is*? They reply "God is." I ask, "Is not Jesus coming again?" Reply, "Jesus is coming." Then we all say "Hallelujah." Well it is a regular raising-the-roof affair. I sometimes wish some of our dear old staid Christians at home could hear it. The shock would produce enough energy and enthusiasm to milk a whole herd of goats and make them give double quantity.

C. T. Studd (1862–1931)

28th November

And this gospel of the kingdom will be preached in the whole world as a testimony to all nations, and then the end will come.
(Matthew 24:14)

When first I came to India I was astonished and grievously

disappointed because I did not see what I had seen in Japan. There, before going on a special campaign, the number I might ask for and receive from Him was usually shown the day before, a day given up to prayer. And as it was shown, so it came to pass, and baptism followed as a matter of course, and open life as a Christian thereafter. Here it was different.

But why? Was not the power of God the same in India as in Japan? So far as I could tell the preparation was the same. Why then were the results different?

It seems to me now, and the missionary reading of years confirms it, that the Sovereign Master of the field sends some to parts of that field where He knows there will be tremendous strain on faith; and he trusts them to go on there, and *be sure* that even there He shall reign.

It is so where individual souls are concerned. "He must reign" (1 Corinthians 15:25). The word has gone forth, and the day will come when we shall hear great voices in heaven, saying, "The kingdoms of this world are become the Kingdom of our Lord and of His Christ" (Revelation 11:15).

We live in the interval between Calvary and that day of days. The Two Witnesses have a word for us. They stand in the Presence. "These are the two olive trees and the two candlesticks standing before the God of earth" (Revelation 11:4). They have power. They have traffic with heaven "as often as they will". But the Beast that ascends out of the bottomless pit shall overcome them and kill them. No waving of palms here – no harvest fields. Defeat, death to all human hopes (Revelation 11:7).

But the end? "The Spirit of Life from God entered into them. And they heard a great voice from heaven saying unto them, Come up hither" (Revelation 11:12).

There can't be any such thing as "no result" if truly and faithfully, and in the power of the Spirit, the message is given.

Amy Carmichael (1867–1951)

29th November

God was reconciling the world to himself in Christ, not counting men's sins against them. And he has committed to us the message of reconciliation. We are therefore Christ's ambassadors, as though God were making his appeal through us. We implore you on Christ's behalf: Be reconciled to God.

(2 Corinthians 5:19–20)

The idea of atonement is the covering of sin by something which God provided, and by the use of which sin loses its accusing power, and its power to derange that grand covenant and relationship between man and God which founds the New Humanity. The [Greek] word *katallessein* (reconciliation) is peculiar to Paul. He uses both words; but the other word, "atonement", you also find in other New Testament writings. Reconciliation is Paul's great characteristic word and thought. . . . First, Christ's work is something described as reconciliation. And second, reconciliation rests on atonement as its ground.

Do not stop at "God was in Christ reconciling the world." You can easily water that down. You may begin the process by saying that God was in Christ in the same way in which He was in the old prophets. That is the first dilution. Then you go on with the homeopathic treatment, and you say, "Oh yes, all He did by Christ was to affect the world and impress it by showing how much He loved it."

Now, would that reconcile anybody really in need of it? When your child has flown into a violent temper with you, and still worse, a sulky temper, and glooms for a whole day, is it any use your sending to that child and saying, "Really, this cannot go on. Come back. I love you very much. Say you are sorry." Not a bit of use. For God simply to have told or shown the evil world how much He loved it would have been a most ineffectual thing. Something had to be *done* – judging or saving. Revelation alone is inadequate. Reconciliation must rest on atonement.

P. T. Forsyth (1848–1921)

30th November

We implore you on Christ's behalf: Be reconciled to God. God made him who had no sin to be sin for us, so that in him we might become the righteousness of God.

(2 Corinthians 5:20–21)

[Continued from yesterday.]

For, as I say, you must not stop at "God was in Christ reconciling the world unto Himself," but go on "not reckoning unto them their trespasses." "He made Christ to be sin for us, who knew no sin." That involves atonement. You cannot blot out that phrase.

And the third thing involved is the idea that this reconciliation, this atonement, means change of relation between God and man – man, mind you, not two or three men, not several groups of men, but man, the human race as one whole. And is it a change of relation from alienation to communion – not simply to our peace and confidence, but to reciprocal communion. The grand end of reconciliation is communion. I am pressing that hard. I am pressing it hard here by saying that it is not enough that we should worship God. It is not enough that we should worship a personal God. It is not enough that we should worship and pay our homage to a loving God. That does not satisfy the love of God. Nothing short of living, loving, holy, habitual communion between His holy soul and ours can realise at last the end which God achieved in Jesus Christ.

P. T. Forsyth (1848–1921)

December

1st December

The sting of death is sin and the power of sin is the law. But thanks be to God! He gives us the victory through our Lord Jesus Christ.
(1 Corinthians 15:56–7)

A man may die greatly; his death may be a triumph; nothing in his life may become him like the leaving of it. But . . . death remains the last enemy. There is something in it monstrous and alien to the spirit, something which baffles the moral intelligence, till the truth dawns upon us that for all our race sin and death are aspects of one thing. If we separate them, we understand neither; nor do we understand the solemn greatness of martyrdom itself if we regard it as a triumph only, and eliminate from the death which martyrs die all sense of the universal relation in humanity of death and sin.

No one knew the spirit of the martyr more thoroughly than St Paul. No one could speak more confidently and triumphantly of death than he. No one knew better how to turn the passion into action, the endurance into a great spiritual achievement. But also, no one knew better than he, in consistency with all this, that sin and death are needed for the interpretation of each other, and that fundamentally, in the experience of the race, they constitute one whole.

Even when he cried, "O death, where is thy sting?" he was

conscious that "the sting of death is sin". Each, so to speak, had its reality in the other. No one could vanquish death who had not vanquished sin. No one could know what sin meant without tasting death. These were not mythological fancies in St Paul's mind, but the conviction in which Christian conscience experimentally lived and moved and had its being. And these convictions, I repeat, furnish the point of view from which we must appreciate the Atonement, namely the truth that forgiveness, as Christianity preaches it, is specifically mediated through Christ's death.

James Denney (1856–1917)

2nd December

Timothy, guard what has been entrusted to your care. Turn away from godless chatter and the opposing ideas of what is falsely called knowledge, which some have professed and in so doing have wandered from the faith.

(1 Timothy 6:20–21)

When we once return to the ancient simplicity of faith, then, and not till then, shall we return to the ancient love and peace. I would recommend then to all my brethren, as the most necessary thing to the Church's peace, that they unite in necessary truths, and bear with one another in things that may be borne with; and do not make a larger creed and more necessaries than God hath done. To that end, let me interest you to attend to the following things.

1. Lay not too great a stress upon controverted opinions, which have godly men, and, especially whole Churches, on both sides.

2. Lay not too great a stress on those controversies that are ultimately resolvable into philosophical uncertainties, as are some unprofitable controversies about free will, the manner of the Spirit's operations, and the Divine decrees.

3. Lay not too great a stress on those controversies that are merely verbal, and which if they were anatomised, would appear to be no more. Of this sort are far more (I speak it confidently upon certain knowledge) that make a great noise in the world and tear

the Church, than almost any of the eager contenders that ever I spoke with do seem to discern, or are like to believe.

4. Lay not too much stress on any point of faith which was disowned by or unknown to the whole Church of Christ, in any age since the Scriptures were delivered to us.

5. Much less should you lay great stress on those of which any of the more pure and judicious ages were wholly ignorant.

6. And least of all should you lay much stress on any point which no one age since the apostles did ever receive, but all held commonly to the contrary.

He that shall live to that happy time when God will heal His broken Churches, will see all that I am pleading for reduced to practice, and this moderation take place of the new-dividing zeal, and the doctrine of the sufficiency of Scripture established; and all men's confessions and comments valued only as subservient helps, and not made the test of church communion, any further than they are the same with Scripture. Till, however the healing age come, we cannot expect that healing truths will be entertained, because there are not healing spirits in the leaders of the church. But when the work is done, the workmen will be fitted for it; and blessed will be agents of so glorious a work.

Richard Baxter (1615–91)

3rd December

The earth is the Lord's, and everything in it, the world, and all who live in it.

(Psalm 24:1)

Prayer is for the religious life what original research is for science – by it we get direct contact with reality . . . Let us nurse our prayer on our *study* of our Bible; and let us not be too afraid of *theological* prayer. True Christian prayer must have theology in it; no less than true theology must have prayer in it and must be capable of being prayed. "Your theology is too difficult." said Charles V to the Reformers; "it cannot be understood without much prayer."

Yes, that is our arduous puritan way. Prayer and theology must interpenetrate to keep each other great, and wide and mighty. The failure of the habit of prayer is at the root of much of our light distaste for theology. There is a conspiracy of influences around us whose effect is to belittle our great work. Earnest ministers suffer more from the smallness of their people than from their sins, and far more from their unkindness. Our public may kill by its triviality a soul which could easily resist the assaults of opposition or wickedness. And our newspapers greatly aid their work.

Now to resist this it is not enough to have recourse to prayer and to cultivate devotion. Unfortunately there are signs in the religious world to show that prayer and piety alone do not save men from pettiness of interest, thinness of soul, spiritual volatility, the note of insincerity, or of foolishness, or of judgement, or even vindictiveness. The remedy is not prayer alone, but prayer on the scale of the whole gospel and at the depth of searching faith. It is considered prayer – prayer which rises above the childish petitions that disfigure much of public pietism, prayer which issues from the central affairs of the kingdom of God. It is prayer with the profound Bible as its book of devotion, and a true theology of faith for half of its power. It is the prayer of a mind that moves in Bible passion and ranges with Bible scope, even when it eschews Bible speech and "the language of Canaan".

P. T. Forsyth (1848–1921)

4th December

All over the world this gospel is bearing fruit and growing, just as it has been doing among you since the day you heard it and understood God's grace in all its truth.

(Colossians 1:6)

I believe that the effect of religious and other instruction is hardly to be calculated on; and I may further say, that not withstanding the high estimation and reverence in which I held the Holy Scripture before I went to the prisons, as believing them to be written by the inspiration of God, and therefore calculated to produce the greatest good; I have seen (in reading the scriptures to those women) such a power attending them, and such an effort on the minds of the most reprobate, as I could not have conceived.

If anyone wants a confirmation of the truth of Christianity, let him go and read the scriptures in prisons to poor sinners; you there see, how the gospel is exactly adapted to the fallen condition of man. It has strongly confirmed my faith, and I feel it to be, the bounden duty of the Government and the country, that these truths should be administered in the manner most likely to conduce to the real reformation of the prisoner; you then go to the root of the matter; – for though severe punishment may in a measure deter them and others from crime, it does not amend the character and change the heart, but if you have really altered the principles of individuals they are not only deterred from crime, because of the fear of punishment, but they go out and set a bright example to others.

Elizabeth Fry (1780–1845)

5th December

Now Ahab told Jezebel everything Elijah had done and how he had killed all the prophets with the sword. So Jezebel sent a message to Elijah to say, "May the gods deal with me, be it ever so severely, if by this time tomorrow I do not make your life like one of them." Elijah was afraid and ran for his life.

(1 Kings 19:1–3)

It is noteworthy that the Bible saints often fail just where we should have expected them to stand. Abraham was the father of those who believe; but his faith failed him when he went down to Egypt, and lied to Pharaoh about his wife. Moses was the meekest of men; but he missed Canaan, because he spoke unadvisedly with his lips. John was the apostle of love; yet in a moment of intolerance, he wished to call down fire from heaven. So Elijah, who might have been supposed to be superior to all human weakness, shows himself to be indeed "a man of like passions with ourselves".

The old castle which from its hill watches over the town of Edinburgh, clustering beneath, was captured only once in the whole history of Scotland; and its capture happened thus. Its defenders thought that, on one side, the steepness of the rock made it inaccessible and impregnable; and they put no sentries there. And so, in the grey mist of the early morning, a little party crept up the precipitous slopes and surprised the garrison into surrender.

Is there not a warning here for us all? It may be that some have been saying boastfully of certain forms of vice, "I shall never yield to this or that. I have no inclination to such forms of sin. This is one of the points in which I am strong to resist." Beware! – it may be that the great enemy of souls has a special design in producing in you a false sense of security; that he may assail and vanquish you in the very point in which you deem yourself impregnable, and so forebare to watch.

What proof is here of the veracity of the Bible! Had it been merely a human composition, its authors would have shrunk from delineating the failure of one of its chief heroes. No artist would think of snapping a column, just as it was tapering to its coronal. Men sometimes complain against the Bible for its uncompromising portraitures. Yet, is this not its glory? It holds the mirror up to human nature, that we might learn what is in man; that we may none of us despair; that we may infer that, if God were able to fashion His choicest ware out of such common earth, it is possible for Him to do as much again, in the most ignorant and degraded of His children.

F. B. Meyer (1847–1929)

6th December

God had planned something better for us, so that only together with us would they be made perfect.

(Hebrews 11:40)

Through one weary century after another, the patriarchs and prophets had waited for the kingdom of God, and their faith had been equal to the prolonged strain. For them there was no real sacrifice for sin. Their access to the Divine presence was imperfect. The spiritual powers by which their holiness was sustained was comparatively feeble. Their knowledge of God was very limited. The great promises on which their hearts rested, began to be fulfilled only at the coming of the Lord Jesus. We might also say that they had nothing in actual possession; that for them everything lay in an indefinite future. It was not so with those to whom this Epistle [Hebrews] was written: it is not so with us.

The Messiah, for whom former ages hoped, has come. The kingdom of heaven has been established. The atonement for sin has been effected. In the person of Christ our nature has been united for ever with the nature of God. We ourselves have become one with Him, and have become temples of the Holy Ghost. Instead of having to rely on an unfulfilled promise, we have begun to thank God that the mystery and wealth of the Divine Word have begun to be unfolded. The process of fulfilment has commenced and is moving forward day by day. What was a matter of simple faith in other ages, is a matter of knowledge and of consciousness to ourselves.

R. W. Dale (1829–95)

7th December

This Ezra came up from Babylon. He was a teacher well versed in the Law of Moses which the Lord, the God of Israel, had given.
(Ezra 7:6)

In the words of the 45th Psalm, Ezra's was already the "pen of a ready writer". By his high birth Ezra was by office a priest; when he cared to do it he could trace his unbroken and unblemished descent back to Aaron himself. But what of that, when there was neither temple, nor altar, nor mercy-seat, nor anything else of all the temple apparatus in Babylon. And had Ezra not discovered other and better work for himself; had Ezra not adapted himself to new circumstances, and fitted himself into his new world, his would have been an idle and a lost and an embittered life in Babylon. But Ezra had the humility and the insight, the genius and the grace, to see that the future seat of spiritual worship, and the true source of spiritual life on earth was not to be a building any more but a book.

Ages and ages before books became what they now are, Ezra was a believer in books, and in the Book of books.

You who make a truly evangelical use of your Bible, and thus have a truly evangelical and a truly intelligent love for your Bible, must not forget what you owe to Ezra; for it was in Babylon, and it was under Ezra's so scholarly and so spiritual hands, that your Bible first began to take on its shape and solidarity. When all other priests and Levites were moping about, not knowing what to do with themselves because they had no traditional altar at which to minister, Ezra struck out a new kind of priesthood and ministry in Israel which has outlasted all the temples and priesthoods in Israel, and which will last till the end of time.

Alexander Whyte (1836–1921)

8th December

But God's word is not chained.

(2 Timothy 2:9b)

There was a great struggle to obtain a proper place for the great works achieved by the Bible Society. There was no difficulty whatever in obtaining abundant space for all the implements of war and of human destruction that the mind of man could imagine; a large proportion of the [Great] Exhibition [of 1851] was taken up with guns, cannons, torpedoes, everything that could annoy and desolate mankind. It was suggested that we should erect for the Bible Society, some place in the great Exhibition where we could show proofs of all that we had done to the praise of God, and all that we were capable of doing; some, however, said we had no right to appear before the public in any form in the Exhibition.

I had a long interview with his Royal Highness the Prince Consort on the subject, and he took the view that the Bible Society had no right to a position there. I said, "Putting aside the religious aspect of the question, I will put it before you from an intellectual point of view. I ask you whether it is not a wonderful proof of intellectual power that the Word of God had been translated into 170 distinct languages, and into 230 dialects? Is it not proof of great intellectual power that the agents of the Bible Society have given a written character to upwards of thirty distinct languages, enabling the people to read the Word of God in their own tongue? He said, "You have proved your right to appear; it is a great intellectual effort, and I will do my best to secure for the Society such a position that their deeds shall be made known."

Lord Shaftesbury (1801–85)

9th December

Christ died for our sins according to the Scriptures.
(1 Corinthians 15:3b)

Instead of depriving His death of the peculiar significance Scripture assigns to it, and making it no more than the termination, or at least the consummation of His life, I should rather argue that the Scriptural emphasis is right, and that His life attains its true interpretation only as we find in it everywhere the power and purpose of His death.

There is nothing artificial or unnatural in this. There are plenty of people who never have death out of their minds an hour at a time. They are not cowards, nor mad, nor even sombre: they may have purposes and hopes and gaieties as well as others; but they see life steadily, and see it whole, of all their thoughts the one which has the most determining and omnipresent power is the thought of the inevitable end. There is death in all their life.

It was not, certainly, as the invisible end, the inevitable "debt of nature", that death was present to the mind of Christ; but if we can trust the evangelists at all, from the hour of His baptism it was present to His mind as something involved in His vocation; and it was a presence so tremendous that it absorbed everything into itself. "I have a baptism to be baptised with, and how I am straitened till it be accomplished."

Instead of saying that Christ's life as well as His death contributed to the Atonement ... we should rather say that His life is part of His death: a deliberate and conscious descent, ever deeper and deeper, into the dark valley where at the last hour the last reality of sin was to be met and borne. And if the objection is made that after all this only means that death is the most vital point of life, its intensest focus, I should not wish to make reply. Our Lord's Passion *is* His sublimest action – an action so potent that all His other actions are sublated to it, and we know everything when we know that He *died* for our sins.

James Denney (1856–1917)

10th December

Samson led Israel for twenty years in the days of the Philistines.
(Judges 15:20)

Samson's tragical story has been treated in three ways. Some commentators on the Book of Judges have treated the story of Samson as an excellent piece of Hebrew folklore. They have collected out of all the ancient books of the world wonderful tales of giants, and heroes, and demigods, with their astonishing feats of strength in war, and in love, and in jealousy and revenge: feats more or less like the feats of strength and of revenge we have in Samson. They have produced remarkable parallels to Samson's exploits out of Atlas and Cyclops, Hercules and Odin, and many suchlike mythological characters. And then their work on Samson has been done when they have illustrated his history with romances and legends of sufficient likeness and richness.

Some evangelical preachers, again, have gone to the opposite extreme, and have displayed Samson to us solely as a type and pattern of Jesus Christ. They have selected texts out of Samson's extraordinary history, and they have suspended excellent New Testament sermons on these adapted texts; hanging great weights on small wires. The former is the mythological way of dealing with Samson's history; the latter is the mystical way. But there is a third way. And the third way is the way that Paul takes, not only with Samson, but with all the patriarchs, and judges, and great men of Old Testament times. We have this apostle's way with all those men and women set before us again and again in his own conclusive words: "For whatever things were written aforetime were written for our learning, that we through patience and comfort of the Scriptures might have hope." And again, "All Scripture is given by inspiration of God, and is profitable for doctrine, for reproof, for correction, for instruction in righteousness." And again, "Now, all these things happened to them for examples, and they are written for our admonition, upon whom the ends of the world are come. Wherefore let him that thinketh he standeth take heed lest he fall."

Alexander Whyte (1836–1921)

11th December

But after me will come one who is more powerful than I, whose sandals I am not fit to carry.

(Matthew 3:11)

It would startle some earnest evangelists if they knew how much of their testimony was about themselves. There is sometimes a suspicion of spiritual pride in it, too. "I *was* this; I AM that." "I *did* this; I DO that." It is fine, of course, to illustrate the difference which Christ has made, but talk of self should be the undertone and the stress should fall on Him.

The Hall where I preach is opposite Westminster Abbey and I often step in. I love to linger in Poets' Corner. Not everything in Poets' Corner is admirable, and I will confess a particular dislike for the memorial to John Milton.

It runs like this:

In the year of Our Lord Christ
One thousand seven hundred thirty and seven
This Bust
of the Author of PARADISE LOST
was placed here by William Benson Esquire
One of the two Auditors of the Imprest
to his Majesty King George the second
formerly
Surveyor General of the Works
to his Majesty King George the first.

Rysback
was the Statuary who cut it.

When my eye first fell on that memorial, I read it twice. "Who is it all about?" I asked myself in bewilderment.

Then I got it. It is all about William Benson. He put up the memorial as a device to get his own unimportant name noticed. Milton is merely the excuse; the stress falls on himself. He has discovered a new way of blowing his own trumpet. He was using the name of the Puritan poet to parade himself before the public eye, and he gets into the Abbey – not by his own distinction, for he had none – but by misusing the name of a very great man.

And that soiled artifice has come to my mind many times when listening to some evangelists. One has wanted to cry aloud, "Less of self and more of Christ."

Here is the rule: Seven words of Him for every word about yourself.

W. E. Sangster (1900–1960)

12th December

How, then, can they call on the one they have not believed in? And how can they believe in the one of whom they have not heard? And how can they hear without someone preaching to them? And how can they preach unless they are sent? As it is written, "How beautiful are the feet of those who bring good news!"

(Romans 10:14–15)

Preaching is the communication of truth by man to men. It has two essential elements, truth and personality. Neither of these can it spare and still be preaching. The truest truth, the most authoritative statement of God's will, communicated in any other way than through the personality of brother man to men is not preached truth. Suppose it written on the sky, suppose it embodied in a book which has been so long held in reverence as the direct utterance of God that the vivid personality of the men who wrote its pages has well nigh faded out of it; in neither of these cases is there any preaching. And on the other hand, if men speak to other men that which they do not claim for truth, if they use their powers of persuasion or of entertainment to make other men listen to their speculations, or do their will, or applaud their cleverness, that is not preaching either. The first lacks personality. The second lacks truth.

And preaching is the bringing of truth through personality. It must have both elements. It is the different proportion in which the two are mingled that the difference between two great classes of sermons and preaching lies. It is in the defect of one or other element that every sermon and preacher falls short of the perfect standard. It is in the absence of one or the other element that a discourse ceases to be a sermon, and a man ceases to be a preacher altogether.

If we go back to the beginning of the Christian ministry we can see how distinctly and deliberately Jesus chose this method of extending the knowledge of Himself throughout the world. Other methods were no doubt open to Him, but he deliberately selected this. He taught His truth to a few men and then He said, "Now go and tell that truth to other men."

Both elements were there, in John the Baptist who prepared the way for Him, in the seventy whom He sent out before His face, and in the little company who started from the chamber of Pentecost to proclaim the new salvation to the world. If He gave them the power of working miracles, the miracles were not the final purpose for which he gave it. The power of miracle was, as it were, a divine fire pervading the Apostle's being and opening his individuality on either side; making it more open God-wards by the sense of awful privilege, making it more open man-wards by the impressiveness and the helpfulness with which it was clothed.

Phillips Brooks (1835–93)

13th December

Then Philip ran up to the chariot and heard the man reading Isaiah the prophet. "Do you understand what you are reading?" Philip asked.

(Acts 8:30)

All this took place in the primitive, simple, unsophisticated east, and we must not measure any part of this by our western habits of intercourse. It would be resented as the height of intrusion and incivility among us if one man were to say to another over his book on the deck of a steamer or in a railway carriage, "Are you understanding what you are reading?" But look at it in this way. Suppose you sat beside a foreigner who was struggling with one of our English guide books, and was evidently missing the sense, till he was starting off in a wrong direction; it would be no intrusion or impertinence if you made up to him and said to him something like this: "I fear our barbarous tongue is not easily mastered by foreign scholars, but it is my native language, and I may be able to be of some use to you in it." "How can I?" said the humble-minded eunuch, "except some man should guide me?"

Now we all think, because we know the letters of it, and are familiar with it, that we understand the Bible: Isaiah, and John, and Paul. But we never made a more fatal mistake. There is no book in the world that is so difficult to read, and to understand, and to love as the Bible. Not having begun to understand it, some of you will turn upon me and will tell me that even a little child can understand it. And you are perfectly right. "A lamb can wade it," said a great Greek expositor of it. But he went on to add that "an elephant can swim in it." And thus it was that, over and above the apostles, all the deacons of intellect and experience were drawn on to expound the Scriptures, first to the learned Council of Jerusalem, then to the sceptical men of Samaria, and then to the Ethiopian in his royal chariot.

And thus it is still that the Church collects into her colleges the very best minds she can lay hold of in all her families, and trains them under her very best teachers, and then says to them, "Go join thyself to this and that vacant pulpit, and make the people understand what they read."

Alexander Whyte (1836–1921)

14th December

And there were shepherds living out in the fields near by, keeping watch over their flocks at night. An angel of the Lord appeared to them, and the glory of the Lord shone around them, and they were terrified.

(Luke 2:8–9)

The angel spoke. The gospel was preached by an angel to Zacharias, to the virgin mother of MESSIAH, now to the Shepherds; and perhaps, to none but these. The angel, who appeared to Cornelius, said nothing to him of Jesus, but only directed him to send for Peter (Acts 10:4–5). The glorious gospel of the blessed God, with respect to its dignity and depth, and importance, may seem a fitter theme for the tongue of an angel than of a man; but, angels never sinned, and though they might proclaim its excellency, they could not from experience, speak of its efficacy. In this respect sinful worms are better qualified to preach to others, concerning him by whom they have, themselves, been healed and saved. Their weakness, likewise, is better suited to shew that the influence and success of the gospel is wholly owing to the power of God.

It has, therefore, pleased God "to put this treasure in earthen vessels", and to commit the ministry of his word, not to angels, but to men. They whom he is pleased to employ in this office, however weak and unworthy in themselves, derive honour and importance from the message entrusted to them, and are so far worthy of the same attention, as if an angel from heaven spoke. They are sinful men, and have reason to think humbly of themselves; nor should they, as the servants of a suffering, crucified Master, either wonder or complain if they meet with unkindness from those whom they wish to serve ...

What the world accounts in us "the foolishness of preaching", is made to those who receive it, "the power and the wisdom of God". To others, even angels would preach in vain. They "who hear not Moses and the prophets", who submit not to the ordinary methods and means of grace which God has appointed "would not be persuaded, though one should rise from the dead."

John Newton (1725–1807)

15th December

Watch your life and doctrine closely. Persevere in them, because if you do, you will save both yourself and your hearers.

(1 Timothy 4:16)

These are the elements in preaching, then – truth and personality. The truth is in itself a fixed and stable element; the personality is a varying and growing element. In the union of the two we have the provision for the combination of identity with variety, of stability with growth, in the preaching of the Gospel.

The truth which you are preaching is the same which your brother is preaching in the next pulpit, or in some missionary station on the other side of the globe. If it were not, you would get no strength from one another. You would not stand back to back against the enemy, sustaining one another as you do now. But the way in which you preach the truth is different, and each of you reaches some ears that would be deaf to the most persuasive tones of the other. The Gospel that you are preaching now is the same Gospel that you preached when you were first ordained, in that first sermon which was at once such a terror and a joy to preach, but if you have been a live man all the time, you are not preaching it now as you did then. If the truth had changed, your life would have lost its unity. The truth has not changed, but you have grown to fuller understanding of it, to a larger capacity of receiving and transmitting it. There is no pleasure in the minister's life stronger than this, – the perception of identity and progress in truth as he grows older. It is like a man's pleasure in watching the growth of his own body or his own mind, or of a tree that he has planted.

It is a common experience of ministers I suppose, to find that sentences in their old sermons which were written years ago contain meanings and views of truth which they hold now but which they never thought of in those early days. The truth was there, but the man had not appropriated it. The truth has not changed, but the man is more sufficient for it.

Phillips Brooks (1835–93)

16th December

And the word of the Lord came to him: "What are you doing here, Elijah?" He replied, "I have been very zealous for the Lord God Almighty. The Israelites have rejected your covenant, broken down your altars, and put the prophets to death with the sword. I am the only one left, and now they are trying to kill me too."

(1 Kings 19:9–10)

Elijah thought that he alone was left as a lover and worshipper of God. It was a great mistake. God had many hidden ones. "Yet I have left Me seven thousand in Israel, all the knees that have not bowed to Baal, and every mouth that hath not kissed him." We know nothing of their names or history. They were probably unknown in camp or court; obscure, simple-hearted, and humble. Their only testimony was one long refusal to the solicitations of the foul rites of idolatry. They groaned and wept in secret; and spake often to one another, while the Lord hearkened and heard. But they were all known to God; and enrolled among his jewels; and counted as a shepherd tells his sheep. He cared for them with an infinite solicitude; and it was for their sake that He raised up the good and gentle Elisha to carry on the nurture and discipline of their souls.

It has often been a subject of wonder to me how these seven thousand secret disciples could keep so close as to be unknown by their great leader. Otto of roses will always betray its presence, hide it as we may. When salt has lost its savour, it cannot be hid. And the work of God in human hearts must, sooner or later, discover itself. It is to be feared, therefore, that the godliness of those hidden ones was very vague and colourless, needing the eyes of omniscience to detect it. But for all that, God did detect it; and He prized it. He did not quench the smoking flax; but fanned it. He did not despise the grain of mustard-seed; He watched it grow with tender love and care.

You may be very weak and insignificant – not counted in the numbers of God's captains; not deemed worthy of a name or a place amongst His avowed servants; and yet, if you have but a spark of faith and love, if you strive to keep yourself untainted by the world, you will be owned by Him whose sceptre is stretched out to the most timid suppliant. But remember: if your inner life be genuine, it will not remain for ever secret – it will break out as a long hidden fire; it will force its way into the light as the buried seed in which there is the spark of life.

F. B. Meyer (1847–1929)

17th December

Then Jesus came to them and said, "All authority in heaven and on earth has been given to me. Therefore go and make disciples of all nations, baptising them in the name of the Father and of the Son and of the Holy Spirit, and teaching them to obey everything I have commanded you. And surely I am with you always, to the very end of the age.

(Matthew 28:18–20)

There seems to be an opinion existing in the minds of some, that because the apostles were extraordinary officers and have no proper successors, and because many things which were right for them to do would be unwarrantable for us, therefore it may not be immediately binding on us to execute the commission, though it was so upon them. To the consideration of such persons I would offer the following observations.

First. If the command of Christ to teach all nations be restricted to apostles, or those under the immediate inspiration of the Holy Ghost, then that of baptising should be so too; and every denomination of Christians, except the Quakers, do wrong in baptising with water at all.

Secondly. If the command of Christ to teach all nations be confined to the apostles, then all ordinary ministers who have endeavoured to carry the gospel to the heathens, have acted without a warrant, and run before they were sent. Yea, and though God has promised the most glorious things to the heathen world by sending his gospel to them, yet whoever goes first, or indeed at all, with that message, unless he have a new and special commission from heaven, must go without any authority for so doing.

Thirdly. If the command of Christ to teach all nations extend only to the apostles, then, doubtless, the promise of the divine presence in this work must be so limited; but this is worded in such a manner as expressly excludes such an idea: "Lo I am with you always, even to the end of the world."

William Carey (1761–1834)

18th December

While they were worshipping the Lord and fasting, the Holy Spirit said, "Set apart for me Barnabas and Saul for the work to which I have called them."

(Acts 13:2)

[Continued from yesterday.]

That there are cases in which even a divine command may cease to be binding is admitted – as for instance: if it be *repealed*, as the ceremonial commandments of the Jewish law; or if there be *no subjects* in the world for the commanded act to be exercised upon, as in the law of Septennial Release, which might be dispensed with when there should be no poor in the land to have their debts forgiven (Deuteronomy 15:4); or if in any particular instance, we can produce a *counter-revelation*, of equal authority with the original command, as when Paul and Silas were forbidden of the Holy Ghost to preach the word in Bithynia (Acts 16:6–7); or, if in any case, there be a *natural impossibility* of putting it into execution. It was not the duty of Paul to preach Christ to the inhabitants of Otaheite, because no such place was then discovered, nor had he any means of coming at them. But none of these things can be alleged by us in behalf of the neglect of the commission given by Christ.

We cannot say that it is repealed, like the commands of the ceremonial law; nor can we plead that there are no objects for the command to exercised upon. Alas! the far greater part of the world . . . is still covered with heathen darkness! Nor can we produce a counter-revelation, concerning any particular nation, like to that to Paul and Silas, concerning Bithynia (Acts 16:7); and if we could, it would not warrant our sitting still and neglecting all the other parts of the world. For Paul and Silas, when forbidden to preach to these heathens, went elsewhere, and preached to others.

Neither can we allege a natural impossibility in the case. It has been said that we ought not to force our way, but to wait for openings and leadings of providence; but it might with equal propriety be answered in this case, neither ought we to neglect those openings in providence which daily present themselves to us . . . Natural impossibility can never be pleaded so long as facts exist to prove the contrary. Have not the popish missionaries surmounted all these difficulties which we have generally thought insuperable? Have not the missionaries of the Unitas Fratrum, or Moravian Brethren, encountered the scorching heat of Abyssinia, and the frozen climes of Greenland and Labrador, their difficult languages and savage manners?

William Carey (1761–1834)

19th December

This gospel of the kingdom will be preached in the whole world as a testimony to all nations, and then the end will come.

(Matthew 24:14)

[Continued from yesterday.]

Or have not English traders, for the sake of gain, surmounted all those things which have generally been counted insurmountable obstacles in the way of preaching the gospel? Witness the trade to

Persia, the East Indies, China and Greenland, yea, even the accursed slave trade on the coasts of Africa. Men can insinuate themselves into the favour of the most barbarous clans, and uncultivated tribes for the sake of gain . . .

It has been said that some learned divines have proved from Scripture that the time has not yet come that the heathen should be converted, and that first the witnesses must be slain, and many other prophecies fulfilled. But admitting this to be the case (which I must doubt) yet if any objection is made from this against preaching to them immediately, it must be founded on one of these things: either that the secret purpose of God is the rule of our duty, and then it must be as bad to pray for them as to preach to them; or else that none shall be converted in the heathen world till the universal downpouring of the Spirit in the last days. But this objection comes too late; for the success of the gospel has been very considerable in many places already.

It has been objected that there are multitudes in our own nation, and within our immediate spheres of action, who are as ignorant as the South Sea savages, and that therefore we have work enough at home, without going into other countries. That there are thousands in our own land as far from God as possible, I readily grant, and that this ought to excite us to tenfold diligence in our work, and in attempts to spread divine knowledge amongst them, is a certain fact; but that it ought to supersede all attempts to spread the gospel in foreign parts seems to want proof. Our own countrymen have the means of grace, and many attend on the word preached if they choose it. They have the means of knowing the truth, and faithful ministers are placed in almost every part of the land, whose sphere of action might be much extended if their congregations were but more hearty and active in the cause. But with them the case is widely different, who have no Bible, no written language (which many of them have not), no ministers, no good civil government, nor any of these advantages which we have. Pity therefore, humanity, and much more Christianity, call loudly for every possible exertion to introduce the gospel amongst them.

William Carey (1761–1834)

20th December

Jesus went through all the towns and villages, teaching in their synagogues, preaching the good news of the kingdom and healing every disease and sickness. When he saw the crowds, he had compassion on them, because they were harassed and helpless, like sheep without a shepherd. Then he said to his disciples, "The harvest is plentiful but the workers are few. Ask the Lord of the harvest, therefore, to send out workers into his harvest field."

(Matthew 9:35–8)

At the invitation of my beloved and honoured friend, Mr George Pearse (then of the Stock Exchange), I went to spend a few days with him in Brighton.

On Sunday, June 25th, 1865, unable to bear the sight of a congregation of a thousand or more Christian people rejoicing in their own security, while millions [of China] were perishing for lack of knowledge, I wandered out onto the sands alone, in great spiritual agony; and there the Lord conquered my unbelief, and I surrendered myself to God for this service. I told Him that all responsibility as to issues and consequences must rest with Him; that as His servant it was mine to obey and to follow Him – His, to direct, to care for, and to guide me and those who might labour with me. Need I say that peace at once flowed into my burdened heart? There and then I asked Him for twenty four fellow workers, two for each of eleven inland provinces which were without a missionary, and two for Mongolia; and writing the petition on the margin of the Bible which I had with me, I returned home with a heart enjoying rest such as it had been a stranger to for months, and with an assurance that the Lord would bless His own work and that I should share in the blessing. I had previously prayed and asked prayer that workers might be raised up for the eleven then unoccupied provinces, and thrust forth and provided for, but had not surrendered myself to be their leader.

James Hudson Taylor (1832–1905)

21st December

But when the time had fully come, God sent his Son, born of a woman, born under law, to redeem those under law, that we might receive the full rights of sons.

(Galatians 4:4–5)

For what man, that ever was, formed a body for himself from a virgin alone? Or what man ever healed so many diseases as the common Lord of all? Or who has restored what was wanting to man's nature, and made one blind from his birth to see? Asclepius was deified among them because he practised medicine and found out herbs for bodies that were sick; not forming them himself out of the earth, but discovering them by science drawn from nature. But what is this to what was done by the Saviour, in that, instead of healing a wound, he modified a man's original nature, and restored the body whole? Heracles is worshipped as a god among the Greeks because he fought against men his peers, and destroyed wild beasts by guile. What is this to what was done by the Word, in driving away from man diseases and demons and death itself? Dionysus is worshipped among them because he has taught man drunkenness; but the true Saviour and Lord of all, for teaching temperance, is mocked by these people. But let these matters pass.

What will they say to the other miracles of his Godhead? At what man's death was the sun darkened and the earth shaken? Lo even to this day men are dying, and they died also before then. When did any such like wonder happen in their case? Or, to pass over the deeds done through the body, and mention those after its rising again; what man's doctrine that ever was has prevailed everywhere, one and the same, from one end of the earth to the other, so that his worship has flown through every land? Or why, if Christ is, as they say, a man, and not God the Word, is not his worship prevented by the gods they have from passing into the same land where they are? Or why, on the contrary, does the Word himself, sojourning here, by his teaching stop their worship and put their deception to shame?

Athanasius (c. 296–373)

22nd December

My frame was not hidden from you when I was made in the secret place. When I was woven together in depths of the earth, your eyes saw my unformed body. All the days ordained for me were written in your book before one of them came to be.

(Psalm 139:15–16)

Every man is to consider himself as a particular object of God's providence; under the same prayer and protection of God as if the world had been made for him alone. It is not by chance that any man is born at such a time, of such parents, and in such a place and condition. It is as certain that every soul coming into the body at such a time, and in such circumstances, by the express designment of God, according to some purposes of His will, and for some particular ends; that is as certain as that it is by the express designment of God that some beings are Angels, and others are men.

It is as much by the counsel and eternal purpose of God that you should be born in your particular state, and that Isaac should be born the son of Abraham, as that Gabriel should be an Angel, and Isaac a man.

The Scriptures assure us, that it was by divine appointment that our blessed Saviour was born at Bethlehem, and at such a time. Now although it was owing to the dignity of his person, and the great importance of His birth, that thus much of the Divine counsel was declared to the world, concerning the time and manner of it; yet we are sure, from the same Scriptures that the time and manner of every man's coming into the world is according to some eternal purpose and direction of Divine providence, and in such time and place and circumstances, as are directed by God for particular ends of His wisdom and goodness.

This we are certain of, from plain revelation, as we can be of anything. For if we are told that not a sparrow falleth to the ground without our heavenly Father; can anything more strongly teach us, that much greater beings, such as human souls, come not into the world without the care and direction of our heavenly Father?

William Law (1686–1761)

23rd December

The angel answered, "The Holy Spirit will come upon you, and the power of the Most High will overshadow you. So the holy one to be born will be called the Son of God. Even Elizabeth your relative is going to have a child in her old age, and she who was said to be barren is in her sixth month. For nothing is impossible with God."

(Luke 1:35–7)

Let us be glad. For there is no proper place for sadness, when we keep the birthday of the Life, which destroys the fear of mortality and brings us to the joy of promised eternity. No one is kept from sharing in this happiness. There is for all one common measure of joy, because as our Lord the destroyer of sin and death finds none free from charge, so is He come to free us all. Let the saint exult that he draws near to victory. Let the sinner be glad that he is invited to pardon. Let the gentile take courage in that he is called to life.

For the Son of God in the fulness of time which the inscrutable depth of the Divine counsel has determined, had taken on him the nature of man, thereby to reconcile it to its Author: in order that the inventor of death, the devil, might be conquered through that (nature) which he had conquered. And in this conflict undertaken for us, the fight was fought on great and wondrous principles of fairness; for the Almighty Lord enters the lists with His savage foe, not in His own majesty but in our humility, opposing him with the same form and the same nature, which shares our mortality, though it be free from all sin . . .

A royal Virgin of the stem of David is chosen, to be impregnated with the divine seed and to conceive the Divinely-human offspring in mind first and then body. And lest in ignorance of the heavenly counsel she should tremble at so strange result, she learns from converse with the angel that what is wrought in her is of the Holy Ghost. Nor does she believe it to be loss of honour that she is soon to the Mother of God.

For why should she despair over the novelty of such conception, to whom the power of the most High has promised to effect it? Her implicit faith is confirmed also by the attestation of a precursory miracle, and Elizabeth receives unexpected fertility: in order that there may be no doubt that He who had given conception to the barren, would give it even to a virgin.

Leo the Great (400–461)

24th December

For the law was given through Moses; grace and truth came through Jesus Christ.

(John 1:17)

We admit the incarnation was a mystery, looked at from a human standpoint, but no greater mystery than many other incarnations taking place all around us, and because a mystery, none the less a necessity. Humanity must have a deliverer *able to save*, and no less than the Almighty deliverer was equal to the task. Here all merely human deliverers, all philosophers and teachers of the world, had failed, because they could only teach, they could not *renew*. They could set up a standard, enunciate a doctrine, but they could not remove man's inability, or endure him with power to reach it. Here even the law of God failed, and that which was ordained to life wrought death. Here was the sunken rock, the bitter maddening failure of all systems and deliverers – they failed to *rectify the heart*; they could not give a new life or impart another spirit . . .

Man needed some being outside of himself, above him, and yet able to understand and pity him in his utmost guilt and misery, and helplessness – able to inspire him with a *new life*, to impart light, love, strength, and endurance, and to do this always, and everywhere, in every hour of darkness, temptation and danger. Humanity needed an exhibition of God, not merely to be told about Him, but to *see* Him; not merely to know that He was an Almighty Creator able to crush him, but that He is a pitiful Father, yearning and waiting to save him.

God's expedient for showing this to man was to come in the flesh. Can the wisest modern philosopher or the most benevolent philanthropist conceive better? How otherwise could God have revealed himself to fallen man? Since the fall man has proved himself incapable of seeing or knowing God; he has ever been afraid of the heavenly, running away from an angel; and when only hearing a voice and seeing the smoke which hid the divinity, he exceedingly feared and quaked, and begged not to hear that voice again (Hebrews 12:18–21). Truly, no man as he is by nature can see God and live. Seeing then, that God desired that man should see Him – that is, know Him – and live, notwithstanding the fall, He promised a Saviour, who should reveal Him all the holiness and benevolence of His character, and in His plenitude of power to save!

Catherine Booth (1829–90)

25th December

Today in the town of David a Saviour has been born to you; he is Christ the Lord.

(Luke 2:11)

Lo! dear friends, today, as it were, an angel is saying to the shepherds: *I bring you good tidings of great joy that shall be to all people.* And suddenly a multitude of angels breaks into praise, saying: *Glory to God in the highest, and on earth peace to men of goodwill*!

As you commemorate these things, dear friends, rejoice that today God is born a man, that there may be glory to God in the highest and on earth peace to men of goodwill. Rejoice that today the infinitely Mighty is born a child, that there may be glory to God in the highest, etc. Rejoice that today a Reconciler is born to reconcile man to God, that there may be glory to God in the highest, etc. Rejoice that today he is born to cleanse sinners from their sin, to deliver them from the devil's power, to save them from eternal perdition, and to bring them to eternal joy, that there may be glory to God in the highest, etc. Rejoice with great joy that today is born unto us a King, to bestow in its fulness upon us the heavenly kingdom, a Bishop to grant His eternal benediction, a Father of the ages to come, to keep us as His children by His side for ever: yea, there is born a Brother beloved, a wise Master, a sure Leader, a just Judge, to the end that there may be glory to God in the highest, etc. Rejoice, ye wicked, that God is born as a Priest, Who hath granted to every penitent absolution from all sins, that there may be glory, etc. Rejoice that today the Bread of Angels – that is, God – is made the Bread of men to revive the starving with His Body, that there may be peace among them, and on earth, etc. Rejoice that God immortal is born, that mortal man may live for ever. Rejoice that the rich Lord of the Universe lies in a manger, like a poor man, that he may make us rich. Rejoice dearly beloved, that what the prophets prophesied has been fulfilled, that there may be glory to God in the Highest, etc. Rejoice that there is born to us a Child all-powerful, and that a Son is given to us, all-wise and gracious, that there may be glory to God in the highest, etc. Oh, dear friends ought there to be but a moderate rejoicing over these things? Nay, a mighty joy! Indeed, the angel saith: *I bring you good tidings of great joy*, for that there is born a Redeemer from all misery, a Saviour of sinners, a Governor of His faithful ones; there is born a Comforter of the sorrowful, and there is given to us the Son of God that we may have great joy, and that there may be glory to God in the highest and on earth peace to men of goodwill. May it please God, born this day, to grant to us this goodwill, this peace, and withal this joy!

Jan Hus (1373–1415)

26th December

He sent them to Bethlehem and said, "Go and make a careful search for the child. As soon as you find him, report to me, so that I too may go and worship him."

(Matthew 2:8)

The day, dearly-beloved on which Christ the Saviour of the world first appeared to the nations must be venerated by us with holy worship. Today those joys must be entertained in our hearts which existed in the breasts of the three magi, when, aroused by the sight and leading of a new star, which they believed to have been promised, they fell down in the presence of the King of heaven and earth. For that day has not so passed away that the mighty work, which was then revealed, has passed away with it, and that nothing but the report of the thing has come down to us for faith to receive and memory to celebrate.

By the oft-repeated gift of God, our times daily enjoy the fruit of what the first age possessed. Although the narrative which is read to us from the Gospel properly records those days on which the three men who had neither been taught by the prophets' predictions nor instructed by the testimony of the law, came to acknowledge God from the furthest parts of the East, yet we behold this same thing more clearly and abundantly carried on now in the enlightenment of all those who are called.

The prophecy of Isaiah is fulfilled. He says, "The Lord has laid bare His holy arm in the sight of all the nations, and all the nations upon earth have seen the salvation which is from the Lord our God"; and again, "and those to whom it has not been announced about Him shall understand". When we see men devoted to worldly wisdom and far from belief in Jesus Christ brought out of the depth of their error and called to an acknowledgement of the true Light, it is undoubtedly the brightness of the Divine grace that is at work.

Whatever of new light illumines the darkness of their hearts, comes from the rays of the same star: so that it should both move with wonder, and going before led to the adoration of God the minds which it visited with its splendour. But if with careful thought we wish to see how their threefold kind of gift is also offered by all who come to Christ with the foot of faith, is not the same offering repeated in the hearts of true believers?

He that acknowledges Christ the King of the Universe brings gold from the treasure of his heart: he that believes the Only-begotten of God to have united man's true nature to Himself, offers myrrh; and he that confesses Him in no wise inferior to the Father's majesty, worships Him in a manner with incense.

Leo the Great (c. 400–461)

27th December

When they saw the star, they were overjoyed. On coming to the house, they saw the child with his mother Mary, and they bowed down and worshipped him. Then they opened their treasures and presented him with gifts of gold and of incense and of myrrh.

(Matthew 2:10–11)

What was it that induced them to worship? For neither was the Virgin conspicuous, nor the house distinguished, nor was any of the things they saw apt to amaze or attract them. Yet they not only worship, but also *open their treasures* and *offer gifts*; and gifts, not as to a man, but as to God. For the frankincense and myrrh were a symbol of this.

What then was their inducement? That which wrought upon them to set out from home, and to come on so long a journey; and this was both the star and the illumination wrought of God in their mind, guiding them by little and little to the more perfect knowledge. For surely, had it not been so, all that was in sight being ordinary, they would not have shewn so great honour.

Therefore none of the outward circumstances was great in that instance, but it was a manger, and a shed, and a Mother in poor estate; to set before thine eyes, naked and bare, those Wise-men's love of Wisdom, to prove to thee, that not as a mere man they approached Him, but as a God and Benefactor. Wherefore neither were they offended by ought of what they saw outwardly but even worshipped, and brought gifts; gifts not only free from Judaical grossness, in that they sacrificed not sheep and calves, but also coming nigh to the self-devotion of the Church, for it was knowledge and obedience and love they offered Him.

John Chrysostom (c. 344/345–407)

28th December

Instead, they were longing for a better country – a heavenly one. Therefore God is not ashamed to be called their God, for he has prepared a city for them.

(Hebrews 11:16)

If heaven is such a blessed world, then let it be our chosen country, and the inheritance that we look for and seek. Let us turn our course this way, and press on to its possession. It is not impossible but that this glorious world may be obtained by us. It is offered to us. Though it be so excellent and blessed a country, yet God stands ready to give us an inheritance there, if it be but the country that we desire, and will choose and diligently seek.

God gives us our choice. We may have our inheritance wherever we choose it, and obtain heaven if we will but seek it by patient continuation in well-doing. We are all of us, as it were, set here in this world as in a vast great wilderness, with diverse countries about it and we are left to our choice what course we will take. If we heartily choose heaven, and set our hearts entirely on that blessed Canaan – that land of love, and if we choose and love the path that leads to it, we may walk in that path; and if we continue to walk in it, it will lead us to heaven at last.

Let what we have heard of the land of love stir us all up to turn our faces toward it, and bend our course thitherward. Is not what we have heard of the happy state of that country, and the many delights that are in it, enough to make us thirst after it, and to cause us, with the greatest earnestness and steadfastness of resolution, to press towards it, and spend our whole lives in travelling in the way that leads thither? What joyful news might it well be to us when we hear of such a world of perfect peace and holy love, and to hear that it is possible, yea, there is full opportunity, for us to come to it, and spend an eternity in its joys!

Jonathan Edwards (1703–58)

29th December

May the God of peace, who through the blood of the eternal covenant brought back from the dead our Lord Jesus, that great Shepherd of the sheep, equip you with everything good for doing his will, and may he work in us what is pleasing to him, through Jesus Christ, to whom be glory for ever and ever. Amen.

(Hebrews 13:20–21)

From this Epistle we have seen reason to infer, that many of the Jewish Christians had sunk into a condition in which it was impossible for them, without passing through a great change, to do the will of God. Their thoughts about their ancient faith and about the Lord Jesus Christ needed re-adjustment. Human passions and spiritual affections were not rightly balanced. Their loyalty to Christ was overborne by their natural sympathy with the patriotic enthusiasm of their countrymen, and by the natural veneration for the institutions and traditions of their fathers. Their dread of present shame and suffering had greater influence than their faith in the Divine promises. The merciful and mighty influence of the Holy Ghost was needed to restore order and harmony, to suppress and subdue the passions which had usurped undue power, and to strengthen principles and convictions which had become too feeble.

Just as a machine which has got out of order must be set right, before it can work easily and well; just as a ship must be equipped and fitted up, before it can safely commence its voyage; so it was necessary that these Jewish Christians should have their whole nature re-organised before their Christian life can be vigorous or happy. The prayer is, that the re-organisation should be such as to make them ready for "every good work"...

This is a prayer which we should offer for ourselves, and offer with confidence in God's willingness to listen to us. If we are to be made ready, or perfectly equipped, for a holy life, we must receive from God a large variety of blessings. Our habits of thought, perhaps, must be greatly modified. There is no necessity that we should receive clearer light on the transitory character of those ritualistic institutions which exerted a fatal power over the hearts of the

Jewish Christians; but we may need clearer light on the transitory character of all earthly things, a brighter vision of the eternal world, a more vivid apprehension of the reality of the Divine anger and the Divine approbation, of the rapid approach of death and judgement, of the glory and the terror which lie beyond.

R. W. Dale (1829–95)

30th December

Early in the morning Joshua and all the Israelites set out from Shittim and went to the Jordan, where they camped before crossing over. After three days the officers went throughout the camp, giving orders to the people: "When you see the ark of the covenant of the Lord your God, and the priests, who are Levites, carrying it, you are to move out from your positions and follow it. Then you will know which way to go, since you have never been this way before."
(Joshua 3:1–4a)

The poetry of all growing life consists in carrying an oldness into a newness, a past into a future, always. So only can our days possibly be bound "each to each by natural piety". I would not for the world think that twenty years hence I should have ceased to see the things which I see now, and love them still. It would make life wearisome beyond expression if I thought that twenty years hence I should see them just as I see them now, and love them with no deeper love because of other visions of their lovableness. And so there comes this deep and simple rule for a man as he crosses the line dividing one period of his life from another, the same rule which he may use also as he passes through any critical occurrence of his life: Make it a time in which you shall realise your faith and also in which you shall expect of your faith new and greater things. Take what you believe and are and hold it in your hand with new firmness as you go forward; but as you go, holding it look on it with continual and confident expectation to see it open into something greater and truer.

No doubt there is something which every critical change in the circumstances of life, or a change from one period of life to another, gives us the chance to cast away and leave behind. No doubt the Israelites left in heaps the accumulated rubbish of their desert journey, – their worn out clothing and their ragged shoes, – on the eastern bank of the Jordan; but they took the ark with them. So let every call that comes to us to enter into new and untried ways be to us the summons to leave our worthless ways and foolish sins behind us, but to tighten our hold on truth and goodness, to renew the covenant of our souls with God before we go on where He shall lead us.

Phillips Brooks (1835–93)

31st December

The land must not be sold permanently, because the land is mine and you are but aliens and my tenants.

(Leviticus 25:23)

It is not merely the physical facts of death and change that make us strangers here, but the directions of our desires, and the true affinities of our nature. If by these we belong to heaven and God, then here we shall feel that we have not to lay our heads, and shall "dwell in tabernacles" because "we look for the city".

What a contrast between the perishable tents of the wilderness and the rock-built mansions of that city! And how short this phase must look when seen from above! You remember how long a year, a week, seemed to you when a child – what do the first ten years of your life look to you now? What must the earthly life of Abel, the first who died, look to him even now, when he contrasts its short twenty or thirty years with the thousands since? and, after thousands and thousands more, how it will dwindle! So to us, if we reach that safe shore, and look back upon the sea that brought us thither, as it stretches to the horizon, miles of billows once so terrible will seem shrunken to a line of white foam.

Cherish, then, constant consciousness of that solemn eternity, and let your eyes be ever directed to it, like a man who sees some great flush of light on the horizon, and is ever turning from his work to look. Use the transient as preparation for the eternal, the fleeting days as those which determine the undying "Day" and its character. Keep your cares and interests in the present rigidly limited to necessary things. Why should travellers burden themselves? The less luggage, the easier marching. The accommodation and equipment in the desert do not matter much. The wise man will say, "Oh, it will do. I shall soon be home."

Alexander Maclaren (1826–1910)

Index

Abraham 3/1, 3/9, 4/9, 5/9, 11/11.
Adam 24/6, 21/7, 23/10, 28/10, 31/10, 4/11.
AMBROSE 14/7, 15/7, 8/11.
Angels 24/1, 21/7, 22/7, 2/11, 14/12.
Animals 28/10, 29/10.
ANSELM 31/10.
Apollos 5/5, 6/5, 7/5.
Armour of God 25/7, 26/7, 27/7.
Ascension 24/1, 12/5, 13/5, 14/5, 25/5.
ATHANASIUS 12/9, 13/9, 21/12.
AUGUSTINE 26/3, 26/5, 5/10.

Baptism of Jesus 15/2, 5/3.
BARTH 1/1, 7/2, 13/5.
BAXTER 28/1, 18/4, 4/5, 8/6, 11/6, 25/6, 26/6, 28/7, 30/7, 16/8, 19/9, 6/10, 2/12.
BEDE 15/9, 16/9, 29/9.
BERNARD 18/1, 12/7, 21/10.
Bible 3/1, 11/1, 26/4, 27/4, 28/4, 4/12, 5/12, 7/12, 8/12, 10/12.
Body of Christ 25/1, 26/1, 27/1, 9/2, 30/5, 6/6, 31/7.
BOOTH 7/3, 28/3, 24/4, 17/5, 18/5, 3/7, 24/7, 7/8, 1/9, 5/9, 7/9, 17/9, 1/10, 24/12.

BROOKS 12/2, 24/2, 12/3, 20/4, 22/5, 6/8, 21/8, 22/8, 18/10, 19/10, 9/11, 10/11, 12/12, 15/12, 30/12.
BUNYAN 3/2, 4/2, 8/4, 9/4, 7/5, 12/6, 3/9, 3/11.

Cana of Galilee 18/2, 25/2.
CAREY 10/4, 15/6, 20/6, 23/8, 24/8, 30/9, 10/10, 23/11, 17/12, 18/12, 19/12.
CARMICHAEL 2/2, 27/3, 20/8, 12/10, 28/11.
Children 10/3, 15/5, 18/5, 23/7, 20/10, 26/10, 5/11, 19/11.
CHRYSOSTOM 26/1, 5/4, 9/5, 10/5, 19/6, 7/10, 16/10, 27/12.
Church 9/2, 24/5, 27/5, 30/5, 5/8.
CLEMENT 19/4, 5/5 ,11/7, 17/10.
Communion 25/1, 31/3, 6/6, 30/8, 26/11.
Compassion 28/3, 15/5.
Conversion 29/1, 30/1, 31/1, 4/4, 23/6, 14/8, 28/8, 29/11, 30/11.
Covet 12/11.
Creation 17/10, 24/10, 25/10.
Cross 22/1, 23/1, 19/2, 8/3, 16/3, 31/3, 1/4, 2/4, 5/4, 8/4, 11/8, 12/8, 13/8,

Cross [cont'd]
25/8, 31/10, 1/12, 9/12.
CYPRIAN 6/4, 3/5, 5/7, 3/8, 14/9.
DALE 15/1, 19/1, 18/3, 3/4, 4/4, 20/5, 3/6, 4/6, 18/6, 4/7, 26/7, 14/8, 6/9, 28/9, 2/10, 25/10, 12/11, 17/11, 6/12, 29/12.
Daniel 22/11.
David 6/4, 14/6, 12/7, 19/7, 10/8, 17/8, 13/10, 14/10, 28/10.
Death 8/1, 9/1, 1/4, 2/4, 9/8, 19/8, 6/10, 1/11, 2/11, 3/11, 1/12.
Decalogue 20/5, 30/10, 11/11, 12/11.
Dedication 8/1, 10/10, 29/12.
DENNEY 29/2, 5/3, 6/3, 16/3, 24/6, 27/6, 8/7, 31/7, 26/8, 25/11, 1/12, 9/12.
DIDACHE 30/8, 31/8, 26/9.
DIOGNETUS 19/3.
Disciple 8/2, 12/2, 18/2, 7/3, 9/3, 13/3, 16/4, 17/4, 29/5, 17/6, 11/8, 9/9, 11/9.
Discipline, church 28/1, 4/5, 8/6.
Doubt 3/2, 4/2, 11/5, 25/6, 26/6.

EDWARDS 12/1, 20/3, 16/4, 1/5, 14/6, 17/6, 29/7, 8/10, 27/10, 28/12.
Easter 25/3, 3/4.
Elijah 11/3, 13/3, 17/3, 13/10, 5/12, 16/12.
Emotion 21/3, 22/6, 23/6, 26/8, 18/9.
Encouragement 27/1, 8/2, 9/2, 10/2, 11/2, 7/5, 8/5, 11/5, 16/8, 16/10, 23/10.
Envy 26/1, 20/3, 29/3, 6/4, 3/5, 9/6, 29/7, 30/7, 27/10.
EUSEBIUS 28/5, 29/8.
Example 18/3, 24/8, 25/8, 29/9.
Ezra 7/12.

Faith 30/1, 29/4, 25/5, 21/6, 30/6, 16/7, 21/8, 27/8, 1/9, 2/9, 3/9, 3/10.
Faithfulness 26/2, 27/2, 3/9.
FINNEY 27/1, 29/1, 9/3, 21/3, 17/4, 8/5, 19/5, 27/5, 4/8, 18/9, 27/9, 21/11.
Forgiveness 29/1, 8/4, 21/5, 26/5, 13/8, 14/8, 17/8, 26/8.
FORSYTH 11/1, 16/1, 17/1, 2/4, 23/4, 31/5, 16/6, 13/8, 3/10, 13/11, 18/11, 29/11, 30/11, 3/12.
FRY 6/1, 10/2, 11/2, 13/4, 25/4, 27/7, 9/8, 10/8, 4/12.

Gethsemane 21/1, 12/3.
Giving 9/3, 16/5, 17/5, 19/5, 15/6.
Grace 7/2.
Great Commission 27/3, 24/11, 17/12, 18/12, 19/12.
Growth 10/1, 13/1, 14/1, 15/1, 20/1, 16/2, 17/2, 18/4, 20/4, 21/4, 23/4, 4/7, 1/8, 2/8, 27/9, 30/12.
Guidance 9/1, 12/3, 12/10, 22/12.

HAVERGAL 21/1, 27/4, 7/7, 26/11.
Heaven 28/2, 19/3, 31/12.
Healing 2/2, 6/2, 2/12.
High Priest 14/5, 25/5.
Holiness 10/1, 12/1, 14/1, 23/2, 6/3, 18/3, 3/7.
HUBMAIER 1/2.
Humility 30/3, 16/4, 5/5, 6/5, 10/6, 12/6, 13/6, 30/7, 7/11.
HUS 5/6, 25/12.

Idol 10/9, 12/9, 13/9, 15/9, 16/9, 8/10, 9/11, 10/11.
Image 30/11.
Incarnation 29/6, 2/10, 4/10, 25/10, 30/10, 21/12, 23/12, 24/12, 25/12.

Job 1/6, 4/7, 5/9.
John the Baptist 1/2, 14/2, 28/2, 29/2, 5/3, 10/6, 12/12.
Joseph 21/4.
Joshua 8/2, 9/6, 14/7, 29/7, 10/9, 11/9, 11/10.
Joy 27/6, 20/8, 15/10, 16/10, 23/12.
Jubilee 5/1, 31/12.

Index

KEMPIS 1/6, 17/7.

LAW 23/2, 29/5, 2/6, 18/7, 9/10, 22/10, 20/11, 22/12.
Leader 19/5, 23/8, 19/9, 20/9, 26/9, 10/10, 13/12, 14/12.
Lent 16/2.
LEO 16/2, 13/3, 14/3, 25/3, 2/5, 11/5, 12/5, 21/5, 11/8, 24/10, 23/12, 26/12.
Love 18/1, 16/3, 9/7, 10/7, 11/7, 12/7, 13/7, 28/7, 21/10.
Luke 18/10, 19/10.

MACLAREN 4/1, 5/1, 22/1, 23/1, 8/2, 15/3, 17/3, 30/4, 20/7, 25/7, 1/8, 2/8, 12/8, 10/9, 11/9, 21/9, 23/9, 11/10, 7/11, 21/12.
Magi 26/12, 27/12.
Marriage 4/3, 22/9.
Martyrdom 20/2, 21/2, 22/2, 5/9, 14/9.
Mary 13/2, 18/2, 18/8.
Messianic Banquet 4/11.
MEYER 13/1, 14/1, 18/2, 25/2, 23/5, 24/5, 7/6, 9/6, 13/6, 19/7, 17/8, 2/9, 8/9, 9/9, 13/10, 14/10, 28/10, 6/11, 5/12, 16/12.
Miracles 26/3, 10/4.
Mission 27/3, 11/4, 12/4, 15/4, 22/4, 15/6, 19/6, 20/6, 29/8, 23/9, 29/9, 30/9, 24/11, 28/11, 17/12, 18/12, 19/12, 20/12.
MOODY 7/1, 14/2, 28/2, 11/3, 22/3, 30/3, 26/4, 12/6, 28/6, 1/7, 6/7, 9/7, 13/7, 15/8, 24/9, 25/9, 4/10, 15/10, 4/11, 22/11.
Moses 18/1, 19/1, 15/2, 11/3, 13/3, 17/3, 9/6, 10/6, 13/6, 29/7, 2/9, 6/11, 7/11, 8/11, 9/11, 10/11.

Name 30/4, 20/7, 28/10.
Nationhood 14/4, 15/4, 11/11, 12/11, 19/11.

NEWTON 2/1, 10/1, 17/2, 8/3, 1/4, 25/5, 29/6, 30/10, 2/11, 14/12.

Passover 31/3, 7/4.
Peace 2/5, 15/11, 23/11, 2/12.

Pentecost 9/5, 10/5, 22/5, 23/5, 26/5, 27/5.
Personality 20/4, 31/5, 15/12.
Physician 26/5, 19/10.
Pilate, Pontius 23/1, 29/3, 6/4, 7/4, 11/11.
POLYCARP 20/2, 21/2, 22/2, 20/9.
Prayer 11/1, 2/2, 16/6, 5/7, 24/9, 25/9, 9/10, 13/11, 20/11, 21/11, 22/11.
Preaching 14/1, 23/4, 25/8, 18/11, 11/12, 12/12, 14/12, 15/12.
Pride 7/2, 11/6.
Prison 6/1, 10/2, 11/2, 25/4, 9/8, 10/8, 4/12.
Psalms 4/8, 17/8, 18/8, 19/8, 20/8.

Reconciliation 28/1, 8/7, 25/11, 29/11, 30/11.
Rejection 13/2, 1/3, 2/3, 3/3, 8/3, 1/4, 21/4, 24/4, 29/4.
Remember 8/2, 20/7, 10/9, 11/10.
Repentance 29/1, 1/2, 4/5, 24/6, 27/8.
Resurrection 3/4, 19/4, 11/5, 27/6, 3/10.
Revival 14/2, 7/6, 1/8, 2/8.
RIEDEMAN 9/2, 19/8, 15/11.
Ruth 21/9, 22/9, 23/9.

Sacrifice 14/5, 18/5, 21/8, 22/8, 14/11.
Salvation 30/1, 31/1, 5/2, 11/3, 8/4, 24/12.
Samson 2/7, 15/7, 10/12.
SANGSTER 2/3, 3/3, 11/12.
SCHLAFFER 6/6.
Second Coming 19/4, 1/11, 26/11, 27/11, 28/11.
Selfishness 8/10.

Service 27/2, 23/3, 30/3, 12/4, 13/4, 15/5, 7/7, 13/10, 14/10, 6/11.
SHAFTESBURY 8/1, 10/3, 14/4, 15/4, 28/4, 15/5, 23/7, 8/8, 20/10, 26/10, 29/10, 5/11, 11/11, 16/11, 19/11, 8/12.
Sheep 24/3, 28/6.
SIMEON 1/3, 27/8.
SIMONS 25/1, 19/2.
Slaves 7/1, 17/1, 12/4, 13/4, 14/4, 15/6, 23/10, 23/11.
Social Concern 17/11, 18/11.
Solomon 20/1, 20/7.
Spring 23/3.
SPURGEON 3/1, 30/1, 27/2, 23/3, 31/3, 23/6, 3/9, 4/9.
Stealing 20/5, 7/8, 8/8.
STUDD 4/3, 16/7, 14/11, 27/11.
Sunday 3/4, 3/6, 4/6.
Suffering 22/1, 6/2, 1/6, 17/6, 4/7, 17/7, 12/8, 5/9, 28/9.

TAYLOR 22/4, 14/5, 21/6, 30/6, 5/8, 1/11, 20/12.
Temperance 1/7, 2/7.

Temptation 6/7, 26/7.
Thankfulness 12/1, 2/6, 16/6, 26/8, 22/10, 6/12.
Time 1/1, 2/1, 4/1, 6/1, 26/2, 31/12.
Tongue 13/2.
Transfiguration 13/3, 14/3, 17/3, 12/6.

Unity 16/1, 17/1, 25/3, 5/5, 5/6, 30/7, 31/7, 3/8, 2/12

War 17/5, 24/7, 14/11.
Wealth 15/5, 16/5, 14/7, 15/7, 6/8, 7/8.
WESLEY 26/2, 29/4, 16/5, 30/5, 22/6, 10/7, 28/8, 23/10.
WHITEFIELD 24/1, 24/3, 21/7, 22/7, 24/11.
WHYTE 20/1, 31/1, 6/2, 13/2, 15/2, 29/3, 7/4, 21/4, 6/5, 7/5, 10/6, 2/7, 18/8, 25/8, 22/9, 7/12, 10/12, 13/12.
Wisdom 4/7.
Witness 18/3, 19/3, 27/3, 30/4, 28/5, 19/6. 16/12.
Worship 29/5, 4/8, 19/8.

ZINZENDORF 9/1, 5/2, 11/4, 12/4.

Sources of Readings

Every effort has been made to trace copyright holders for the material used, but in some cases without success. If in due course further information comes to light, we shall be happy to make acknowledgement in any reprint.

JANUARY

1. p. 40 *Call for God*, London, SCM Press, 1967.
2. p. 572 *The Works of the Rev. John Newton*, Edinburgh, Peter Brown and Thomas Nelson, 1834.
3. p. 137 *Sermons*, London, Thomas Nelson and Sons, n.d.
4. p. 162 *Expositions of Holy Scripture, Isaiah and Jeremiah*, London, Hodder and Stoughton, 1906.
5. p. 269 *Expositions of Holy Scripture, Exodus and Leviticus*, London, Hodder and Stoughton, 1906.
6. p. 120 *Memoir of the Life of Elizabeth Fry*, Vol. 2, London, Charles Gilpin, 1847.
7. p. 122 *Conversion, Service and Glory*, London, Marshall, Morgan and Scott, n.d.
8. p. 7 *Lord Shaftesbury*, Florence M. G. Higham, London, SCM Press, 1945.
9. Hymn 544 *The Baptist Hymn Book*, London, Psalms and Hymns Trust, 1962.
10. p. 210 *The Works of the Rev. John Newton*, Edinburgh, Peter Brown and Thomas Nelson, 1834.
11. p. 79 *The Soul of Prayer* (1916), Reprint, London, Independent Press, 1966.
12. p. 240 *Charity and Its Fruits* (1852), Reprint, Edinburgh, Banner of Truth, 1969.
13. p. 40 *Five "Musts" of the Christian Life*, London, Marshall, Morgan and Scott, n.d.
14. Ibid.

In Good Company

15. p. 298 *Epistle to the Hebrews*, London, Hodder and Stoughton, 1882.
16. p. 49 *The Church and the Sacraments* (1917), London, Independent Press, Sixth Impression, 1964.
17. Ibid.
18. p. 62 *Life and Works of St Bernard of Clairvaux*, Vol. 4, London, John Hodges, 1896, altd.
19. p. 78 *The Jewish Temple and the Christian Church*, London, Hodder and Stoughton, 1871.
20. p. 194 *Bible Characters, Gideon to Absalom*, London, Oliphant, n.d.
21. p. 837 *The Poetical Works of Frances Ridley Havergal*, London, Nisbet and Co., n.d.
22. p. 192 *Bible Class Expositions, Matthew*, Vol. 2, London, Hodder and Stoughton, 1897.
23. Ibid.
24. p. 170 *Whitefield's Works*, Vol. 7, London, E. and C. Dilly, 1771.
25. p. 208 *Anabaptism in Outline*, Scottdale, P. A. Herald Press, 1981.
26. p. 434 *Library of the Fathers*, Vol. 5, Oxford, John Henry Parker, 1839.
27. p. 212 *Lectures on Revivals of Religion*, 13th edition, London, Simpkin, Marshall and Co., 1840
28. p. 98 *The Reformed Pastor*, Glasgow, William Collins, 1829, altd.
29. p. 211 *Lectures on Revivals of Religion*, 13th edition, London, Simpkin, Marshall and Co., 1840
30. p. 87 *Spurgeon the Early Years*, Edinburgh, Banner of Truth, 1962.
31. p. 132 *Bible Characters, Ahithopel to Nehemiah*, London, Oliphant, Anderson and Ferrier, n.d..

FEBRUARY

1. p. 42 *Anabaptism in Outline*, Scottdale, P. A. Herald Press, 1981.
2. p. 76 *Fragments that Remain*, edited by Bee Trehane, London, SPCK, 1987.
3. p. 191 *The Pilgrim's Progress and Holy War*, London, R. E. King, n.d.
4. Ibid.
5. Hymn 208 *The Baptist Hymn Book*, London, Psalms and Hymns Trust, 1962.
6. p. 202 *Bible Characters, Stephen to Timothy*, London, Oliphant, Anderson and Ferrier, 1904.
7. p. 78 *Call for God*, London, SCM Press, 1967.
8. p. 89 *Expositions of Holy Scripture, Deuteronomy to 1 Samuel*, London, Hodder and Stoughton, 1906.
9. p. 132 *Anabaptism in Outline*, Scottdale, P. A. Herald Press, 1981.
10. p. 380 *Memoir of the Life of Elizabeth Fry*, Vol. 1, London, Charles Gilpin, 1847.

11. Ibid.
12. p. 24 *The Light of the World*, London, Macmillan and Co. 1899.
13. p. 13 *Bible Characters, Joseph and Mary to James*, London, Oliphant, Anderson and Ferrier, 1904.
14. p. 107 *Bible Characters*, London, Morgan and Scott, n.d.
15. p. 243 *Bible Characters, Adam to Achan*, London, Oliphant, Anderson and Ferrier, 1903.
16. p. 154 *A Select Library of Nicene and Post Nicene Fathers*, Oxford, James Parker and Co. 1895.
17. p. 328 *The Works of the Rev. John Newton*, Edinburgh, Peter Brown and Thomas Nelson, 1834, altd.
18. p. 106 *Five "Musts" of the Christian Life*, London, Marshall, Morgan and Scott, n.d.
19. p. 97 *Anabaptism in Ouline*, Scottdale, P. A. Herald Press, 1981.
20. p. 159 *The Apostolic Fathers*, London, Griffith, Farran, Okeden and Welsh, n.d., altd.
21. Ibid.
22. Ibid.
23. p. 98 *A Serious Call*, London, Griffith, Farran, Okeden and Welsh, 1888.
24. p. 345 *The Light of the World*, London, Macmillan and Co., 1899.
25. p. 111 *Five "Musts" of the Christian Life*, London, Marshall, Morgan and Scott, n.d.
26. p. 50 *The Works of the Rev. John Wesley*, 3rd edition, Vol. 13, London, John Mason, 1831.
27. p. 358 *Spurgeon's Sermons*, London, Passmore and Alabaster, n.d.
28. p. 106 *Bible Characters*, London, Morgan and Scott, n.d.
29. p. 262 *Jesus and the Gospel*, London, Hodder and Stoughton, 1909.

MARCH

1. p. 72 *Charles Simeon*, H. G. Moule, London, Methuen, 1892, altd.
2. p. 56 *Westminster Sermons*, Vol. 1, London, Epworth Press, 1960.
3. Ibid.
4. p. 31 *Fool and Fanatic?* Compiled by Jean Walker, Bulstrode, WEC, n.d.
5. p. 251 *The Christian Doctrine of Reconciliation*, London, Hodder and Stoughton, 1907.
6. Ibid.
7. *Popular Christianity*, London, The Salvation Army Book Department, n.d.
8. p. 434 *The Works of the Rev. John Newton*, Edinburgh, Peter Brown and Thomas Nelson, 1834.

9. p. 362 *Lectures on Revivals of Religion*, 13th edition, London, Simpkin, Marshall and Co., 1840.
10. p. 161 *The Life and Work of the 7th Earl of Shaftesbury*, Vol. 2, Edwin Hodder, London, Cassell and Co. Ltd, 1887.
11. p. 42 *Addresses*, London, Morgan and Scott, n.d.
12. p. 120 *The Light of the World*, London, Macmillan and Co., 1899.
13. p. 163 *A Select Library of Nicene and Post Nicene Fathers*, 2nd Series, Vol. 13, Oxford, James Parker and Co., 1895.
14. Ibid.
15. p. 178 *Expositions of Holy Scripture, Deuteronomy to 1 Samuel*, London, Hodder and Stoughton, 1906.
16. p. 150 *Studies in Theology*, London, Hodder and Stoughton, 1895.
17. p. 144 *Bible Class Expositions, Matthew*, Vol. 2, London, Hodder and Stoughton, 1897.
18. p. 250 *The Jewish Temple and the Christian Church*, London, Hodder and Stoughton, 1871.
19. p. 60 *The Epistle of Diognetus*, London, SPCK, 1908.
20. p. 22 *Charity and Its Fruits* (1852), Reprint, Edinburgh, Banner of Truth, 1969.
21. p. 360 *Lectures on Revivals of Religion*, 13th Edition, London, Simpkin, Marshall and Co., 1840.
22. p. 51 *Anecdotes, Incidents and Illustrations*, London, Morgan and Scott, n.d.
23. p. 181 *Spurgeon's Sermons*, London, Passmore and Alabaster, n.d.
24. p. 436 *Whitefield's Works*, Vol. 7, London, E. and C. Dilly, 1771.
25. p. 186 *A Select Library of Nicene and Post Nicene Fathers*, 2nd Series, Vol. 13, Oxford, James Parker and Co. 1895, altd.
26. *Sermons on Selected Lessons of the New Testament*, Vol. 1, Oxford, 1844.
27. p. 3 *Fragments That Remain*, edited by Bee Trehane, London, SPCK, 1987.
28. p. 74 *Popular Christianity*, The Salvation Army Book Department, n.d.
29. p. 130 *Bible Characters, Joseph and Mary to James*, London, Oliphant, Anderson and Ferrier, 1904.
30. p. 90 *The Faith which Overcomes*, London, Morgan and Scott, n.d.
31. p. 37 *Spurgeon's Sermons*, London, Passmore and Alasbaster, n.d.

APRIL

1. p. 328 *The Works of the Rev. John Newton*, Edinburgh, Peter Brown and Thomas Nelson, 1834.
2. p. 356 *Positive Preaching and the Modern Mind*, London, Hodder and Stoughton, 1907.
3. p. 642 *The Life of R. W. Dale*, A. W. W. Dale, London, Hodder and Stoughton, 1898.
4. p. 15 *The Living Christ and the Four Gospels*, London, Hodder and Stoughton, 1891.
5. p. 41 *Library of the Fathers*, Vol. 4, Oxford, John Henry Parker, 1836.
6. p. 267 *The Treatises of Cyprian*, Oxford, John Henry Parker, 1840.
7. p. 131 *Bible Characters, Joseph and Mary to James*, London, Oliphant, Anderson and Ferrier, 1904.
8. p. 22 *The Pilgrim's Progress and Holy War*, London, R. E. King, n.d.
9. p. 209 *The Pilgrim's Progress and Holy War*, London, R. E. King, n.d.
10. p. 75 *The Enquiry* (1792). Reprint, London, The Carey Kingsgate Press Ltd, 1961, altd.
11. Sections 40–41, pp. 53–73, *Outline of a History of Protestant Missions from the Reformation to the Present Time*, Gustav Werneck, New York, Fleming H. Revell Co., 1902.
12. Ibid.
13. p. 194 *Memoir of the Life of Elizabeth Fry*, Vol. 2, London, Charles Gilpin, 1847.
14. p. 471 *The Life and Work of the 7th Earl of Shaftesbury*, Vol. 2, Edwin Hodder, London, Cassell and Co., 1887.
15. Ibid.
16. p. 150 *Charity and Its Fruits* (1852), Reprint, Edinburgh, Banner of Truth, 1969.
17. p. 352 *Lectures on Revivals of Religion*, 13th Edition, London, Simpkin, Marshall and Co., 1840.
18. p. 82 *The Reformed Pastor*, Glasgow, William Collins, 1829, altd.
19. p. 171 *The Apostolic Fathers*, London, Griffith, Farran, Okeden and Welsh, n.d.
20. p. 38 *The Joy of Preaching* (Lectures on Preaching, 1895), Grand Rapids, Michigan, Kregel Publications, 1989.
21. p. 201 *Bible Characters, Adam to Achan*, London, Oliphant, Anderson, and Ferrier, 1903.
22. p. 60 *Retrospect*, London, Overseas Missionary Fellowship Books, 18th edition.
23. p. 103 *Positive Preaching and the Modern Mind*, London, Hodder and Stoughton, 1907.
24. p. 137 *Papers on Practical Religion*, London, S. W. Partridge Ltd, n.d.

25. p. 344 *Memoir of the Life of Elizabeth Fry*, Vol. 1, London, Charles Gilpin, 1847.
26. p. 82 *Addresses*, London, Morgan and Scott, n.d.
27. p. 836 *The Poetical Works of Frances Ridley Havergal*, London, Nisbet and Co., n.d.
28. p. 464 *The Life and Work of the 7th Earl of Shaftesbury*, Vol. 3, Edwin Hodder, London, Cassell and Co., 1887.
29. p. 233 *The Works of the Rev. John Wesley*, 3rd edition, Vol. 1, London, John Mason, 1829.
30. p. 111 *The Victor's Crown*, London, Christian Commonwealth Co. Ltd, n.d.

MAY

1. p. 87 *Charity and Its Fruits* (1852), Reprint, Edinburgh, Banner of Truth, 1969.
2. p. 205 *A Select Library of Nicene and Post Nicene Fathers*, 2nd Series, Vol. 12, Oxford, James Parker and Co., 1895.
3. p. 266 *The Treatises of Cyprian*, Oxford, James Henry Parker, 1740, altd.
4. p. 85 *The Reformed Pastor*, Glasgow, William Collins, 1829.
5. p. 182 *The Apostolic Fathers*, London, Griffith, Farran, Okeden and Welsh, n.d.
6. p. 269 *Bible Characters, Stephen to Timothy*, London, Oliphant, 9th edition, n.d.
7. Ibid.
8. p. 369 *Lectures on Revivals of Religion*, 13th edition, London, Simpkin, Marshall and Co., 1840.
9. p. 11 *Homilies on Acts*, Oxford, John Henry Parker, 1751.
10. Ibid.
11. p. 163 *A Select Library of Nicene and Post Nicene Fathers*, 2nd Series, Vol. 13, Oxford, James Parker and Co., 1895, altd.
12. p. 187 *A Select Library of Nicene and Post Nicene Fathers*, 2nd Series, Vol. 12, Oxford, James Parker and Co., 1895.
13. p. 79 *The Heidelberg Catechism for Today*, London, Epworth Press, 1964.
14. p. 74 *Union and Communion*, Reprint, London, China Inland Mission, 1962.
15. p. 164 *The Life and Work of the 7th Earl of Shaftesbury*, Vol. 2, Edwin Hodder, London, Cassell and Co. Ltd, 1887.
16. p. 227 *Wesley's Works*, 3rd edition, Volume 13, London, John Mason, 1831.

Sources of Readings

17. p. 104 *Popular Christianity*, London, The Salvation Army Book Department, n.d.
18. Ibid.
19. p. 213 *Lectures on Revivals of Religion*, 13th edition, London, Simpkin, Marshall and Co., 1840.
20. p. 196 *The Ten Commandments*, London, Hodder and Stoughton, 1884.
21. p. 174 *A Select Library of Nicene and Post Nicene Fathers*, 2nd Series, Vol. 12, Oxford, James Parker and Co., 1895.
22. p. 226 *The Candle of the Lord*, London, Macmillan and Co., 1905.
23. p. 80 *Five "Musts" of the Christian Life*, London, Marshall, Morgan and Scott, n.d.
24. Ibid.
25. p. 9 *Select Sermons*, London, Religious Tract Society, 1799.
26. p. 240 *Sermons on Selected Lessons of the New Testament*, Vol. 2, Oxford, 1844.
27. p. 339 *Lectures on Revivals of Religion*, 13th edition, London, Simpkin, Marshall and Co., 1840.
28. p. 190 *Eusebius* (1850), Reprint, Grand Rapids, Michigan, Baker Books, 1955.
29. p. 16 *A Serious Call*, London, Griffith, Farran, Okeden and Welsh, 1888.
30. p. 471 *The Works of John Wesley*, 3rd Edition, Vol. 12, London, John Mason, 1830.
31. p. 262 *Positive Preaching and the Modern Mind*, London, Hodder and Stoughton, 1907.

JUNE

1. p. 19 *The Imitation of Christ*, London, Griffith, Farran, Okeden and Welsh, n.d.
2. p. 164 *A Serious Call*, London, Griffith, Farran, Okeden and Welsh, 1888, altd.
3. p. 100 *The Ten Commandments*, London, Hodder and Stoughton, 1884.
4. Ibid.
5. p. 61 *Letters of John Hus*, London, Hodder and Stoughton, 1905.
6. p. 196 *Anabaptism in Outline*, Scottdale, P. A. Herald Press, 1981.
7. p. 59 *Five "Musts" of the Christian Life*, London, Marshall, Morgan and Scott, n.d.
8. p. 98 *The Reformed Pastor*, Glasgow, William Collins, 1829.
9. p. 156 *Moses*, London, Morgan and Scott, 1909.

10. p. 280 *Bible Characters, Adam to Achan*, London, Oliphant, Anderson and Ferrier, 1903.
11. p. 135 *The Practical Works of the Rev. Richard Baxter*, Vol. 17, London, 1830.
12. p. 82 *The Faith which Overcomes*, London, Morgan and Scott, n.d.
13. p. 127 *Moses*, London, Morgan and Scott, 1909.
14. p. 88 *Charity and Its Fruits* (1852), Reprint, Edinburgh, Banner of Truth, 1969.
15. p. 84 *The Enquiry* (1792), Reprint, London, The Carey Kingsgate Press Ltd, 1961.
16. p. 62 *The Soul of Prayer* (1916), London, Independent Press, 5th Impression, 1966.
17. p. 258 *Charity and Its Fruits* (1852), Reprint, Edinburgh, Banner of Truth, 1969.
18. p. 20 *The Epistle of James*, London, Hodder and Stoughton, 1895.
19. p. 212 *Library of the Fathers*, Vol. 11, Oxford, John Henry Parker, 1863.
20. p. 81 *The Enquiry* (1792), Reprint, London, The Carey Kingsgate Press, 1961.
21. p. 42 *A Retrospect*, London, China Inland Mission/Marshall Morgan and Scott, 8th impression.
22. p. 312 *The Works of the Rev. John Wesley*, 3rd Edition, Vol. 13, London, John Mson, 1831.
23. p. 43 *Spurgeon's Sermons*, London, Passmore and Alabaster, n.d.
24. p. 324 *The Christian Doctrine of Reconciliation*, London, Hodder and Stoughton, 1917.
25. p. 239 *The Practical Works of the Rev. Richard Baxter*, Vol. 17, London, James Duncan, 1830.
26. Ibid.
27. p. 170 *Studies in Theology*, London, Hodder and Stoughton, 1895.
28. p. 104 *Moody's Stories*, New York, Fleming H. Revell, 1899.
29. p. 1 *Select Sermons*, London, Religious Tract Society, 1799.
30. p. 116 *A Retrospect*, London, China Inland Mission/Marshall, Morgan and Scott, 8th impression.

JULY

1. p. 120 *Moody's Stories*, New York, Fleming H. Revell, 1899.
2. p. 38 *Bible Characters, Gideon to Absalom*, London, Oliphant, n.d.
3. p. 14 *How Christ Transcends the Law, A Sermon by Mrs Booth*, London, n.d.
4. p. 10 *The Epistle of James*, London, Hodder and Stoughton, 1895.
5. p. 180 *The Treatises of Cyprian*, Oxford, John Henry Parker, 1840.

Sources of Readings

6. p. 53 *Moody's Stories*, New York, Fleming H. Revell, 1899.
7. p. 25 *The Poetical Works of Frances Ridley Havergal*, London, Nisbet and Co., n.d.
8. p. 24 *The Christian Doctrine of Reconciliation*, London, Hodder and Stoughton, 1917.
9. p. 105 *Anecdotes, Incidents and Illustrations*, London, Morgan and Scott, n.d.
10. p. 464 *The Works of the Rev. John Wesley*, 3rd Edition, Vol. 12, London, John Mason, 1830.
11. p. 18 *The Ante Nicene Fathers*, Vol. 1, Buffalo, Christian Publishing Co., 1887, altd.
12. p. 962 *The Life and Works of St Bernard of Clairvaux*, Vol. 4, London, John Hodges, 1896.
13. p. 77 *Anecdotes, Incidents, and Illustrations*, London, Morgan and Scott, n.d.
14. p. 63 *A Select Library of Nicene and Post Nicene Fathers*, 2nd Series, Vol. 10, Oxford, James Parker and Co., 1896.
15. Ibid.
16. p. 43 *Fool and Fanatic?* Compiled by Jean Walker, Bulstrode, WEC, n.d.
17. p. 18 *The Imitation of Christ*, London, Griffith, Farran, Okeden and Welsh, n.d.
18. p. 282 *A Serious Call*, London, Griffith, Farran, Okeden and Welsh, 1888.
19. p. 46 *David*, London, Marshall, Morgan and Scott, 1960 Impression.
20. p. 176 *Expositions of Holy Scripture, 2 Samuel to 2 Kings 7*, London, Hodder and Stoughton, 1906.
21. p. 408 *Whitefield's Works*, Vol. 7, London, E. and C. Dilly, 1771.
22. Ibid.
23. p. 254 *The Life and Work of the 7th Earl of Shaftesbury*, Vol. 2, Edwin Hodder, London, 1887.
24. p. 94 *Popular Christianity*, The Salvation Army Book Department, n.d.
25. p. 358 *Expositions of Holy Scripture, Ephesians*, London, Hodder and Stoughton, 1909.
26. p. 428 *The Epistle to the Ephesians*, London, Hodder and Stoughton, 1872.
27. p. 156 *Memoir of the Life of Elizabeth Fry*, Vol. 2, London, Charles Gilpin, 1847.
28. p. 203 *The Practical Works of the Rev. Richard Baxter*, Vol. 17, London, James Duncan, 1830.
29. p. 112 *Charity and Its Fruits* (1854), Reprint, Edinburgh, Banner of Truth, 1969.

30. p. 198 *The Practical Works of the Rev. Richard Baxter*, Vol. 17, London, James Duncan, 1830.
31. p. 188 *Studies in Theology*, London, Hodder and Stoughton, 1895.

AUGUST

1. p. 52 *Expositions of Holy Scripture, Isaiah and Jeremiah*, London, Hodder and Stoughton, 1906.
2. Ibid.
3. p. 132 *The Treatises of Cyprian*, Oxford, John Henry Parker, 1840, altd.
4. p. 224 *Lectures on Revivals of Religion*, 13th edition, London, Simpkin, Marshall and Co., 1840.
5. p. 19 *Union and Communion* (1962), Reprint, London, China Inland Mission.
6. p. 42 *The Influence of Jesus*, London, H. R. Allenson, 1895.
7. p. 136 *Popular Christianity*, London, The Salvation Army Book Dept, n.d.
8. p. viii *These Fifty Years*, London, London City Mission, n.d.
9. p. 310 *Memoirs of the Life of Elizabeth Fry*, Vol. 1, London, Charles Gilpin, 1847.
10. Ibid.
11. p. 172 *A Select Library of Nicene and Post Nicene Fathers*, Oxford, James Parker and Co., 1895.
12. p. 90 *Expositions of Holy Scripture, Isaiah 49–66*, London, Hodder and Stoughton, 1906.
13. p. 295 *Positive Preaching and the Modern Mind*, London, Hodder and Stoughton, 1907.
14. p. 14 *The Living Christ and the Four Gospels*, London, Hodder and Stoughton, 1891.
15. p. 80 *Anecdotes, Incidents and Illustrations*, London, Morgan and Scott, n.d.
16. p. 84 *The Reformed Pastor*, Glasgow, William Collins, 1829.
17. p. 149 *David*, London, Marshall, Morgan and Scott, 1953, Reprint.
18. p. 143 *Bible Characters, Gideon to Absalom*, London, Oliphant, n.d.
19. p. 131 *Anabaptism in Outline*, Scottdale, P. A. Herald Press, 1981.
20. p. 116 *Fragments that Remain*, Edited by Bee Trehane, London, SPCK, 1987.
21. p. 29 *The Candle of the Lord*, London, Macmillan and Co., 1905.
22. Ibid.
23. p. 72 *The Enquiry*, (1792), Reprint, London, The Carey Kingsgate Press Ltd, 1961, altd.
24. p. 115 *Faithful Witness*, Timothy George, Leicester, I.V.P. 1992.

25. p. 136 *Bible Characters, Stephen to Timothy*, London, Oliphant, n.d.
26. p. 13 *The Christian Doctrine of Reconciliation*, London, Hodder and Stoughton, 1907.
27. p. 189 *Charles Simeon*, H. C. G. Moule, London, Methuen, 1892.
28. p. 103 *The Works of John Wesley*, Vol. 1, 3rd Edition, London, John Mason, 1829.
29. p. 122 *Eusebius* (1850), Reprint, Grand Rapids, Michigan, Baker Books, 1955.
30. p. 174 *The Apostolic Fathers*, London, Griffiths, Farran, Okeden and Welsh, n.d.
31. Ibid.

SEPTEMBER

1. p. 83 *Papers on Practical Religion*, London, Partridge and Co., n.d.
2. p. 22 *Moses*, London, Morgan and Scott, 1909.
3. p. 413 *Spurgeon's Sermons*, London, Passmore and Alabaster, n.d.
4. p. 655 *Spurgeon's Sermons*, London, Passmore and Alasbaster, n.d.
5. p. 146 *Papers on Practical Religion*, London, Partridge and Co., n.d.
6. p. 82 *The Epistle of James*, London, Hodder and Stoughton, 1895.
7. p. 7 *How Christ Transcends the Law, A Sermon by Mrs Booth*, London, n.d.
8. p. 21 *Five "Musts" of the Christian Life*, London, Marshall Morgan and Scott, n.d.
9. Ibid.
10. p. 183 *Expositions of Holy Scripture, Deuteronomy to 1 Samuel*, London, Hodder and Stoughton, 1906.
11. Ibid.
12. p. 80 *Athanasius on the Incarnation*, Edinburgh, D. Nutt, 1891.
13. Ibid.
14. p. xiii *The Treatises of Cyprian*, Oxford, John Henry Parker, 1740, altd.
15. p. 94 *Bede's Ecclesiastical History of England*, London, George Bell and Sons Ltd., 1907.
16. Ibid.
17. p. 126 *Popular Christianity*, London, The Salvation Army Book Dept., n.d.
18. p. 349 *Lectures on Revivals of Religion*, 13th edition, London, Simpkin, Marshall and Co., 1840.
19. p. 41 *The Reformed Pastor*, London, SCM, 1956.
20. p. 145 *The Apostolic Fathers*, London, Griffiths, Farran, Okeden and Welsh, n.d.

21. p. 262 *Expositions of Holy Scripture, Deuteronomy to 1 Samuel*, London, Hodder and Stoughton, 1906.
22. p. 53 *Bible Characters, Gideon to Absalom*, London, Oliphant, n.d.
23. p. 264 *Expositions of Holy Scripture, Deuteronomy to 1 Samuel*, London, Hodder and Stoughton, 1906.
24. p. 79 *Prevailing Prayer*, London, Marshall, Morgan and Scott, n.d.
25. Ibid.
26. p. 176 *The Apostolic Fathers*, Griffiths, Farran, Okeden and Welsh, n.d., altd.
27. p. 395 *Lectures on Revivals of Religion*, 13th Edition, London, Simpkin, Marshall and Co., 1840, altd.
28. p. 33 *The Epistle of James*, London, Hodder and Stoughton, 1895.
29. p. 89 *Bede's Ecclesiastical History of England*, London, George Bell and Sons, 1907.
30. p. 60 *William Carey*, Mary Drewery, London, Hodder and Stoughton, 1978.

OCTOBER

1. p. 90 *Popular Christianity*, London, The Salvation Army Book Department, n.d.
2. p. 103 *Christian Doctrine*, London, Hodder and Stoughton, 1894.
3. p. 118 *The Holy Father and the Living Christ*, London, Hodder and Stoughton, 1897.
4. p. 67 *Addresses*, London, Morgan and Scott, n.d.
5. p. 213 *Augustine on Christian Doctrine and Catechising*, Edinburgh, T. and T. Clark, 1873.
6. p. 563 *The Practical Works of the Rev. Richard Baxter*, Vol. 17, London, James Duncan, 1830.
7. p. 382 *Library of the Fathers*, Vol. 7, Oxford, John Henry Parker, 1841.
8. p. 184 *Charity and Its Fruits* (1852), Reprint, Edinburgh, Banner of Truth, 1969.
9. p. 141 *A Serious Call*, London, Griffith, Farran, Okeden and Welsh, 1888.
10. p. 64 *William Carey*, J. B. Middlebrook, London, The Carey Kingsgate Press, 1961.
11. p. 121 *Expositions of Holy Scripture, Deuteronomy to 1 Samuel*, London, Hodder and Stoughton, 1906.
12. p. 131 *Fragments that Remain*, edited by Bee Trehane, London, SPCK, 1987.
13. p. 139 *David*, London, Marshall, Morgan and Scott, 1960 Impression.
14. Ibid.

15. p. 82 *Addresses*, London, Morgan and Scott, n.d.
16. p. 383 *Library of the Fathers*, Vol. 7, Oxford, John Henry Parker, 1841.
17. p. 11 *The Ante Nicene Fathers*, Vol. 1, Buffalo, Christian Literature Publishing Company, 1887.
18. p. 216 *The Light of the World*, London, Macmillan and Co., 1899.
19. Ibid.
20. p. 156 *The Life and Work of the 7th Earl of Shaftesbury*, Vol. 3, Edwin Hodder, London, Cassell and Co. Ltd, 1887.
21. p. 307, *The Life and Work of St Bernard of Clairvaux*, Vol. 4, London, John Hodges, 1896, altd.
22. p. 48 *A Serious Call*, London, Griffin, Farran, Okeden and Welsh, 1888.
23. p. 127 *The Works of the Rev. John Wesley*, 3rd edition, Vol. 13, London, John Mason, 1831.
24. p. 122 *A Select Library of Nicene and Post Nicene Fathers*, Second Series, Vol. 12, Oxford, James Parker and Co., 1895.
25. p. 2 *Funeral Sermons*, London, James Paul, 1850.
26. p. 305 *The Life and Work of the 7th Earl of Shaftesbury*, Vol. 1, Edwin Hodder, London, Cassell and Co. Ltd, 1887.
27. p. 118 *Charity and Its Fruits* (1852), Reprint, Edinburgh, Banner of Truth, 1969.
28. p. 36 *David*, London, Marshall, Morgan and Scott, 1960 Impression.
29. p. 273 *The Life and Work of the 7th Earl of Shaftesbury*, Vol. 3, Edwin Hodder, London, Cassell and Co. Ltd, 1887.
30. p. 2 *Select Sermons*, London, Religious Tract Society, 1799.
31. p. 38 *Why God Became Man*, London, Religious Tract Society, n.d.

NOVEMBER

1. p. 201 *Hudson Taylor and the China Inland Mission*, Dr and Mrs Howard Taylor, London, China Inland Mission, 1943.
2. p. 12 *Select Sermons*, London, Religious Tract Society, 1799.
3. p. 210 *The Pilgrim's Progress and Holy War*, London, R. E. King, n.d.
4. p. 5 *Addresses*, London, Morgan and Scott, n.d.
5. p. 290 *The Life and Work of the 7th Earl of Shaftesbury*, Vol. 3, Edwin Hodder, London, Cassell and Co., 1887.
6. p. 33 *Moses*, London, Morgan and Scott, 1909.
7. p. 28 *Expositions of Holy Scripture, Exodus and Leviticus*, London, Hodder and Stoughton, 1906.
8. p. 82 *A Select Library of Nicene and Post Nicene Fathers*, 2nd Series, Vol. 10. Oxford, James Parker and Co., 1896.
9. p. 229 *The Joy of Preaching* (Lectures on Preaching, 1895), Grand Rapids, Michigan, 1989.

10. Ibid.
11. p. 503 *The Life and Work of the 7th Earl of Shaftesbury*, Vol. 3, Edwin Hodder, London, Cassell and Co. Ltd, 1887.
12. p. 235 *The Ten Commandments*, London, Hodder and Stoughton, 1884.
13. p. 35 *The Soul of Prayer* (1916), Fifth Impression, London, Independent Press.
14. p. 107 *Fool and Fanatic?* Jean Walker, Bulstrode, WEC, n.d.
15. p. 277 *Anabaptism in Outline*, Scottdale, P. A. Herald Press, 1981.
16. p. 14 *The Life and Work of the 7th Earl of Shaftsbury*, Vol. 3, Edwin Hodder, London, Cassell and Co. Ltd, 1887.
17. p. 42 *Christ and the Controversies of Christendom*, London, Hodder and Stoughton, 1869.
18. p. 166 *Positive Preaching and the Modern Mind*, London, Hodder and Stoughton, 1907.
19. p. 154 *The Life and Work of the 7th Earl of Shaftesbury*, Vol. 1, Edwin Hodder, London, Cassell and Co. Ltd, 1887.
20. p. 240 *A Serious Call*, London, Griffith, Farran, Okeden and Welsh, 1988.
21. p. 351 *Lectures on Revivals of Religion*, 13th Edition, London, Simpkin, Marshall and Co., 1840.
22. p. 48 *Bible Characters*, London, Morgan and Scott, n.d.
23. p. 77 *The Enquiry* (1792), Reprint, London, The Carey Kingsgate Press Ltd, 1961.
24. p. 78 *Whitefield's Works*, Vol. 7, London, E. and C. Dilly, 1771, altd.
25. p. 176 *The Christian Doctrine of Reconciliation*, London, Hodder and Stoughton, 1917.
26. p. 492 *The Poetic Works of Frances Ridley Havergal*, London, Nisbet and Co., n.d.
27. p. 51, 54 and 41 *Fool and Fanatic?* Jean Walker, Bulstrode, WEC, n.d.
28. p. 4 *Fragments that Remain*, edited by Bee Trehane, London, SPCK, 1987.
29. p. 56 *The Work of Christ*, London, Independent Press, 1938.
30. Ibid.

DECEMBER

1. p. 75 *The Atonement of the Modern Mind*, London, Hodder and Stoughton, 1908.
2. p. 102 *The Reformed Pastor*, London, SCM, 1956.
3. p. 78 *The Soul of Prayer* (1916) London, Independent Press, 1966.
4. p. 208 *Memoir of the Life of Elizabeth Fry*, Vol. 2, London, Charles Gilpin, 1847.

5. p. 101 *Elijah*, London, Morgan and Scott Ltd, 1909.
6. p. 251 *The Jewish Temple and the Christian Church*, London, 1871.
7. p. 212 *Bible Characters, Ahithophel to Nehemiah*, London, Oliphant, Anderson and Ferrier, 1903.
8. p. 342 *The Life and Work of the 7th Earl of Shaftsbury*, Vol. 2, Edwin Hodder, London, Cassell and Co., 1887.
9. p. 108 *The Atonement and the Modern Mind*, London, Hodder and Stoughton, 1908.
10. p. 33 *Bible Characters, Gideon to Absalom*, London, Oliphant, n.d.
11. p. 98 *Let Me Commend*, London, Wyvern (Epworth Press), 1961.
12. p. 25 *The Joy of Preaching* (Lectures on Preaching, 1895), Grand Rapids, Michigan, Kregel Publications, 1989.
13. p. 24 *Bible Characters, Stephen to Timothy*, London, Oliphant, n.d.
14. p. 12 *Selected Sermons*, London, Religious Tract Society, 1799.
15. p. 39 *The Joy of Preaching* (Lectures on Preaching, 1895), Grand Rapids, Michigan, Kregel Publications, 1989.
16. p. 129 *Elijah*, London, Morgan and Scott Ltd, 1909.
17. p. 8 *The Enquiry* (1792), Reprint, London, The Carey Kingsgate Press Ltd, 1961.
18. Ibid.
19. Ibid.
20. p. 114 *Retrospect*, London, Overseas Missionary Fellowship Books, 18th edition, n.d.
21. p. 86 *St Athanasius on the Incarnation*, Edinburgh, D. Nutts, 1891.
22. p. 260 *A Serious Call*, London, Griffith, Farran, Okeden and Welsh, 1888.
23. p. 128 *A Select Library of Nicene and Post Nicene Fathers*, Second Series, Vol. 12, Oxford, James Parker and Co., 1895.
24. *Popular Christianity*, London, The Salvation Army Book Department, n.d.
25. *Letters of John Hus*, London, Hodder and Stoughton, 1905.
26. p. 150 *A Select Library of Nicene and Post Nicene Fathers*, Second Series, Vol. 13, Oxford, James Parker and Co., 1895.
27. p. 107 *Library of the Fathers*, Vol. 11, Oxford, John Henry Parker, 1863.
28. p. 363 *Charity and Its Fruits* (1852), Reprint, Edinburgh, Banner of Truth, 1969.
29. p. 289 *The Jewish Temple and the Christian Church*, London, Hodder and Stoughton, 1871.
30. p. 297 *The Light of the World*, London, Macmillan and Co., 1899.
31. p. 276 *Expositions of Holy Scripture, Exodus and Leviticus*, London, Hodder and Stoughton, 1906.